PROFESSIONAL MEDICAL CODING AND BILLING FOUNDATIONS

ONLINE EDUCATION & TRAINING SOLUTIONS

Career Step, LLC
Phone: 801.489.9393
Toll-Free: 800.246.7837
Fax: 801.491.6645
careerstep.com

Product Number: HG-PR-11-119
Generation Date: July 29, 2013

TABLE OF CONTENTS

Health Information Management

Module

1

UNIT 1

Introduction

INTRODUCTION TO HEALTH INFORMATION MANAGEMENT

Learning Objectives

At the conclusion of this module, the learner will be able to:

1. Identify data sources by describing types of medical records and the information found in each record.
2. Describe the role medical records take in coding and billing.
3. Describe the structure and use of health information.
4. Identify record data collection tools.
5. Discuss healthcare data sets.
6. Discuss appropriate health record documentation.
7. Describe data quality and integrity.
8. Discuss health information systems, including specialty coding systems.
9. Describe the archival, retrieval, and imaging systems used in health information.
10. Identify data retrieval, maintenance, security, and integrity processes.
11. Discuss the evolution of the electronic health record (EHR) and the personal health record (PHR).

The patient's medical record is vital to the medical coder/biller because analyzing the medical record is required in the coding process. An understanding of the importance of this record and a responsibility to safeguard the personal information it contains is vital knowledge for any coding professional. The Health Information Management module focuses on the patient's medical record. Specifically, this module will discuss the creation, content, integrity and confidentiality of the medical record information.

UNIT 2
Structure of Healthcare Data

STRUCTURE OF HEALTHCARE DATA – INTRODUCTION

Structure and Use of Health Information

According to AHIMA a health record is "a paper or computer-based tool for collecting and storing information about the healthcare services provided to a patient in a single healthcare facility also called a patient record medical record, resident record, or client record, depending on the healthcare setting."

There are primary uses and secondary uses for the medical record. The primary uses are to deliver patient care to the patient and to manage that care. Further, the record is the communication tool to the entire healthcare team and provides patient care support for data analysis of trends. During the course of treatment, the information in the record is used for financial and administrative purposes to collect payment for services. An additional use is for patient self-management as patients become more active in monitoring and participating in their healthcare treatment and maintaining their own personal health record (PHR).

Secondary uses of the medical record do not involve direct patient care, but rather the use of the medical record to assist in research, education, regulations, public health, homeland security, and policy making.

The primary user of the medical record is the healthcare team, but many others use the record. In addition to the patient care providers, other individual users might be patient care managers and support personnel, coding and billing staff, patients, employers, lawyers, law enforcement, researchers, and government policy makers.

Organizations also use data from medical records. Examples of users are third-party payers, medical review organizations, research and accreditation organizations, licensing agencies and policy-making bodies.

Many of these users use the specific identifying information in the medical record, while others use what is called aggregate data. Aggregate data consists of data extracted from individual patient records and it is de-identified information that makes it possible to compare and analyze data about many patients. An example of aggregate data would be the numbers and causes of death of all patients in the state, or the number of patients discharged and then readmitted within 30 days with a diagnosis of congestive heart failure. In these types of statistics, the patient is not identified, but rather only the numbers of cases involved.

1. Patient visits physician
2. Physician documents care provided (either written, dictated, or selected in computer)
3. Report completed (either written, transcribed or available in electronic health record (EHR))
4. Coder codes encounter using documentation
5. Coded information is abstracted into system or entered onto bill
6. Encounter is billed to third party payer
7. Completed documents are filed (either in paper format or electronic format)

This graphic illustrates how the healthcare documentation process is the process by which the medical record containing the details of a patient's healthcare visit(s) is created and stored. The patient provides personal and health information at the beginning of a visit and throughout the healthcare documentation process. This helps the physician document the information correctly either through written notes, dictation or templates. A report might be dictated, and then transcribed by a transcriptionist, followed by coding, and billing for insurance purposes. In other instances, speech recognition software translates the physicians' dictations, in which case a medical transcription editor might edit the data. Some organizations have computer assisted coding (CAC) software which automatically assigns codes based on the documentation in the electronic health record (EHR). In this case, the coder becomes the editor, checking for accuracy of assigned codes by the computer.

The main function of the medical record is to collect patient data and store it so that it is accessible for all needing access. This record should be of the highest quality, secure, flexible, efficient and connected. The ability of the record to be connected is allowed by the creation of the electronic health record (EHR). This movement to EHRs will be discussed later in this course. For now, data sources and healthcare data sets will be covered with a focus on the discussion of health record documentation.

The quality of the health record is vital to patient care, and all members of the healthcare team rely on the accuracy in the record. The information is collected from many different sources and this information is then collected on a paper record or in electronic form, making up the medical record. In order to provide quality care, the organization must have mechanisms in place to identify the patient health record and to ensure that authorized users have access to the information when needed.

PATIENT INFORMATION

The critical element to be added to complete the healthcare documentation process is **patient information**. Patient information includes facts about the patient (also known as **patient demographics**), as well as personal and medical information, such as his or her living situation, symptom (a change in health function experienced by a patient), symptom onset, personal and medical history, family history, and other relevant information. The patient's personal information can be obtained verbally, in writing, or using a combination of both.

Demographic and personal information, reason for admission, and usually some patient-supplied information form the foundation for the medical record. Then the physician and other healthcare workers provide the medical data to the record that has been initiated by registration or clerical staff. By the time the physician or healthcare worker providing treatment sees the patient, the process of gathering information has already begun!

The process of gathering this information actually begins when the appointment is made. The scheduling secretary would ask (and make note of) the primary reason for requesting the appointment. If the patient is a new patient, demographic and medical information is collected through a form or series of forms as soon as the patient registers.

The forms provide information from the patient regarding insurance information and past medical care. This information is vital in evaluating patient complaints and providing treatment. Personal information is also extremely important in processing medical claims and submitting bills.

I. TRUE/FALSE.
Mark the following true or false.

1. Patient demographics are basic facts about the patient.
   ○ true
   ○ false

2. The patient's demographics and personal information can only be obtained in writing.
   ○ true
   ○ false

3. The foundation of the medical record is formed only of demographic information.
   ○ true
   ○ false

4. The process of gathering patient information begins when the appointment is made.
   ○ true
   ○ false

PATIENT DEMOGRAPHICS

At some point in the process, virtually every healthcare worker is involved in gathering patient information. As noted earlier, the receptionist (medical secretary, admissions clerk or registration staff) makes the first entries into the patient's medical record by collecting **patient demographics** when the patient arrives for treatment. Demographics include basic information such as:

- name
- address
- telephone number
- gender
- date of birth
- insurance/billing information

Highlights

What is a healthcare worker?
A healthcare worker is a person who participates directly or indirectly in providing healthcare services to a patient.

A healthcare worker can be a: physician, medical secretary, nurse, physician's assistant, nurse's aide, admissions clerk, laboratory or radiology technician, and many others.

This information is important, and it is updated and verified as necessary throughout patient care and the healthcare documentation process. Weeks or months after the initial visit, medical billing specialists or office staff may contact the patient to ask for additional or corrected demographic information.

Patient information—age, gender, insurance, medical history—is an important factor for establishing and managing healthcare.

COLLECTION OF PATIENT INFORMATION

Once basic patient demographics are collected, the process of gathering more detailed health and personal information comes next. The patient provides the first information by completing a form or forms such as the one below.

We've placed a multi-page visual aid in the appendix on pages 345-347.

Not all healthcare providers will gather this information by having the patient fill out forms. For example, for most emergency room visits, an admitting or evaluating nurse (triage nurse) conducts a brief interview with the patient or patient's family member and documents the patient's reason for admission: symptoms, brief history, etc. This is also the point at which vital signs—height, weight, temperature, respiratory rate, pulse, and blood pressure—are taken and recorded.

After step one in the healthcare documentation process is completed, the medical record is moved to the healthcare provider actually providing treatment to the patient. Only now, the medical record contains enough information for the doctor to know who the patient is and why he or she is seeking treatment. During treatment, a consent is signed by the patient to give permission for care or treatment or for surgery to be performed.

SUBJECTIVE/OBJECTIVE DATA

Once the patient has provided basic information, healthcare personnel begin collecting and recording more detailed and pertinent information. The treating nurse, physician, or other provider will ask the patient more detailed questions and record the answers, as well as make observations about the way the patient looks, acts, interacts, and appears on physical examination.

Patient information is continuously updated by the healthcare provider to ensure complete and accurate patient information.

Different methods are used to obtain patient information. The first method involves asking questions, obtaining descriptions, and interviewing and filling out forms. The second involves observing, examining, and recording results. These are commonly known as **subjective** and **objective**.

SUBJECTIVE means dependent on the mind or on an individual's perception for its existence.

OBJECTIVE means factual or not influenced by personal feelings or opinions.

In simpler terms, subjective information is the information provided by a patient or patient's family describing how he or she feels, what happened, where it hurts, or what's causing the problem.

Subjective examples:

"I fell and hit my head. The top of my head hurts when I touch it."
"I'm running a fever. I feel hot and flushed."

Objective information is the data collected from observation and examination: measuring, looking, touching, or testing.

Objective examples:

Head exam: The patient has a 2-inch cut on the top of the head.
Temperature: 100.1 degrees F

All of the information—demographics, patient-supplied information, subjective/objective statements, and results recorded—is compiled into a medical record. As you can imagine, the medical record is filled with personal, sensitive information and is getting larger each minute.

COLLECTING PATIENT INFORMATION

Patient information can be collected prior to and after treatment. It is common practice to receive follow-up calls after care has been completed. This process is very common for patients undergoing same day or outpatient surgery. This is done a day or two after treatment, by a nurse or other provider. Usually the patient is called to query about any complications such as fever, severe pain, etc. Also the patient might be reminded of postoperative or postcare instructions. This is an example of patient information being collected in the period following treatment.

Patient information may also be collected prior to the patient receiving care. It is quite common to "pre-register" for care. Common examples are for a lab or x-ray test or a same-day surgery visit. Registration staff collects personal data to begin the medical record and provide any pre-surgery or pre-test information prior to arrival at the facility. This is patient information collected prior to (sometimes weeks in advance) admission for treatment.

HEALTH RECORD DATA COLLECTION TOOLS

Efforts are being made to standardize data sets (or a list of uniform data elements that are well defined) to standardize and compare data collected on patients. For example, the Uniform Hospital Discharge Data Set (UHDDS) is a series of definitions collected on all hospital inpatients. Examples include the principal diagnosis, principal procedure, discharge date, discharge status, etc. These data sets will be discussed in more detail in the Reimbursement module. In order to collect this information at discharge, standard abstracting systems are used. The coded information is entered into the abstracting program to collect and store this information into databases at the facility. The purpose is so that the data and statistics can be retrieved, and also to compare data with other organizations and with external users such as payers, government agencies, etc.

I. **MULTIPLE CHOICE.**
   Choose whether the following example is subjective or objective.

   1. Patient feels nauseated and has feelings of disorientation. (◯ subjective, ◯ objective)

   2. Patient has a temperature of 101.2 degrees F. (◯ subjective, ◯ objective)

3. Patient has a burst left eardrum. (◯ subjective, ◯ objective)

4. Patient feels pain in their left ear. (◯ subjective, ◯ objective)

II. TRUE/FALSE.
Mark the following true or false.

1. The UHDDS is used in the hospital inpatient setting to collect data on discharged patients.
   ◯ true
   ◯ false

2. Abstracted patient information is used only internally.
   ◯ true
   ◯ false

3. UHDDS means Uniform Healthcare Discharge Data Set.
   ◯ true
   ◯ false

UNIT 3
Outpatient Medical Reports

OUTPATIENT MEDICAL REPORTS – INTRODUCTION

Data Sources

The final product of the healthcare documentation process is the patient's medical record. A **medical record** is not a single document; it's a folder (paper and/or electronic) containing a collection of several individual documents. The record contains the demographic information collected from the patient, signed patient confidentiality forms, treatment forms, and documents where the details of patients' encounters are recorded.

Support service healthcare professionals use the patient's financial record for patient contact information and insurance records, maintaining compliance with **Health Insurance Portability and Accountability Act (HIPAA)**, and as the source documents for medical coding and medical billing.

Medical coding specialists refer to the medical record to identify diagnoses, procedures, treatments, ancillary services, and any other information necessary to properly code the medical record. This unit will focus on the collection of documents in the medical record where medical details of patient encounters are recorded.

Highlights

Financial information is kept separate from the patient's medical record. Bills, insurance denials, payment records, and other financial documents are not part of the patient's medical record, although a copy of the patient's insurance card is often included in the medical record.

The collection of documents contained in an outpatient medical record will depend on the type of outpatient treatment the patient receives. The collection of documents contained in the medical record and the organization of those documents will vary depending on where the patient receives treatment, the treatment received, and the policies/procedures of the healthcare provider. The medical record, whether inpatient or outpatient, is the who, what, where, when, and how of patient care.

Medical Humor

A man goes to the doctor and says to the doctor:
"It hurts when I press here," (pressing his side)
"And when I press here," (pressing the other side)
"And here," (his leg)
"And here, here and here." (his other leg, and both arms)
So the doctor examined him all over and finally discovered what was wrong. "You've got a broken finger!"

OUTPATIENT MEDICAL RECORD CONTENT

Note: it is important to remember that not all outpatient records will contain all of these reports. "Outpatient" is a term that can mean many things, from a physician encounter, a same day or outpatient surgery, an emergency room visit, or even a simple ancillary test such as a chest x-ray or blood test.

In general, a patient's medical record is made up of some or all of the following types of reports:

Report Types	Types	Sample Elements
Face Sheet	patient registration demographic form intake assessment	Patient name, date of birth, etc.
Progress Notes	first visit notes physician notes/orders[1] nurses' notes medication administration records treatment notes SOAP (subjective/objective/assessment/plan) clinic notes	Patient identification Date of progress note Documentation of the reason for the encounter/visit Tests and procedures performed Results of tests and procedures Treatment plan Signature of author Relevant dates
Consultations	consultation report specialists' report	Patient identification Name of physician who requested the consultation Name of consultant Reason for the consultation Date of examination/review by consultant Pertinent lab/exam findings Consultant's opinion, diagnosis, or impression Consultant's recommended diagnostic tests and/or treatment Signature, credentials, and specialty of the consultant
History and Physical (H&P)	history and physical preoperative H&P prenatal H&P routine H&P intake H&P	Patient identification Relevant dates Reason for visit/chief complaint History of present illness Past medical history, surgical history Social history Health habits Race/ethnicity Family history Allergies, medications Physical examination Assessment and plan

Emergency Room Reports	ER Summary	Patient identification Time and means of arrival (ambulance, car, etc.) Pertinent history Chief complaint/reason for visit Onset of injury/illness Significant physical findings Lab, x-ray, EEG, or other test findings Treatment rendered Results of treatment Change in physical findings and symptomatology Discharge conclusions/diagnosis Disposition of patient, including transfer or discharge home Condition of patient at discharge or transfer Discharge instructions
Operative (OP) Reports	operative (OR) summary procedure notes	Patient identification Preoperative and postoperative diagnoses Indications/reasons for operation Description of procedures performed Description of normal and abnormal findings Description of organs explored and specimens removed Description of patient's medical condition before, during, and after the surgical procedure Estimated blood loss, ligatures, sutures, number of packs, drains and sponges used Descriptions of any unique or unusual events during course of procedure Complications Names of surgeons and their assistants Relevant dates Signature of principal physician, credentials Type of anesthesia Allergies

Ancillary Reports/ Records	ancillary reports/records pathology reports laboratory reports radiology studies cardiac studies – EKG medication administration records many others	Patient identification Relevant dates Signatures of technicians Lab values Normals for comparison Study findings/results Printouts/strips Description of findings Pertinent history Chief complaint/reason for study Physician signatures as appropriate
Other Documents	correspondence – letters from attorneys, patient, family members, specialists medical record requests physician referral forms HIPAA release forms (notice of privacy practices) privacy statements consent for treatment advanced directives property and valuables list privacy statements	

Documentation varies from provider to provider and visit to visit. Some reports in the medical record may contain every element listed and more; others may include only one or two of the elements listed. This is why the column describing elements in the record is specified as "sample elements." The Medical Record Organization unit in this module will cover common elements of medical records in more detail.

Footnotes:

1. Provider notes/orders and in some settings other physician-documented (signed) portions of the patient record are the only ones that medical coders can use to code the document. This will be explained in the Official Coding Guidelines in subsequent courses. For coding, the term "provider" is used to mean physician or any qualified healthcare practitioner who is legally accountable for establishing the patient's diagnosis. In many states this could be a nurse practitioner or a physician assistant.

MEDICAL RECORD CONTENT

Medical records are usually created by the healthcare team as the patient moves through the healthcare process and are compiled over a visit or series of visits. Standardized forms for every type of report or encounter do not exist. One healthcare encounter might have physicians, nurses, nursing assistants, and other providers chart their progress notes on simple lined medical record paper in chronological order. The example below illustrates one method of recording progress notes.

We've placed a visual aid in the appendix on page 348.

Other encounters might have one physician progress note document, separate physician order documents, and a separate sheet where nurses chart their patient notes.

In a perfect world, each report in the medical record would be complete, well-organized, and legible. Actually the patient's medical record will not always be complete, logically organized, or (in some cases) legible. It is part of the Health Information manager's responsibility to correct these deficiencies. Remember a patient's medical record is compiled as the patient moves through the process of receiving healthcare in one visit or multiple visits over time. Generally several different people contribute to creating and compiling a medical record.

Medical coding specialists analyze the medical record in order to find the information they need to assign the proper codes. Medical record content is the basis for medical coding. Several examples are provided of different types of documentation that make up a patient's medical record.

We've placed a visual aid in the appendix on page 349.

We've placed a visual aid in the appendix on page 350.

We've placed a visual aid in the appendix on page 351.

MEDICAL RECORD EXAMPLES

Roland is at the park playing softball with his family. He slides into first base and feels a pop in his right ankle followed by immediate pain. His family takes him to the emergency room for treatment. On arrival in the emergency room, he is evaluated by the triage nurse. The triage nurse's notes are followed by the physician's notes and the order for ankle x-ray. (Notice the physician and the nurse charts are on different forms at this clinic). These are all compiled together to make up Roland's medical record.

We've placed a visual aid in the appendix on page 352.

We've placed a visual aid in the appendix on page 353.

We've placed a visual aid in the appendix on page 354.

We've placed a visual aid in the appendix on page 355.

Another example might be 4-year-old Jennifer who came in 2 weeks ago because of an earache and is back. Notice in this clinic visit both the physician and the nurse include their notes on the same record.

We've placed a visual aid in the appendix on page 356.

FACE SHEET

Report Types	Types	Sample Elements
Face Sheet	patient registration demographic form intake assessment	Patient name, date of birth, etc.

Demographic information and the patient-supplied personal and medical history, a sample Patient History form have been reviewed. The information gathered from the patient makes up the **face sheet** in the patient medical record. The face sheet has different names:

The face sheet provides good information about the patient, but is not complete for coding.

- patient history
- patient registration
- demographics form
- intake assessment
- patient information sheet

Physician offices and emergency rooms, physical therapy offices and outpatient radiology clinics, and all other outpatient settings have some sort of face sheet.

Sample face sheets:

> We've placed a visual aid in the appendix on page 357.

> We've placed a visual aid in the appendix on page 358.

> We've placed a visual aid in the appendix on page 359.

I. **MULTIPLE CHOICE.**
   Review the history form above for this patient and answer the following questions.

   1. The patient reports an allergy to _____.
      - ○ aspirin
      - ○ penicillin
      - ○ Crestor
      - ○ dust

   2. Which of the following medical problems are NOT reported in the family history?
      - ○ diabetes
      - ○ osteoporosis
      - ○ hypertension
      - ○ renal disease

3. A social history is reviewed and is negative for _____.
   - ○ daily alcohol intake
   - ○ smoking
   - ○ jogging
   - ○ use of caffeine products

4. The patient's past medical history is positive for _____.
   - ○ rotator cuff tear
   - ○ osteoporosis
   - ○ urinary tract infection
   - ○ heart disease

5. On the history form, the patient reports several problems. Which one was reported?
   - ○ frequent headaches
   - ○ chest pain
   - ○ dizziness
   - ○ shortness of breath

PROGRESS NOTES

Report Types	Types	Sample Elements
Progress Notes	first visit notes physician notes/orders* nurses' notes treatment notes SOAP (subjective/objective/assessment/plan) notes clinic notes	Patient identification, including name and medical record number Date of progress note Documentation of the reason for the encounter/visit Tests and procedures performed Results of tests and procedures Treatment plan Signature of author

Although non-physician progress notes can be helpful to direct physician queries or clarify information, medical coders can only code provider documented diagnoses and treatments.

Virtually all direct healthcare providers document their patient interactions, called **progress notes**. Progress notes can be informal notes or formal, typewritten documents. Often these are pre-printed forms with check boxes or fill-in-the-blank forms.

Medical coders can only code provider-documented diagnoses and treatments.

Take a look at the examples below:

We've placed a multi-page visual aid in the appendix on pages 360-361.

We've placed a visual aid in the appendix on page 362.

PHYSICIAN PROGRESS NOTES AND PHYSICIAN'S ORDERS

Physician progress notes in an outpatient setting, such as a physician's office, document the reason for the encounter/visit and direct the treatment plan. By reviewing the physician progress notes one can develop a sense of the focus of treatment. The primary care physician, consulting physician, and other physicians who see a patient in an outpatient setting create a progress note for each visit.

In the inpatient setting, physician progress notes describe the patient's course throughout their stay in the hospital. During an inpatient stay, an admitting physician, resident physician such as a hospitalist, consulting physician, and/or other physician provider may add physician note documentation to the chart. As with outpatient notes, physician notes can help provide clarification when coding diagnoses or procedures.

Progress notes can be typewritten, formalized documents or quickly scrawled "chart notes."

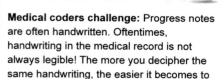

Highlights

Medical coders challenge: Progress notes are often handwritten. Oftentimes, handwriting in the medical record is not always legible! The more you decipher the same handwriting, the easier it becomes to read.

Progress notes are reviewed to help determine the primary diagnosis. They are also reviewed for any procedures or tests that were performed during the encounter/visit and any secondary diagnoses that affected the treatment or management of the patient.

Physician's orders are instructions either written by the physician or verbally given to and documented by another healthcare professional regarding the care plan/treatment of the patient or entered directly into a computer physician order entry system (COPE).

Diagnostic and **therapeutic orders** include orders for medications, diagnostic tests, therapeutic tests, ancillary medical services, and medical devices provided to patients. Although orders can initially be given as verbal orders, they must be followed by written orders signed and dated by the physician.

Physician's orders help medical coders identify the focus of treatment and support the selection of the primary diagnosis. They also assist the medical coder in identifying significant secondary diagnoses.

A word of caution before you move on; make sure to verify all documentation. Assumptions can't be made based on orders alone; always look at the full medical record, not just one report.

PHYSICIAN'S ORDERS

Read the following physician's orders and answer the questions below.

We've placed a visual aid in the appendix on page 363.

I. MULTIPLE CHOICE.
Choose the best answer.

1. What type of diet was ordered by the physician?
   - ⃝ ADA 2000
   - ⃝ regular
   - ⃝ low salt, low fat

2. Review the physician's order sheet. Under #1, the physician checked where the patient was to go after surgery. Where did the physician order the patient to go following surgery?
   - ⃝ home
   - ⃝ admitted to hospital
   - ⃝ PAR
   - ⃝ transferred to another hospital

3. For which foot did the physician order elevation and checking of the circulation?
   - ⃝ right
   - ⃝ left
   - ⃝ information not available
   - ⃝ neither

4. Which type of training did the physician order for the patient?
   - ⃝ cast shoe removal
   - ⃝ weightbearing and weight shifting
   - ⃝ weight transfer training
   - ⃝ crutch train

5. The physician ordered _____ for the patient.
   - ⃝ an x-ray
   - ⃝ crutches
   - ⃝ a mini-mental exam
   - ⃝ a CBC

NURSE'S NOTES

The nursing staff takes vital signs, gives medications, changes dressings, and does many other tasks as they carry out the care instructions given by the physician. All these activities are documented. The nursing staff is responsible for the notes regarding the patient's progress during the encounter/visit. These notes become a part of the patient's outpatient medical record. All notes are dated and signed with the nurse's name and professional designation. Some examples of notes the nursing staff are responsible for include the following:

Nurse's Progress Notes

The nursing staff begins writing progress notes in the patient's medical record when the patient presents for the encounter/visit. These progress notes provide a complete record of the patient's encounter/visit and continue until the patient is released from treatment.

Medication Records

The medication record includes a list of all the medications administered to the patient during the encounter/visit. The record includes the date and time each drug was administered, the name of the medication, the form of administration, and the medication's dosage and strength. The entry for each medication is signed and dated by the individual who administered the drug.

Nursing Assessment

The nursing assessment contains clinical and personal information about the patient and is usually performed shortly after the patient presented for the encounter/visit. It includes the date and time, patient's current condition, and vital signs.

These notes provide detailed information about the patient's care, treatment, diagnoses, and procedures for the patient's encounter/visit. Nursing entries should contain objective data, such as stating the quantity of fluids taken, as opposed to subjective statements, such as intake is "poor" or "good." The primary care physician must confirm any diagnoses and procedures documented in these notes. Coders do not report any diagnoses or procedures documented in these notes without the provider documenting their clinical significance.

Read the following note and answer the questions below.

We've placed a visual aid in the appendix on page 364.

I. **MULTIPLE CHOICE.**
   Choose the best answer.

   1. Using a drug reference book, choose the medication on the patient's medication administration record that is used to treat diabetes.
      ○ Glucophage
      ○ Evista
      ○ Synthroid
      ○ gemfibrozil

   2. Read the information at the top of the medication administration record and identify the patient's diagnosis.
      ○ diabetes
      ○ ORIF left ankle
      ○ neuropathy
      ○ creatinine reduction

3. Using a drug reference book, determine which medication from this patient medication administration record is used to treat hyperlipidemia.
   ○ Percocet
   ○ gemfibrozil
   ○ Inapsine
   ○ Evista

4. Using a drug reference book, determine what type of medication Percocet is.
   ○ bone resorption inhibitor
   ○ neuroleptic
   ○ opiate analgesic
   ○ antilipemic

5. How many mg of gemfibrozil was the patient administered?
   ○ 16 mg
   ○ 60 mg
   ○ 1000 mg
   ○ 600 mg

CONSULTATIONS

Report Types	Types	Sample Elements
Consultations	consultation report specialists' reports	Patient identification Name of physician who requested the consultation Name of consultant Reason for the consultation Date of examination/review by consultant Pertinent lab/exam findings Consultant's opinion, diagnosis, or impression Consultant's recommended diagnostic tests and/or treatment Signature, credentials, and specialty of the consultant

Physicians can be generalists or specialists. Often physicians will seek the advice of other physicians on one or more of the patient's symptoms before making final diagnostic and therapeutic decisions. A third-party payer, a patient, or a patient's family may also request a consult for a second opinion. **Consultation reports** contain an opinion about a patient's condition by a physician other than the primary care (attending) physician. This opinion is requested by the primary care physician and is based on a review of the patient's medical record, an examination of the patient, and a conference with the primary care physician. The primary care physician must formally request a consultation indicating the symptoms or findings for which an opinion is desired. The consulting physician examines the patient and documents the findings in a consultation report, making recommendations for treatment of the patient.

The consultation report should be reviewed for the cause of the patient's symptoms for which the consultation was requested. The cause of these symptoms should be coded as the primary diagnosis for the visit to the consulting physician's office. It is also important to identify any significant secondary diagnoses documented in the consultation report.

HISTORY AND PHYSICAL REPORTS

Report Types	Types	Sample Elements
History and Physical (H&P)	history and physical preoperative H&P prenatal H&P routine H&P intake H&P	Patient identification Relevant dates Reason for visit/chief complaint History of present illness Past medical history, surgical history Social history Health habits Race/ethnicity Family history Allergies, medications Physical examination Assessment and plan

History and Physical reports (commonly called H&Ps) can be stand-alone documents or incorporated into other documents in the medical record. A clinic note or progress note might include some physical exam or history elements, but an H&P is usually a more detailed, focused history and physical exam with a specific purpose and associated assessment and plan. It is often a good place to pick up key chronic and past history conditions.

For example, a preoperative H&P is done prior to surgery. A preoperative H&P details the patient's medical and surgical history and includes a detailed physical exam to help the provider determine if the patient has high risks for complications or has certain conditions that might require special considerations during surgery. A prenatal H&P is done to help the provider determine what factors may affect the pregnancy or delivery, such as a prior history of miscarriages or a family history of blood clots. A thorough H&P helps determine the type of care needed throughout the pregnancy.

H&Ps are important documents in both inpatient and outpatient records.

Read the following H&P and answer the questions below.

Medical Record

HISTORY AND PHYSICAL

PATIENT NAME: Janet Jong

MEDICAL RECORD NUMBER: 25-85-21

HISTORY OF PRESENT ILLNESS: This established patient was seen preoperatively for blepharoplasty due to some ptosis, which may require levator tightening.

The risks, benefits, alternatives, and different options of the procedure were discussed with the patient. The patient did not wish to do any significant Americanizing of the eyes or anything like this. Her main concern was the redundant skin and excess weight on her eyes.

She understands that the scarring involved with darker skin or Asian skin is less predictable, as well as the scarring to the levator structures underneath, which could end up causing more or less of a crease than she would like. She denies any significant medical problems.

PAST SURGICAL HISTORY: She had neck surgery in the past; otherwise, no major or significant surgeries.

ALLERGIES: No known allergies.

MEDICATIONS: None.

SOCIAL HISTORY: Nonsmoker, nondrinker.

REVIEW OF SYSTEMS: All systems individually reviewed and all findings were negative other than for the redundant skin on the upper eyelids.

PHYSICAL EXAMINATION:

CONSTITUTIONAL: General: She is 5'3" and 130 lbs. Alert and oriented x 3. WDWN, regular pulse, regular rate, afebrile. No acute distress.

HEENT: Head is atraumatic, normocephalic. No sinus tenderness. EYES: Pupils are equally round and reactive to light. Extraocular movements are intact.

EARS, NOSE, and OROPHARYNX are normal without abnormality.

NEUROLOGIC: Cranial nerves II-XII intact.

PSYCHIATRIC: Normal affect and mood.

NECK: Supple, full ROM, trachea is midline. NO JVD. No thyroid gross abnormality.

LUNGS: Clear to auscultation A&P. Normal respiratory effect.

HEART: RRR, without murmur. No gross edema, or significant varicosities.

ABDOMEN: Soft, nontender, nondistended. No hepatosplenomegaly or masses. Normal bowel sounds.

EXTREMITIES: Within normal limits.

MUSCULOSKELETAL: Generally unremarkable. Normal gait. No asymmetry. Normal range of motion.

LYMPHATIC: No adenopathy, neck and axilla.

SKIN: No visual or palpable gross irregularities on areas examined.

ASSESSMENT/PLAN: The patient has ptosis of the upper eyelids, which requires blepharoplasty and possible levator tightening. We will go ahead and proceed with the surgery tomorrow morning as scheduled.

I. MULTIPLE CHOICE.
Choose the best answer.

1. Read the ASSESSMENT/PLAN. What is the preoperative diagnosis?
   - ○ excess skin
   - ○ levator tightening
   - ○ ptosis of the upper eyelids
   - ○ redundant skin

2. The patient reported that she has what?
   - ○ significant medical problems
   - ○ no significant medical problems
   - ○ abdominal pain
   - ○ constant headaches

3. Which procedure is the patient scheduled to have performed?
   - ○ levator tightening
   - ○ upper lid excision
   - ○ excision of excess skin
   - ○ blepharoplasty

4. Which of the following was discussed with the patient?
   - ○ risks and benefits of the procedure
   - ○ alternatives to the procedure
   - ○ different options for the procedure
   - ○ all of the above

5. When is the patient scheduled to undergo surgery?
   - ○ next week
   - ○ tomorrow morning
   - ○ two weeks
   - ○ next month

EMERGENCY ROOM (ER) REPORTS

Report Types	Types	Sample Elements
Emergency Room Reports	ER summary	Patient identification Time and means of arrival (ambulance, car, etc.) Pertinent history Chief complaint/reason for visit Onset of injury/illness Significant physical findings Lab, x-ray, EEG, or other test findings Treatment rendered Results of treatment Change in physical findings and symptomatology Discharge conclusions/diagnosis Disposition of patient, including transfer or discharge home Condition of patient at discharge or transfer Discharge instructions

Emergency departments provide urgent care to patients. Patients treated in emergency departments and discharged the same day are considered hospital outpatients. The increased use of emergency room services for more routine care has resulted in a large volume of healthcare documentation for ER outpatients.

Read the following emergency room report and answer the questions below.

Medical Record

EMERGENCY ROOM REPORT

Patient Name: Fred Smith

Medical Record Number: 15-85-72

The patient was seen with a medical student. The patient has COPD. The patient complains of a cough for approximately 1 week. The patient has had no travel, no new pets, and no one else is sick, per se. The patient is coughing up thick white phlegm. He is having some difficulty being able to bring it up.

The patient states he has increasing short of breath starting this morning. He comes in today for evaluation.

PHYSICAL EXAMINATION: Afebrile at 96.8, pulse 84, respiratory rate 20, blood pressure 194/101; however, the patient did not take his medications today. LUNGS: good airflow throughout. There were occasional inspiratory and expiratory wheezes. HEART: Regular rate and rhythm.

IMPRESSION: Bronchitis.

PLAN: Plenty of rest and plenty of fluids. We gave him Augmentin 875 mg and given some Robitussin 2 teaspoons q.4 hours. He is to follow up if he is no better, or worsens.

I. MULTIPLE CHOICE.
Choose the best answer.

1. What is the patient's complaint on admission?
   - ◯ fever
   - ◯ COPD
   - ◯ cough
   - ◯ bronchitis

2. Use your drug reference book to select the correct drug classification for Augmentin.
   - ◯ antibiotic
   - ◯ antiviral
   - ◯ antifungal
   - ◯ anti-inflammatory

3. What does the doctor indicate is his impression or primary diagnosis for this patient?
   - ◯ inspiratory and expiratory wheezes
   - ◯ cough
   - ◯ shortness of breath
   - ◯ bronchitis

4. Use your drug reference book to select the correct drug classification for Robitussin.
   - ◯ antiemetic
   - ◯ nonopioid analgesic
   - ◯ expectorant
   - ◯ antibiotic

5. This record indicates that the patient has a chronic condition that had been diagnosed prior to this visit. What chronic condition does the patient have?
   - ◯ COPD
   - ◯ shortness of breath
   - ◯ bronchitis
   - ◯ cough

OPERATIVE REPORTS

Report Types	Types	Sample Elements
operative (OP) reports	operative (OR) summary procedure notes	Patient identification Preoperative and postoperative diagnoses Indications/reasons for operation Description of procedures performed Description of normal and abnormal findings Description of organs explored and specimens removed Description of patient's medical condition before, during, and after the surgical procedure Estimated blood loss, ligatures, sutures, number of packs, drains and sponges used Descriptions of any unique or unusual events during course of procedure Complications Names of surgeons and their assistants Relevant dates Signature of principal physician, credentials Type of anesthesia Allergies

An **operative report** (OP) is used to describe the surgical procedures performed on the patient. This detailed report describes the entire surgical process from administration of anesthesia through wound closure. The principal surgeon dictates/provides content for the report. The operative report is usually dictated immediately after surgery and filed in the patient's medical record.

> ## Highlights
>
> The procedures performed have an impact on the amount of reimbursement the surgeon receives. It is imperative all procedures are accurately coded and billed—a missed code results in missed revenue; and most importantly assertions of fraudulent claims submission.

The entire operative report should be read to identify all the diagnoses documented and all the procedures performed. The majority of the time the diagnoses are documented under the preoperative and postoperative headings. However, the physician may also document pertinent diagnoses in the body of the report. These will also need to be coded. The same is true of the procedures performed. The procedures are mainly documented under the heading operations performed but may also be documented in the body of the report.

Read the following operative report and answer the questions below.

Medical Record

OPERATIVE REPORT

PATIENT NAME: Janet Johnson

MEDICAL RECORD NUMBER: 25-85-74

DATE OF OPERATION: 2/25/2004

PREOPERATIVE DIAGNOSIS: Right ring and long fingers pain.

POSTOPERATIVE DIAGNOSIS: Trigger finger, right ring and long fingers.

OPERATION PERFORMED: Right ring and long fingers A1 pulley release.

SURGEON: ___ [NAME], M.D.

INDICATIONS: The patient is a 32-year-old with significant right ring finger and long fingers pain which interferes with activities of daily living.

DESCRIPTION OF PROCEDURE: The patient was taken to the operating room, at which time Anesthesia initiated a Bier block. The patient was then prepped and draped in the normal sterile fashion. A transverse incision was made at the level of the distal palmar crease in the right hand. Careful longitudinal dissection was carried out. The digital nerves were identified to the long finger and the A1 pulley was released in its entirety to the long finger. We then directed our attention to the ring finger. The digital nerves were identified, and the A1 pulley was released there as well. The patient tolerated the procedure well. There were no complications. A bulky hand dressing was applied, and she was taken to recovery in good condition.

I. MULTIPLE CHOICE.
Choose the best answer.

1. What is the principal diagnosis for this procedure? *Hint: The diagnosis after (post) surgery.*
   - ⃝ finger pain
   - ⃝ nerve injury
   - ⃝ trigger finger
   - ⃝ A1 pulley release

2. What is the principal procedure performed?
   - ⃝ A1 pulley release
   - ⃝ finger pain
   - ⃝ tendon repair
   - ⃝ trigger finger

3. What type of anesthesia was used for this procedure?
   - ○ general
   - ○ local
   - ○ topical
   - ○ Bier block

4. Where was the patient taken at the end of the procedure?
   - ○ anesthesia room
   - ○ recovery room
   - ○ physician office
   - ○ home care

ANCILLARY REPORTS

Report Types	Types	Sample Elements
Ancillary Reports/Records	ancillary reports/records pathology reports laboratory reports radiology studies cardiac studies – EKG medication administration records many others	Patient identification Relevant dates Signatures of technicians Lab values Normals for comparison Study findings/results Printouts/strips Description of findings Pertinent history Chief complaint/reason for study Physician signatures as appropriate

Ancillary reports/records contain all of the documentation of the tests, procedures, and treatments ordered for the patient. Diagnoses are made from observation of the patient, review of symptoms, tests, and procedures. The results of tests and procedures are reported in a variety of ways. EKG machines print a strip showing the electrical activity of the heart. Ultrasounds and x-rays result in films, accompanied by an interpretation of the results by a radiologist. **Laboratory work**—blood analysis, urine analysis, or pathology—biopsies—are reported on data sheets as values, findings, and results.

ANCILLARY REPORTS – LABORATORY

Laboratory reports consist of various types of analyses or examinations of body substances collected from the patient. They include blood, urine, spinal fluid, and other fluids and substances. The results are documented in a laboratory report. All laboratory tests require a physician's order. The samples for testing are generally collected from patients by nurses or phlebotomists. After the tests have been performed and the results are available, they are returned to the physician who ordered the tests. These results should be filed in the medical record within 24 hours of completion.

Read the following report and answer the questions below.

> We've placed a visual aid in the appendix on page 365.

I. **MULTIPLE CHOICE.**
   Choose the best answer.

1. In the report above, H represents a result above normal (high). How many of the lab test results for hematology were in the above normal (high) range?
   - ○ 3
   - ○ 2
   - ○ 5
   - ○ 1

2. In the report above, L represents a lower than normal value. Which lab test results are reported as low under hematology?
   - ○ Band % and Lymph %
   - ○ Hgb and Seg %
   - ○ RBC and Band %
   - ○ Hct and Lymph %

3. In the report above, how many of the lab test results were reported low in the chemistry results section?
   - ○ 5
   - ○ 3
   - ○ 2
   - ○ 4

4. In the report above, which lab test result is high under chemistry?
   - ○ Sodium
   - ○ Glucose
   - ○ Potassium
   - ○ Creatinine

ANCILLARY REPORTS – PATHOLOGY

Ancillary reports also include physician diagnostic reports and studies, such as pathology reports and radiology reports. Pathology examinations consist of microscopic and/or gross description of tissue performed every time a specimen or foreign object is removed from a patient during a surgical procedure. Pathology is the study of the essential nature of disease—the underlying changes in tissue or structure that cause or are caused by disease. When a specimen is removed, the pathologist studies it by gross examination, measuring it, describing color and texture and determining any masses present. The specimen is then sectioned into thin slices for further examination. Microscopic slides are made by allowing formalin fixation to view the specimen.

The specimen is hardened and embedded in hot wax to form a tissue block. The slides are reviewed by the pathologist and compared to the gross findings and the pathologist prepares the pathology report.

The diagnoses documented in a pathology report are based on the pathologist's findings. The pathologist is a physician. In outpatient coding, when a pathologist's report provides greater specificity to the diagnosis than the attending physician documented, it is used in coding the diagnosis listed in the pathology report.

Read the following report and answer the questions below.

PATHOLOGY REPORT

SPECIMEN: Right breast mass and left breast mole.

GROSS DESCRIPTION:

Part A: The specimen is labeled "right breast mass, fresh" and consists of a firm fresh fibroadipose tissue specimen aggregating 2.8 x 2.1 x 1.5 cm. As the specimen is serially sectioned, several areas are noted to have a very gritty, firm appearance. A representative section is frozen for receptor studies. The remainder of the specimen is submitted in its entirety in cassettes A1-4.

Part B: The specimen is labeled "left breast mole" and consists of one grey-tan soft tissue fragment in aggregate measures 0.4 x 0.3 x 0.3 cm. The specimen is bisected and submitted in its entirety in 1 cassette.

MICROSCOPIC:

Part A: Multiple H&E sections were reviewed which showed neoplasm composed of glandular cribriform-like structures. The cells making up the cribriform structures are pleomorphic, hyperchromatic, showing occasional minute nucleoli. These malignant cells are not only in clusters, but are seen to infiltrate surrounding stromal tissue, and in Indian-file filtration. A desmoplastic reaction is noted with the neoplasm.

Part B: The histologic sections show dermal fibrosis and edema.

DIAGNOSIS:

Part A: Right breast mass: infiltrating ductal carcinoma.

Part B: Left breast mole, excision: dermal fibrosis.

I. MULTIPLE CHOICE.
Choose the best answer.

1. How many specimens were submitted for pathological examination?
   - ◯ 3
   - ◯ 2
   - ◯ 4
   - ◯ 1

2. What is the diagnosis in the pathology report for the right breast mass?
   - ◯ dermal fibrosis
   - ◯ breast mass
   - ◯ infiltrating ductal carcinoma
   - ◯ mole

3. For outpatient encounters you can code the diagnoses directly from the _____.
   - ◯ laboratory report
   - ◯ pathology report
   - ◯ radiology report
   - ◯ operative report

4. What is the diagnosis in the pathology report for the left breast mole?
   - ◯ infiltrating ductal carcinoma
   - ◯ mole
   - ◯ breast mass
   - ◯ dermal fibrosis

ANCILLARY REPORTS – RADIOLOGY

Radiology services include both diagnostic and therapeutic services. The **diagnostic services** are used to diagnose medical conditions. Diagnostic services can include x-ray, radioactive scanning, thermography, xerography and ultrasonography. With these methods, the results are projected into a visual form. Usually the radiologist writes or dictates a description of what is seen and the implications for the patient. The interpretation (which the radiologist must sign) becomes the report. For **therapeutic purposes**, radiation and/or radioactive materials may be administered. The amount of the dose, the date, and the time are documented.

A summary of the treatment is provided and signed by the radiologist and becomes a part of the medical record. Nuclear medicine and interventional cardiology procedures can be either diagnostic or therapeutic treatment for diseases, such as cancer and heart conditions.

Diagnostic Examples:

- computed tomography (CT scan)
- magnetic resonance imaging (MRI)
- ultrasound

Therapeutic Examples:

- radiopharmaceutical therapy
- radiation treatment
- brachytherapy

The diagnoses documented in a radiology report are based on the radiologist's findings. The radiologist is a physician. In outpatient coding, when a radiologist's report provides greater specificity to the diagnosis than the attending physician documented, code the diagnosis listed in the radiology report.

Read the following radiology report and answer the questions below.

Medical Record

MRI SCAN

INDICATION: Left knee with physical exam findings and history suggestive of medial meniscus tear. Rule out medial meniscus tear.

LEFT KNEE MRI: The left knee was scanned in sagittal projection utilizing proton density, T2, and gradient echo imaging sequences, and in coronal projection utilizing a T1 weighted imaging sequence. The cruciate ligaments are well visualized and appear intact. The collateral ligaments are not as well visualized, but appear to be intact. There is an area of low signal intensity within the anterior aspect of the lateral femoral condyle on the T1 weighted sequence. This becomes brighter on the more progressively T2 weighted sequences and on the gradient echo sequence. This is compatible with subchondral bony marrow edema due to marrow injury in the lateral femoral condyle. The underlying meniscus appears normal, however, without evidence of tear. There is a minimal grade I signal intensity within the posterior horn of the medial meniscus, but no evidence for tear. A moderate-sized joint effusion is present. The cartilaginous surfaces are somewhat difficult to evaluate at the site of marrow edema, although there is a suggestion of at least focal cartilage thinning.

IMPRESSION

1. Evidence of subchondral bony injury to the anterior aspect of the lateral femoral condyle.
2. A joint effusion is present.
3. No ligament tear or meniscal tear is identified.

I. MULTIPLE CHOICE.
Choose the best answer.

1. Which knee was the MRI performed on?
   - ○ left
   - ○ right

2. Review the indications and choose the reason the MRI was performed.
   - ○ knee effusion
   - ○ evidence of subchondral bone injury
   - ○ ligament tear
   - ○ rule out medial meniscus tear

3. These were *not well visualized, but appear to be intact.*
   - ○ lateral femoral condyle
   - ○ underlying meniscus
   - ○ cruciate ligaments
   - ○ collateral ligaments

4. According to the IMPRESSION, what type of effusion is present?
   - ○ meniscal tear
   - ○ subchondral bone
   - ○ joint
   - ○ ligamentous

OTHER DOCUMENTS

Report Types	Types
Other Documents	correspondence—letters from attorneys, patient, family members, specialists medical record requests physician referral forms HIPAA release forms privacy statements

Both inpatient and outpatient medical records contain some or all of the documents described above. Correspondence, written notes from phone conversations with the patient, requests for copies of the medical record, fall under the "other" category.

There had been debate about whether patient records from other facilities should be part of the receiving facility's medical record. HIPAA regulations now require that all such information, including patient health information from other facilities is made part of the health record.

Release of information requests (with what was released, to who released and the date) are maintained in the medical record. This is filed with, but not released when patient information is released. Federal regulations now also require that facilities provide an "accounting of disclosure" under HIPAA.

UNIT 4

Inpatient Medical Reports

INPATIENT MEDICAL REPORTS – INTRODUCTION

A coder who works with inpatient medical records will have a slightly different approach to coding the record than coding an outpatient record. The inpatient record contains many different documents that can span days, weeks, or months of treatment. To code accurately, the coder reviews, analyzes contents of the file a and applies appropriate guidelines and rules to code the complete stay and all care received by the patient.

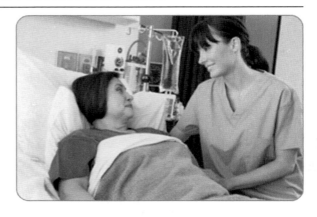

Outpatient medical records and inpatient medical records are not completely different they contain many of the same reports. Consultations, History and Physicals, Operative Reports, and Progress Notes will all be part of the inpatient files. Additional reports such as a discharge summary are also found in the inpatient medical record. All reports are helpful and used in the coding function in the inpatient setting.

The content of a patient's inpatient medical record will vary depending on the type of treatment the patient receives. An otherwise healthy individual who has an overnight stay in the hospital following a surgery will obviously have a very different medical record than an elderly patient with multiple medical problems receiving inpatient treatment for chronic disease. Again, every patient's medical record won't necessarily contain every report type.

Let's look at some of the reports found in an inpatient medical record. Notice the bolded report types. Those are the report types that are found **only in inpatient reports**.

Report Types	Types	Sample Elements
Discharge Summaries	discharge summary interim summary death summary	Patient identification Summary date Reason for visit Admission/Discharge diagnosis History (past, social, surgical, family) Physical exam Laboratory data Course summary Discharge instructions Medications
Consultations	consultation report specialists' report	Patient identification Name of physician who requested the consultation Name of consultant Reason for the consultation Date of examination/review by consultant Pertinent lab/exam findings Consultant's opinion, diagnosis, or impression Consultant's recommended diagnostic tests and/or treatment Signature, credentials, and specialty of the consultant

History and Physical (H&P)	history and physical preoperative H&P prenatal H&P routine H&P intake H&P	Patient identification Relevant dates Reason for visit/chief complaint History of present illness Past medical history, surgical history Social history Health habits Race/ethnicity Family history Allergies, medications Physical examination Assessment and plan
Operative (OP) Reports	operative (OR) summary procedure notes	Patient identification Preoperative and postoperative diagnoses Indications/reasons for operation Description of procedures performed Description of normal and abnormal findings Description of organs explored and specimens removed Description patient's medical condition before, during, and after the surgical procedure Estimated blood loss, ligatures, sutures, number of packs, drains and sponges used Descriptions of any unique or unusual events during course of procedure Complications Names of surgeons and their assistants Relevant dates Signature of principal physician, credentials Type of Anesthesia Allergies
Progress Notes	first visit notes physician notes/orders* nurses' notes medication administration records treatment notes SOAP (subjective/ objective/assessment/ plan) clinic notes	Patient identification Date of progress note Documentation of the reason for the encounter/visit Tests and procedures performed Results of tests and procedures Treatment plan Signature of author Relevant dates

Death Summary		Time and Date of Death/Expiration DNR status Cause of Death (may or may not be known at time of dictation) If family requested an autopsy Pathology/Pending Lab Reports
Autopsy	forensic (for medicolegal purposes) clinical (for research) coroner's (self-explanatory)	Manner of Death Cause of Death Findings/Summation Laboratory Results General Appearance Identification External Examination Injuries Toxicology Photography Trace Evidence X-Rays Microscopic Examination

DISCHARGE SUMMARY

A discharge summary is just what its name implies, a summary of a patient's hospital stay. The discharge summary should include the reason(s) for the hospitalization (principal and secondary diagnoses), procedures performed (principal and secondary procedures), test results, summary of hospital stay, complications, prescribed medications, and the recommended future plan of care. The discharge summary is a vital report in the medical record, and it is very helpful to the coder. Many times, in fact most of the time, the coder is actually coding the record before the discharge summary is available.

Following is a description of each elements of the report. This is not an inclusive list of the different elements of a discharge summary; however, these are the most common elements. Other elements which are not discussed in detail include past medical history, physical exam, lab tests, and radiology tests (x-rays).

Patient's name – Patient's first name, middle initial, and last name should be clearly identified on the report.

Medical record number – Each patient is assigned a unique number by which he or she is identified. This number is called the medical record number.

Date of admission – Date the patient was admitted to the hospital. This date needs to include the month, day, and year of the admission.

Date of discharge – Date the patient was discharged from the hospital. This date needs to include the month, day, and year of the discharge.

Admission diagnoses – Reason or condition the patient was admitted to the hospital for treatment or additional workup. The admission diagnosis is not always the same as the principal diagnosis.

Discharge diagnoses – List of all pertinent diagnoses for the hospital stay.

Procedures – Description of all the procedures performed during the patient's hospital stay.

History of present illness – History of present illness is a description of the patient's present illnesses—signs, symptoms, onset, progression prior to admission and prior treatment.

Hospital course – Hospital course is a narrative summary of the patient's time in the hospital. The summary includes treatment the patient received, complications, interventions, and the outcome of treatment. The hospital course might consist of a few short sentences or be a lengthy, detailed description of the patient's day-to-day hospital stay.

Discharge status – The discharge status can include several factors relating to the patient's discharge, such as condition on discharge (poor, much improved) and discharge disposition (to home, to nursing home, to managed care).

Discharge medications – List of the medications the physician prescribed for the patient which the patient will continue to take after discharge from the hospital.

Discharge instructions – Discharge instructions include any treatment the patient will continue to receive, tests ordered, followup appointments, and other information the physician or hospital deems important for the patient's ongoing care after discharge.

Discharge summary reports will not always break down nicely into headings, and individual providers will sometimes use different names for similar sections. For example, "Discharge status" information might be found under the heading "Disposition." As you become more familiar reading discharge summaries, you will recognize the components quickly and be able to find what you are looking for.

DISCHARGE SUMMARY – EXERCISES

The discharge summary is helpful in determining the principal diagnosis and principal procedure codes. Discharge summaries can contain much of the information necessary for coding. However, it often cannot and should not be the only report used to determine which diagnoses and procedure codes need to be reported. The entire medical record is used to locate all the diagnoses and procedures pertinent to each inpatient medical record.

    I. **MULTIPLE CHOICE.**
        Using the Discharge Summary, choose the best answer.

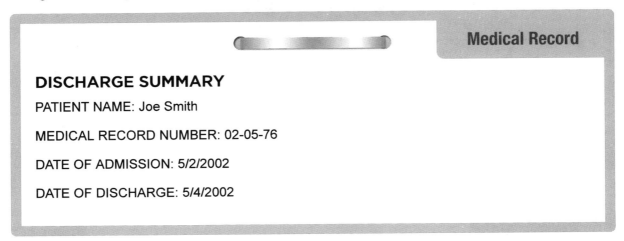

Medical Record

DISCHARGE SUMMARY

PATIENT NAME: Joe Smith

MEDICAL RECORD NUMBER: 02-05-76

DATE OF ADMISSION: 5/2/2002

DATE OF DISCHARGE: 5/4/2002

ADMISSION DIAGNOSIS:
Left knee pain status post left total knee arthroplasty.

DISCHARGE DIAGNOSIS:
Failed left total knee arthroplasty.

PROCEDURE:
Revision of tibial component on the left total knee arthroplasty.

HISTORY OF PRESENT ILLNESS: Mr. ___ [NAME] is a 53-year-old gentleman who underwent a total knee arthroplasty two years ago. Since his revision, he has had continued problems and pain in that knee, especially along the tibial joint line.

He was evaluated extensively for infected knee and had no evidence of infection. There was concern he may probably have had some loosening in his tibial component. The patient was counseled as to the risks and benefits of nonoperative and operative intervention. He understood these risks and benefits and desired the procedure done. The patient is otherwise healthy with no other significant medical problems.

HOSPITAL COURSE: He was admitted to the hospital after his total knee revision without any complications or problems. He was managed in the hospital with a patient-controlled anesthesia (PCA) pump for the first day, and his pain was well under control. He was switched over to oral pain medication. He was started on physical therapy and had a continuous passive motion (CPM) machine while he was in the hospital.

Prior to his discharge, the patient was ambulating with crutch assistance and had 0 to 90 degrees range of motion. His pain was well controlled with oral analgesics.

DISCHARGE DISPOSITION: The patient was discharged back home.

DISCHARGE MEDICATIONS:
He was given a prescription for Percocet 1–2 tablets p.o. q. 4–6 hours p.r.n. pain, #40 (forty).

DISCHAGE INSTRUCTIONS:
1. He has a physician in ___ [PLACE] who will take out his staples.
2. He will give us a telephone call if he has any problems, concerns, or questions.
3. Otherwise, he will follow up in around six weeks to make sure he continues to do well and/ or give us a call and we can decide at that point whether or not he needs to come down.

1. How many discharge medications was the patient given a prescription for?
   ○ 3
   ○ 1
   ○ 2
   ○ 5

2. What is the patient's discharge status?
   ○ acute care hospital
   ○ home health
   ○ home
   ○ skilled nursing facility

3. What is the patient's principal diagnosis?
   ○ failed total knee arthroplasty
   ○ revision left total knee arthroplasty
   ○ knee pain
   ○ status post left knee total arthroplasty

4. What type of medication is Percocet?
   ○ anti-infective
   ○ opiate analgesic
   ○ anti-inflammatory
   ○ corticosteroid

5. What is the patient's principal procedure?
   ○ knee pain
   ○ failed total knee arthroplasty
   ○ status post left total knee arthroplasty
   ○ revision left tibial knee arthroplasty

HISTORY AND PHYSICAL

The history and physical (H&P) examination is another common report included in the medical record. It consists of two main portions: the history and physical examination. The **history** portion is a summary of the patient's illness as told by the patient to the examining physician. (Review the term *subjective* from the last unit). The history is data the physician uses to establish a tentative provisional diagnosis on which to base the treatment of the patient. It provides information about the patient's condition before admission to the hospital. The **physical examination** portion includes an assessment by the examining physician of the body areas and organ systems (this is *objective*). The history and physical generally concludes with an assessment and basic treatment plan.

A complete history and physical is required for each patient who is admitted to the hospital within 24 hours of admission as an inpatient. Many of the care providers treating the patient during the hospital stay refer to the history and physical to gain an overview of the patient's admitting problems/condition. Again, the comprehensive nature of this report makes it an excellent resource for the coder seeking information about a patient receiving inpatient care.

The content of the history and physical should include the following elements:

Patient's name – The patient's first, middle initial and last name should be clearly identified on the report.

Medical record number – Each patient is assigned a unique identification number upon admission. This number is called the medical record number.

Date of admission – Date the patient was admitted to the hospital. This date needs to include the month, day, and year of the admission.

Chief complaint – The nature and duration of the symptoms causing the patient to seek medical attention, as stated in the patient's own words.

History of present illness – A detailed, chronological description of the development of the patient's present illnesses, signs and symptoms from the appearance of the first symptom to the present time. This can also contain the chief complaint.

Past medical history – Past medical history includes a summary of childhood and adult illnesses, such as infectious diseases, pregnancies, allergies and drug sensitivities, accidents, operations, prior hospitalizations, and current medications.

Family history – Family history describes information about parents, siblings, and children in which heredity or contact may play a role, such as allergies, infectious diseases, mental, metabolic, endocrine, cardiovascular, renal diseases, or neoplasms. The health of immediate relatives, ages at death, and causes of death should be included.

Social history – Social history should include habits, marital status, dietary, sleeping, exercise patterns, use of coffee, alcohol, other drugs and tobacco, occupation, environment, daily routine, and outlook on life.

Medications – List of medications the patient is taking at the time of admission.

Review of systems – Review of systems is an inventory of the patient's signs and symptoms by body systems. The review should include general information as well as a close review of each of the body systems. It is designed to reveal information the patient could have forgotten to describe or which at the time seemed relatively unimportant.

Physical examination – Physical examination provides baseline data about the patient to assist in determining a diagnosis. The examination should include all body areas and organ systems. The degree of detail depends upon the patient's symptoms and possible other physical findings or laboratory data.

Assessment/Plan – Reason or condition(s) for which the patient was admitted to the hospital for treatment. The physician records a tentative diagnosis or an impression based on the history and physical examination findings. There may be several diagnoses possible, often referred to as differential diagnoses. A treatment plan is recommended for the treatment of the condition(s).

The history and physical examination report is an integral part of the inpatient medical record. It can assist the coder in determining whether the principal diagnosis was present on admission. The **principal diagnosis** is the condition established, after study, to be chiefly responsible for occasioning the admission of the patient to the hospital for care. For inpatient records, it is necessary to indicate whether all diagnoses are present on admission or occurred after admission.

HISTORY AND PHYSICAL – EXERCISES

I. MULTIPLE CHOICE.
Using the History and Physical report, choose the best answer.

HISTORY AND PHYSICAL

Patient Name: John Jones

Medical Record Number: 11-15-22

Date of Admission: 7/14/2005

HISTORY OF PRESENT ILLNESS: This is a 78-year-old white male, with a past medical history significant for coronary artery disease with 3-vessel CABG and atrial flutter who was admitted to the ___[PLACE] for medical cardioversion using propafenone.

The patient developed an atrial flutter after undergoing a CABG procedure eight to nine years ago. Previously the patient was DC cardioverted for the atrial flutter. The patient did respond to the DC cardioversion and returned to a normal sinus rhythm for three weeks. However, the patient eventually reverted back to an atrial flutter rhythm after being cardioverted. The patient then underwent an ablation therapy for the atrial flutter but the procedure was unsuccessful.

The patient is currently asymptomatic. However, the patient's symptoms are usually confined to lethargy during episodes of irregular heartbeat that he can notice.

The patient denies any paroxysmal nocturnal dyspnea, any orthopnea, or any decrease in exercise tolerance.

PAST MEDICAL HISTORY
1. Three-vessel coronary artery bypass graft.
2. Atrial flutter refractory to sotalol, DCCV, and ablation therapy.
3. Diabetes mellitus.

FAMILY HISTORY
1. Mother died of Hodgkin's disease.
2. Father died at age 94 due to natural causes.

SOCIAL HISTORY: The patient has a 120-pack-year history for smoking. The patient is a social drinker and he denies any illicit drug use.

MEDICATIONS ON ADMISSION:
Coumadin 3 mg per day, simvastatin 30 mg at night, potassium chloride 10 mEq every other day, ranitidine 150 mg at night, nitroglycerin sublingual p.r.n. for chest pain, metoprolol 50 mg b.i.d., felodipine 5 mg q.d., glipizide 2.5 mg q.a.m., digoxin 0.125 mg q.d., and nitroglycerin patch 0.2 mg remove at night.

REVIEW OF SYSTEMS: GENERAL: The patient denies any fevers, chills, and excessive weight gain or weight loss. The patient denies any recent history of trauma or headaches. EYES: The patient denies any discharge from the eyes, itchiness of the eyes, or double vision. EARS: The patient denies any discharge from the ears or tinnitus. NOSE: The patient denies any rhinorrhea or difficulty breathing. THROAT: The patient denies any thyromegaly or difficulty swallowing. CARDIOVASCULAR: The patient denies any paroxysmal nocturnal dyspnea, orthopnea, or decrease in exercise tolerance. RESPIRATORY: The patient denies any history of TB, pneumonia, or shortness of breath. GASTROINTESTINAL: The patient denies any blood in stools, any diarrhea, constipation, nausea, or vomiting. ENDOCRINE: The patient denies any excessive weight gain or weight loss, any excessive heat or cold intolerance. NEUROLOGICAL: The patient denies any seizures, numbness, tingling, or memory loss. RENAL: The patient denies any polyuria, dysuria, or difficulty urinating.

PHYSICAL EXAMINATION
VITAL SIGNS showed a pulse of 54, blood pressure 123/68, temperature 97.5, and a respiratory rate of 14. GENERAL: The patient is alert and oriented in no acute distress, and is a well-developed, well-nourished male. HEENT: Showed a patient who has a normocephalic, atraumatic head. Extraocular muscles are intact. Pupils were equal, round, and reactive to light bilaterally. No evidence of jugular venous pulsations. No thyromegaly, no scleral icterus, and no evidence of lymphadenopathy. CARDIOVASCULAR EXAMINATION revealed S1 and S2 to be present with a regularly irregularly heartbeat and distant heart sounds. No murmurs, gallops, or rubs were appreciated. LUNGS were clear to auscultation bilaterally with good air entry. No accessory muscles were being used. No rales, rhonchi, or wheezing was appreciated. ABDOMEN EXAMINATION showed no tenderness, no distention, no masses, and positive bowel sounds. EXTREMITIES revealed no clubbing, cyanosis, or edema. Pedal pulses were present and there was evidence of scars secondary to the fem-popliteal procedure. NEURO EXAMINATION showed cranial nerves II-XII to be grossly intact, and no focal deficits.

ASSESSMENT/PLAN: Atrial flutter. The patient will be converted using propafenone. Cardiology will start this medication and titrate appropriately. We will restart the patient on his home medications. We will obtain serial EKGs in the morning. The patient will also get blood results of PT, PTT, basic metabolic panel, magnesium, and phosphate, and Cardiology will continue to follow this patient.

1. What is the patient's principal diagnosis?
   - ◯ coronary artery disease
   - ◯ atrial flutter
   - ◯ coronary artery bypass graft
   - ◯ tobacco abuse

2. Which condition is the medication nitroglycerin sublingual used to treat?
   - ◯ atrial flutter
   - ◯ diabetes
   - ◯ history of coronary artery disease
   - ◯ chest pain

3. How many laboratory tests were ordered?
   - ○ 2
   - ○ 3
   - ○ 5
   - ○ 7

4. Which medication is being used to treat the atrial flutter?
   - ○ propafenone
   - ○ Coumadin
   - ○ potassium chloride
   - ○ metoprolol

CONSULTATION

Physicians can be generalists or specialists. Often physicians will seek the advice of other physicians on one or more of the patient's symptoms before making final diagnostic and therapeutic decisions. **Consultation reports** contain an opinion about a patient's condition by a physician other than the attending or primary care physician. This opinion is requested by the attending physician and is based on a review of the patient's medical record, an examination of the patient, and a conference with the attending physician. The attending physician must formally request a consultation indicating on which symptoms or findings an opinion is desired. The

consulting physician examines the patient and documents the findings in a consultation report, making recommendations for treatment of the patient. The consultation report becomes part of the patient's medical record.

Consultation reports usually contain the following types of information:
- name of physician who requested the consultation
- consultant being asked to see the patient
- reason for the consultation
- date the patient is seen and examined by the consultant
- pertinent findings on the examination
- consultant's opinion, diagnosis, or impression
- recommendations by the consultant for diagnostic tests and/or treatment
- signature, credentials, and specialty of the consultant

The consultation report should be carefully reviewed for support of the potential principal diagnosis, as well as significant secondary diagnoses. It is important to thoroughly review the consultation report to identify the diagnoses to be coded. This could be the only place in the patient's medical record these diagnoses are well-documented well-documented.

CONSULTATION – EXERCISES

In the example report below, notice the patient was admitted for treatment of a cerebrovascular accident (CVA). The CVA would be reported as the principal diagnosis. The metatarsal shaft fracture would be reported as a secondary diagnosis code since the fracture occurred after admission to the hospital.

I. **MULTIPLE CHOICE.**
   Using the Consultation report, choose the best answer.

CONSULTATION

Physician requesting consultation is Dr. _____.

REASON FOR CONSULTATION: Right foot pain.

HISTORY OF PRESENT ILLNESS: The patient is a 55-year-old male who was admitted to the hospital three days ago for an acute CVA with right hemiplegia. During the course of his hospitalization, he was walking to the bathroom when he twisted his right foot, felt a loud pop and immediate pain in the area.

Two-view x-rays of the foot were obtained showing a fracture of the fifth metatarsal. Orthopedics was consulted for further evaluation and treatment.

PAST MEDICAL HISTORY is significant for hypertension, coronary artery disease, COPD, aortic stenosis, degenerative joint disease, bilateral carpal tunnel, left elbow epicondylitis, eczema, GERD.

MEDICATIONS include Tylenol, fosinopril, zolpidem, atorvastatin, albuterol, salmeterol, metoprolol, lansoprazole, beclomethasone, aspirin, and Percocet.

EXAMINATION:

VITAL SIGNS: Temperature 97.2, pulse 66, respirations 20, blood pressure 99/51.

EXTREMITIES: Focusing on his right foot, his toes are pink and warm. He is sensate to light touch in all nerve distributions. He is tender over the lateral portion of his forefoot around the fourth and fifth metatarsals. There is significant swelling and edema with ecchymosis present in the area. He is nontender over the medial aspect of the talofibular ligament. He is able to move all of his toes and his ankle without difficulty.

X-RAY shows a mid-shaft fracture of this fifth metatarsal. This is a spiral fracture which is minimally displaced with about 10 degrees of angulation.

ASSESSMENT/PLAN: Right fifth metatarsal shaft fracture. We would ideally treat this in a nonweightbearing short-leg cast; however, given the fact he has recently had a CVA and has had some right-sided hemiplegia and is in need of aggressive rehabilitation, we would place him in a cam walker which should be worn at all times, except to shower, and he may partially weight bear. We would like to follow him a little closer than usual because of this to prevent any displacement. We would see him in one week with x-rays of the foot.

1. What is the reason for the consultation?
   - ○ acute CVA
   - ○ right foot pain
   - ○ hemiplegia
   - ○ metatarsal fracture

2. Where did the patient injure his foot?
   - ○ home
   - ○ store
   - ○ work
   - ○ hospital

3. What is this patient's principal diagnosis?
   - ○ metatarsal shaft fracture
   - ○ foot pain
   - ○ acute CVA
   - ○ hemiplegia

4. Which medication is used for treatment of COPD?
   - ○ albuterol
   - ○ Percocet
   - ○ fosinopril
   - ○ lansoprazole

5. What is the recommended treatment for this patient's fracture?
   - ○ short-leg cast
   - ○ surgery
   - ○ cam walker
   - ○ no treatment

PHYSICIAN PROGRESS NOTE

Up to this point, the reports reviewed have been generalized reports that give overviews of diagnoses, histories, procedures, and medications. Physician progress reports are different in that the treatment is documented in chronological order.

Physician progress notes are specific statements that document the course of the patient's illness, response to treatment, and status at discharge. By reviewing the progress notes the focus of treatment is evident. The attending physician is required to record continuing observations of the patient's progress each time the patient is examined during the hospital stay. The physician's final progress note usually describes the patient's status upon discharge. Progress notes are also written by ancillary professionals providing services to the patient. These would include occupational therapists, respiratory therapists, etc. Frequently, nursing progress notes are separate from the physician and ancillary professional notes.

Physician progress notes usually contain the following information:

- date of progress note
- time of progress note
- documentation of the patient's response to treatment
- significant change in patient's condition
- significant change in patient's diagnosis
- results of test/procedures
- progress toward discharge
- signature of physician

Translation: Christina J. Washburn

PHYSICIAN PROGRESS NOTE – EXERCISES

I. **MULTIPLE CHOICE.**
   Using the Progress Note, choose the best answer.

Medical Record

PROGRESS NOTE #1

Date: 2/12/2006
Time: 9:45 AM

Denies illicit drug use other than heroin. Drinks occasional beer. Last two urine tests have been positive for heroin.

No new psychosocial difficulties. Seemingly spending more time at home and reports no difficulties at work.

Brief physical shows that his BP continues elevated at 152/92.

Reports he attends NA weekly and continues in the weekly support group.

Impression
1. Heroin drug addiction.
2. Participating in program of recovery and by self-report is using Subutex as directed.
3. Mild blood pressure elevation.

Rx Plan
1. Continue Subutex 16 mg daily.
2. Discussed BP elevation and the importance of developing an exercise program and low salt diet.
3. Discharge after detoxification from heroin.

1. What is this patient's principal diagnosis?
   ○ mild blood pressure elevation
   ○ heroin drug addiction
   ○ drinks occasional beer
   ○ detoxification from heroin

2. Is the patient addicted to any other drug beside heroin?
   ○ yes
   ○ no
   ○ not enough information given

3. Name the secondary diagnosis that needs to be coded.
   ○ heroin drug addiction
   ○ detoxification from heroin
   ○ mild blood pressure elevation
   ○ drinks occasional beer

4. How often does the patient drink beer?
   ○ daily
   ○ monthly
   ○ never
   ○ occasionally

5. How was the heroin addiction treated while in the hospital?
   ○ Subutex and detoxification
   ○ exercise program
   ○ low salt diet
   ○ NA support group

II. MULTIPLE CHOICE.
Choose the best answer.

RENAL

This 24 y/o male has ESRD due to IgA nephropathy - on C.A.P.D. Now admitted for renal transplant - brother with 7 antigen match is donor. His lab tests are acceptable. C.A.P.D. dose up until the pm. May have had peritonitis, cleared now - has been on antibiotics. Feeling well. I feel we can proceed with transplant tomorrow without further dialysis. His K is 3.7. Will likely have immediate function from graft. I will follow with you.

Final crossmatch before surgery reported negative by H&I lab. See printed report.

CSR

___[NAME] is a 24 y/o male with CKD 2 degrees to glomerulonephritis. He has been on home peritoneal dialysis since ___[DATE]. He has had 2 episodes of catheter-associated peritonitis, the last being 2 weeks ago. We plan an LRD renal transplant this am. His brother will be the donor.

1. Why was this patient admitted to the hospital?
   ○ peritoneal dialysis
   ○ renal transplant
   ○ peritonitis
   ○ nephropathy

2. Who is the kidney donor for this patient?
   ○ mother
   ○ cadaver
   ○ father
   ○ brother

3. Name the reason for the kidney transplant.
   ○ end-stage renal disease due to IgA nephropathy
   ○ acute renal failure
   ○ peritonitis
   ○ chronic kidney disease

4. How long ago did the patient have peritonitis?
   - ◯ three weeks
   - ◯ one month
   - ◯ two weeks
   - ◯ four months

5. What type of dialysis was the patient receiving?
   - ◯ hemodialysis
   - ◯ peritoneal dialysis
   - ◯ hemoperfusion
   - ◯ hemofiltration

DEATH SUMMARY

A death summary report is a description of the hospitalization and care the patient received up to and through the time of death. The attending physician should complete a death summary once the cause of death has been determined. A death summary report can be filed in the patient's medical record in the place of a discharge summary.

Death summaries usually include the following information:

- patient identification, including name and medical record number
- date of admission
- date and time of death
- cause of death
- history of present illness
- hospital course
- discharge disposition (funeral home, medical examiner, or coroner)

The death summary is helpful in determining the principal diagnosis and any secondary diagnoses pertinent to the patient's hospital stay. It may also list any procedures that need to be reported. The principal diagnosis is not always the cause of death. The patient may have been admitted for a specific condition and then developed complications that caused the patient's death. In this instance the condition for which the patient was admitted would be the principal diagnosis, and the cause of death would be reported as a secondary diagnosis. It is also important to identify where the patient's body was taken following death.

DEATH SUMMARY – EXERCISES

I. **MULTIPLE CHOICE.**
   Using the Death Summary, choose the best answer.

DEATH SUMMARY

PATIENT NAME: Susan Smith

MEDICAL RECORD NUMBER: 19-25-87

ADMISSION DATE: 08/20/1982

DATE OF DEATH: 08/22/1982

CAUSE OF DEATH: Ventricular fibrillation secondary to cardiomyopathy secondary to hypertensive emergency.

HISTORY: This was a 45-year-old previously healthy woman with no known history of heart or kidney disease or hypertension who had been complaining of upper respiratory tract symptoms for the past week.

She was seen by a cardiologist and was noted to have a systolic blood pressure of around 260. She was sent to the Emergency Room for further evaluation. She had an episode of nausea and vomiting and then began to feel sick after receiving some fluid and was admitted to the hospital.

HOSPITAL COURSE: The patient was admitted to the hospital with a hypertensive emergency and end organ dysfunction as specified by her renal insufficiency and left ventricular hypertrophy on EKG.

Patient was immediately started on an Esmolol drip without significant reduction in her blood pressure. Thus, a Nipride drip was initiated since she was refractory to Esmolol. Her blood pressure was difficult to manage even on a Nipride drip; thus, she was also given hydralazine for additional blood pressure control. She was later switched to a labetalol drip and oral labetalol as the nitroprusside drip was weaned off. She was also given clonidine as well.

For her acute renal insufficiency, she was placed on a Lasix drip after a bolus. She eventually did respond somewhat to the Lasix drip and was making some urine within the next 24 hours.

As for the etiology of her hypertension, we were concerned this patient had hyperaldosteronism as evidenced by her significant hyperkalemia on presentation. Her RAN and aldosterone were elevated. A renal ultrasound was done which showed the patient had a left renal mass suggestive of an infiltrative mass.

An echocardiogram was done which revealed an ejection fraction of 30–40% with left ventricular hypertrophy; normal left atrial size, normal right ventricular size. The left ventricular hypertrophy was consistent with hypertrophic cardiomyopathy.

Given the patient had an elevated white count as well as right lower lobe infiltrate and prior symptoms of upper respiratory tract infection, we presumed the patient had community-acquired pneumonia and was started on cefotaxime and azithromycin.

The patient suffered a cardiac arrest and was intubated for airway access and oral airway protection. Cardiac arrest was secondary to RNT, and she subsequently went into torsade. She was resuscitated from her ventricular fibrillation and torsades after receiving an amiodarone drip.

She was taken to the cardiac cath lab. She was found to have normal coronary arteries, but the patient arrested while being transported back to the Intensive Care Unit. She received prolonged cardiopulmonary resuscitation for greater than 30 minutes, massive doses of epinephrine, atropine, and was rebolused with amiodarone, lidocaine, as well as given bicarbonate, calcium gluconate, and numerous cardioversions.

She was then started on drip for significant hypotension. She was transported successfully back to the Intensive Care Unit; however, that night, she went back into severe bradycardic episode as well as developed asystole requiring repeat attempts at CPR as well as transvenous pacing.

Patient was elected to be DNR by the family, but to maintain close support until family members could arrive. The patient was maintained on the ventilator as well as blood pressure support throughout the day as we awaited the arrival of family members prior to withdrawal of support. The patient went into ventricular fibrillation and torsades. No intervention was taken to keep the patient alive as her final family members had arrived just about 10 minutes prior to this episode. All monitors were turned off and the family was allowed to be at the patient's bedside. She became asystolic and neurological examination was done. The patient was pronounced dead at 8:04 p.m. on ___ [DATE].

Cause of death was ventricular fibrillation secondary to hypertrophic cardiomyopathy secondary to hypertension. She also had severe acute renal failure. The patient's family did allow a full autopsy to be done, and the patient's body was taken to autopsy several hours after her death.

1. Where was the patient admitted to the hospital from?
   ○ nursing home
   ○ transferred from another hospital
   ○ emergency room
   ○ home

2. What is the patient's cause of death?
   ○ acute renal failure
   ○ hypertension
   ○ cardiomyopathy
   ○ ventricular fibrillation

3. Was an autopsy performed?
   - ○ yes
   - ○ no
   - ○ not enough information given

4. What condition are the medications cefotaxime and azithromycin used to treat?
   - ○ hypertension
   - ○ acute renal failure
   - ○ cardiomyopathy
   - ○ pneumonia

5. Was the patient placed on a ventilator?
   - ○ yes
   - ○ no
   - ○ not enough information given

AUTOPSY

Autopsy reports are unique to inpatient medical records. An **autopsy report** is a description by a pathologist of the examination of the patient's body after he or she has died. The report usually contains a summary of the history of the patient's illness and treatment, a detailed report of gross findings, microscopic findings, and the anatomical diagnosis at the time of autopsy. Autopsies are usually performed when there is a question concerning the cause of death or when information is needed for legal purposes. The purpose of an autopsy is to determine or confirm the cause of death. Autopsies also provide valuable information about the human body, disease processes,

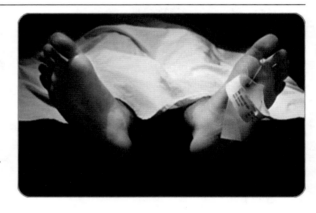

and help further education, research and development in the ongoing effort to cure diseases and develop treatments.

When local authorities suspect a patient's death may have been the result of a crime, a local medical examiner (also a pathologist) may perform the autopsy instead of the hospital pathologist. In the majority of states, medical examiners are required to issue a provisional autopsy report within three days of the autopsy and the final report within sixty days.

The authorization for an autopsy, signed either by the patient's next of kin or by a law enforcement official, should be filed in the patient's medical record. A copy of the provisional autopsy report and final autopsy report should also be filed in the patient's medical record.

The autopsy report may contain the following headings:

- Autopsy Face Sheet
- Historical Summary
- Examination Type, Date, Time, Place, Assistants, Attendees
- Presentation, Clothing, Personal Effects, Associated Items

- Evidence of Medical Intervention
- Postmortem Changes
- Postmortem Imaging Studies
- Features of Identification
- External Examination
- Internal Examination
- Summary of Injuries
- Ancillary Procedures, Laboratory Tests, and Results
- Block Listing and Histologic Description
- Findings and Diagnoses
- Summary and Comments
- Cause of Death Statement
- Amendments

The attending physician is responsible for reviewing the autopsy report and updating the medical record to include the diagnoses documented in the autopsy report (if they are not already documented in the patient's medical record). If the autopsy lists new, different, or additional diagnoses the attending physician has not documented in the medical record, these diagnoses cannot be coded without physician query.

AUTOPSY – EXERCISES

I. **MULTIPLE CHOICE.**
   Using the Autopsy report, choose the best answer.

Medical Record

AUTOPSY FACE SHEET

Case Number:
Name:
Age/Race/Sex:
Date and Time of Death:
Date of Autopsy:

History
The deceased was found in bed at home with an apparent self-inflicted gunshot wound to the head. He had reportedly been complaining of recent headaches. He was transported to the hospital, where death occurred 30 minutes after arrival.

Clinical Procedures
1. Emergency treatment including attempted resuscitation, vascular line placement, fluid administration, endotracheal tube placement.

Findings and Diagnoses
1. Contact gunshot wound of right parietal area of head
A. Perforating brain injury
B. Fracture of left parietal bone
C. Diffuse subarachnoid hemorrhage

D. Cerebral edema
E. Recovery of bullet from left parietal bone (no exit wound)
F. Wound track right to left and slightly upward
2. Berry aneurysm, left anterior communicating cerebral artery
3. Resolving subungual hematoma, left thumb
4. External hemorrhoid
5. Concentric left ventricular hypertrophy, heart
6. Benign prostatic hyperplasia
7. Degenerative osteoarthritis, spinal column
8. Remote amputation of distal portion of left fifth finger
9. Surgical scar, left inguinal area; probable remote hernia repair

Cause-of-Death Statement
Perforating brain injury due to gunshot wound of head

Pathologist:
Date of Report:

AUTOPSY REPORT

HISTORICAL SUMMARY
This 57-year-old male was reportedly found in his bed with a gunshot wound to the head and a handwritten suicide note on the bed stand. He was transported to the hospital by emergency medical services but died in the emergency room. He had a history of recent headaches. Additional details are contained in the investigator's report contained in the medical examiner case file.

EXAMINATION TYPE, DATE, TIME, PLACE, ASSISTANTS, ATTENDEES
Under the provisions of the Death Investigation Act, a complete autopsy is performed in the County Morgue on ___ [Date], beginning at _____ [Time] with the assistance of ___ [Name].

PRESENTATION, CLOTHING, PERSONAL EFFECTS, ASSOCIATED ITEMS
The body is contained in a white plastic body bag bearing a tag with the deceased's name on it and an identification number. The hands are covered with paper bags secured at the wrists with rubber bands. A pair of white briefs is present in the pelvic area and is stained with a small amount of yellow fluid with an odor of urine. A gold colored ring is present on the left ring finger. The briefs are discarded and the ring is removed and forwarded with the body. No other items are present with the body.

EVIDENCE OF MEDICAL INTERVENTION
An endotracheal tube exits from the right side of the mouth. Multiple perimortem needle puncture wounds are present in each subclavian region. An intravascular cannula is inserted in the right cubital fossa. A small needle mark with underlying hematoma is present in the left

radial fossa. Electrocardiographic conductor pads are located over each shoulder anteriorly and in the left lateral midthoracic area. A gauze pad is taped to the right side of the forehead and covers a wound that will be described in further detail below.

POSTMORTEM CHANGES
Rigor mortis is generalized and well developed. Livor mortis is well developed, dorsal, the usual violet color, and blanches with light pressure. The eyes show early corneal clouding. The vermilion borders of the lips are slightly dry. Other postmortem changes are absent.

POSTMORTEM IMAGING STUDIES
Postmortem radiographs of the head show a density beneath the inner table of the left parietal bone, consistent with a medium-caliber bullet.

FEATURES OF IDENTIFICATION
A hospital band on the right wrist bears the deceased's name. The body is unembalmed and that of a male appearing slightly older than the stated age. Height measures 68 inches, and weight is 160 lb. The physique is mesomorphic. The head hair is black, coarse, measures about 1 inch in greatest length, and shows frontoparietal balding. The irides are brown. The teeth are natural with some amalgam restorations. An oblique, well-healed, 4-inch scar with crosshatched suture marks is located in the left inguinal area. The penis is uncircumcised. No tattoos are noted. The distal phalanx of the left fifth finger has been previously amputated and is well healed. No other distinctive external markings are present.

EXTERNAL EXAMINATION
General
Body habitus and hair distribution are normal for age and gender. There is no evidence of malnutrition or dehydration. No peculiar odors or color changes are noted. There is no visible or palpable lymphadenopathy.

Head
A penetrating wound, consistent with a gunshot entry wound, is present on the right side of the head, just above the top of the right ear, 2 inches above the external auditory meatus. The wound is located 64 inches above the heel and 6 inches to the right of the anterior midline. The wound consists of a 3/8-inch circular hole from which extend radial tears measuring up to 1/2 inch in length. A 1/4-inch concentric rim of purple contusion surrounds the hole. Within the superficial wound track, prominent deposits of soot and gunshot residue are visible. No soot or stippling is present on the skin surface surrounding the wound. Dry blood streaks are present posterior to the wound and within the hair. The ear canals are free of blood. The face shows no evidence of trauma. The scalp and soft tissues of the head are otherwise normal, except for palpable lump beneath the skin overlying the left midparietal skull just above the left ear. The nasal and facial bones are without palpable fracture. The conjunctival vessels are slightly congested, and there are no ocular or facial petechiae. A small amount of blood-tinged fluid is present in each nasal vestibule. The lips, gums, teeth, tongue, and buccal mucosa are normal and free of injury. The pinnae and mastoid regions are normal.

Neck
The neck shows no indication of abrasion, contusion, swelling, asymmetry, or other abnormality.

Torso

The torso is free of injury and is symmetrical. No subcutaneous emphysema or cutaneous lesions are noted. The abdomen is moderately distended with gas. Two testes are palpable in the scrotum, which is otherwise normal. The external genitalia, perineum, and anorectal areas are normal except for a small external hemorrhoid at the 2 o'clock position. The inguinal regions and buttocks are normal.

Upper Extremities

The upper extremities are symmetrical, muscular, and well developed. No pigmented or scarred needle tracks are seen, and there are no hesitation marks or healed incised wounds. A 0.5 cm, resolving, subungual hematoma is present beneath the left thumbnail. No soot or gunshot residue is visible on the hands.

Lower Extremities

The lower extremities are well developed and symmetrical. There is slight hair loss bilaterally in a sock like distribution, and the toenails are somewhat thickened and untrimmed.

Evidence of Injury

External evidence of injury is limited to an apparent gunshot wound of the head, a resolving subungual hematoma of the left thumb, and evidence of medical intervention as described above.

Summary

External examination shows a well-developed male with no significant findings except an apparent gunshot wound of the right side of the head.

INTERNAL EXAMINATION

Torso

Evisceration/Dissection Method. The thoracic and abdominal organs are removed using the Virchow technique (individually).

Chest and Abdomen Walls and Cavities.

The skin of the chest and abdomen is reflected using the usual Y-shaped incision. Subcutaneous fat and musculature are normal and free of injury. There are no abnormal fluid collections in the chest or abdomen. The ribs and sternum are intact and without fracture. No unusual odors or color changes are identified. Examination of the organs in situ shows normal organ morphology and relationships. The viscera are congested. The diaphragm is normal. The stomach is distended with air.

Organ Weights.

Heart, 485 g Left lung, 450 g Right lung, 510 g Liver, 1650 g Kidneys, 160 g each Spleen, 140 g

Cardiovascular System.

The left ventricle demonstrates concentric hypertrophy with a left ventricular wall thickness of 2.1 cm. The coronary arteries are normally distributed and are widely patent throughout their lengths, with minimal, soft, atherosclerotic plaques focally. The epicardium, valve leaflets, chordae, and endocardium appear normal. The myocardium is reddish-tan throughout, and no focal myocardial lesions are observed. The thoracoabdominal aorta and major branches show

moderate, yellow, atherosclerotic streaking without ulceration. There are no vascular perforations. The carotid arteries are pliable and patent.

Respiratory System.
The trachea and bronchi are grossly normal except for focal mucosal contusion adjacent to the endotracheal tube cuff, which is positioned appropriately. The hilar nodes and structures are normal. The major pulmonary vessels are normally distributed and free of gross abnormalities. The lungs appear similar, and each lung is congested and moderately edematous, exuding a pink-white foam on manual compression. There is no aspirated blood. No consolidation is observed. There is no indication of thrombosis, embolism, infarction, or neoplasia. The visceral and parietal pleura are free of hemorrhage or perforating defects.

Digestive System.
The serosa, wall, and mucosa of the esophagus, stomach, small bowel, colon, and rectum are grossly normal. The stomach is distended with air and contains approximately 1 cup of partially digested food, primarily consisting of green vegetable material. Hepatobiliary System and Pancreas. The liver shows intense congestion. There is no indication of fatty change or cirrhosis. No focal intrahepatic lesions are noted. The gallbladder contains about 15 cc of viscous green bile, no stones, and is grossly normal. The extrahepatic biliary ducts are patent. The pancreas shows the usual lobular architecture, mild autolysis, and is otherwise normal.

Reticuloendothelial System.
The spleen has a tense capsule and is acutely congested. The red and white pulp is normal. Nodes of the axillary, hilar, mediastinal, abdominal, and cervical area appear normal, except to note mild anthracosis of hilar nodes. The thymus is involuted. Bone marrow of the vertebral bodies appears normal and without focal lesions or masses.

Urogenital Systems.
The kidneys are symmetrical and each shows congestion of the cortex and medulla. The capsules strip easily and the cortical surfaces are smooth. The corticomedullary ratio and junction are normal, as are the pyramids, calyces, pelves, and vessels. The ureters are of normal caliber. The urinary bladder is normal and contains approximately 100 cc of amber urine. The seminal vesicles are normal, and the prostate is firm and nodular with slight enlargement.

Endocrine System.
The thyroid gland is normal size, symmetrical, tan, and free of nodularity, hemorrhage, or cysts. The parathyroids are not identified grossly. The adrenals are of normal size and are free of nodularity or hemorrhage.

Head
The scalp is reflected with the standard intermastoidal incision. There is no indication of scalp trauma, except for a 4-inch circular area of full-thickness soft tissue hemorrhage around the gunshot wound in the right parietal area and a 2-inch circular area of full-thickness soft tissue hemorrhage in the left midparietal region above the left ear. The right temporoparietal bone shows a 3/8-inch circular hole with sharply defined margins on the outer table and beveling of the inner table. The outer table of skull around the hole shows black discoloration from gunshot residue, which is also visible in the diploic spaces. The left midparietal bone contains a 1/2-inch circular fracture, which is displaced into the overlying parietal soft tissues 2.5 inches

directly above the left auditory meatus. Adjacent to the inner table of the bone fragment is a medium-caliber, slightly deformed, fully jacketed, round nose, copper-colored projectile, which is retrieved for submission to the Crime Laboratory. The bullet shows prominent lands and grooves. The dura shows ragged, roughly circular, 3/8-inch, perforating defects in both parietal areas in locations corresponding to overlying defects in the skull. Diffuse subarachnoid hemorrhage is present over the convexities. Brain weight is 1540 g. There is no evidence of significant herniation or midline shift. Coronal sections demonstrate a hemorrhagic wound track extending from the right midparietal region transversely through the brain to the left midparietal cortical surface. The wound track extends through the upper cerebral peduncles. Small cortical contusions are present on the inferior aspect of the frontal poles bilaterally. The circle of Willis contains a 0.5 cm berry aneurysm of the anterior communicating artery on the left. No focal or mass lesions are seen within the brain, and the cortex is normal to palpation. Moderate cerebral edema is noted. The basilar skull and atlanto-occipital region are intact.

Neck and Pharynx
The skin of the neck is dissected up to the angle of the mandible. There is no evidence of soft tissue trauma to the major airways or vital structures in the lateral neck compartments. The hyoid bone and thyroid cartilages are free of fracture. The carotid vessels are pliable and patent. The epiglottis is not inflamed or swollen. There is no airway mucosal edema. No foreign objects are present in the upper airway except for an endotracheal tube. The anterior cervical spine is intact. The tongue is normal.

Spinal Column and Cord
The thoracolumbar spinal column shows mild degenerative osteophytic lipping. The spinal cord is not removed or examined.

Additional Dissection
None.

SUMMARY OF INJURIES
Examination shows an apparent contact gunshot wound of the right parietal area with perforating brain injury and recovery of a projectile in the left midparietal area. No other acute injuries are present.

ANCILLARY PROCEDURES, LABORATORY TESTS, AND RESULTS
1. Vitreous for chemistries: Na, 135; K, 8.0; Cl, 120
2. Peripheral blood for ethanol quantitation: Negative
3. Urine for drug abuse screen: Negative
4. Documentary photographs are prepared and filed in the case folder
5. Retrieved bullet is forwarded to Crime Lab for firearms examination; the Crime Lab will report results

BLOCK LISTING AND HISTOLOGIC DESCRIPTION
Block 1 Heart and lungs
Block 2 Liver, spleen, pancreas, kidney
Block 3 Adrenal, thyroid, pancreas
Block 4 Routine sections of cerebrum, cerebellum, and basal ganglia
Block 5 Routine sections of esophagus, stomach, small and large bowel

Block 6 Prostate
Block 7 Gunshot entry wound
The heart shows mild hypertrophic change; prostate shows benign prostatic hyperplasia. The gunshot wound shows hemorrhage, extensive gunpowder particles, and thermal changes in the collagen. Other sections are not contributory.

FINDINGS AND DIAGNOSES
1. Contact gunshot wound of right parietal area of head
A. Perforating brain injury
B. Fracture of left parietal bone
C. Diffuse subarachnoid hemorrhage
D. Cerebral edema
E. Recovery of bullet from left parietal bone (no exit wound)
F. Wound track right to left and slightly upward
2. Berry aneurysm, left anterior communicating cerebral artery
3. Resolving subungual hematoma, left thumb
4. External hemorrhoid
5. Concentric left ventricular hypertrophy, heart
6. Benign prostatic hyperplasia
7. Degenerative osteoarthritis, spinal column
8. Remote amputation of distal portion of left fifth finger
9. Surgical scar, left inguinal area; probable remote hernia repair

SUMMARY AND COMMENTS
Investigation and autopsy show that death resulted from a self-inflicted gunshot wound of the head. No other significant injuries were observed. The finding of a cerebral artery berry aneurysm is the cause of the history of recent headaches. Cardiac findings suggest a history of hypertension.

CAUSE-OF-DEATH STATEMENT
Perforating brain injury due to contact gunshot wound of head. Based on the circumstances, the manner of death is classified as suicide.

AMENDMENTS
None as of ___ [Date].

1. In the cause of death statement section of the autopsy, what is this patient's cause of death?
   - ◯ cerebral edema
   - ◯ perforating brain injury
   - ◯ fracture of left parietal bone
   - ◯ diffuse subarachnoid hemorrhage

2. In the summary and comments section of the autopsy report, name the cause of the injury.
   - ◯ accidental gunshot wound
   - ◯ fall from ladder
   - ◯ self-inflicted gunshot wound
   - ◯ fall down stairs

3. In the summary and comments section of the autopsy report, what is the cause of the patient's recent headaches?
   - ◯ cerebral artery berry aneurysm
   - ◯ fracture of left parietal bone
   - ◯ diffuse subarachnoid hemorrhage
   - ◯ cerebral edema

4. In the examination type, date, time, place, assistants, attendees section of the autopsy report, where was the autopsy performed?
   - ◯ hospital morgue
   - ◯ medical examiners office
   - ◯ state donor office
   - ◯ county morgue

5. In the history section of the autopsy report, how long after arrival to the hospital was the patient pronounced dead?
   - ◯ two days
   - ◯ 30 minutes
   - ◯ one day
   - ◯ five hours

UNIT 5

Medical Record Organization

MEDICAL RECORD ORGANIZATION – INTRODUCTION

While hard and fast rules do not exist for report organization, medical record organization does have some common practices and formats.

So far this course has concentrated on common types of medical reports. This Medical Record Organization unit discusses how reports are organized—the structure and flow of medical reports—so that all reviewing the record sees a consistent structure.

SUBJECTIVE, OBJECTIVE, DESCRIPTIVE INFORMATION, ASSESSMENT, AND PLAN

Hard and fast rules do not exist for report organization, but there are some common elements you will see in actual practice. These were referred to in the last unit as *sample elements* and are the report headings/formats and ways to present information commonly used to organize medical record content. Having this knowledge will allow the medical coding specialist to focus on certain key parts of the medical record to assign and verify the proper codes.

> While hard and fast rules do not exist for report organization, medical record organization does have some common practices and formats.

Virtually all of the content within a medical report fits into one of five broad categories: subjective, objective, descriptive information, assessment, and plan. Although these headings may or may not literally appear in the document, most of the information contained in a medical report falls into one of these areas.

Subjective – Of, relating to, or designating a symptom or condition perceived by the patient and not by the examiner.

Objective – Not influenced by personal feelings, interpretations, or prejudice; based on facts; unbiased; an objective opinion. Medicine/Medical – Regarding a symptom, discernible to others as well as the patient.

Descriptive Information– Story or account of events, experiences, or the like.

Assessment – The act of assessing; appraisal; evaluation; rendering an opinion; summary of findings.

Plan – A series of steps to be carried out or goals to be accomplished; a scheme, program, or method worked out beforehand for the accomplishment of an objective.

SUBJECTIVE

Subjective: Of, relating to, or designating a symptom, condition, or history perceived by the patient and not by the examiner.

As defined above, subjective information is the information contained in the report "as the patient sees it, feels it, or reports it." In the subjective portions of the healthcare document, the healthcare provider documents what the patient reports to them and not what they have observed first hand.

EXAMPLE 1

CHIEF COMPLAINT/ HISTORY OF PRESENT ILLNESS: This is a 53-year-old female who presents complaining of painful flatfoot deformity and torn tibialis posterior tendon and painful arthritis, left foot, times many months' duration. Patient has exhausted all forms of conservative treatment with no relief and relates continued pain with ambulation and shoe gear and limitation of activities. Patient asks for surgical intervention at this time.

EXAMPLE 2

CHIEF COMPLAINT: Right upper quadrant pain and headache.
HISTORY OF PRESENT ILLNESS: This is a 65-year-old Caucasian female complaining of 3 days of right upper quadrant pain, which is sharp and constant without radiation. The pain is localized. There is no change with position or eating. The pain is accompanied by intermittent nausea and headache.

EXAMPLE 3

This is a 5 month, 28 day old baby girl born full term, no complications, here with both parents. Around 7 p.m., acute onset of fever. T-max 103. Tylenol was given. Did not go down until Motrin given. Had cold symptoms prior to it. No vomiting. No diarrhea. Positive recent wet diaper.

EXAMPLE 4

This is a 53-year-old male who, while at home, accidentally lacerated his left index finger on a glass table as it broke. He denies any loss of function of the finger or any numbness.

Subjective information also includes information provided by the patient as the healthcare provider probes for additional detail about the current condition/complaint and about the patient's history.

EXAMPLE 1

PAST MEDICAL HISTORY: Significant for asthma and degenerative joint disease.
MEDICATIONS: Singulair, Maxair inhalers, estrogen.
ALLERGIES: IV DYE.
SOCIAL HISTORY: No tobacco, occasional alcohol usage.
FAMILY HISTORY: Noncontributory.
REVIEW OF SYSTEMS: No nausea, no shortness of breath.

EXAMPLE 2

REVIEW OF SYSTEMS: She denies any fever, chills, night sweats, chest pain, shortness of breath, vomiting, hematochezia, weakness, or paresthesias. No back pain. She does admit to abdominal pain,

nausea, headache, and a decreased appetite.
PAST MEDICAL HISTORY: Significant only for cataracts.
MEDICATIONS: Include Ativan p.r.n., lithium, Prevacid, ophthalmic drops for her cataracts.
ALLERGIES: PERCOCET, PERCODAN, AND ALL ANTIBIOTICS.
PAST SURGICAL HISTORY: Significant for cataracts, appendectomy, and hemorrhoidectomy.
SOCIAL HISTORY: Fifty pack-years of tobacco. She denies any alcohol use.

EXAMPLE 3

REVIEW OF SYSTEMS: As above. No difficulty swallowing and no stiff neck. No abdominal distention. Positive recent void. No rash.
PAST MEDICAL HISTORY: Full term. No complications.
NO KNOWN ALLERGIES TO ANTIBIOTICS.
IMMUNIZATIONS: Are up to date.

SUBJECTIVE HEADINGS

The following table shows some common subjective headings found in outpatient medical reports, although subjective information can be dispersed throughout reports. Key words to indicate subjective content may be "complained," "stated," and "reported." Medical reports generally contain one or more elements of subjective information.

Common Subjective Headings	Definition
History of Present Illness (HPI)	Patient's description of the history and development of the current illness(es) or injury(ies).
Chief Complaint (CC)/Reason for Visit	Patient's description of the symptom(s) which caused them to seek medical treatment.
Review of Systems (ROS)	An overall review of patient's body systems as stated by the patient or family member to the healthcare provider.
Past Medical History/ Medications	Patient's description of past illnesses, injuries, surgeries, hospitalizations, medications, and allergies.
Past Family History	Patient's description of medical conditions, medical illnesses, congenital anomalies, and/or cause of death of an immediate family member.
Past Social History	Patient's description of the patient's occupation, marital status, personal habits (i.e., tobacco use, drinking habits), and living conditions.
Allergies; Medications	A list of current medications, reported by the patient, of the medications the patient is currently taking; A list of allergies reported by the patient.

REVIEW: SUBJECTIVE

I. **MULTIPLE CHOICE.**
   Using the discharge summary below, choose the best answer.

Medical Record

DISCHARGE SUMMARY

____[NAME] ,____[NAME]

DISCHARGE DATE: 12-18-00.

ADMITTING DIAGNOSES:
1. History of chronic falls.
2. Hypoglycemia.
3. Questionable compliance issues.
4. History of coronary artery disease.
5. History of cerebrovascular accident with right mild hemiparesis.
6. History of carotid stenosis.
7. History of poorly controlled hypertension.
8. Chronic anemia.
9. History of peptic ulcer disease in the past.
10. Noninsulin-dependent diabetes mellitus.
11. Chronic renal insufficiency.
12. Mild aortic stenosis.
13. History of bradycardia.
14. History of non-Q myocardial infarction.
15. Osteoporosis.
16. Chronic peripheral edema.

DISCHARGE DIAGNOSES:
1. Hypoglycemia.
2. Symptomatic anemia.
3. Active peptic ulcer disease.
4. Generalized weakness and joint pain.

CONSULTATIONS:
1. Gastroenterology.
2. Nephrology.
3. Physical therapy.

PROCEDURES:
1. EGD.
2. Colonoscopy.

HISTORY OF PRESENT ILLNESS: The patient is a 79-year-old white male who was admitted for hypoglycemia and having some medical management difficulties at home. The patient has a history of mild right hemiparesis and leads a very sedentary lifestyle. He basically walks to the bathroom and the refrigerator and spends most of his time in a recliner chair. He has problems with peripheral vascular disease including venous stasis and recently was being managed by the chronic wound team. Some notes indicate that the wife was having some difficulties managing him at home. There was some question about adding HBPC. Over the last two weeks, the patient had two events where he was walking and slowly got so weak he slowly crumbled to the floor, there was no loss of consciousness, there was no trauma. The patient usually walks with a walker. His last fall was difficult as he got stuck in the bathroom. He was brought in by EMS. At the time of these incidents, the patient denies any visual changes or any loss of consciousness. He denied any chest pain, rapid pulse, no nausea or vomiting, diarrhea. He had no fever, chills, or night sweats. The patient was hypoglycemic at the time of arrival on this admission.

PHYSICAL EXAMINATION ON ADMISSION: Height: 70". Weight: 184 lbs. Temperature 98, blood pressure 129/58, pulse 75. In general, the patient was in no apparent distress, he was adequately nourished. HEENT exam: Within normal limits with dry scaly scalp. Lungs: Clear to auscultation, no wheezes or rales, he had good air movement. Cor: Regular rate and rhythm, no murmur was appreciated. Abdomen: Soft, nontender, nondistended, no hepatosplenomegaly. Extremities: He had left leg edema 2+ and 3+ at the foot, right leg had less edema with 1+ to 2+ with more edema again at the foot. The patient has chronic peripheral edema with the left leg always larger than the right. Skin: Thin with some appearance of scarring or breakdown, but no active infection. There were some venous stasis changes and mild erythema. He had severe onychomycosis and the toenail on the right toe looked impacted. Cranial nerves were intact. Strength: Left side had 4+ strength upper and lower extremity, right side had 3+ strength upper and lower extremity, otherwise was grossly intact.

LABORATORY DATA ON ADMISSION: Blood sugar was 30 to 40 upon admission. WBC 10.4, hemoglobin 8.9, on discharge hemoglobin was 11.6, hematocrit 26.7, platelet count 228. INR 1.01. Fecal occult blood was positive x 2. Helicobacter was negative. Urinalysis was clear with no microbes, urine leuko esterase, or protein. Glucose on admission 33, BUN 77, creatinine 2.6, potassium 5.3, calcium 7.9, magnesium 3.1, total protein 7.4, albumin 3.6, alkaline phosphatase 100, AST 30. LDH 532, CK 247. Troponin 1.8. Total bilirubin 0.1. Cholesterol 155. Iron 30, TIBC 223, ferritin 109, folic acid 10.5. TSH 1.3.

HOSPITAL COURSE: The patient was admitted to the medicine floor. He was transfused two units of PRBCs for symptomatic anemia and felt much improved. The patient was evaluated by gastroenterology and found to have active peptic ulcer disease. Prep on colonoscopy was poor. The patient was also rehydrated. The following issues were addressed during this hospitalization: 1. Generalized weakness due to symptomatic anemia. The patient is post transfusion. He will continue with iron and Epogen therapy. Follow up with nephrologist within one month and see if this needs to be adjusted. He will be on Prevacid for 60 days and have reevaluation of Hemoccult stool as a followup. HBPC will be called to follow up with patient.

2. Chronic renal insufficiency remained stable during his stay. Peripheral venous stasis did better with hospital bed and is recommended that patient get hospital bed for adequate elevation of legs. He had been worked up in the past for DVT and has chronic venous stasis with one leg enlarged. He has no history of DVT.

3. Deconditioning. The patient was evaluated by physical therapy. After transfusion he apparently was at his baseline. The patient refused any further rehab which was offered to him. He will be discharged home with HBPC for assistance and will have followup with podiatry.

DISCHARGE MEDICATIONS:
1. Prevacid 30 mg p.o. q.d.
2. Cephradine 250 mg p.o. q.i.d.
3. Fosinopril 40 mg p.o. q.h.s.
4. Epogen 8000 units every Wednesday.
5. Nitro patch 0.4 mg p.o. q.d.
6. Lasix 80 mg p.o. q.d.
7. Aspirin 325 mg p.o. q.d.
8. Terazosin 40 mg p.o. q.h.s.
9. Clonidine 0.4 mg p.o. b.i.d.
10. Isosorbide dinitrate 40 mg p.o. b.i.d.
11. Ferrous sulfate 325 mg p.o. t.i.d.
12. Nifedipine 60 p.o. q.d. (Adalat CC).
13. Aspirin 81 mg p.o. q.d.
14. Glipizide 2.5 mg p.o. b.i.d.
15. Colace 100 mg p.o. b.i.d.
16. Terazosin 4 mg p.o. q.h.s.
17. Nitroglycerin transdermal patch apply topically q.d., remove q.p.m.

DISCHARGE DIET: Low potassium, 60 g protein, low fat, no added salt.

DISCHARGE ACTIVITY: Slowly increase as tolerated.

DISCHARGE FOLLOWUP: Follow up with nephrology within one month, podiatry within one month, and HBPC within the week.

1. Which information provided above would NOT be considered subjective information?
   ○ Spends most of his time in a recliner.
   ○ Patient denies any visual changes.
   ○ Cranial nerves were intact.
   ○ He denied any chest pain.

2. Which heading in the discharge summary contains subjective information?
   ○ HISTORY OF PRESENT ILLNESS
   ○ CONSULTATIONS
   ○ PROCEDURES
   ○ DISCHARGE MEDICATION

3. Which information provided in the report would be considered in the subjective?
   ○ Blood sugar was 30 to 40 upon admission.
   ○ His last fall was difficult as he got stuck in the bathroom.
   ○ Lungs: Clear to auscultation, no wheezes or rales, he had good air movement.
   ○ He will be on Prevacid for 60 days and have reevaluation of Hemoccult stool as a followup.

4. Which information provided in the report would be considered in the subjective?
   ○ Follow up with nephrology within one month.
   ○ The patient is post transfusion.
   ○ Urinalysis was clear with no microbes.
   ○ Some notes indicate that the wife was having some difficulties managing him at home.

II. MULTIPLE CHOICE.
Using the outpatient clinic note below, choose the best answer.

Medical Record

CLINIC NOTE

CHIEF COMPLAINT/ HISTORY OF PRESENT ILLNESS: This is a 53-year-old female who presents complaining of painful flatfoot deformity and torn tibialis posterior tendon and painful arthritis, left foot, times many months' duration. Patient has exhausted all forms of conservative treatment with no relief, and relates continued pain with ambulation and shoe gear and limitation of activities. Patient asks for surgical intervention at this time.

PAST MEDICAL HISTORY: Significant for asthma and degenerative joint disease.

MEDICATIONS: Singulair, Maxair inhalers, estrogen.

ALLERGIES: IV DYE.

SOCIAL HISTORY: No tobacco, occasional alcohol usage.

FAMILY HISTORY: Noncontributory.

REVIEW OF SYSTEMS: No nausea, no shortness of breath.

All labs and x-rays reviewed. Radiographic studies also reviewed, being consistent with physical exam.

PHYSICAL EXAMINATION: General: Patient alert and oriented times 3, in no apparent distress. Integument: No open lesions, no signs of infection bilaterally. Skin warm, dry, supple bilaterally. Vascular: DP and PT 1/ 4 bilaterally. Cap refill time less than 3 seconds bilaterally. No edema bilaterally. Neurologic: Grossly intact sensation bilaterally. DTRs 1/4 bilaterally. Musculoskeletal: Positive pain on palpation along the course of tibialis posterior tendon.

Decreased medial arch with valgus rotation of the calcaneus and forefoot abduction. Mild pain with passive range of motion of the hindfoot tritarsal joint complex, left foot. No ankle joint pain with active or passive range of motion. Muscle strength: Decreased plantar flexion inversion strength bilaterally, worse on the left. All other muscle strengths are within normal limits. Adequate dorsiflexion and range of motion, left ankle joint. No calf tenderness bilaterally, antalgic gait.

ASSESSMENT

1. Painful flatfoot deformity, left foot.

2. Painful degenerative joint disease, left tritarsal joint complex.

PLAN: A triple arthrodesis with possible harvest of iliac bone graft, left foot. Patient A&O times 3. Consent signed and witnessed in chart. Patient to be seen and cleared by medicine and anesthesia. All risks, benefits, and expected outcomes explained to patient. All questions answered. No guarantees given or implied. Patient on call to OR per ____ [NAME].

1. Which information provided above would NOT be considered subjective information?
   - ○ A triple arthrodesis with possible harvest of iliac bone graft, left foot.
   - ○ Allergy to IV dye.
   - ○ Occasional alcohol use.
   - ○ Patient complains of painful flat feet.

2. The presentation of subjective information can be listed under different headings. Which would NOT be a common subjective heading?
   - ○ ALLERGIES
   - ○ PAST MEDICAL HISTORY
   - ○ SOCIAL HISTORY
   - ○ PHYSICAL EXAMINATION

3. Which of the following statements from the above report is subjective?
   - ○ DTRs 1/4 bilaterally.
   - ○ Patient to be seen and cleared by medicine and anesthesia.
   - ○ Painful flatfoot deformity, left foot.
   - ○ ...relates continued pain with ambulation and shoe gear and limitation of activities.

4. Which of the following statements from the above report is subjective?
   - ○ The patient is A&O times 3.
   - ○ Patient asks for surgical intervention at this time.
   - ○ Adequate dorsiflexion and range of motion...
   - ○ All risks, benefits and expected outcomes explained to the patient.

OBJECTIVE

Objective: Not influenced by personal feelings, interpretations, or prejudice; based on facts; unbiased: an objective opinion. *Medicine/Medical. Regarding symptoms, discernible to others as well as the patient.*

Objective information is the "reporting of the facts." The healthcare provider tests, examines, and observes, and the results are documented. Objective headings contain information not based on the patient's report, but based on test results, facts, or provider observation.

EXAMPLE 1

PHYSICAL EXAMINATION: General: Patient alert and oriented times 3, in no apparent distress. Integument: No open lesions, no signs of infection bilaterally. Skin warm, dry, supple bilaterally. Vascular: DP and PT 1/4 bilaterally. Cap refill time less than 3 seconds bilaterally. No edema bilaterally. Neurologic: Grossly intact sensation bilaterally. DTRs 1/4 bilaterally. Musculoskeletal: Positive pain on palpation along the course of tibialis posterior tendon. Decreased medial arch with valgus rotation of the calcaneus and forefoot abduction. Mild pain with passive range of motion of the hindfoot tritarsal joint complex, left foot. No ankle joint pain with active or passive range of motion. Muscle strength: Decreased plantar flexion inversion strength bilaterally, worse on the left. All other muscle strengths are within normal limits. Adequate dorsiflexion and range of motion, left ankle joint. No calf tenderness bilaterally, antalgic gait.

EXAMPLE 2

LABORATORY DATA: CBC shows a white count of 7.6, H&H of 13.6 and 41.4, platelet count of 282. Differential is normal. BMP has a sodium of 140, a potassium of 4.5, a chloride of 106, bicarb of 24, BUN and creatinine of 12 and 1.0 respectively, glucose of 104, osmolality of 289, calcium 9.4. Lipase is 160. Total bilirubin is 0.5. Alk phos 62. AST 27. ALT 9. Albumin 4.4.
Urinalysis is positive for leukocyte esterase, but there is no bacteria or white blood cells.
Head CT was done which was negative.
Rib films showed no obvious fracture although we are awaiting final results.
Patient did have an MRI in ___ [DATE] that showed a small region of white matter with ischemic change and small vessel disease.
In ___ [DATE] she had a stress thallium test, which was negative for ischemia, normal LV function and an EF of 63%.

EXAMPLE 3

Examination today confirmed the presence of a 2nd papule of a pink color, more proximal to the graft site and otherwise a healing wound. He shows very severe solar damage, with generalized freckling and multiple solar keratoses of the scalp and arms.

His benign nevus count is less than 50, and no dysplastic nevi were detected. The graft site is clear of any clinical involvement.
His nodes and liver were not palpable.
Incidental finding of BCC showing on the posterior left shoulder, right upper chest, right and left shin and an SCC in-situ on the left popliteal region.

EXAMPLE 4

SLEEP STUDY: The mean oxygen saturation (SaO2)% while awake was 96% and during sleep was 94%. The minimum SaO2 in REM was 80% and NREM was 81% with maximum SaO2 of 96% and 96% respectively. The percentage of time spent above 89% was 89.5. The minimum SaO2 recorded was 80%. 0 Total desaturations recorded.

Once again, as with subjective information, objective information can be found under many headings. Objective information can provide important clues to help medical coding specialists find codable diagnoses and treatments or to seek clarification from the healthcare provider.

OBJECTIVE HEADINGS

The following table shows some common objective headings found in medical reports. Objective information can be dispersed throughout the report. Subjective, assessment, descriptive, or plan information can be inserted under an "objective" heading.

Common Objective Headings	Definition
Physical Examination (PE)	The description of the physical findings resulting from examination of the patient and recorded by the healthcare provider performing the examination.
Laboratory Data	Results of laboratory tests performed on the patient's body fluids or tissues.
Radiologic Studies	Results of radiologic studies performed on the patient including mammography, plain film x-rays, or complex radiologic studies such as CT, MRI.
Studies Performed; Study Performed; Results*	Examples of the many general objective headings for reporting results of studies for such things as sleep studies, swallowing studies, EKG, neurologic studies, nerve conduction studies.
Medications	A documented list of current medications the patient is currently taking. (If patient provides the information and it is not documented by the dictator, it could be considered subjective information.)
Procedure(s) Performed; Primary Procedure; Secondary Procedure	Brief description of the type of procedure being performed.

*In many cases, objective information simply follows the name of the test, i.e. SLEEP STUDY, SMA-7, and so forth.

Objective studies are often simply titled based on the type of study being reported.

REVIEW: OBJECTIVE

With the objective criteria in mind, review the following report and answer the questions.

Medical Record

PREOPERATIVE HISTORY AND PHYSICAL

CHIEF COMPLAINT/ HISTORY OF PRESENT ILLNESS: This is a 53-year-old female who presents complaining of painful flatfoot deformity and torn tibialis posterior tendon and painful arthritis, left foot, times many months' duration. Patient has exhausted all forms of conservative treatment with no relief, and relates continued pain with ambulation and shoe gear and limitation of activities. Patient asks for surgical intervention at this time.

PAST MEDICAL HISTORY: Significant for asthma and degenerative joint disease.

MEDICATIONS: Singulair, Maxair inhalers, estrogen.

ALLERGIES: IV DYE.

SOCIAL HISTORY: No tobacco, occasional alcohol usage.

FAMILY HISTORY: Noncontributory.

REVIEW OF SYSTEMS: No nausea, no shortness of breath.

LABORATORY DATA: CBC shows a white count of 7.6, H&H of 13.6 and 41.4, platelet count of 282. Differential is normal. BMP has a sodium of 140, a potassium of 4.5, a chloride of 106, bicarb of 24, BUN and creatinine of 12 and 1.0 respectively, glucose of 104, osmolality of 289, calcium 9.4. Lipase is 160. Total bilirubin is 0.5. Alk phos 62. AST 27. ALT 9. Albumin 4.4.

Urinalysis is positive for leukocyte esterase, but there is no bacteria or white blood cells.

MRI of the left foot was consistent with the physical findings.

PHYSICAL EXAMINATION: General: Patient alert and oriented times 3, in no apparent distress. Integument: No open lesions, no signs of infection bilaterally. Skin warm, dry, supple bilaterally. Vascular: DP and PT 1/ 4 bilaterally. Cap refill time less than 3 seconds bilaterally. No edema bilaterally. Neurologic: Grossly intact sensation bilaterally. DTRs 1/4 bilaterally. Musculoskeletal: Positive pain on palpation along the course of tibialis posterior tendon. Decreased medial arch with valgus rotation of the calcaneus and forefoot abduction. Mild pain with passive range of motion of the hindfoot tritarsal joint complex, left foot. No ankle joint pain with active or passive range of motion. Muscle strength: Decreased plantar flexion inversion strength bilaterally, worse on the left. All other muscle strengths are within normal limits. Adequate dorsiflexion and range of motion, left ankle joint. No calf tenderness bilaterally, antalgic gait.

ASSESSMENT

1. Painful flatfoot deformity, left foot.
2. Painful degenerative joint disease, left tritarsal joint complex.

PLAN: A triple arthrodesis with possible harvest of iliac bone graft, left foot. Patient A&O times 3. Consent signed and witnessed in chart. Patient to be seen and cleared by medicine and anesthesia. All risks, benefits, and expected outcomes explained to patient. All questions answered. No guarantees given or implied. Patient on call to OR per ___ [NAME].

I. MULTIPLE CHOICE.
Choose the best answer.

1. Which of the following statements from the report above is objective information?
   - ○ This is a 53-year-old female who presents complaining of painful flatfoot deformity and torn tibialis posterior tendon and painful arthritis, left foot, times many months' duration.
   - ○ REVIEW OF SYSTEMS: No nausea, no shortness of breath.
   - ○ Total bilirubin is 0.5.
   - ○ PLAN: A triple arthrodesis with possible harvest of iliac bone graft, left foot.

2. Which of the following headings would NOT be a common objective heading?
   - ○ PAST MEDICAL HISTORY
   - ○ RADIOLOGIC FINDINGS
   - ○ LABORATORY DATA
   - ○ PHYSICAL FINDINGS

3. The statement "Urinalysis is positive for leukocyte esterase, but there is no bacteria or white blood cells" would be considered _____.
   - ○ subjective
   - ○ objective

4. The statement "The patient reports no nausea or shortness of breath" would be considered

   _____.
   - ○ subjective
   - ○ objective

5. The statement "On physical exam, the patient is in no acute distress" would be considered

   _____.
   - ○ subjective
   - ○ objective

DESCRIPTIVE INFORMATION

> **Descriptive Information:** Story or account of events, experiences, or the like.

This section includes portions of the record that don't fit neatly into subjective, objective, assessment, or plan. These portions generally involve accounts of what's happening with or to the patient. The information in this first example is the detailed description of the mechanics of the operative procedure (OPERATION IN DETAIL):

Medical Record

OPERATIVE REPORT

OPERATIVE PROCEDURE: Right fifth metacarpal fracture with correction of malrotation and angulation, difficult in nature since initial injury was almost 2 weeks old.

DIAGNOSIS: Complex metacarpal fracture of the right fifth digit.

OPERATION IN DETAIL: After regional block anesthesia using lidocaine, an ulnar block at the dorsal branch of the ulnar nerve, and then testing the patient for effectiveness of the block, an area with residual sensation near the fracture was also anesthetized using a 30 gauge needle. After good anesthesia was achieved of the entire digit, multiple attempts were made at reducing and correcting the malrotation. Since the fracture was 2 weeks old, it took considerably more time and 5 separate attempts to complete the alignment. Typically this reduction would be completed in a single attempt, which would be completed in 1 hour to 1 1/2 hours, but because of the delay in treatment, it required 5 attempts and at least 2 hours longer than normal to achieve correction of the malrotation Total operating time was between 3 and 3 1/2 hours. The angulation was also corrected to an adequate degree, whereas the patient should not have any significant problems, according to the statistics in the literature.

The angulation originally was close to 50 degrees and after the reduction it was more in the 20-degree range. As far as the dorsal angulation and the malrotation, there was none. It was totally corrected. The finger was buddy-taped to the fourth digit. The fracture was stable. It was splinted with specialized casting material, using Orthoplast fiberglass splinting material, with both a dorsal and a volar splint, double thickness in continuity, in order to prevent noncompliance and reinjury of the fracture by the patient. Extra support using extra Ace bandages was also used.

The patient tolerated the procedure well. Post reduction films were adequate and no further procedures will be required as long as the patient continues to be compliant.

The second and third examples are the description of the patient's course in the emergency room:

Medical Record

EMERGENCY DEPARTMENT REPORT

EMERGENCY DEPARTMENT COURSE: Patient was given Imitrex 6 mg subcutaneously with no change in her symptomatology. Repeated temperature while in the emergency department showed some increase up to 38.3 level. Patient did receive Demerol and Vistaril, again with only minimal relief of her pain. She was subsequently given some fentanyl with only mild improvement.

Medical Record

EMERGENCY DEPARTMENT REPORT

E.D. COURSE: This patient's primary neurologist, ____[DOCTOR], was contacted and he felt that if the patient did not have any significant gross loss of strength, that we should not consider starting him on a steroid at this time and he should continue medications as previously prescribed. Furthermore, he has agreed to move up his appointment in the Neurology Clinic to ___ [DATE] at 8 o'clock. The patient will be seen should he have any acute loss of strength between now and his upcoming neurology appointment.

The fourth is the step-by-step account of an injection:

Medical Record

EMERGENCY DEPARTMENT REPORT

PROCEDURE: Patient seated. After sterile prep and drape, local anesthetic was injected into the skin and subcutaneous tissue. Epidural space was entered using the loss-of-resistance technique with an 18 gauge two-way needle. No blood, no CSF, and no paresthesias were noted. The patient was injected with 60 mg of triamcinolone and 2 cc of normal saline. He tolerated the procedure well.

DESCRIPTIVE INFORMATION HEADINGS

The following table shows some common descriptive headings found in medical reports. Descriptive information can be dispersed throughout the report.

Descriptive Information	Definition
Summary; ER Course; Note; Hospital Course; Death Summary; Interim Summary	Record of the details of the course of the patient's visit/hospitalization.

79

Observation	Record of the observations of the healthcare provider(s) of the patient during the visit.
Description of Procedure(s); Operative Summary	Description of the details of the operation/procedure, may include anesthesia, type of sutures, instrument used, and condition of the patient at the end of the procedure.

These categorizations are not absolute or rigid. In other words, a paragraph under a common descriptive heading might contain objective statements or assessment information. Keep in mind that these categories are to help identify general patterns and categories of information.

I. **MULTIPLE CHOICE.**
Using the discharge summary below, choose the best answer.

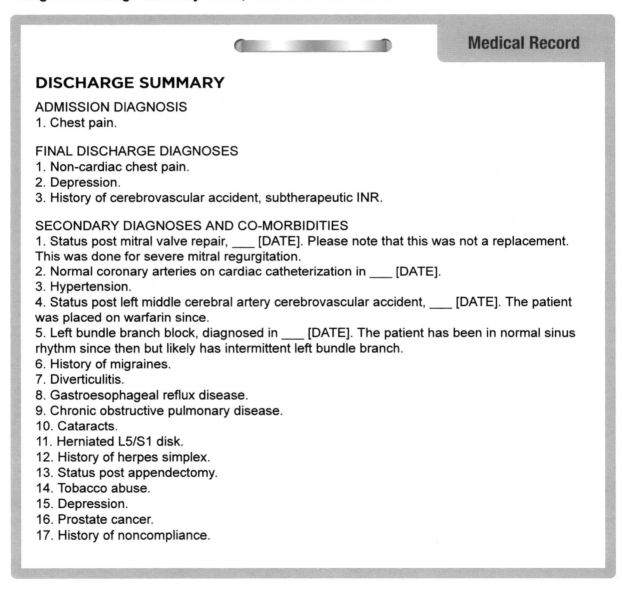

Medical Record

DISCHARGE SUMMARY

ADMISSION DIAGNOSIS
1. Chest pain.

FINAL DISCHARGE DIAGNOSES
1. Non-cardiac chest pain.
2. Depression.
3. History of cerebrovascular accident, subtherapeutic INR.

SECONDARY DIAGNOSES AND CO-MORBIDITIES
1. Status post mitral valve repair, ___ [DATE]. Please note that this was not a replacement. This was done for severe mitral regurgitation.
2. Normal coronary arteries on cardiac catheterization in ___ [DATE].
3. Hypertension.
4. Status post left middle cerebral artery cerebrovascular accident, ___ [DATE]. The patient was placed on warfarin since.
5. Left bundle branch block, diagnosed in ___ [DATE]. The patient has been in normal sinus rhythm since then but likely has intermittent left bundle branch.
6. History of migraines.
7. Diverticulitis.
8. Gastroesophageal reflux disease.
9. Chronic obstructive pulmonary disease.
10. Cataracts.
11. Herniated L5/S1 disk.
12. History of herpes simplex.
13. Status post appendectomy.
14. Tobacco abuse.
15. Depression.
16. Prostate cancer.
17. History of noncompliance.

CONSULTS
1. Psychiatry.

PROCEDURES
1. Electrocardiogram, revealing left bundle branch block.
2. Chest x-ray, ___ [DATE]. Poor inspiratory effort. No infiltrate. Possible component of vascular congestion.
3. Ventilation perfusion scan, ___ [DATE]. This was normal.

HISTORY OF PRESENT ILLNESS: This is a 72-year-old, white male with the above medical history. He presented to the ___ [PLACE] with right-sided chest discomfort. The patient admitted to being very depressed on initial evaluation. He was admitted to the ___ [PLACE] team and then converted to the Medicine team for further evaluation.

REVIEW OF SYSTEMS: On initial evaluation on the ___ [PLACE] team, the patient expressed feelings of depression due to the recent death of his wife and daughter. The patient denied any suicidal ideation. The patient stated he had been noncompliant with his medications and had not been eating. The patient was chest pain free on initial evaluation by the Medicine team. The remainder of his review of systems was negative.

ADMISSION DATA: Troponin less than 0.03 times three sets. Normal CBC and normal chemistry-7. His INR was subtherapeutic at 1.5. His LDL was 146. His urinalysis was normal. An ABG revealed 7.43/31/52 with 82% saturations on room air.

PHYSICAL EXAMINATION ON ADMISSION
GENERAL APPEARANCE: On initial evaluation, the patient appeared depressed and was often tearful.
VITAL SIGNS: He was afebrile. His vital signs were stable.
NECK: There was no jugular venous distention.
HEART: His heart was regular without murmurs, rubs or gallops.
LUNGS: His pulmonary examination did reveal some bibasilar rales.
EXTREMITIES: There was no peripheral edema.

HOSPITAL COURSE BY PROBLEM
1. Non-cardiac chest pain: The patient was ruled out with cardiac markers, and his left bundle branch block, which was old, was thought to be intermittent. On review of the patient's chart, he had a normal coronary angiogram done in ___ [DATE] as preoperative for his mitral valve repair. No further workup was indicated, as this left bundle branch block is likely due to the patient's mitral valve disease.

2. Depression: On initial evaluation, the patient was depressed. He had the recent death of his wife and daughter, and the patient admitted to anhedonia, weakness, lack of appetite, etc. The patient denied any suicidal ideation.

The patient was seen by the ___ [PLACE] team, and they agreed with continuing the patient on his selective serotonin reuptake inhibitor. The patient did not meet criteria for an acute psychiatric admission. The patient agreed with this plan, and throughout his hospital stay he improved.

3. History of cerebrovascular accident, subtherapeutic INR: On initial evaluation, the patient's INR was 1.5. This was consistent with his stated history of noncompliance with his medications due to his depression.

The patient was restarted on warfarin, and his INR was 2.4 at the time of discharge. The patient will be re-enrolled in the ___ [PLACE], and his dose will be adjusted accordingly. The patient has been on warfarin since ___ [DATE] when he had a left middle cerebral artery cerebrovascular accident.

DISCHARGE DATA: Hematocrit 38.7, INR 2.4.

COMPLICATIONS: None.

DISPOSITION: The patient was discharged to home.

DISCHARGE MEDICATIONS: The patient will resume his home medications, which include:
1. Oxybutynin 5 mg p.o. t.i.d.
2. Terazosin 5 mg p.o. q. h.s.
3. lansoprazole 15 mg p.o. q.d.
4. Gabapentin 900 mg p.o. t.i.d.
5. Docusate 100 mg p.o. b.i.d. p.r.n.
6. Diltiazem 240 mg p.o. q.d.
7. Albuterol inhaler 2 puffs q.i.d. p.r.n.
8. Acetaminophen 500 mg p.o. q. 6 hours p.r.n.
9. Sertraline 100 mg p.o. q. a.m.
10. Warfarin 5 mg p.o. q.d. except for Tuesday and Thursday, to be further adjusted by the ___ [PLACE].
11. Warfarin 2.5 mg p.o. q.d. on Tuesday and Thursday, to be further adjusted by the ___ [PLACE].
12. Simvastatin 20 mg p.o. q. h.s.

DIET: Cardiac.

ACTIVITY: As tolerated.

FOLLOWUP
1. The patient will follow up with the ___ [PLACE] on ___ [DATE].
2. The patient will follow up with Dr. ___ [NAME] on ___ [DATE], who is his primary care physician.

1. Information found under the heading LUNGS would be considered _____.
   ○ subjective
   ○ objective
   ○ other information

2. Information found under the heading HISTORY OF PRESENT ILLNESS would be considered _____.
   ○ subjective
   ○ objective
   ○ other information

3. Information found under the heading HOSPITAL COURSE BY PROBLEM would be considered _____.
   ○ subjective
   ○ objective
   ○ other information

4. Information found under the heading VITAL SIGNS would be considered.
   ○ subjective
   ○ objective
   ○ other information

5. Information found under the REVIEW OF SYSTEMS heading would be considered _____.
   ○ subjective
   ○ objective
   ○ other information

ASSESSMENT

Assessment: The act of assessing; appraisal; evaluation; rendering an opinion; summary of findings.

The assessment or diagnosis portion of the medical record is the place where the physician documents his or her conclusions regarding the patient's condition.

Healthcare providers, particularly physicians, determine the underlying causes of, and prescribe the treatments for, a patient's healthcare issues. From the medical coding specialist's point of view, the healthcare provider's assessment is one of the most critical pieces of information contained in the medical record. Diagnosis coding is often done from the physician's assessment.

EXAMPLE 1

ASSESSMENT: Sarcoma with an ECOG performance status of 4, bed bound on home oxygen.

Highlights

Medicine is not an exact science. Diagnosis is often a process of elimination and/or educated guess based on evaluation.

EXAMPLE 2

ASSESSMENT: Arthritis of the metacarpophalangeal joint, possibly degenerative joint disease, possibly inflammatory, possible history of rheumatoid arthritis.

EXAMPLE 3

IMPRESSION: The patient has degenerative joint disease of both knees.

ASSESSMENT HEADINGS

The following table shows some common assessment headings found in medical reports. The healthcare provider's assessment, like any other type of information, can be clearly stated under a heading or mixed in with other subjective, objective, descriptive, or plan information.

Common Assessment Headings	Definition
Preoperative Diagnosis	The diagnosis for which surgery is to be performed.
Postoperative Diagnosis	The diagnosis documented by the surgeon after the procedure is performed.
Assessment; Opinion; Conclusion; Impression; Post-Procedure Diagnosis, Condition During Procedure	Provider's assessment of patient condition.
Diagnosis; Final Diagnosis; Primary Diagnosis, Secondary Diagnosis, Differential Diagnoses; Axis Diagnosis	Provider's diagnosis(es), often listed by order of importance.

REVIEW: ASSESSMENT

Medical Record

CLINIC NOTE

The patient is seen for followup of multiple problems. She reports that four days ago, after going to the Steeler exhibition game, she walked to her car. She had discomfort the next day in the area of the Achilles tendon on the left side as well as both knees, although the right tended to have more of a sense of giving way. She also developed some hip and back pain. She has had no referred pain and no complaints of paresthesias.

Physical exam for the back demonstrates discomfort with lateral flexion and rotation. Symptoms are localized to the left oblique muscles. There is also some discomfort with palpation of the trochanteric bursa, and there is discomfort with manual muscle testing as well as stretch of the hip abductors. There is full flexion and extension of the lumbar spine as well as rotation to the right without significant discomfort. The lumbar spine, paraspinal muscles, sciatic notch, and sacroiliac joints are nontender with palpation.

Examination of both knees demonstrates discomfort on palpation of the patella facets. There is significant reduction in quadriceps tone, in particular on the left side more so than the right, although both appear decreased. The quadriceps and patellar tendons are nontender with palpation. Circumduction maneuvers produce no frank clunk, but do produce some discomfort. There is no pain with valgus or varus stress at 0 and 30 degrees of flexion. Lachman test is negative.

Examination of the patient's left Achilles tendon does demonstrate significant discomfort with some thickening. There is no evidence of swelling. Negative posterior impingement test is noted. Generalized weakness of the ankle musculature is present.

ASSESSMENT: Left Achilles tendonopathy, hip abductor strain with trochanteric bursitis and external oblique strain. Exacerbation of patellar subluxation.

PLAN: The patient will be started on nitroglycerine patches cut in quarters to be applied to the Achilles tendon. She will be given a prescription for Vicodin 5/500 #30 to be used on an as needed basis for pain. She will start a course of physical therapy for her hips and continue therapy for her knees. She will follow up with me over the next six weeks.

I. **MULTIPLE CHOICE.**
   Choose the best answer.

   1. Which of the terms listed below is NOT synonymous with the term assessment?
      ○ axis diagnosis
      ○ conclusion
      ○ plan
      ○ postoperative diagnosis

   2. Which of the following statements is part of the assessment?
      ○ Exacerbation of patellar subluxation.
      ○ Physical exam for the back demonstrates discomfort with lateral flexion and rotation.
      ○ She also developed some hip and back pain.
      ○ Lachman test is negative.

3. Which of the following statements from the above report is subjective?
- ◯ There is no pain with valgus or varus stress at 0 and 30 degrees of flexion.
- ◯ She reports that four days ago, after going to the Steeler exhibition game, she walked to her car.
- ◯ She will start a course of physical therapy for her hips and continue therapy for her knees.
- ◯ Exacerbation of patellar subluxation.

4. Which of the following statements from the above report is objective?
- ◯ The quadriceps and patellar tendons are nontender with palpation.
- ◯ She has had no referred pain and no complaints of paresthesias.
- ◯ Exacerbation of patellar subluxation.
- ◯ She will follow up with me over the next six weeks.

5. Which of the following statements from the above report is part of the physician's assessment?
- ◯ She will follow up with me over the next six weeks.
- ◯ The lumbar spine, paraspinal muscles, sciatic notch, and sacroiliac joints are nontender with palpation.
- ◯ Left Achilles tendinopathy, hip abductor strain with trochanteric bursitis and external oblique strain.
- ◯ Symptoms are localized to the left oblique muscles.

PLAN

Plan: A series of steps to be carried out or goals to be accomplished; A scheme, program, or method worked out beforehand for the accomplishment of an objective.

Assessment and Plan often go together. In many reports, the plan of action for the patient's treatment, followup, disposition, or intervention is given as part of the assessment.

ASSESSMENT/PLAN

1. Congestive heart failure. The patient is well compensated at present. Continue medications.
2. Upper respiratory tract infection. I will give him Septra DS b.i.d. for 10 days. The patient will follow up with me in 3 months.

Whether contained in a separate heading or combined in the assessment, the plan or recommendations are important to the medical coding specialist. Plan-related headings can include comprehensive recommendations and instructions, or plans can be scattered throughout a number of headings detailing the patient's recommended medication, followup care, and so forth.

EXAMPLE 1 (OUTPATIENT)

PLAN: I told her that it is extremely important she lose weight. I gave her leg extension exercises to perform and will fit her for orthotics. She may continue with medications. However, I would caution that if she stays on Naprosyn she should have either Cytotec or proton pump inhibitor to prevent any stomach ulcers, as she is at increased risk due to her age. She will follow up in 3 months for reevaluation.

EXAMPLE 2 (OUTPATIENT)

ASSESSMENT/PLAN: Hypertension. Blood pressure is still elevated with a systolic blood pressure of 140s to 150s. The patient had not stopped his hydrochlorothiazide/triamterene medications. Today he was instructed to stop this medication because being on fosinopril 40 mg two tablets a day, helps retain potassium and currently his potassium is normal. We will decrease his potassium to 10 mEq q.d. We will increase his felodipine to 20 mg q.d. to help with his blood pressure. His Isordil has been changed to 20 mg b.i.d. since the patient cannot remember to take it 3 times a day. He was instructed to take Simvastatin 1 1/2 tablets of a 40 mg tablet every q.h.s.

We will plan to have the patient back to clinic in approximately 8 days with another blood pressure and BMP check at that time. Further recommendations, if necessary will be done at that visit.

EXAMPLE 3 (INPATIENT)

PLAN
1. Coagulopathy: We will give ____ [NAME] 2 units of fresh frozen plasma as well as 20 mg of vitamin K. We will hold her Coumadin and check INR daily. We will start Lovenox when the INR is less than 3.
2. Anemia: Transfuse cross and screened packed red blood cells with a goal of a hematocrit of approximately 30. We will check the hematocrit posttransfusion.
3. Angina: Almost certainly related to severe anemia. No sign of MI on EKG and cardiac enzymes negative.
4. Gastrointestinal: She will n.p.o. for now. We will discuss the case with Dr. ____ [NAME] in the morning. She will be n.p.o. except we will continue her essential medications.

PLAN HEADINGS

The following table shows some common plan headings found in medical reports. The healthcare provider's plan, like any other type of information, can be clearly stated under a heading or mixed in with other subjective, objective, descriptive, or assessment information.

Common Plan Headings	Definition
Plan; Recommendations, Suggestions, Advised To	The healthcare provider's recommended treatment/plan/course of action for the patient's condition(s).
Disposition	Description of the final settlement of the patient's visit or hospitalization.
Discharge Medications	Medications recommended on discharge; prescriptions.
Instructions; Recommended Followup	Instructions for followup care; patient education.

REVIEW: PLAN

I. **MULTIPLE CHOICE.**
   Choose the best answer.

> PLAN: I advised her it is extremely important that she lose weight. I gave her leg extension exercises to perform and will fit her for orthotics. She may continue with medications. However, I would caution that if she stays on Naprosyn she should have either Cytotec or proton pump inhibitor to prevent any stomach ulcers, as she is at increased risk due to her age. She will follow up in 3 months for re-evaluation.

1. Which of the following was not a recommendation made by the provider?
   - ○ lose weight
   - ○ leg extension exercises
   - ○ discontinue Naprosyn
   - ○ return for followup in 3 months

> RECOMMENDATIONS: I discussed with this patient the fact he would not tolerate any therapy at all, and the fact that he has a sarcoma, he probably would not get much benefit from chemotherapy in the first place. So our basic recommendation is that we need to think seriously about home hospice care and recommended that they come and talk to him and see what they can do for him at home.
>
> DISCHARGE MEDICATIONS: We did give him prescriptions for oxycodone SA 10 mg 1 p.o. q.12 hours to start as well as oxycodone 5 mg 1 to 2 p.o. q. 4-6 hours p.r.n.
>
> DISPOSITION: I want to see him back in a month and see how he is doing with pain control.

2. The recommendations, discharge medications, and disposition are all parts of the discharge plan.
   - ○ true
   - ○ false

3. Part of the plan was for the patient to begin chemotherapy.
   - ○ true
   - ○ false

4. Which was not a part of the plan?
   - ○ continue pain medications
   - ○ consider home hospice care
   - ○ consider resuming chemotherapy
   - ○ return for follow-up visit in one month

DISCHARGE MEDICATIONS:

1. Prescriptions for medications. Will write Isordil 10 mg t.i.d. in place of the isosorbide mononitrate 30 mg q.d.

2. Prescribe sulfasalazine 500 mg q.i.d.

3. Prescribe simvastatin 20 mg q.d. in place of the Lipitor 10 mg q.d.

PLAN:

1. Schedule a primary care physician appointment with laboratories and EKG, morning appointment.

2. Obtain the medical records from ___ [PLACE].

5. In the example above is the section labeled discharge medications part of the plan for the patient?

○ yes
○ no

6. Which of the following is not included in the discharge plan?

○ return for followup
○ change Lipitor to simvastatin
○ obtain medical records
○ schedule PCP appointment

DEMOGRAPHICS/ANCILLARY INFORMATION

Every medical record document contains some patient-identifying information (demographics) for tracking, storing and retrieval.

Additionally, headings and pieces of information are included in medical records to provide important information to healthcare providers, consultants, and healthcare support staff. An example of this is the physician name and physician signature.

DEMOGRAPHICS/ANCILLARY HEADINGS

The chart in this section is not comprehensive, but it gives the types of demographics and ancillary information that complete medical record content.

Demographics/Ancillary information	Definition
Medical record number; Account number	Number generated by the healthcare facility when the patient is registered for care, usually used for all patient visits to the provider.
Patient name	Patient name.
Date of birth	Date of birth.
Attending physician; Primary surgeon; Assistants	Attending physician; Primary surgeon; Assistants.
Date of visit	Date of visit.

We've placed a visual aid in the appendix on page 366.

We've placed a visual aid in the appendix on page 367.

We've placed a visual aid in the appendix on page 368.

The patient information in all of the example documents used in this program is fictitious, made up to protect patient confidentiality.

MEDICAL RECORD CONTENT

Medical record content and report organization varies from healthcare provider to healthcare provider. Some healthcare organizations have strict guidelines for documentation, including pre-set report formats and templates. Other healthcare providers (individual and institutional) may use little, if any, standardized formatting. All types of documentation is encountered such as headings, handwritten documents, typed documents with pre-set formats, pre-printed forms with fill-in-the-blank documentation, demographics on the top, bottom, side, as well as scanned documents, faxed documents, and many other electronic and paper records. All medical record content, however, contains some or all of the same basic elements: subjective, objective, descriptive information assessment, plan, and demographics/ancillary information.

UNIT 6

Health Information Processes

HEALTH INFORMATION PROCESSES – INTRODUCTION

This course has previously discussed the actual structure and use of the health record, and has focussed on health record documentation. Data sources and data sets have been explored. This unit will focus on other operational functions in the health information department. After the record is created, it is critical that it can be retrieved, stored and archived.

Most health information management (HIM) departments have several main functions or services. They may be:

- Record processing/completion
- Storage and retrieval
- Transcription
- Release of information
- Clinical coding, abstracting and data analysis

MASTER PATIENT INDEX

A very important index used by the HIM department is the master patient index (MPI). This index consists of a permanent record of all patients seen in the facility. This is the guide to being able to locate or retrieve data about the patient's demographic information previously discussed. This information is entered into the MPI. The amount of data entered depends on particular facilities, but the recommended core data elements per AHIMA are:

- Patient identification number (medical record number)
- Name
- Birth date
- Gender
- Race
- Ethnicity
- Address
- Telephone number
- Alias/previous/maiden names
- Social Security Number
- Facility Identification
- Account or visit number
- Admission date
- Discharge date
- Encounter service type
- Encounter service location
- Primary physician
- Patient disposition

Because the MPI is such an important and robust data base, it is important that there are quality control processes in place to monitor for duplicates or overlap of medical record numbers. The medical record or health record number is the most important data element in the MPI and it is a unique identifier used in paper-based filing systems to retrieve records.

The **enterprise-wide master patient index** (EMPI) references all patients in multiple facilities. This is information from overlapping patient populations. These EMPIs link several smaller organization level **master patient indexes (MPIs)** together. The EMPI can be used to identify, match, merge, and cleanse patient records to create a master index that may be used to obtain a complete and single view of a patient.

I. **TRUE/FALSE.**
   Mark the following true or false.

   1. The MPI allows retrieval of patient information.
      ○ true
      ○ false

   2. The primary physician is the most important data element in the MPI.
      ○ true
      ○ false

   3. The MPI is used in paper-based systems.
      ○ true
      ○ false

FILING SYSTEMS

The following types of paper record filing systems describe methods used to store and retrieve health information.

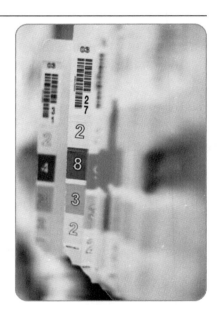

Alphabetic Filing

This is the simplest filing method and may be used in some small facilities and clinics. The patient's last name is the first source of identification, and then first name, followed by middle initial are used in filing the record.

Straight Numeric Filing

This kind of filing is good for large organizations—and is exactly what its name implies—just straight numbers. It's easy to know exactly where a file will be in numerical order. To make it easier, some color-coding may be used. The health record number is used, and the records are arranged consecutively in number order.

Alpha-Numeric Filing

This is a combination of the first two methods. This is a very accurate method, leading to ease of filing and access. An example is a system where records are filed using the first two letters of a patient's last name and the last four digits of a unique identifier.

Terminal Digit Filing

This type is common in larger organizations, such as hospitals. The last digit or group of digits is the primary unit for filing. This is then followed by the middle unit and then the last unit of numbers. This is the only type of filing system that allows for expansion in the file area.

Record filing is a function that is eliminated or reduced in the EHR.

Retrieval of Health Records

For paper based records, it is common for an outguide to be placed in the file area to indicate the location of the record. Certainly this is one HIM function that is much improved in an electronic world. Chart-tracking and requisition systems track the movement of the physical paper record for easy retrieval.

Maintenance of Medical Records

Certainly it is optimal that records are kept forever, but this is not always possible. There is only so much permanent storage room available. Typically facilities store paper records for a certain time period and then convert them to microfilm or microfiche which condenses the record into an image. There are federal and state laws regarding destruction timelines and requirements. AHIMA also has guidelines regarding retention standards. record into an image. There are federal and state laws regarding destruction timelines and requirements. AHIMA also has guidelines regarding retention standards.

Go to the following website and review the AHIMA Practice Brief: Retention and Destruction of Health Information

Read the information in the link above, paying special attention to Appendix D which contains AHIMA's recommendations for minimum record retention time periods in the absence of any federal, state, or accreditation requirements. Then answer the following questions.

I. **MULTIPLE CHOICE.**
   Choose the best answer.

1. What is the age of majority?
   - ○ 18
   - ○ 21
   - ○ Defined by state law
   - ○ 13

2. How long does the FDA require research records on cancer patients be retained?
   - ○ 10 years
   - ○ Permanently
   - ○ 20 years
   - ○ 30 years

3. How long does AHIMA suggest records be maintained for adults?
   - ○ 10 years
   - ○ 5 years
   - ○ Permanently
   - ○ 20 years

4. How long does AHIMA suggest the MPI be maintained?
   - ○ 10 years
   - ○ 5 years
   - ○ Permanently
   - ○ 20 years

5. How long does AHIMA suggest that x-rays be maintained for minors?
   - ○ 5 years
   - ○ 5 years after age of majority
   - ○ Permanently
   - ○ 10 years

ARCHIVAL AND DOCUMENT IMAGING SYSTEMS

There are several ways to archive medical records to reduce space needs. Microfilm and microfiche have been used for many years to accomplish this.

Microfilm

Microfilm can be in roll form which holds thousands of images on a long roll that stores images. It is read on a special reader. A disadvantage to this is that the entire health record for the patient is not stored on one roll of film. Microfilm can also be in a jacket format. The roll is cut into jackets with sleeves to hold the images. An advantage to this is that the sleeves can be stored into a folder with all records on a particular patient.

Microfiche

While this looks similar to the microfilm jacket, it is actually a copy of it and it is made of Mylar film. When copies are needed during the release of information process, copies of the microfiche are made using a duplicator.

OFF-SITE STORAGE SYSTEMS

When storage is a problem and microfilm is prohibitive because of costs, many facilities contract with off-site storage services to store health records.

Image-Based Storage Systems

The use of these digital document imaging systems has been increasing especially as facilities move toward the EHR. During the conversion process from paper to an electronic record, facilities use a hybrid record that is part paper and part electronic. The paper documents may be scanned into the electronic system. These scanned images are then stored in an electronic format, such as on magnetic or optical disk.

RELEASE OF INFORMATION (ROI)

There are many examples of when patient information is released to a requestor. Patients may request copies for other physicians or consultants, attorneys, and for personal use. Because of state and federal privacy and security laws, there are strict guidelines on how this ROI is processed. Patient confidentiality is of utmost importance. The request should be entered into a database and the authorization for the release verified. It must be a valid authorization, and the patient's identity is also verified. To process the request, the record is retrieved and only the authorized information is released to the requestor.

SECURITY

No matter what type of medical record or method of storage, expectations are that healthcare providers will protect and respect the privacy of their patients. The privacy, security and confidentiality of patient information are all related but actually the terms are slightly different. According to AHIMA, the following definitions apply:

- Privacy – the right of individuals to control access to their personal health information
- Confidentiality – the expectation that the personal information shared by an individual with a healthcare provider during the course of care will be used only for its intended purpose
- Security – the protection of the privacy of individuals and the confidentiality of health records. Security allows only those authorized users to access the information.

UNIT 7
Data Quality and Integrity

DATA QUALITY AND INTEGRITY – INTRODUCTION

The importance of complete, accurate and timely medical record documentation and protecting the confidentiality of the medical record cannot be overemphasized. Physicians and other members of the healthcare team rely on the information in the medical record to make decisions about patient care. Administrators rely on quality data to make decisions about the future of the healthcare facility. The patient relies on quality data to ensure quality care is delivered. The health record must be accurate, complete, permanent and legible. In addition, this data must be secure and private. Many laws such as the Health Insurance Portability and Accountability Act (HIPAA), American Recovery and Reinvestment Act (ARRA) and other laws monitor compliance to minimize risks. Access controls must be in place for all electronic health record (EHR) and paper records and information systems. Also a patient is entitled to assurance that their personal health information is treated in a confidential manner.

Here are a few scenarios to illustrate importance of accurate, timely, and confidential medical records.

SCENARIO 1:

The patient is scheduled to undergo a surgical procedure on the left leg, but the documentation in the medical record inaccurately states the surgery is to be performed on the right leg. The patient is taken to the operating room where the operation is performed on the wrong leg.

SCENARIO 2:

A child is brought to the emergency room following an accident and is admitted to the hospital. A history is taken, including the fact that she is allergic to penicillin, but the report is not returned to the medical record for several days. Because of infection the child is given an injection of penicillin. She goes into anaphylactic shock and comes close to death.

SCENARIO 3:

A patient visits a local clinic for blood work and learns she has AIDS. The clinic's computer is "hacked" into and her personal information and AIDS status are printed on an anti-homosexual flyer in her hometown.

SCENARIO 4:

A family member suffers from depression, and is treated with medication and counseling and copes well with family and work. He applies for a promotion but is denied because his boss heard from his neighbor, a nurse at the clinic, about the depression and thinks it might affect his ability to do a good job.

Each of these scenarios represents a serious breach in the handling of private healthcare information. Data quality is an important component of quality patient care. This unit will discuss data quality and integrity, common documentation errors, and the role medical coding/billing professionals play in ensuring integrity and confidentiality in the medical record.

Whether the medical record is in a paper-based system or an electronic system, measures must be in place to ensure quality of the medical record content. In addition, all medical records must be secure, accessible and timely. The organization must develop standards and monitoring to control the quality of the health record. One way to do this is to perform analysis of the record. The entire healthcare team depends on the medical record quality to provide patient care. Missing, incomplete or inaccurate information can be disastrous to patient care. A missing laboratory or x-ray report may negatively impact the outcome of the patient.

Qualitative analysis: Review of the medical record to ensure that standards are met and to determine accuracy of record documentation.

Quantitative analysis: Review of the medical record to determine its completeness and accuracy.

QUALITATIVE AND QUANTITATIVE ANALYSES

After the health record is assembled, it is analyzed to review for any missing reports or signatures. Reviewing these deficiencies is quantitative analysis. This can be done in a concurrent review process while the patient is in the hospital, or retrospectively after discharge. The review involves several steps during a concurrent or retrospective review. According to AHIMA, the main steps for quantitative analysis involve:

- Review of all forms and reports to ensure that correct patient identification is included.
- Analysis to ensure that all forms and reports are present and accounted for.
- Review of authentication on reports requiring signatures.

Qualitative analysis is also performed to ensure the quality of the medical record. The types of qualitative analysis pertaining to the coding function involve audits of the coded data to ensure that accurate codes are assigned and billed correctly.

Medical records documentation audits of individual records and provider records should be done consistently. Audits can be internal or external. The HIM professionals would conduct internal audits, while external reviews are conducted by special consultants or third-party payers.

During a coding/billing audit the focus should be on areas of high risk, such as MS-DRG coding accuracy, discharge status, medical necessity, evaluation and management services, and chargemaster description for example. A random sample of records should be selected, to ensure a good cross section is reviewed. After the reviews are completed, action must be taken to provide education and to correct any errors.

Which definition is qualitative analysis and which definition is quantitative analysis?

TYPES OF ANALYSIS

There are three other types of reviews or audits you should be aware of:

Review or Audit	Meaning
Concurrent review	Review of the medical record carried out while the patient is actively receiving care.
Occurrence screening	Review technique of medical records of current and discharged patients with the goal of identifying events not consistent with routine. Used to identify and correct problems and to prepare for legal defense.
Retrospective review	Review of the medical record after the patient has been discharged.

Concurrent reviews are conducted while the patient is receiving treatment. HIM professionals and document authors review the records as they are created and compiled. The benefit of this type of review is that documentation issues can be identified at the time of patient care and rectified (if necessary) in a timely manner.

Occurrence screening is a **risk management-related** audit. The reviewer looks for accidents, omissions, or medical errors that resulted or could potentially result in a personal injury or loss of property. Occurrences include instances when the wrong surgery was performed or an informed consent for a procedure was not obtained. These reports are considered very confidential documents and they are never filed in the patient record. They identify potentially compensable events that are defined as unexpected events that either cause or could cause injury. They may result in a claim being filed against the organization.

Retrospective review does not allow for timely identification of documentation issues. However it is still very useful for identifying and addressing weaknesses in documentation processes, areas where staff need additional training, and, where appropriate, addressing deficiencies in individual records.

REVIEW: CONSISTENCY AND AUDITING

I. MATCHING.
Match the term and the definition. Enter the letter for the corresponding definition next to the term.

1. ____ concurrent review
2. ____ qualitative analysis
3. ____ occurrence screening
4. ____ retrospective review
5. ____ quantitative analysis

A. Medical record review performed after the patient has been discharged.
B. Review of the medical record to identify potential medical errors.
C. Review of the medical record while the patient is still a patient.
D. Review of medical record to ensure that documentation standards are met.
E. Medical record review for completeness.

II. FILL IN THE BLANK.

Select the word or phrase from the box which best completes the sentence. Complete the sentence by entering the selected word or phrase in the blank provided.

1. A(n) _____ can identify documentation issues (which can be rectified in a timely manner) while the patient is in the hospital.

2. A(n) _____ is the review of the medical record to identify potential medical errors.

3. A(n) _____ is performed to ensure the accuracy of documentation in the medical record.

4. A(n) _____ is used to determine the completeness of the medical record.

5. A(n) _____ does not allow for timely identification of documentation problems but is useful for identifying trends and areas where improvements are needed.

concurrent review
retrospective review
qualitative analysis
occurrence screening
quantitative analysis

COMMON DOCUMENTATION ERRORS

The job of implementing and managing the documentation standards will not usually be the job of the medical coding/billing specialist (although many medical coders and billers choose the career path of HIM department manager or risk management supervisor). The medical coder is one of the first HIM professionals to review documents in the medical record. To be effective and efficient as a medical coder/biller and ensure quality documentation, coders should become familiar with common documentation errors and deficiencies. The following is a list of some common errors and deficiencies:

- missing/incorrect patient identification (name, medical record number, gender, etc.)
- diagnoses/procedures or other text inconsistencies, ambiguities, or insufficiencies
- missing physician signatures
- location discrepancies (left/right, inconsistencies in description of wound or illness)
- date inconsistencies

When these types of errors or deficiencies are identified in the patient's medical record, they need to be reported using a deficiency slip. Most healthcare organizations have developed automated systems for tracking errors or deficiencies. HHealth information personnel create a deficiency either on paper or via computer to indicate the error or deficiency. If paper, this placed in the patient's medical record, and the record is filed in a specially designated area of the HIM department. This is commonly known as the **incomplete record file.** The physician, the appropriate HIMs staff, or the appropriate healthcare provider accesses the incomplete record file to provide clarification, additional information, or whatever is necessary to correct or complete the file.

There is an image available online for you to view on page 79.

I. **FILL IN THE BLANK.**

   Using the word/word parts in the box, fill in the blanks.

   1. Health information personnel create a _____ indicating an error or deficiency in a medical record.

   2. The _____ is one of the first HIM professionals to review documents in the medical record.

   3. The _____ is a specially designated area of the HIM department for files with documentation errors.

   4. A common deficiency in documentation is a missing physician _____.

incomplete record file
medical coder
deficiency slip
signature

COMMON ERRORS – SCENARIO 1

Review the following report and answer the question below.

PROCEDURE NOTE

PATIENT NAME:

MEDICAL RECORD NUMBER: 18-65-76

OPERATION DATE: 8/25/2001

SURGEON: Dr. Smith

PREOPERATIVE DIAGNOSIS: Obstruction in esophagus due to carcinoma.

PROCEDURE PERFORMED: Dilatation of esophagus and replacement of nasogastric feeding tube.

FINDINGS: This patient had radiation therapy for squamous cell carcinoma located in the mid thorax beginning at below the aortic arch. The radiation therapy has not opened the esophagus and the patient cannot swallow satisfactorily around the 18-French nasogastric tube. The patient was brought in for dilation of his esophagus and possible pharyngogastric tube insertion; however, the patient developed tachycardia and shortness of breath and it appeared that his condition was fragile.

It is known this patient has severe coronary artery disease with ejection fraction of 15% and cardiomyopathy of severe degree. Therefore, the procedure was stopped after dilating the esophagus up to 30-French.

The nasogastric tube, which was previously placed and pulled back up, was passed down into the stomach and fixed in this position. The patient tolerated the procedure satisfactorily, although the full extent of the planned surgery was not performed. The patient's pulse returned back to 100 with no change in blood pressure with nasal oxygen saturation remaining normal. The patient was sent to post-anesthesia care unit.

I. MULTIPLE CHOICE.
Choose the best answer.

1. What information is incorrect or missing from this report?
   - ○ operation date
   - ○ patient name
   - ○ medical record number
   - ○ preoperative diagnosis

COMMON ERRORS – SCENARIO 2

Review the following report and answer the question below.

Medical Record

CLINIC NOTE

PATIENT NAME: John Smith

MEDICAL RECORD NUMBER: 25-85-96

DATE: 2/18/2004

PHYSICIAN: Dr. Jones

HISTORY: This is a 54-year-old male with a history of seizure disorder, likely etiology was alcohol related. No history of head injury or coma. She has not had any seizures in more than six months. He has slowed down on his alcohol use and is complaining of some dizziness, usually worsened with a quick change in position. She has also quit smoking and is using the patch. He was on Neurontin, but it has been discontinued. He is currently taking doxepin 150 mg h.s.

Neurological exam is unremarkable, and there is no change from the previous visit.

ASSESSMENT: Dizziness

PLAN: If EEG (electroencephalogram) is negative, plan to give Antivert 12.5 to 25 mg p.o. p.r.n. for dizziness. Again, I stressed to her to stop drinking. His follow up appointment will be in six months.

I. **MULTIPLE CHOICE.**
   Choose the best answer.

   1. What information is incorrect or missing from this report?
      ◯ patient name
      ◯ date
      ◯ gender inconsistency
      ◯ medical record number

COMMON ERRORS – SCENARIO 3

Review the following report and answer the question below.

CLINIC NOTE

PATIENT NAME: Jane Jones

MEDICAL RECORD NUMBER: 25-87-52

DATE: 7/27/2000

PHYSICIAN: Dr. Smith

This 65-year-old lady was seen today 7/25/2000 in the ____ [PLACE] for evaluation of her MP joint. Her left great toe was submitted to a procedure on August 16th of last year for an advanced hallux rigidus deformity.

At the time of the operation, the spurs of the metatarsal head were properly removed, and the base of the proximal phalanx resected. An intramedullary pin and Kirschner wire were placed to maintain the joint space. Unfortunately, in the followup, the joint space completely obliterated and presently the appearance of the MP joint was back to its preoperative condition with the spur formation and only a slight shortening of the great toe. The bunion was properly removed, and the alignment of the great toe is very satisfactory.

On clinical examination, there is considerable tenderness over the MP joint of the great toe, and there is a very limited range of motion that is exceeding 5 to 8 degrees.

I explained to the patient that at this point in time only a fusion of the MP joint could relieve her of the pain and recommended such an intervention.

With her consent, I made arrangements for her to see Dr. ____ [NAME] in the first part of December for arrangement for this intervention.

In the meantime, I prescribed clog shoes to see how much relief of the symptoms they could afford.

I. **MULTIPLE CHOICE.**
   Choose the best answer.

   1. What information is incorrect or missing from this report?
      ○ gender inconsistency
      ○ patient name
      ○ medical record number
      ○ date inconsistency

COMMON ERRORS – SCENARIO 4

Review the following report and answer the question below.

OPERATIVE REPORT

PATIENT NAME: Bob Smith

MEDICAL RECORD NUMBER: 29-85-11

OPERATION DATE: 4/25/2003

SURGEON: Dr. Johnson

PREOPERATIVE DIAGNOSIS: Right temple lesion.

POSTOPERATIVE DIAGNOSIS: Right temple lesion.

PROCEDURE: Excision of left temple lesion.

ANESTHESIA: Local.

SPECIMENS: Right temple lesion.

ESTIMATED BLOOD LOSS: 5 mL.

COMPLICATIONS: None.

INDICATIONS: Mr. ___ [NAME] presents with a right temple lesion which is ulcerating consistent with basal cell carcinoma.

OPERATIVE DESCRIPTION: After informed consent was obtained from the patient, he was taken to the operating room and placed in the supine position and prepped and draped in the usual fashion. An elliptical incision was made following skin tension lines. The lesion was excised and sent to pathology for permanent section. Hemostasis was obtained with bipolar cautery.

The wound was closed in layered fashion with 4-0 Vicryl and 5-0 nylon running suture and dressed with Bacitracin.

I. **MULTIPLE CHOICE.**
   Choose the best answer.

1. What information is incorrect or missing from this report?
   - ○ location discrepancy
   - ○ patient name
   - ○ operation date
   - ○ date

COMMON ERRORS – SCENARIO 5

Review the following report and answer the question below.

Medical Record

CLINIC NOTE

PATIENT NAME: John Doe

MEDICAL RECORD NUMBER: 54-98-85

DATE: 5/8/2004

PHYSICIAN: Dr. Jackson

Mr. ___ [NAME] is a 69-year-old white male who is followed for multiple medical problems.

The patient states he was recently hospitalized for cellulitis of his leg and presumably for review of his other multiple problems. Unfortunately, the discharge summary is not yet available from that admission. He states his cellulitis has completely resolved.

The patient has congestive heart failure and states his breathing is stable.

He does have type II diabetes. He does home glucose monitoring every morning and states his blood sugars were in the 80s when he was hospitalized. When he is less compliant with his diet at home they are somewhat higher but still less than 150. He denies hypoglycemic reactions.

He has obesity, has seen the dietitian, and is attempting to lose weight.

He has sleep apnea. It is unclear what further evaluation has been done to follow up on this problem.

He has hypercholesterolemia, no history of coronary artery disease, is following his low cholesterol diet, and taking his simvastatin regularly.

OBJECTIVE: Patient is alert and in no acute distress. Blood pressure today was 148/80. He had multiple physical examinations while recently hospitalized. Last lab showed glucose was down to 74 while patient was hospitalized and was carefully following his diet.

ASSESSMENT:

1. Congestive heart failure.
2. Type I diabetes.
3. Obesity.
4. Sleep apnea.
5. Hypercholesterolemia.
6. History of cellulitis of the leg.

PLAN:

1. Patient education.
2. Continue current therapy for now.

3. He states that he also has occasional gastroesophageal reflux which is well controlled with p.r.n. Maalox. He does have refills on the Maalox.
4. At my last visit with this patient we talked about having his glucometer checked out because there were some discrepancies in his readings. He has not yet had an opportunity to do this. If his blood sugar reading and glucometer reading are divergent at the next visit, we will attempt again to have this checked out.
5. Return to clinic in two months.

I. MULTIPLE CHOICE.
Choose the best answer.

1. What information is incorrect or missing from this report?
   - ○ date
   - ○ diagnosis discrepancy
   - ○ medical record number
   - ○ gender inconsistency

PRIMARY AND SECONDARY DATA USE

Healthcare documentation falls into two basic categories: primary and secondary data. Both are important for the medical world.

Primary data is what we've been discussing up to this point—the medical record. Treatment and other medical information is recorded by the medical professionals who provided it and pertains specifically to the patient and their medical record.

Secondary data is taken from the primary data but has a different purpose. When a patient's primary data is entered into a medical registry or database, it becomes a searchable secondary data source. Where the primary data is patient-specific, secondary data is known as **aggregate data**. It may still contain patient-specific information (such as names in a registry), but the purpose of secondary data use is to collect data on groups of patients with a specific healthcare issue, such as in cancer registries.

Because it can be difficult and time-consuming to collect large amounts of information from primary data, secondary data is extremely useful when studying certain medical conditions. Secondary data can quickly provide information on the effectiveness of treatment, or demonstrate trends such as survival rates. Data can be used by individuals inside the healthcare facility (internal users), or outside the facility by groups such as state health departments (external users).

1. Another name for the medical record is primary data.

   ○ true
   ○ false

2. Secondary data is known as aggregate information.

   ○ true
   ○ false

3. Secondary data usage is only possible within the healthcare facility.

   ○ true
   ○ false

SECONDARY DATA SOURCE TYPES

There are three basic types of secondary data sources: facility-specific indexes, population-based registries, and healthcare databases.

Indexes

Facility-specific indexes help healthcare facilities organize and locate information on diagnoses, procedures, and physicians. Some, like the master population/patient index (MPI), contain patient-identifiable data. These can help easily and quickly retrieve data on specific patients. Disease and operation indexes help facilities identify patient-specific information on disease diagnoses and operations in the facility. A physician index helps the facility retrieve information on specific doctors in their facility.

Registries

Registries typically contain much more extensive data than indexes. They collect data that refers to a certain diagnosis, condition, or procedure, and they include information from multiple facilities as well as more detailed information from patient records. Registries also have very specific case definitions—a strict definition of all cases in the registry, such as a diagnosis falling within a certain range of codes. Once medical records that fit the case definition are found at various facilities—a process called case finding—they are entered into the registry database.

Registries provide data from health records around the country, and even around the world, to users who need them. Some registries even include follow-up information. Registries are typically population-based, meaning they focus on trends and changes in the incidences (new cases) in the case definition covered by the registry.

Some examples of registries are the National Cancer Registrars Association (NCRA), trauma registries like The American Trauma Society, various birth defect registries, diabetes registries, implant and transplant registries, and immunization registries.

Healthcare Databases

Healthcare information can also be used for a variety of other purposes, such as for government uses or research into reimbursement issues. For example, some databases are developed for Medicare claims, to track medical malpractice payments, and to track healthcare fraud and abuse. Public health agencies also use databases to keep track on the health status of their populations.

Vital statistics—such as births, deaths, marriages, and divorces—are another example of healthcare databases. Clinical trials track new drugs, treatments, and tests to determine safety and efficacy.

I. **TRUE/FALSE.**
   Mark the following true or false.

   1. Registries typically contain much more data than indexes.
      ○ true
      ○ false

   2. Indexes are intended for broad use of information by parties outside a healthcare facility.
      ○ true
      ○ false

   3. Registries never include follow-up information.
      ○ true
      ○ false

   4. An *incidence* is a new case of a particular health trend.
      ○ true
      ○ false

   5. Healthcare databases are rarely used to track reimbursement issues.
      ○ true
      ○ false

COLLECTING AND MAINTAINING SECONDARY DATA

In this day and age, most databases and registries are electronic, but most data collection is still done manually. The most common method is called **abstracting**. Abstracting is when someone reviews a patient's health record and enters the appropriate pieces into the database. Some databases may download data from other registries or systems also. Healthcare institutions can either use a vendor system or facility-specific system for their databases and collections processes.

Because data is entered mostly by hand there is, of course room, for error. The database is only as good as its data. It's important that data entered is valid, reliable, and complete, so data-entry personnel need to be extra careful. And it's important that the data be secure and confidential. After all, databases are still dealing with personal medical records.

UNIT 8

Technology and the Health Record

TECHNOLOGY AND THE HEALTH RECORD – INTRODUCTION

Because you will be utilizing a computer in your future employment, and because maximizing your competency and employability are goals of our program, we have included this module in your training. Technology is not only generally improving processes within the healthcare industry, it will significantly improve your ability to function as a medical professional. The medical coding industry has developed software that significantly enhances efficiency and performance. Additionally, there is an expectation of employers that people they hire are proficient on any software they will be working in regularly, or at the very least are proficient in a similar product and will have a relatively short learning curve.

In this module you will be introduced to coding software, online coding tools, and medical billing software. The Electronic Health Record and associated clinical documentation are discussed, as are affiliated software. Finally, we will look at ways various software and technology can improve the quality of medical care and medical records.

COMPUTER NETWORKS

Computer networks in healthcare allow the exchange of information and the establishment of virtual Health Information Management (HIM) departments. Some of the terms that might be used in these networks are discussed here. Because organizations have formed healthcare enterprises or integrated delivery systems, the networks allow sharing of information. The ability of various systems to actually network and share and exchange information is known as **interoperability**.

A computer network is a group of computers and hardware that are interconnected allowing sharing of this information and resources. A **local area network** (LAN) would connect limited computers, such as in a certain area or close proximity such as a school, or office building. The **wide area network** (WAN) covers a much larger geographic area such as a city, a country, or even involves other countries.

A **virtual private network** (VPN) might be used to connect remote workers within the organization and allows this remote work. This uses access such as the internet to transport data and connect the network nodes. Encryption and special security measures are used so that only authorized users gain access to these VPNs. When dealing with patient medical records, it is required that security is in place so that information cannot be intercepted.

Organizations might use an **intranet** or private network. This requires the internet to be in place, and this same technology also supports information communication solely within the organization. Many organizations use this method to communicate news and announcements to employees. Many organizations are using their intranets to share the ICD-10-CM/PCS implementation progress and awareness with staff. It is also a way to share education and archived video or audio of training sessions missed. When an organization elects to share some of their private network with other stakeholders, clients, partners or customers, it is known as an **extranet**. These intranets and extranets are extensions of computer networks, usually a LAN.

A **firewall** is used to protect the intranet from unauthorized access. A firewall can be software or hardware-based and it keeps the network secure. It analyzes incoming and outgoing data to identify if it should be allowed through. Firewalls keep others out, but allow the organization access to the Internet. A firewall can also be used with VPNs to provide privacy while still sharing the transmission of the data. Remember that the data would be encrypted before sent, but then is decrypted when received. This all allows sensitive patient medical information to be transmitted.

Networks also allow for **electronic data interchange** (EDI). An example of this is the electronic transmission of health insurance claims rather than paper-based claims. It is important that there are standards and procedures in place so that the receiving computer can interpret the data transmitted.

Highlights

With the advent of this ability to network computers has come the ability to do many HIM functions remotely and the coding and abstracting functions are certainly a primary function that is being performed remotely in many organizations. Many coders are excited about the option of working at home and usually are offered the ability to select their own hours. With the coder shortage, many organizations have most or all staff working remotely. It is important to note that this option is not likely available to a new coder. Even after taking an intense coding course, coders require a great deal of on the job training to become proficient at coding complex cases using and applying all guidelines and payment policies. Working at home can certainly be an option after a few years of experience, so it is a goal one might strive for.

I. **MULTIPLE CHOICE.**
   Choose the best answer.

1. This type of network allows the connection of large geographic areas.
   - ○ Intranet
   - ○ WAN
   - ○ LAN
   - ○ all of the above

2. Which is an example of processing health insurance claims electronically?
   - ○ VPN
   - ○ LAN
   - ○ interoperability
   - ○ EDI

3. What is used to provide security to data?
   - ○ encryption
   - ○ firewalls
   - ○ both a. and b.
   - ○ neither a. nor b.

ELECTRONIC HEALTH RECORD

The vast world of computer technology continues to provide abundant tools for the documentation of patient care. Historically a written record of a patient visit was created, then as technology evolved, a record of the visit was dictated, including the history, diagnosis, and other findings. Now the electronic health record (EHR) has evolved allowing direct entry into the computer using the keyboard, voice or templates. Lab reports, x-rays, and other reports can be electronically linked to the record via network connections with other medical providers, thus creating a comprehensive electronic medical file.

The Electronic Health Record

The definition for the **electronic health record (EHR)** has evolved over time and has become complex. An earlier term that was also used is the **electronic medical records (EMR).** AHIMA defines these two terms as:

EHR: an electronic record of health-related information on an individual that conforms to nationally recognized interoperability standards and that can be created, managed, and consulted by authorized clinicians and staff across more than one healthcare organization.

EMR: An electronic record of health-related information on an individual that can be created, gathered, managed, and consulted by authorized clinicians and staff within a single healthcare organization.

The main difference then is the ability of the EHR to be **interoperable** (using standards so systems work together) and shared across the continuum of care. During the transition to a totally electronic record, hybrid records are common. The hybrid record contains paper and electronic elements.

Bridging technology such as document imaging is used to replace hard copy documents with paperless electronic copies to better help collect these reports. Included in this information are patient demographics, progress notes, or physician orders. When the written document is scanned into the optical or electronic system, more of the health record is electronic for retrieval purposes.

HIPAA and Confidentiality and Release of Information

Easily accessible healthcare information in an electronic format is the goal but issues of protection from fraud and safeguarding privacy and confidentiality become critically important. The federal government included security regulations and restrictions in the **Health Insurance Portability and Accountability Act (HIPAA)** to protect patient rights. When visiting a health care provider, patients sign a form stating notification of HIPAA rights. HIPAA requires that medical facilities take action to protect confidential patient information from reaching anyone who does not have a legitimate need for, or right to, the information. Custody or transfer of medical records and information must be closely tracked, and the medical office can be held legally liable for improperly using or releasing records. Third parties accessing the records to process their own claims, make their own evaluations, or perform sub-contracted work for the primary caregiver must protect the records and information as if they were the primary caregiver. The act applies to all persons or companies that legally come in contact with private patient information. Medical professionals—coders, physicians, nurses, lab techs, and anyone else who accesses personal medical information—are under serious obligation to protect private information In conjunction with medical software, the electronic health record can assist medical professionals with necessary patient followup and treatment follow-up. Automated audits of lab results and other data collected can alert the medical staff of significant test results, abnormal findings, or other medical issues that require review or action. Treatment planning and review can be scheduled and queued for better followup and tracking.

The electronic health record also helps to protect the integrity of the information. Increasing accuracy in clinical documentation, in theory, should provide for better patient care and improved treatment outcomes. Documentation that is photocopied, re-written, or re-typed generally experiences degradation as errors creep in. When done properly, electronic transfer and maintenance of records reduces errors and provides for data to be stored in multiple locations as originally input and recorded. The electronic health record, when needed elsewhere for evaluation or emergency treatment, can easily be transferred for review and use.

PATIENT AND MEDICAL PROFESSIONAL EDUCATION

Increasingly, the Internet and software programs are being used to better educate and to provide resources for the public at large and for medical professionals themselves. Virtually gone are the days of time-consuming library research. The exhaustive building of personal or clinic reference libraries, which must be updated and maintained regularly, is also becoming obsolete.

Patients now have access to a wealth of medical information via the Internet. This access can lead to a better understanding of diagnosed medical conditions and their treatments. A few comprehensive sites include www.webmd.com and www.medlineplus.gov. Sites like these allow individuals to research their own conditions to better understand treatments prescribed by the physician.

Pharmaceutical information is now readily available as well, so the patient can better understand the drug action and its risks and side effects. There are a myriad of drug websites out there, but www.fda.gov, www.rxlist.com and www.drugs.com are options.

Physicians, nurses, technicians, and other medical professionals now have access to a vast amount of medical and pharmaceutical information via the Internet and specialized software. This allows them to improve their training and knowledge from their office or home, helping them to stay abreast of the increasing volume of changes, breakthroughs, and improvements in modern medical care. Classes are offered by universities and associated experts via telecommunications to provide expanded and up-to-date training to medical professionals throughout the United States and the world. Traditionally, such information and updated training was only available through printed journals, specialized conferences, or mini-courses provided by medical schools. The newer technology makes resources more readily available and makes training time much more efficient.

PAPER HEALTH RECORDS

Though the EHR is becoming more prevalent, it is by no means the only way of storing health care records, as discussed throughout this course. Paper records may still be in use in many settings. Paper records use different types of filing systems, such as alphabetical or numerical, which were previously discussed.

While they are certainly more secure and even fairly simple to access, paper records can also be complicated. For example, when patients are transferred between facilities, sharing the paper medical records can be more difficult than sharing the EHR. Paper records can also be cumbersome to store, difficult to retrieve, and are not accessible to multiple members of the healthcare team simultaneously.

TECHNOLOGY AND THE MEDICAL RECORD

When information in patient medical records was all stored on paper and was only transferable to other healthcare providers via confidential mail and private telephone calls, it was relatively difficult for outsiders to gain access to it, but it wasn't particularly accessible either! Healthcare providers, like consulting physicians and nurses, had to wait for the piece of paperwork to be located and shuffled around to get the information they needed.

Now information can be instantly transferred via e-mail, fax, Internet sites, voice files, video, and even small hand-held portable devices.

These advances in modern technology have enhanced the opportunities for collaboration because patient information can be shared quickly for the best possible medical care available.

Highlights

Technology has enabled exciting breakthroughs for patients and the medical community, such as video conferencing. Video conferencing allows physicians an opportunity to consult "face-to-face" with their patients, other professionals, or both. In some cases, video conferencing has enabled "supervised" medical procedures to be performed in remote areas under the direction of capable clinicians, nurses, or physicians. This technology has also been instrumental in saving lives.

However, there may be a trade off to having easily available information, and that trade off is **security**. The free flow of information means an increased risk of personal data and medical details being intercepted. As long as the potential risks of electronically transferred data are managed, technology provides enhanced health information management and information sharing.

EVOLUTION OF ELECTRONIC HEALTH RECORD (EHR)

The **EHR**, or **electronic health record**, is a medical record that exists entirely in electronic format. A patient's EHR can be a compilation of information from a single visit or contain information from multiple healthcare-related visits. For those healthcare providers in-between an entirely paper-based system and a completely computer-based (electronic) system a hybrid record is being used.

In the near future more and more healthcare providers will migrate to electronic health records to store and transmit their patients' health information. Standard accepted practices have been developed for collecting, maintaining, and transferring healthcare information among computer systems making it possible for healthcare providers to select and maintain an appropriate EHR system for their documentation needs.

THE ADVENT OF EHR

Brief History of the EHR

1960s: The idea of electronic records seems viable with newest technology. The first electronic format in the U.S. is developed.

1970s: Some clinics use electronic medical records internally, sometimes inconsistently and only within specific departments (e.g., Radiology's records are all computerized but not accessible by other departments). Some larger hospitals adopt an electronic system. The biggest innovation in EHR progression is the integration of medical and procedural information into the systems, allowing physicians instant access to best practices.

1980s: Many new proprietary platforms are developed and the first inpatient/outpatient systems are used. Departmental records are integrated and can be accessed throughout a facility.

1990s: Computer network capabilities and large medical facility networks make integrating between/among multiple institutions possible and beneficial.

2000s: The Federal government enters the scene. As part of the 2009 economic stimulus plan, the government offers monetary incentives to those facilities that adopt the EHR.

Beyond: Many advancements and government initiatives have been implemented since 2009.

Go to the AHIMA Practice Brief: Managing the Transition from Paper to EHRs at http://library.ahima.org/ xpedio/groups/public/documents/ahima/bok1_048418.hcsp?dDocName=bok1_048418. Read the article and then answer the questions.

With the technology, the benefits, and the incentives, come hurdles to a comprehensive EHR.

   Lack of standardized systems: There are many platforms available, but they all require training and they do not interface well.

   Dependability: Computerized systems are still able to be harmed by floods, fires, power problems, and deliberate malicious attacks.

   Centralization: A patient who sees various specialists will have an extensive record. Who should be responsible for housing, maintaining, and making the record accessible?

   Privacy: With so many users accessing the facilities' networks, patient information could get into the hands of someone not authorized to have the information.

   I. **FILL IN THE BLANK.**

   Enter the correct word in the blank provided.

      1. The American Recovery and Reinvestment Act (ARRA) encourages healthcare organizations to adopt the _____.

      2. There must be a formal process and guidelines addressing _____, confidentiality, security, print control, spoliation mitigation, disclosure, and e-discovery.

      3. A loss of confidentiality is the unauthorized disclosure of _____.

II. TRUE/FALSE.
Mark the following true or false.

1. The organization must have a standard definition for the legal health record.
    ○ true
    ○ false

2. HIM professionals are not involved in the implementation of the EHR.
    ○ true
    ○ false

3. The transition to EHR has an impact on coding staff.
    ○ true
    ○ false

THE CHALLENGES OF CHANGE

Paper records are less efficient and more complicated to transfer than EHR. So why aren't all medical providers using EHR?

While EHR is beneficial in keeping medical records secure, organized, contained in a small area, and easily transferred to other medical facilities, it is also time consuming and costly to implement. Let's take a look at a few specific complications:

*   EHR systems are costly to install and maintain, costing thousands to tens of thousands of dollars each year.
*   Installing an EHR system requires reorganization of all files, perhaps including the difficult process of digitizing current paper records.
*   New training for all employees on the EHR system must occur.
*   While generally secure, EHR systems can be hacked and private medical information exposed.
*   Many companies sell different types of EHR systems, it can be difficult to find the one that will work best for a particular facility.

It's easy to see that, despite the benefits of EHR, it will take some time for all facilities and practitioners to overcome the challenges of changing to a new system.

THE EHR SOFTWARE AND CERTIFICATION

There are many different ways to store and retrieve EHR. Various companies have developed software specifically designed for different healthcare specialties (acute care organizations, physicians offices, etc.) to manage their EHR. These programs help maintain health informatics standards within the EHR. The Certification Commission for Health Information Technology (CCHIT), a non-profit organization, has developed its own certification system for what it views as quality EHR products. You can visit www.cchit.org for more information.

Certification for EHR products are becoming the standard in the United States. The Health Information Technology for Economic and Clinical Health Act (HITECH), part of the 2009 stimulus bill, is promoting that all Americans have an EHR by 2014. As part of the process, incentives and other programs have been implemented by legislation. The HITECH is providing incentives for "meaningful use (MU) of certified EHR technology," This consists of sanctions in the form of a downward adjustment to Medicare reimbursements.

There are many other organizations and groups who have different roles interests and responsibilities concerning health information technology and the EHR.

Health Level Seven (HL7) is a non-profit organization concerning itself with international healthcare informatics interoperability standards. HL7, among other things, developed **clinical document architecture (CDA)** an XML-based markup standard for electronic exchange of clinical documents (like a progress note or discharge summary).

The **Office of the National Coordinator (ONC)** is the name of the U.S. government agency tasked with guiding the nationwide implementation of health information technology.

The **Regional Health Information Organization (RHIO)** is the organization that promotes the exchange of healthcare data within a defined geographic location. They are generally charged with governing health information exchange to improve health and care.

HEALTH INFORMATION EXCHANGE (HIE)

Health information exchange (HIE) is the term used for electronically transferring medical records between facilities around the country. HIE helps improve patient care by making it easier, cheaper, and faster to transfer a patient's records from one facility to another.

While HIE can save health care providers money in not having to transfer paper records, the systems themselves can be costly for the organizations that provide them. Many of these organizations work with grants and support from state, federal, and private sources.

ELECTRONIC HEALTH RECORD APPLICATIONS

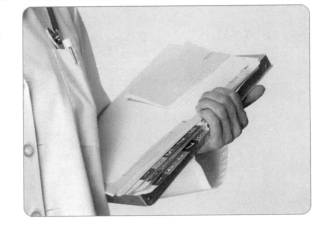

There are many different types of computerized applications that all go togther to make up the EHR. They can be divided into broad categories:

- Clinical information systems
- Administrative information systems
- Management support systems
- Research/data analytics systems

In order for all of these systems to work together, they must be integrated with each other.

Clinical Information Systems

The types of clinical information systems all support patient care and include the following:

- Admission-discharge-transfer systems (ADT) – computer systems that register and track patient encounters.
- Laboratory information systems – collect, verify and report results for laboratory tests.
- Pharmacy information systems – streamline dispensing of medication, control inventory and automate drug orders improving quality patient care.
- Radiology information systems – generate, analyze and manage imaging
- Nursing information systems – automate nursing assessment and evaluations.

- Emergency medical systems – computerized information in the emergency room.
- Patient monitoring systems – automate the collection and storage of many various patient monitoring systems such as fetal, vital sign and oxygen saturation.
- Computerized provider order entry (CPOE) – application accepting physician orders electronically to replace handwritten or verbal orders and prescriptions.
- Clinical decision support systems – assist in the actual diagnosis and treatment of patients using alerts and reminders.

Other Electronic Systems

Other types of computerized systems are used besides clinical systems. Financial information systems, human resource management systems, and materials management systems are utilized to enhance services throughout the organization. Management Information Systems (MISs) are used to provide reports and information regarding organizations statistics.

HEALTH INFORMATION SPECIALTY SYSTEMS (CODING)

Several electronic tools are utilized in the coding function. They are discussed below.

Coding and Abstracting

The medical coder assigns appropriate diagnosis and procedure codes for the encounter and then enters these codes into a computer database abstracting system. During the abstracting process, many other fields of data are captured, such as dates, admit source, transfer and discharge information, etc. This is all per established data sets. To assist in the coding process, encoders may be used. The encoder takes the manual process of coding and assists in computerizing it to the point that there are online references, groupers for inpatient or outpatient prospective system calculations, and built-in logic prompts. The function of the encoder is to improve speed and efficiency in the coding process.

In an entirely EHR environment, computer-assisted coding (CAC) software can actually generate the codes.

I. **TRUE/FALSE.**
   Mark the following true or false.

   1. CPOE provides electronic physician orders.
      ○ true
      ○ false

   2. All computerized systems involve clinical systems.
      ○ true
      ○ false

3. Alerts and reminders are used in MIS systems in actual patient care.

○ true
○ false

4. An encoder generates codes.

○ true
○ false

EHR BENEFITS — LESSON 1

There are many benefits for healthcare providers to switch from a **paper-based record** (medical record data printed and stored on paper in a hard copy format) to an **electronic-based record** (medical record data stored in an electronic format in a computer system or systems). These benefits include the following:

Ease of storage – The more visits a patient makes to his or her healthcare provider, the larger the patient's medical record becomes. Many healthcare providers see hundreds or even thousands of patients. Record storage can take up a lot of space in any office. Storing patient's health information in an electronic health record (EHR) simply saves space.

> **Highlights**
>
> Benefits of the EHR: Ease of storage, accessibility, efficiency, searchability, collaboration, uniformity & standardization, reduction in errors.

Accessibility – Authorized users can access EHR information from on-site or remote computers. If a healthcare provider needs information, they no longer have to physically go to a record storage area or request a file clerk retrieve documents from a physical record in a records room. Authorized users have immediate access to information. Information is stored and indexed for easy retrieval on demand.

Efficiency – Easy access leads directly to efficiency. As soon as information is entered, it's accessible. The end user (patient, physician) does not have to wait for the document to travel from healthcare provider to medical transcriptionist to medical coder to medical biller before they have access to it. The original document is available and additions can be made efficiently until the document reaches a final form.

Searchability – It takes less time to search for a specific item in an electronic document than in a hard copy document. Software tools and features make searching quick and easy. This is a benefit for providing patient care to an individual patient and it is a time saver as well.

I. MATCHING.
   Enter each term in the space provided. Read the definition and description for each term.

1. ____ Ease of storage
2. ____ Accessibility
3. ____ Efficiency
4. ____ Searchability
5. ____ Paper-based record
6. ____ Electronic-based record

A. Medical record data stored in an electronic format in a computer system or systems.
B. An EHR benefit that expedites the time it takes to search for an item and makes it easier to find.
C. An EHR benefit that helps save space when storing records.
D. Medical record data printed and stored on paper in hard copy format.
E. An EHR benefit wherein information is accessible the moment it is entered to whoever needs it.
F. An EHR benefit that offers easy and immediate access to information.

EHR BENEFITS — LESSON 2

Collaboration

Accessibility and efficiency make collaboration and information sharing easier. Many providers can simultaneously view a record simply by accessing the record electronically. This collaborative process—or the use of information technology to improve the quality, safety, efficiency, and confidentiality of healthcare through simultaneous access to patient health information by multiple healthcare providers—is known as **health information exchange (HIE)**. Simply stated, it means patient care is improved when everyone providing care has access to patient health information simultaneously.

Uniformity and Standardization

Most electronic health record systems adhere to **structure and content standards**—common elements and definitions to be included in an electronic health record. These standards identify each data element collected in various data field and then defined in a data dictionary.

Electronic health record programs can control the order of information within a document and the order of documents within a file, can create required information fields, and can provide or restrict access to information so that **users enter and update information in compliance standards**. The program sets the structure and content standards; the user must enter information in accordance with the structure and content standards.

Reduction in Medical Errors

When records are available quickly, are easily searched, and updates are easy to make, the opportunities for patient care errors are reduced. Additionally, handwritten entries in a patient record can be challenging to read. A totally integrated EHR eliminates handwritten entries and reduces the risk of errors made trying to decipher illegible handwriting.

EHR CHALLENGES

To balance out the benefits of an EHR, some challenges are also presented.

Cost

The main disadvantage to fully implementing an EHR is the cost. There is no national standardized EHR program. So designing, implementing, and maintaining an EHR is a significant undertaking. Healthcare providers must invest dollars to develop or purchase, then install and maintain an EHR system that adequately meets their needs.

> **Highlights**
>
> **EHR Concerns**
>
> - Cost
> - Confidentiality
> - Security

Confidentiality and security

The biggest concerns are maintaining confidentiality and security of the patient's health information. Identity theft and unauthorized use of personal information are constant.

> *The Department of Veterans Affairs recently announced that a computer containing personal information on more than 26.5 million veterans and their spouses was stolen.*
>
> *Initial reports stated that the information was on veterans discharged since 1975. Further reports revealed that the information on 30,000 active-duty Navy personnel and 20,000 National Guard and Reserve personnel were also "potentially included." Records at risk also included any veteran who left the service before 1975 but had submitted any VA claims.*
>
> *Unfortunately, social security numbers were included in the information that was stolen, exposing veterans and their spouses to the potential of identity theft. The laptop containing the records was stolen from the Maryland home of a Department of Veterans Affairs analyst who was not authorized to remove the data from the VA office.*
>
> (AARP. www.aarp.com)

Let's face it. It would have been much more difficult for this data analyst to take home 26.5 million hard copy records!

A series of privacy laws over the years has sought to address the issues of security and confidentiality—eventually leading to the drafting and implementation of the **Health Insurance Portability and Accountability Act (HIPAA)**, the law that protects confidentiality and security of electronically transmitted information. There is a lot to be said about HIPAA, and we've just finished saying a lot about other things. It's probably a good time to have some exercises and review before you are ready to start absorbing more information.

I. TERMINOLOGY.
Enter each term in the space provided. Read the definition and description for each term.

1. **Collaboration** _____

An EHR benefit wherein information sharing is made easier.

2. **Health information exchange** _____

The use of information technology to improve the quality, safety, efficiency, and confidentiality of healthcare through simultaneous access to patient health information by multiple healthcare providers.

3. **Uniformity and standardization** _____

An EHR benefit in which health record systems adhere to structure and content standards.

4. **Structure and content standards** _____

Common elements and definitions to be included in an electronic health record.

5. **Reduction in medical errors** _____

An EHR benefit in which health record systems adhere to structure and content standards.

6. **Cost** _____

A disadvantage to EHR wherein a great deal of money must be spent to design, implement, and maintain an EHR.

7. **Confidentiality and security** _____

An EHR disadvantage wherein confidentiality and security of patient's records can be more easily compromised.

PERSONAL HEALTH RECORD

The personal health record (PHR) is a fairly new concept that is being used to encourage patients to take responsibility in their health information. AHIMA defines the PHR as an electronic, universally available, lifelong resource of health information needed by individuals to make health decisions. Certainly an electronic PHR is preferred; but many patients use a paper PHR. The patient owns and manages the information in their PHR. Certainly the PHR is in evolution as is the EHR. Many patients have not embraced this technology yet.

AHIMA has a website dedicated to the PHR. Go to http://www.myphr.com and review the website. Use the tab "Start a PHR" and answer the following questions:

I. TRUE/FALSE.
Mark the following true or false.

1. An EHR and a PHR are the same thing.
   - ○ true
   - ○ false

2. Patients should have access to their complete health information.
   - ○ true
   - ○ false

3. PHRs can include information the physician doesn't have.
   - ○ true
   - ○ false

4. PHRs are legal health records.
   - ○ true
   - ○ false

5. All PHRs are electronic.
   - ○ true
   - ○ false

6. The website provides different PHR options either for purchase or as free software.
   - ○ true
   - ○ false

II. MULTIPLE CHOICE.
Choose the best answer.

1. The physical health record belongs to the healthcare provider and the information in it belongs to:
   - ○ healthcare provider
   - ○ patient
   - ○ physician
   - ○ all of the above

2. Under HIPAA the patient has which right?
   - ○ right to access, inspect and copy health information
   - ○ right to request correction or amend health information
   - ○ right to request accounting of disclosures of health information and who has received it
   - ○ all of the above

Healthcare Delivery Systems

Module

2

UNIT 1

Introduction

INTRODUCTION TO HEALTHCARE DELIVERY SYSTEMS

Learning Objectives

In this module, the student will explore the structure and organization of the healthcare system in the United States. At the conclusion of this module, the learner will be able to:

1. Explain the main structure and organization of healthcare services in the United States.
2. Differentiate between the various healthcare settings.
3. Differentiate between healthcare providers.
4. Identify the structure of hospitals in the United States.
5. Explain the purpose of healthcare licensure, certification and accreditation in healthcare facilities.
6. Differentiate between healthcare registries and their purpose.
7. Identify the various stakeholders throughout the healthcare delivery system.
8. Describe current trends in healthcare delivery.

When working in any capacity within the healthcare system, it is helpful to have a basic understanding of how the system itself works. This module is designed to help you as a medical coder to better understand the structure, organization, and inner workings of the current healthcare system in the United States. This includes things that are clearly visible, like the buildings and places where healthcare is performed, as well as the doctors and different staff who fill them. But it also includes the "behind the scenes" things you may not be as familiar with like the licensing, evaluations, and associations that greatly influence how our healthcare works today.

UNIT 2

Healthcare Structure and Organization

HEALTHCARE STRUCTURE AND ORGANIZATION - INTRODUCTION

In the United States, ranges of professionals in numerous settings provide healthcare delivery. The goal is to provide patients with the **right care, at the right time, from the right provider.**

In addition to traditional hospital and physician office services, healthcare may be provided in the home, clinics, or long-term care facilities. The range of services varies from preventative care (such as immunizations) to complex surgeries or specialty care from burn hospitals.

For the past several decades, the trend is for healthcare organizations formed by physician groups and hospitals to develop a network that is referred to as an *integrated delivery system* (IDS). The goal is for the patient to be able to move among the continuum of care without fragmentation. The patient's healthcare needs are matched with the appropriate level of care.

Highlights

All of the services were coordinated through an integrated delivery system. Many IDS are investing in electronic health record systems so that all caregivers can access the patient's health record.

> Example: A patient is seen in the Emergency Department at Memorial Hospital (part of integrated delivery system-IDS) after collapsing at home. After tests, it was determined that the patient had a stroke. His primary care physician who is also a member of the IDS admits the patient to Memorial Hospital. After acute care treatment, the patient is transferred to a rehabilitation hospital (part of IDS).

CATEGORY OF HEALTHCARE FACILITIES

Healthcare facilities are frequently categorized by ownership and services they provide.

One general category designation is *for-profit* and *non-for-profit.*

For-profit A privately owned facility with the excess income distributed to the shareholders and owners. An example of a proprietary hospital would be HCA (Hospital Corporation of America).

Not-for-profit The excess income is reinvested in the facility. An example of not-for-profit hospitals includes the VA Medical Centers, which are supported by the Department of Veterans Affairs (VA), a government supported network.

TYPES OF HOSPITALS

Healthcare services can be provided in a variety of settings, as listed below:

Hospitals – "Acute care" facilities that provide services to patients who have serious, sudden acute injuries or illnesses. Hospitals provide a range of services, including emergency and critical care, surgery, and obstetrics. Patients admitted to the hospital are called inpatients, and the stay is typically less than 30 days unless it is medically necessary to extend beyond the 30 days.

Critical Access Hospitals – These hospitals are located more than 35 miles from any other hospital and are certified as being a necessary provider of care to the residents in the area.

Specialty Hospitals – These hospitals concentrate on providing care to a particular population such as burn patients, children, or cancer treatment.

Rehabilitation Hospitals – Specialty hospitals devoted to rehabilitation of patients with various neurological, musculoskeletal and other conditions following stabilization of their acute illness. For example, a patient who has a head injury and no longer needs acute care may need physical and speech therapy to continue their recovery.

Behavioral Health Hospitals – The hospitals specialize in treatment of individuals with mental health diagnoses.

UNIT 3

Healthcare Settings

HEALTHCARE SETTINGS – INTRODUCTION

When we talk about healthcare, we typically think of a hospital or doctor's office. However, there many types of medical conditions that exist, and many varied treatments that they require. Consequently, there are also many different places where treatment is given. This unit will cover some of the several settings where patients can receive healthcare.

AMBULATORY CARE

Healthcare delivery is more than hospital-related care. This unit will explore the various settings and the care that is provided. One general, broad category of care is **Ambulatory Care (or Outpatient Care).**

Ambulatory care allows patients to receive care without the need for inpatient hospitalization. Care may be provided by a hospital-based center or a freestanding facility. The following table displays typical outpatient services and their definition.

Facility	Definition
Outpatient Surgery	Patients undergo surgical treatment and return home after recovery, typically hours after the procedure.
Physician Office	Physicians offer primary care or medical/surgical specialty care. The physicians may belong to an integrated delivery system or have private medical practices that are physician-owned entities.
Outpatient Diagnostic or Therapeutic Services	A freestanding facility, hospital department or a satellite facility provides a variety of services. The services range from an Imaging Center (such as MRI, CT scan), Infusion Center (provides continuous or intermittent infusion), or cancer treatment.
Neighborhood Health Clinics	Care is provided to economically disadvantaged, and treatment is family-centered.
Public Health Department	Provides preventive medicine services such as well-baby clinics.
Urgent Care Center	An on-duty physician provides immediate care for non life-threatening conditions. Many patients elect to use the center after the physician's office is closed.

HOME CARE

Home care allows patients to remain at home and be treated by nurses, social workers, therapists or other licensed healthcare professionals. A variety of care can be provided by the healthcare team, including:

- Assessment and monitoring of illnesses
- Intravenous (IV) medication administration
- Wound care

EXAMPLE OF HOME HEALTH CARE PATIENT

A patient with a diagnosis of Type 1 diabetes mellitus with peripheral neuropathy has an ulcer of the left leg that required surgical debridement at the local hospital. The patient was discharged from the hospital and receives home care for wound management. The nurse visits the patient to evaluate the progress of the wound. In addition, a nutritionist sees the patient at home to discuss management of her diabetes.

HOSPICE CARE

Hospice care provides comprehensive medical and supportive care to terminally ill patients and their families. Hospice is based on the philosophy of palliative care, providing comfort rather than curative care (therapeutic treatment). An interdisciplinary team (nursing, spiritual care, social workers) provides care to the hospice patients. In addition to home care, some hospitals and long-term care facilities offer hospice services.

EXAMPLE OF HOSPICE PATIENT

A 79-year-old female patient with terminal cancer is nearing the end of life and chooses not to have an artificial or mechanical effort to prolong life. A care team includes nursing, psychological and pharmacological support to the patient.

LONG-TERM CARE

Long-term care includes services delivered in a variety of settings, such as skilled nursing facilities (nursing homes); residential care facilities, hospice and adult day-care programs. Characteristically, the length of stay is greater than 30 days. Although residents of these facilities are typically elderly, other patients may also need long-term care after an injury or extended illness. Long-term care facilities provide a range of services, including custodial, intermediate, rehabilitation and skilled nursing care. As with hospitals, the facilities may be for-profit or not-for-profit. The following table summarizes the types of long-term care services.

Type	Description
Skilled Nursing Facility (SNF) or Nursing Facility (NF)	A team of healthcare professionals provides medical necessary services on a daily basis. Patients are often transferred from acute care (hospital) for continuing 24-hour medical care.
Retirement Communities	These communities provide a variety of care based on the residents' needs. Different levels of care range from independent living to skilled care.
Assisted Living Facilities	Assisted living is for adults who need help with everyday tasks. Patients may need help with dressing, bathing, or using the bathroom, but they do not need full-time nursing care. Some assisted living facilities are part of retirement communities.
Adult Day-Care Programs	Adult day-care programs offer a range of services during daytime hours. The goal of the program is to provide respite for caregivers and avoid costly alternatives. Some centers specialize in caring for special conditions such as Alzheimer's disease.

UNIT 4

Organization of Hospital Services

ORGANIZATION OF HOSPITAL SERVICES – INTRODUCTION

A hospital is far more than a building full of doctors and medical equipment. They can be very complex, with many different roles and responsibilities to fill. All of them are important to make sure patients visiting a hospital receive quality, reliable care. The unit will cover the different responsibilities of physicians and medical staff, as well as the many support and administrative roles.

GOVERNING BOARD AND ADMINISTRATION

Most hospitals are organized in a top-down format, with the authority and responsibility flowing downward through a chain of command. The overall legal authority for the hospital's operation resides with a governing board (also called board of trustees or board of directors). The board members are either elected or appointed depending on the type of hospital and form of ownership. The governing board hires a chief executive officer (CEO) to carry out the mission and goals of the organization. In addition to the CEO, the executive leadership may include a chief financial officer (CFO), chief information officer (CIO) and chief operating officer (COO).

MEDICAL STAFF

The medical staff consists of licensed physicians and other licensed providers permitted by law, such as a licensed nurse practitioner. Through an application process, physicians are granted permission to practice medicine. Traditionally, physicians were not employed by the hospital but this has changed within the last decade. The medical staff agrees on policies called medical staff bylaws, which spell out the qualifications for physicians to become part of the medical staff.

ROLE OF PHYSICIAN

The role of the physician is central in the healthcare delivery system. The physician is the "conductor" of patient care. Physicians perform examinations, orders tests, prescribe medications and evaluate signs and symptoms to confirm diagnoses.

In the delivery of healthcare, the term **attending physician** means the physician who has been selected by or assigned to the patient and who has assumed primary responsibility for treatment and care of the patient.

Physicians may also participate in patient care in other roles such as **consulting physician**. An attending physician may ask another physician for their professional advice.

> **EXAMPLE:**
>
> *A patient is admitted to the hospital by the orthopedic surgery for a hip replacement. During the hospital stay, the patient experiences chest pains and the orthopedic surgeon requests a consultation from a cardiologist.*

DIAGNOSTIC AND THERAPEUTIC SERVICES

Although physicians and nurses perform most of the direct patient care for inpatients, many other supportive services are provided within the hospital. Diagnostic services include clinical laboratory, radiology and nuclear medicine. Therapeutic services include radiation therapy, occupational therapy and physical therapy. The following table outlines several departments and their services.

Department	Diagnostic Services
Clinical Laboratory Services	Conducts diagnostic tests on body fluids, tissues and body wastes. A pathologist, a physician employed by the facility, oversees the department. Clinical laboratory technologist and technicians perform tests.

Radiology	Provides image-guided procedures for inpatients and outpatients. Examples of tests include computerized tomography (CT scan) and magnetic resonance imaging (MRI). A radiologist, a physician employed by the facility, oversees the department. Radiology technicians are trained to operate the equipment and perform tests.
Nuclear Medicine and Radiation Therapy	Nuclear medicine is the specialty that uses radioactive substances to diagnose and treat patients. Radiation therapy uses radiation to treat human diseases.

REHABILITATION

A team of physicians and therapists often provides rehabilitation services to eliminate or lessen the patient's disability. Examples of rehabilitation departments and their services are listed below.

Department	Therapeutic Services
Occupational Therapy	Occupational therapists and/or assistants help patients participate in everyday activities after loss of a function. Therapy interventions include helping patients recover from an injury to regain skills.
Physical Therapy	Therapists and/or assistants use physical agents of exercise, massage and other modalities to help patients recover.
Speech and Language Pathology	Therapists evaluate and assist patients with speech, language and swallowing difficulties.

OTHER CLINICAL SUPPORT

The healthcare team also includes several other allied health professionals, such as those listed below:

Nutrition – Registered dietitians provide nutritional care.

Pharmacy – Pharmacists review medication orders, manage the patient's medication profile and offer consulting services to the healthcare team.

Respiratory – Therapists treat patients who have lung disorders such as pneumonia or asthma.

ANCILLARY SUPPORT SERVICES

Ancillary units within the hospital provide clinical and administrative support services, such as those listed below:

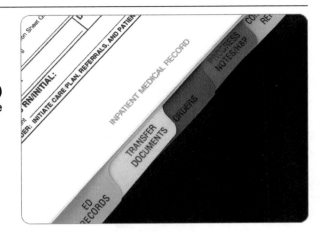

Health Information Management (Medical Records) – The department practices the maintenance and care of health records; traditional (paper-based) and electronic health records.

Social Service – Licensed social workers assist patients and families in locating resources that are specific to their healthcare needs.

UNIT 5

Healthcare Providers

HEALTHCARE PROVIDERS – INTRODUCTION

This unit focuses on healthcare providers involved in primary care, nursing care and specialty care.

The governing body delegates authority and responsibility for patient care to the medical staff. The medical staff is organized into clinical departments according to medical specialties that are defined by their scope of practice. For example, an Ear, Nose and Throat (ENT) physician would not be able to perform open-heart surgery.

MEDICAL SPECIALTIES

In the medical community the term **generalist** often refers to medical doctors (MDs) and doctors of osteopathic medicine (DOs) who specialize in internal medicine, family practice, or pediatrics. Physician assistants (PAs) are trained in a variety of services and work in collaboration with an MD or DO. In some case, the primary care physician will refer a patient to a doctor of a certain specialty, such as:

Specialty Area	Description
Anesthesiology	General anesthesia or spinal block for surgeries and some forms of pain control
Cardiology	Heart disorder
Dermatology	Skin disorders
Endocrinology	Hormonal and metabolic disorders, including diabetes
Gastroenterology	Digestive system disorders
General Surgery	Common Surgeries involving any body part
Hematology	Blood disorders
Immunology	Disorders of immune system
Infectious disease	Infections affecting the tissues of any part of the body
Nephrology	Kidney disorders
Neurology	Nervous system disorders
Obstetrics/ gynecology	Pregnancy and women's reproductive disorders
Oncology	Cancer treatment
Ophthalmology	Eye disorders and surgery
Orthopedics	Bone and connective tissue disorders
Otorhinolaryngology	Ear, nose and throat (ENT) disorders
Psychiatry	Emotional or mental disorders

Pulmonary (lung)	Respiratory tract disorders
Rheumatology	Pain and other symptoms related to joints and other parts of the musculoskeletal system
Urology	Disorders of the male reproductive and urinary tracts and the female urinary tract

NURSING CARE

Registered nurses (RNs) have graduated from a nursing program and successfully complete a state board examination and are licensed by the state. Licensed practical nurses (LPNs) are state-licensed who have been trained to care for the sick.

Advanced practice nurses have education and experience beyond the basic training and licensing required of all RNs. This includes nurse practitioners (NPs) and certified nurse midwives (CNMs) and certified registered nurse anesthetists (CRNAs). Their scope of practice is determined by state regulations.

UNIT 6

Licensure, Certification, and Accreditation

LICENSURE, CERTIFICATION, AND ACCREDITATION – INTRODUCTION

Licensure, certification, and accreditation have had an impact on the quality of healthcare services in the United States. In addition to government sponsored programs, many private agencies develop standards to regulate the U.S. Healthcare delivery system. This unit will highlight the standards developed to regulate management of healthcare facilities.

ROLE OF THE GOVERNMENT

Medicare is the government-sponsored healthcare program for qualified seniors and the disabled. Medicaid is a joint state and federal healthcare program for qualified individuals who lack resources to pay for healthcare. In order for healthcare facilities to receive federal funding for Medicare and Medicaid, they have to meet certain requirements. Before exploring the requirements, it important to discuss the agencies responsible for overseeing and governing the federal programs.

Department of Health and Human Services (DHHS)

The Department of Health and Human Services (DHHS) is the federal agency tasked with governing and regulation healthcare in the United States. DHHS is divided into offices and agencies.

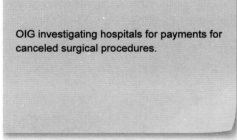

OIG investigating hospitals for payments for canceled surgical procedures.

Centers for Medicare and Medicaid Services (CMS)

The Centers for Medicare and Medicaid Services (CMS) is an agency of the Department of Health and Human Services. CMS administers the Medicare and Medicaid programs by setting standards and regulations.

Office of Inspector General (OIG)

The Office of Inspector General monitors and tracks the use of taxpayer dollars through audits, inspections, evaluations and investigations. The OIG department is under the U.S. Department of Commerce. OIG publishes a yearly Work Plan that outlines the initiatives for the upcoming year.

LICENSURE

State laws require healthcare facilities to obtain licensure before serving patients. The licensing agency sets standards that must be met before a "license to operate" is granted.

The state department of health issues the license after reviewing the facility's compliance to state standards.

Examples of standards include staffing levels and the safety requirements, such as the installation of a sprinkler system and fire alarms. The types of facilities licensed, and standards vary from state to state.

CERTIFICATION FOR MEDICARE PARTICIPATION

Certification is the result of a process that determines if the facility meets required standards. In order for a facility to receive federal healthcare funding (Medicare and Medicaid), they must comply with regulations called *Conditions of Participation (CoP)*. The regulations (standards) are the foundation for improving quality and protecting health and safety for patients. The certification process is conducted by state agencies and the regulations are published on the website of the Centers for Medicare and Medicaid Services (CMS). CMS is an agency of the Department of Health and Human Services that administers the Medicare and Medicaid programs. *Conditions of Participation's* standards apply to numerous healthcare organizations, such as: Ambulatory Surgical Centers, Critical Access Hospitals, Home Health Agencies, Hospice, Hospitals and Clinics.

The following is an excerpt from the CoP Manual that describes the hospital's obligation to protect the confidentiality of the patient's record:

§482.24(b)(3) – The hospital must have a procedure for ensuring the confidentiality of patient records. Information from or copies of records may be released only to authorized individuals.

CONDITIONS OF PARTICIPATION FOR HOSPITALS

Download the following excerpt from the *Conditions of Participation* to answer the support questions:

We've placed a multi-page visual aid in the appendix on pages 369-370.

I. MULTIPLE CHOICE.
Choose the best answer.

1. According to the Conditions of Participation, medical records must be retained:
   - ○ forever
   - ○ for 1 year
   - ○ for 5 years
   - ○ for 10 years

2. If a patient is discharged from the hospital on July 1st, the medical record must be completed by:
   - ○ July 15th
   - ○ August 1st
   - ○ September 1st
   - ○ October 1st

II. TRUE/FALSE.
Mark the following true or false.

1. On April 15th, a patient is seen by his primary care physician with complaints of abdominal pain. During that encounter, a history and physical examination was performed. On April 20th the patient was admitted to General Hospital with acute cholecystitis. According to the *Conditions of Participation*, the history and physical examination from April 15th is acceptable documentation for the inpatient record.
   - ○ true
   - ○ false

2. The attending physician in charge of the patient must authenticate all medical record entries.
   - ○ true
   - ○ false

ACCREDITATION

Accreditation is a voluntary process that a healthcare facility undergoes to demonstrate that it has met standards beyond what is required by law. There are many accrediting bodies, such as The Joint Commission and the American Osteopathic Association.

The Joint Commission is a private, nonprofit organization that establishes guidelines and standards for the operation and management of healthcare facilities. These standards are considered more rigorous than regulations. Organizations apply for accreditation and participate in a formal evaluation process by external reviewers to determine whether they comply with the standards.

The Centers of Medicare and Medicaid (CMS) states that if a facility is accredited by The Joint Commission, the Healthcare Facilities Accreditation Program (American Osteopathic Association) or Det Norske Veritas Healthcare, Inc. they are deemed to be in compliance with the *Conditions of Participation* and do not have to undergo a separate certification process. In other words, organizations seeking Medicare approval may choose to surveyed either by an deemed accrediting body (The Joint Commission, HFAP DNV, or by state surveyors) on behalf of CMS.

The following table displays one aspect, the survey frequency, for the three organizations.

	The Joint Commission	Healthcare Facilities Accreditation Program (HFAP)	Det Norske Veritas Healthcare, Inc. (DNV)
Survey Frequency	On-site surveys of hospitals every three (3) years. An annual self-assessment with Periodic Performance Review is prepared by the hospital.	On-site surveys of hospitals once every three (3) years.	An annual on-site survey.

EXAMPLE OF THE JOINT COMMISSION STANDARD

The Joint Commission Manual of Standards is available for purchase on their website. The following is example of a standard for a History and Physical Examination:

The history and physical examination must be completed and documented within 24 hours following admission of the patient, but prior to surgery or a procedure requiring anesthesia services.

OTHER ACCREDITING ORGANIZATIONS

In addition to the previously mentioned accrediting bodies, the following table outlines some of the other healthcare accrediting organizations.

Accrediting Body	Description
Accreditation Association for Ambulatory Health Care (AAAHC)	An organization committed to developing Standards that advance and promote patient safety, quality healthcare, and value in ambulatory healthcare settings.
Commission on Accreditation of Rehabilitation Facilities (CARF)	An accrediting organization for rehabilitation facilities.
National Committee for Quality Assurance (NCQA)	Organization assessments the quality of managed care plans. Developed the Health Plan Employer Data and Information Set (HEDIS) that is a tool for measuring quality of care. Example of a HEDIS measure: cancer screening and prenatal care.

UNIT 7

Public Health and Registries

PUBLIC HEALTH AND REGISTRIES - INTRODUCTION

Public health is the science and art of preventing disease, prolonging life and promoting health. In the United States, one of the methods for evaluating healthcare services and trends is collecting information through registries. **Registries** are an organized system for collection, storage, retrieval, analysis and dissemination of information on individual persons who have either a particular disease or condition (such as a risk factor). Some of the most common registries will be explored in this unit.

Highlights

For example, registry data has documented the rapid increase in the occurrence among women of lung cancer.

USES OF REGISTRIES

The following list outlines some of the uses of healthcare registries in the United States:

- Estimating magnitude of a problem
- Determining the incidence of disease
- Examining trends of disease over time
- Identifying groups at high risk for specific diseases
- Conducting research
- Estimating survival analysis
- Evaluating health effects of specific exposures

SPONSORS OF REGISTRIES

Registries are operated by many different entities, including:
- Federal government (National Exposure Registry)
- State government (sexually transmitted diseases)
- Universities (cancer and trauma registries)
- Groups of Hospitals (Assembled for research purposes)
- Non-profit organizations (United States Eye Injury Registry)
- Private Groups (transplant registries)

VITAL STATISTICS

The National Center for Health Statistics (NCHS) is the federal agency responsible for maintaining official vital statistics for the country. Vital statistics includes registration of births, deaths, marriages and divorces. Birth certifications are often completed by the hospital and forwarded to the local vital statistic office. The local office is responsible for sending the certificate to the state and then the state submits the form to NCHS.

The federal government controls several other registries such as the Center for Disease Control's Agency for Toxic Substances.

LIST OF REGISTRIES

The following table provides a snapshot of some registry programs in the United States:

Registry	Sponsor	Description
Cancer Registry	Healthcare facilities and state and federal agencies	Collects information about patients being treated for cancer.
Immunization Registry	State and federal agencies	Population-based registry that collects vaccination data about persons within a geographic area.
Implant Registries	Various organizations depending on type of implant	Tracks implant and analyzed data on failure. Example: National Breast Implant Registry.
Insulin-Dependent Diabetes Mellitus Registries	National Institutes of Health (NIH)	Determines incidence of insulin dependent diabetes mellitus in defined populations for research studies.
National Trauma Data Bank	American College of Surgeons	Organization creates and distributes data sets that can be used by researchers concerning treatment of trauma patients.

UNIT 8

Professional and Trade Associations Related to Healthcare

PROFESSIONAL AND TRADE ASSOCIATIONS RELATED TO HEALTHCARE – INTRODUCTION

This module has included many of the professional and trade associations that influence the practice of medicine and the delivery of healthcare services in the United States (such as, The Joint Commission, American Osteopathic Association).

A trade organization is a group of people that form an organization because of common interests, goals or purpose. Trade organizations allow individuals to band together and have a strong, unified voice to influence regulation, shape policy, provide information, and share information. The associations are generally organized on a national, state or local level. The trade associations hold meetings, provide education and permit interaction for their members. Examples of trade organizations include the American Occupational Therapy Association and the American Health Information Management Association.

AMERICAN MEDICAL ASSOCIATION (AMA)

The main mission of the AMA is to promote the art and science of medicine and the betterment of public health. The association acts as an accrediting body for medical schools and residency programs. In addition, it also maintains and publishes the *Current Procedural Terminology (CPT®)* coding system. CPT coding is the basis for reimbursement for physician's services. AMA published *CPT Assistant*, which provides official coding advice for CPT coding.

AMERICAN HOSPITAL ASSOCIATION (AHA)

This national organization represents and serves hospitals, healthcare networks and their patients and communities. Their services include advocacy activities for the healthcare facilities they represent.

AHA serves over 5,000 hospitals and 40,000 individual members

AHA publishes *Coding Clinic*, which provides official coding advice for ICD-9-CM, ICD-10-CM and HCPCS.

AMERICAN COLLEGE OF HEALTHCARE EXECUTIVES (ACHE)

ACHE is an international professional society of healthcare executives who lead hospitals, healthcare systems and other healthcare organizations.

The society published books and textbooks on healthcare services management.

AMERICAN HEALTH INFORMATION MANAGEMENT ASSOCIATION (AHIMA)

The mission of this professional organization is to lead the health informatics and information management community to advance professional practice and standards. The organization supports the philosophy that *"quality information promotes quality healthcare."*

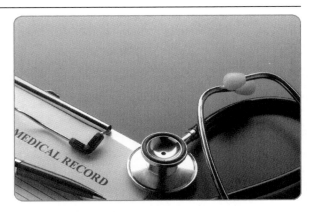

OTHER HEALTHCARE-RELATED ORGANIZATIONS

There are many other associations that provide education, certification and accreditation services to support healthcare professionals. Example of those organizations include:

- American Dental Association
- American League for Nursing
- American Dietetic Association
- American Association of Nurse Anesthetists

UNIT 9

Trends in Healthcare

TRENDS IN HEALTHCARE - INTRODUCTION

The cost of healthcare in the United States has escalated significantly which has lead to many initiatives to control costs without compromising quality. Several trends in the healthcare industry will be explored in this unit.

FOCUS ON QUALITY

Healthcare organizations are being pressured to delivery higher value care and accountability. The focus is to reduce costs and improve quality and safety. Healthcare leaders are promoting operating efficiencies with optimal outcomes.

TECHNOLOGY

Healthcare organizations continue to integrate the use of technology to improve patient care and eliminate waste. The federal government has created incentives to promote the use of electronic health records for initiatives such as e-prescribing (electronic prescribing) to reduce medication errors.

BEST PRACTICES

Using evidence-based medicine to help make decisions about the care of patients continues to be a focus in healthcare facilities. Evidence-based medicine is the phrase that means healthcare providers combine their individual experience and knowledge with clinical based research to make decisions.

The Agency for Healthcare Research and Quality (AHRQ), a federally funded organization, is committed to advancing excellence in healthcare. AHRQ developed Quality Indicators (QI) that provides measures for hospital quality and safety.

GROWTH OF MANAGED CARE

Managed care is a phrase for healthcare reimbursement system that manages cost, quality and access to services. Typically, managed care organizations do not provide patient care but contract for services with hospitals, physicians, etc. They employ several methods to control costs, including precertification (permission) for healthcare services such as surgery and utilization review processes.

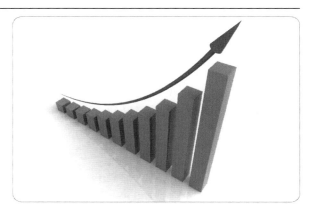

In order to manage costs and maintain quality, many managed care organizations have developed programs such as:

- Wellness Programs
- Patient Education
- Disease Prevention

Legal and Compliance

Module

3

UNIT 1

Introduction

INTRODUCTION TO LEGAL AND COMPLIANCE

LEARNING OBJECTIVES

In this module, the student will discover the laws and regulatory practices that impact healthcare professionals:

1. Explain the legislative and regulatory processes in the United States.
2. Describe the laws and regulations pertaining to health information.
3. Define Health Insurance Portability and Accountability Act (HIPAA).
4. Adhere to privacy and security policies.
5. Identify the components of the Code of Ethics and Standards of Ethical Coding.

Healthcare is a complex industry. There are many laws and regulations controlling the proper use and security of healthcare records. In this module, you will learn about the legal practices, processes, and policies, including HIPAA, that govern healthcare professionals. You will also have the opportunity to study and apply the principles outlined in the the Standard of Coding Ethics.

UNIT 2
Legislative Process Overview

LEGISLATIVE PROCESS OVERVIEW – INTRODUCTION

Laws are classified as public or private. **Public** laws deal with relationships between individuals and government. Examples of public law crimes include healthcare fraud; such as a physician billing for patients he/she did not treat. **Private** (civil) laws deal with the legal rights and relationships of private individuals. A wrongful act (**tort**) such as a surgeon leaving forceps in the abdominal cavity during surgery would be a civil suit. The sources of laws include administrative, case or statutory.

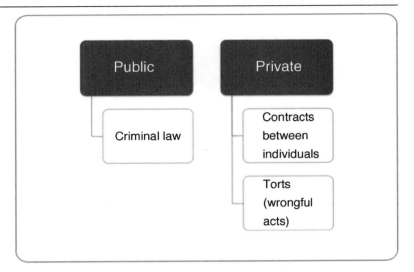

SOURCES OF LAWS

In the U.S. legal system, laws are passed by a legislative body (such as Congress) and the government enforces it. In addition to the Constitution of the United States and individual state constitutions, sources of law include:

Administrative law – created by administrative agencies of government

Case law (also called common law) – based on judicial decision

Statutory law – passed by legislative body

EXAMPLES:

The Code of Federal Regulations (CFR) is a type of administrative law.

The Health Insurance Portability and Accountability Act of 1996 was passed by Congress, making it a statutory law.

LEGAL DISPUTES

Resolving legal disputes is primarily through the court system. The Supreme Court is the highest court in the system and the district courts are the lowest tier. The court of appeals addresses appeals on decisions made at the district court level.

Besides courtroom decisions, there are alternative dispute resolution methods such as arbitration or mediation. During **arbitration,** a third party or panel of experts settles the dispute. During **mediation**, a third party is requests to facilitate agreement between the disputing parties. The mediator does not make a decision; they are seeking solutions to the dispute.

LEGAL PROCESS

During a lawsuit, the **plaintiff** initiates the process against the **defendant** by filing a **complaint** in court. The burden of proof resides with the plaintiff. **Discovery** is the legal process lawyers use to obtain information regarding all aspects in the case. A **deposition** is a form of discovery used to learn answers to certain questions such as a sworn statement from a witness. Sometimes during the deposition process, a subpoena is issued for the health information professional to bring the health record to the deposition. The role of the health information professional is to testify that the health record was compiled in the normal course of business and not altered in any way. Each state has different rules governing the production of health records in litigation.

Subpoena duces tecum is a court summons to appear and bring the documents (such as health record).

LEGAL HEALTH RECORD

The **legal health record** is the official business record created by or for the healthcare organization. Although standards may vary depending on state laws and type of health care setting, the health record must be maintained according to accreditation standards (such as Joint Commission), legal principles (federal and state laws), practice standards and regulations (such as the Conditions of Participation).

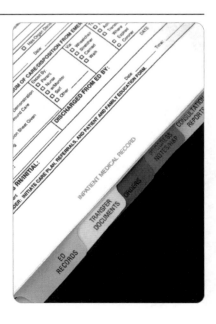

Organizations should develop and maintain an **inventory of documents** and data that comprise the legal health record, such as electronic documents as well as paper. Facilities must evaluate whether other types of information are considered part of the legal health record, such as:
- fetal monitoring strips
- diagnostic images
- digital photography
- email correspondence

LEGAL DOCUMENTS

Informed Consent

The health record includes several documents developed for the legal aspect of healthcare. For example, the patient is required to give consent for treatment. In addition, a separate consent form is required if the patient has surgery. **Informed consent** is the process of advising a patient about treatment options.

Note the following excerpt from a patient's operative report:

Medical Record

OPERATIVE REPORT

After obtaining informed consent from the patient and having an extensive discussion with his wife regarding the high risk of this patient's current medical condition and surgery, the patient was brought to the operating room where upon smooth induction of general anesthesia was performed.

Advance Directives

A patient record must document whether the individual has executed an **advance directive**, which is a legal document in which patients provide *instructions as to how they want to be treated* in an event they become unable to communicate their wishes. These instructions can direct physicians to refrain from various kinds of cardiopulmonary resuscitation or aggressive medical interventions.

Highlights

Example of Directive: Due to religious beliefs, a patient may have an advance directive that states that a healthcare provider *not* administer a blood transfusion.

RETENTION OF THE HEALTH RECORD

The retention of health records depends on two main factors: **type of organization and federal/state laws.** Providers can elect to retain the records longer than required but policies must comply with the laws. Some research facilities maintain health records far beyond what is required for educational purposes. In addition, Children's Hospitals maintain records for a longer period of time.

Health records should be retained for at least the period specified by the state's statute of limitations for malpractice, and other claims.

The Medicare Conditions of Participation requires hospitals, long-term care facilities, specialized providers and home-health agencies to retain medical records for a period of **no less than five years.** Health information of a minor should be retained until the patient reaches the age of majority (as defined by state law).

UNIT 3
Confidentiality and HIPAA

CONFIDENTIALITY AND HIPAA – INTRODUCTION

Any information communicated by a patient to a health care provider is considered **privileged communication**. Patients have the right to have their medical information confidential. A **breach of confidentiality** occurs when patient information is disclosed to others who do not have a right to access the information.

HEALTH INSURANCE PORTABILITY AND ACCOUNTABILITY ACT (HIPAA)

The Health Insurance Portability and Accountability Act of 1996 (HIPAA), Public Law 104-191, governs the **privacy and security of health information**. There are several components to HIPAA but the "accountability" aspect protects health data integrity, availability and confidentiality. HIPAA defines patient rights such as access to his/her medical information.

HIPAA also protects health insurance coverage for workers and their families when they change or lose their jobs.

THE PRIVACY AND SECURITY RULE

The HIPAA standards for privacy of individually identifiable health information (simply called the **Privacy Rule)** include provisions that protect privileged communication. The HIPAA **Security Rule** includes standards and safeguards to protect health information that is collected, maintained, used or transmitted **electronically.** The safeguards must be implemented to ensure that facilities, equipment and patient information are safe from damage, loss, tampering, theft, or unauthorized access.

COVERED ENTITIES

Individuals, organizations and agencies that meet the definition of a covered entity must comply with the HIPAA rules to protect health information. In simple terms, a **covered entity** means an organization that routinely handles protected health information. If a covered entity contracts with other businesses to help carry out health care activities and functions, the business associate must also comply with the HIPAA rules. The image below outlines types of covered entities:

Health Care Provider	Doctors Clinics Psychologists Dentists Chiropractor Nursing Homes Pharmacies
Health Plans	Health Insurance Companies HMOs Company health plans Government programs such Medicare/Medicaid

PROTECTED HEALTH INFORMATION (PHI)

Protected Health Information (PHI) is information that identifies an individual such as name, address, date of birth, and social security number. Under HIPAA's privacy rule there are specific guidelines for PHI to be disclosed in any form, whether verbal, electronic or paper-based.

Patient must be told about their rights and be provided an opportunity to object to disclosure of PHI.

Highlights

Anyone in a facility could have access to PHI and needs to understand the privacy rules. This would include a dietary worker using the computer to see if there are any special nutritional instructions for the patient.

PATIENT RIGHTS

Under HIPAA, patients have several rights regarding their protected health information (PHI) such as those listed below. For example, a patient may not want communications about a particular episode of treatment to be sent to his/her home address where other family members may see the information.

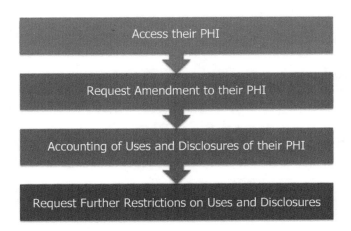

AUTHORIZATION OF PHI

Patients authorize the use or disclosure of information when they provide **written permission** to providers so that PHI may be released. Authorizations are required for many uses or disclosures of PHI for purposes **other than treatment, payment or healthcare operations**. For example, an authorization is not required from a hospitalized patient when a physician calls a consultant to offer an opinion on treatment.

Psychotherapy notes are a special type of PHI with special protections under HIPAA.

We've placed a multi-page visual aid in the appendix on pages 371-372.

AUTHORIZATION NOT REQUIRED

There are many situations where the use or disclosure of PHI *does not require* the individual's authorization. In addition to treatment, payment and operations, the patient does not have the opportunity to agree or object to disclosure in circumstances, such as:

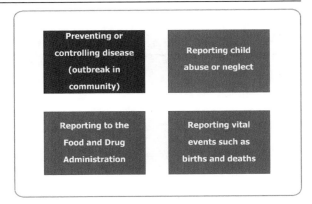

TRACKING DISCLOSURES OF PHI

The HIPAA privacy rule requires tracking of the release of protected health information. A tracking system should include the following:

- Date of disclosure
- Name and address of the person who received the PHI
- Description of the PHI disclosed
- Statement of reason for disclosure (or a copy of written request)

HIPAA SECURITY RULE – LESSON 1

Individuals who work for a healthcare organization have the responsibility for maintaining confidentiality of protected health information. The Security Rule provides **standards to protect confidentiality**. Healthcare facilities must develop policies and procedures to prevent, detect, contain, and correct security violations, such as:

- Risk analysis: Assess potential risks
- Risk management: Reduce risks
- Sanction policy: Penalties for those who do not comply with security policies
- Information system activity review: Audit logs, tracking reports, monitoring

Much of healthcare information is stored in **electronic form**, which has made protecting patient privacy more challenging. HIPAA addresses measures to **prevent accidental or intentional disclosure** to unauthorized persons. In addition, healthcare providers (covered entities under HIPAA) must protect information from being altered, damaged or destroyed accidentally or deliberately.

Accidental disclosure could easily occur if health information is faxed or emailed to the wrong person.

HIPAA SECURITY RULE – LESSON 2

Noncompliance may occur intentionally or unintentionally. The following list provides examples of **noncompliance** with HIPAA:

- Leaving a sheet of paper containing PHI at the front desk which is visible to others
- A computer screen that is unattended and logged in to PHI
- Knowingly releasing PHI to unauthorized individuals
- Selling PHI to marketing firms

There are penalties for HIPAA noncompliance that include fines and prison time.

There are many administrative, physical and technical safeguard "to do" items so that patient information is protected. The **safeguards** can include policies to change passwords, data backup processes, login monitoring and disaster recovery plan. Users are often limited to only applicable sections of the health record to assist with risk management. An example of a security safeguard would be a computer "shut-down" feature after inactivity in a public accessible location such as a nursing station.

Coding Professionals Working at Home:

Many coding professionals work from home and use computers to access protected health information. It is not unusual for managers to perform a home office evaluation to ensure compliance with policies and procedures. Security measures such as eliminating the print function and closely monitoring activity would help with management of risk.

BEST PRACTICES UNDER HIPAA

HIPAA has emphasized the importance of maintaining confidentiality of patient information. The following is a list of **common employee best practices** for complying with HIPAA:

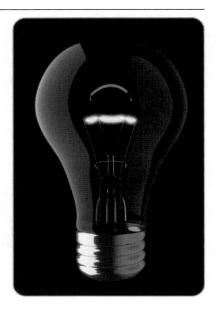

- Do not discuss or disclose any patient information with others, including family and friends, who do not have a need to know the information.
- Only access patient information for which you have specific authorization to access in order to perform your job duties.
- Keep computer passwords confidential.
- Report any security breaches to your supervisor or Privacy Office.

HITECH AND PATIENT PROTECTION AND AFFORDABLE CARE ACT

Since Congress passed HIPAA in 1996, two additional laws have been enacted that add requirements to HIPAA and strengthen various aspects of administrative simplification. These laws are:

Health Information Technology for Economic and Clinical Health Act (HITECH) – Enacted by part of the American Recovery and Reinvestment Action of 2009 (ARRA) and addresses the privacy and security concerns associated with the electronic transmission of health information, in part, through several provisions that strengthen the civil and criminal enforcement of HIPAA rules.

Patient Protection and Affordable Care Act of 2010 (ACA) – ACA builds upon HIPAA with new and expanded provisions and requires a unique, standard Health Plan Identifier.

UNIT 4

Ethics, Compliance, and Risk Management

ETHICS, COMPLIANCE, AND RISK MANAGEMENT – INTRODUCTION

The largest purchaser of healthcare in the United States is the government. As a duty to the taxpayers, federal agencies initiated several pieces of legislation related to investigating, identifying and **preventing healthcare fraud and abuse**. Several government agencies are involved in this initiative, including the Office of Inspector General (OIG). HIPAA authorized the OIG to investigate cases of healthcare fraud that involve private and federally funded programs. In addition to investigating healthcare fraud, the OIG issues compliance program guidance to prevent fraud and abuse.

An example of fraud and abuse is billing for services that were not provided.

OVERVIEW OF CODE OF ETHICS

Ethical codes are adopted by organizations to assists members with difficult decisions and state what behavior is considered ethical or "right." For example, AHIMA (American Health Information Association) publishes a code of ethics for health information management and coding. AHIMA's Code of Ethics establishes a framework for behavior and responsibilities.

Examples of dishonesty are included in section 4.8 of the document, such as:

- assigning codes without physician documentation
- coding an inappropriate level of service
- violating the privacy of individuals

We've placed a multi-page visual aid in the appendix on pages 373-380.

AHIMA publishes Standards of Ethical Coding based on their Code of Ethics. These principles reflect expectations of professional conduct for coding professionals.

I. MULTIPLE CHOICE.
   Use the link to the Standards of Ethical Coding above to answer the following questions. Apply elements of the Standards of Ethical Coding to the case scenarios below.

1. It is difficult for the coder to determine from the documentation if the patient's pneumonia was community acquired or acquired in the hospital. According to Standards of Ethical Coding, what is the appropriate action?
   - ⃝ Assign the code of pneumonia, unspecified.
   - ⃝ Call the physician's office and ask his/her secretary.
   - ⃝ Query the physician for clarification.
   - ⃝ Assign the code for community acquired pneumonia.

2. The surgeon dictates that he accidentally cut the ureter during the colorectal surgical procedure. According to the Standards of Ethical Coding, what is the appropriate action?
   - ⃝ Call the Chief of Medical Staff and ask for guidance.
   - ⃝ Assign the code for acquired deformity of ureter.
   - ⃝ Assign the code for surgical complication.
   - ⃝ Do not assign a code for the cutting of the ureter, only code colorectal procedure.

3. Which of the following is the appropriate practice for locating a poisoning of a drug that is not indexed by the trade name (such as Xanax) in the Table of Drugs and Chemicals?
   - ⃝ Research the appropriate generic name/classification of the drug.
   - ⃝ Assign the code for "unspecified."
   - ⃝ Assign the code for "other" drug.
   - ⃝ Call the pharmacy and ask for guidance.

GUIDANCE FOR COMPLIANCE PROGRAM

The OIG provides guidance for a corporate compliance program that results in improvements in the quality of patient care and prevents criminal and unethical conduct.

The OIG outlines the following **elements** as a minimum for a compliance program:

1. Develop and distribute written standards of conduct.
2. Designate a chief compliance officer.
3. Develop and implement educational and training programs.
4. Maintain a process (such as a hotline) to receive complaints and protect anonymity of whistleblowers.
5. Develop a system to respond to allegations and enforce disciplinary actions.
6. Ongoing monitoring and auditing to detect and reduce identified problem areas.
7. Investigate and remediate systemic problems.

CODING PRACTICE AND COMPLIANCE

One area of the corporate compliance program involves coding. The accuracy and completeness of coding determines payment; therefore a **strong coding compliance program** helps to prevent fraud and abuse. At a minimum, a coding compliance program should include policies and procedures, education/training and a plan for ongoing auditing. Auditing assists in identifying areas of risk. There are many "best practices" for performing coding audits. For example, selections of the cases for auditing may include one of the following:

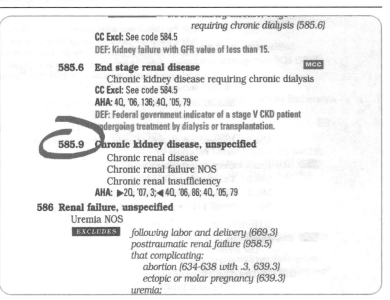

- Most common diagnosis and procedure codes
- High dollar cases
- Unusual patterns in code assignments

HIPAA AND CODING

A major portion of HIPAA focused on identifying medically unnecessary services, upcoding, unbundling and billing for services not provided. **Upcoding** is the practice of assigning a diagnosis or procedure code specifically for the purpose of obtaining a higher level of reimbursement (payment). **Unbundling** is the practice of using multiple codes that describe individual components of a procedure rather than an appropriate single code that describes all steps of the procedure performed.

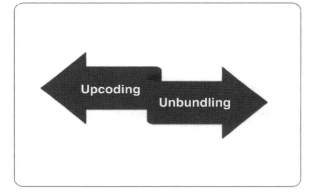

RECOVERY AUDIT CONTRACTOR PROGRAM

The Tax Relief and Health Care Act of 2006 gave way to a program using **recovery audit contractors** (RACs) to investigate claims submitted by physicians, providers, facilities and supplies. Through the use of data mining and "hands-on" reviews of the health record, RAC makes claims determinations with the goal of saving federal healthcare dollars in improper Medicare payments. One of the levels of auditing includes reviewing the record for incorrect application of coding rules.

Reimbursement Methodologies

Module

4

UNIT 1

Introduction

INTRODUCTION TO REIMBURSEMENT METHODOLOGIES

LEARNING OBJECTIVES

At the conclusion of this module, the learner will be able to:

1. Define commercial, managed care, and federal insurance plans.
2. Identify various compliance strategies and reporting.
3. Define and list payment methodologies and systems (such as capitation, prospective payment systems, RBRVS, MS-DRGs).
4. Describe the billing processes and procedures (such as claims, EOB, ABN, electronic data interchange).
5. Explain chargemaster maintenance.
6. Describe regulatory guidelines.
7. Discuss reimbursement monitoring and reporting.

Getting paid for providing services is what healthcare reimbursement is all about. A healthcare provider (individual or institution) performs a healthcare service for a patient and receives payment in return for the service. Building on what you learned in prior modules about healthcare documentation, structure, and organization, let's take a look at healthcare reimbursement.

Regardless of who pays the claim, the healthcare reimbursement process has the same basic elements:

1. documentation – medical record/ financial record
2. code assignment
3. claim preparation
4. claim to payer(s)
5. claim review
6. claim resolution

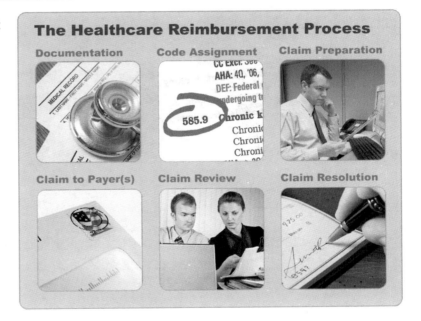

The Healthcare Reimbursement Process

Documentation | Code Assignment | Claim Preparation
Claim to Payer(s) | Claim Review | Claim Resolution

The details, such as how much is billed, how much is paid, and what forms are used, may vary from claim to claim, but the billing process is the same for all healthcare services.

UNIT 2

Medical Billing Basics

MEDICAL BILLING BASICS – INTRODUCTION

The first topic discussed is basics of coding and healthcare reimbursement for outpatients. From a medical coding specialist's perspective, there are two types of outpatient coding situations: coding for physicians and coding for facilities.

BILLING PROCESS

In many cases, the medical coder is also the medical biller. In situations where this is not the case, the medical billing specialist and the medical coding specialist work closely together during the healthcare reimbursement process. As the patient is seen in the outpatient setting, the information is compiled and at the conclusion of the visit it is routed to the medical billing specialist.

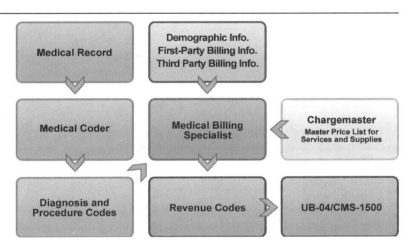

DEMOGRAPHIC INFORMATION

Collection of demographic information is a standard part of the healthcare documentation process and is essential for the healthcare reimbursement process. The medical biller uses the demographic information as the foundation for determining who should receive the bill(s) and who has responsibility for payment.

Demographic information is collected by the front office either during a pre-registration or registration for patient care process. Demographic information may be collected by a front office staff person who then performs the coding and billing for each patient in a physician's office or clinic. Demographic information may also be done by an admissions or registration department collecting demographic information for all patient care services throughout a large multi-use facility. The staff who collect the demographic information in an acute care hospital admission area, for example, would likely never see the coded medical record or the bills generated.

Coding and billing specialists for radiologists, emergency room physicians, or other patient care providers are likely to receive demographic information secondhand through the facility where the patient received the services.

ACCURATE DEMOGRAPHICS

Collecting accurate and complete demographic information allows accurate billing to occur and is an important part of maintaining a financially healthy business. When the time from service to payment is extended because of bad demographic information (such as returned mail from an incorrect or inaccurate third-party payer information on a CMS-1500 or UB-04), a provider can experience cash flow problems. When most claims are paid in a timely manner because patient contact information, third-party payer information, and other demographic information is accurately collected up front, a provider can more easily absorb the bad debts and occasional denials that are an inevitable part of doing business.

Demographics include some or all of the following:

- Patient name
- Patient date of birth
- Patient address
- Patient phone number
- Patient e-mail address
- Patient social security number
- Patient's employer
- Employer's phone number

- Spouse's name (if patient is married)
- Spouse's date of birth
- Spouse's phone number (other than home)
- Responsible party name
- Responsible party address (if different from patient)
- Responsible party phone number
- Emergency contact name
- Emergency contact number

- Third-party payer name
- Third-party payer address
- Third-party payer policy number(s)
- Subscriber's name
- Subscriber's employer (if subscriber is different from patient)
- Employer phone number
- Copy of third-party coverage card
- Copy of driver's license or photo I.D.

Once collected, demographic information is accessed by the medical biller electronically or in hard copy and entered into the provider's billing system. The demographic information is used to determine who will receive a bill for the services: patient or patient representative (first-party payer) or third-party payer and patient or patient representative.

Even when a third-party payer is billed, the patient/responsible party is furnished with a copy of the bill both as a receipt for services and in the event the third-party payer only pays the claim partially or denies the claim.

CHARGE DESCRIPTION MASTER

The charge description master (CDM) or chargemaster is a healthcare provider's comprehensive price list of all supplies, services, and equipment usage fees for patient care.

All chargemasters generally contain the following items:

- CPT/HCPCS Procedure code
- Charge Description
- Revenue Code
- Charge
- Department Code
- Charge Code
- Charge Status

Coders perform the coding on procedures that vary from patient to patient (soft coding) while the CDM automatically assigns codes based on a unique identifier number for routine services (hard coding).

The chargemaster is a large database that contains the price list for all services provided to its patients. The fee (or charge) is the price established and assigned to a unit of medical or other service in the facility. An example would be a visit to a physician or a day in a hospital. The fee for a service may be unrelated to the actual cost of providing the service.

Codes are uniform from provider to provider since they must match the procedure code system (CPT®, and HCPCS) adopted in the United States.

The fees, however, vary from provider to provider. One provider may charge $130 for a routine office visit; another provider may charge $110.

The chargemaster is updated annually (at a minimum). The chargemaster must be maintained whenever new services are added, when codes change, or when charges change.

The actual coding of procedures occurs for surgical procedures, evaluation & management (E&M) codes and other services that vary or may be unique to the patient. For routine services such as laboratory or radiology services however, the charges are actually posted using the CDM. During the order entry, (electronic or paper) a special identifier number for each service is entered. This identifier then triggers a charge from the CDM that is posted on the patient's account. This is known as **hard coding.**

Highlights

Charge description master (CDM) or Chargemaster is a large database used to collect information on all the goods and services provided to patients.

We've placed a visual aid in the appendix on page 381.

I. **MULTIPLE CHOICE.**
   Choose the best answer.

   1. All chargemasters contain which item(s)?
      - ○ procedure code
      - ○ description
      - ○ charge
      - ○ all of the above

   2. The healthcare provider's comprehensive price list of all supplies, services, and equipment usage fees is referred to as the chargemaster or _____.
      - ○ procedure codes
      - ○ provider schedule
      - ○ CDM
      - ○ master list

3. The charges on the chargemaster _____.
   - ○ are always the same
   - ○ vary from provider to provider
   - ○ are set by the procedure code system
   - ○ do not include tax

4. How often is the chargemaster or fee schedule updated?
   - ○ every day
   - ○ every year (at a minimum)
   - ○ every five years (at a minimum)
   - ○ never

CDM MAINTENANCE

It is very important that the CDM is regularly updated. Yearly updates are critical because CPT/HCPCS codes change annually. The management of the CDM can be done by one individual or unit, but the maintenance of the CDM is a joint effort between all involved. It is important to have collaboration by ancillary departments knowledgeable of services and charges. For example, if new services are provided by the organization, they must be added to the CDM.

The CDM may also be called service master, price list, charge list or service item master.

This maintenance of the CDM is very critical to minimize risk of compliance violations for the organization. One wrong or outdated CPT code can continue to be reported when linked or mapped to a specific charge code. This would certainly cause overpayment, underpayment or claims rejections which could result in fines or penalties.

Go to the link:

http://library.ahima.org/xpedio/groups/public/documents/ahima/bok1_047258.hcsp?dDocName=bok1_047258

Review the AHIMA Practice Brief: The Care and Maintenance of Chargemasters. March 2010.

This Practice Brief has basic information on chargemasters, including a CDM example, definitions of each data element, and suggested composition of the CDM committee. Carefully review the three pages in the document and answer the following questions.

I. MATCHING.
Match the correct term to the definition.

1. ____ charge description
2. ____ CPT or HCPCS code
3. ____ revenue code
4. ____ charge
5. ____ department code
6. ____ charge code
7. ____ charge status

A. activity date element
B. fee for the service
C. also known as item description
D. identifies the specific service or procedure
E. used for accounting purposes to distribute revenue to appropriate location
F. internally assigned unique number identifying each item listed
G. four-digit code identifying accommodation, ancillary service, or billing calculation required for Medicare

II. TRUE/FALSE.
Mark the following true or false.

1. Outdated chargemasters can result in over or undercharging.
   ○ true
   ○ false

2. The chargemaster maintenance ideally should be done by one person.
   ○ true
   ○ false

3. There is a high risk that one error in the CDM can replicate and cause multiple errors.
   ○ true
   ○ false

4. CPT codes change every 2 years, and this is the recommended time to perform maintenance.
   ○ true
   ○ false

5. All departments that create charges should be represented on the Chargemaster Committee.
   ○ true
   ○ false

CHARGE SHEET/BILLING MASTER/ENCOUNTER FORM

Inpatient providers compile a patient charge list during an inpatient stay. Each service, supply, or procedure the patient receives is "submitted" by the department providing the service. By the end of the hospital stay, the patient's charge list detailing each service is complete and ready for use in preparing the patient's billing statement/ insurance claim.

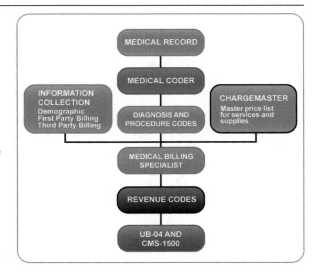

Different providers have different names for the tracking of individual patient charges. Many physician offices call them billing master, encounter forms, charge sheets, charge tickets, communication forms, or superbills. Outpatient facilities may simply call them charges. An example follows for the "charge" process in two different outpatient settings: physician office and outpatient surgery clinic.

There are four main parts to a superbill:
1. Provider information – includes name, degree, service location, and signature.
2. Patient information – patient's name, DOB, and insurance information.
3. Service information – date of service, CPT and ICD-10-CM codes, modifiers, time, units, quantity for drugs, and authorization information.
4. Additional information – notes and comments.

We've placed a visual aid in the appendix on page 382.

CHARGE SHEETS

When a patient completes an outpatient visit to a physician, the physician uses the charge sheet to record the diagnoses and the procedures performed. The charge sheet in a physician's office or small clinic usually reflects the most commonly diagnosed conditions and common procedures and supplies. The charge sheet accompanies the patient from the patient care area to the check-out area.

In this example, the patient was seen for hoarseness and sinus pressure and congestion. The physician diagnosed chronic sinusitis and hoarseness and performed a flexible laryngoscopy.

The patient takes the charge sheet to the front desk for checkout. The front office staff checks the charge sheet and, based on services, calculates the cost of the visit to be $235. The front office staff then checks the patient demographic information and, noting the patient has third-party coverage, collects a partial payment from the patient of $47 and informs the patient the third-party coverage will be billed.

The charge sheet provides the first summary of diagnosis, procedure, and supply information. Charge sheets for physician offices and other limited-service outpatient providers usually list the most common diagnoses and procedures. In many cases, the charge sheet will have a space for the physician or other provider to hand-write additional items.

EXAMPLE CHARGE LIST

The next example is for an outpatient surgery center. The lists of supplies, procedures, and equipment used in an outpatient surgery center are much longer and more complex than in a physician's office. In these settings, the charge list is compiled during and after the patient's care by healthcare providers and support staff.

A surgeon's office contacts the outpatient center to schedule the surgery and provides the diagnosis of chronic tonsillitis and a tonsillectomy procedure is needed. The charge list for the patient is begun when the office staff selects the diagnosis and procedure for the patient and submits the changes.

Diagnosis: Chronic tonsillitis
Procedure: Tonsillectomy

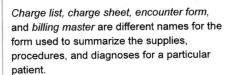

Highlights

Charge list, charge sheet, encounter form, and *billing master* are different names for the form used to summarize the supplies, procedures, and diagnoses for a particular patient.

When the patient presents for the surgery, the medical record creation begins and, at the same time, the healthcare staff enters items on the patient's charge list, as they are ordered/used during surgery.

Patient Name: Marcia Brady
Patient Age: 12 years old

Medical record documented IV hydration.

Charge: IV hydration 1 HR 96360
Each add'l HR 96360

After discharge from the outpatient surgery center, all of the details are summarized on a charge sheet.

Patient Name: Marcia Brady
Patient Age: 12 years old
Diagnosis: Chronic tonsillitis
ICD-10-CM Code: J35.01
Procedure: Tonsillectomy
CPT® Code: 42826
IV hydration 1 HR 96360
IV hydration add'l HR 96360

The charge list is a compilation of diagnoses, procedures, and supplies.

MEDICAL RECORD, MEDICAL CODER, AND CODES

The charge sheet is not a substitute for a medical coder. Remember, the medical codes, descriptions, and charges must accurately reflect the information in the patient's medical record. On discharge from a healthcare visit, the patient's medical record is often still a work in progress—waiting for dictation and transcription of documents, lab results, or signatures.

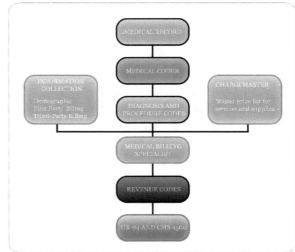

Let's reconsider the example used for the outpatient surgery center. The charge list shows the procedure as a tonsillectomy based on the scheduling of the surgery. If the surgeon found the adenoids to be scarred and removed them during the surgery, that would be reviewed in the operative report and coded by the coder.

Remember the difference between hard and soft coding. A chargemaster only selects charges for repetitive procedures such as X-rays and laboratory tests. An encounter form or list of charges is like a rough draft listing all charges including supplies. The medical coder codes the appropriate diagnoses, procedures, and supplies from the medical record and passes the information to the medical biller. When the information does not match the charge list, the charge sheet is updated to reflect the correct information based on the medical record. The medical coder works with the medical biller, the medical record, and the encounter form to go from rough draft to final form.

Highlights

Auditors compare medical records, codes, and bills for consistency. Charging for services not documented in the patient record is a fraudulent practice.

The demographic information, third-party billing information, charge list reflecting final diagnosis codes, procedure codes, and supply codes are the basic elements necessary for creating the UB-04 or CMS-1500 and the patient's statement.

REVENUE CODES

Once the four necessary components are gathered, the medical biller is ready to review the revenue codes and create the UB-04. Revenue codes are only required for UB-04.

Let's look at each component:

1. demographics, including payer information
2. fee for each service from the chargemaster
3. charge list, with description
4. correct diagnosis, procedure, and supply codes

The medical biller assigns revenue codes, often helped by an automated/integrated medical billing program. Only the UB-04 requires revenue codes. Revenue codes are 4-digit codes; they indicate inpatient or outpatient, the department (cost center) where the service(s) originated, and each 4-digit code represents a range of services. Services described by revenue codes include room (accommodation) or an ancillary service. (The leading zeros are often dropped on revenue codes, making them appear as 3-digit codes).

For example, a patient who is seen in the emergency room would have a 4-digit emergency room revenue code, a newborn in the newborn nursery would have a nursery accommodation revenue code assigned. If the patient had an x-ray performed in the emergency room, a 4-digit revenue code would be assigned for the radiology department. If the patient had lab work done, there would be a laboratory revenue code.

Revenue codes are assigned based on the departments submitting charges to the charge list. The CPT® and HCPCS codes may be assigned automatically from the chargemaster or by the medical coder for certain surgical or outpatient records. Revenue codes describe the same information for inpatient (hospital) stays; however, CPT® or HCPCS codes are not assigned in the inpatient setting.

We've placed a visual aid in the appendix on page 383.

UB-04, CMS-1500, AND PATIENT STATEMENT

The last step in the medical billing process is the preparation of the patient statement and UB-04 or CMS-1500. Let's take a look at and identify these forms.

We've placed a visual aid in the appendix on page 384.

We've placed a visual aid in the appendix on page 385.

We've placed a visual aid in the appendix on page 386.

THE ROLES OF THE OUTPATIENT MEDICAL BILLER

It is typical for larger medical organizations to employ medical billing specialists and medical coding specialists. In smaller settings, such as in physician services, the processes of coding and billing may be combined and provided by one individual.

Keep in mind as you progress in your training and your career how important it is to continue to learn and expand your knowledge. The most employable people with the most employment opportunities are those with the widest set of professional skills.

Another important piece of information to consider in the study of the healthcare reimbursement process is that although the basic elements of the process are the same in each healthcare setting, the methods and procedures themselves may vary greatly. One provider may operate mostly in hard copy; another provider may be totally electronic. The software for one office might automatically insert the medical coder's diagnosis, procedure, and supply codes directly onto the appropriate billing form; another office may function so that only the medical biller can add or delete information from the bill.

Regardless of the methodologies used by organizations, it is important to understand the healthcare reimbursement process and the elements of the billing process.

REVIEW: OUTPATIENT BILLING PROCESS

I. TRUE/FALSE.
Mark the following true or false.

1. Revenue codes are reported on both the CMS-1500 and UB-04 claim forms.
   - ○ true
   - ○ false

2. A charge sheet can be used as a substitute for a medical coder.
   - ○ true
   - ○ false

3. The chargemaster is the price list of all the supplies, services, and equipment usage fees for patient care.
   - ○ true
   - ○ false

4. Demographic information is used to determine who has responsibility for payment of medical services.
   - ○ true
   - ○ false

5. All providers refer to the form used to track individual patient charges as a charge sheet.
   - ○ true
   - ○ false

CODING AND BILLING AT THE PHYSICIAN'S OFFICE

Physicians' offices, whether a single physician or a group of physicians, have specialized processes for coding and billing. When a physician provides care in an office where the physician owns the equipment and facility, the professional services of the physician and the equipment and supply charges are bundled together and billed on a CMS-1500 form. Third party payers consider procedure codes billed by a provider on the CMS-1500 to include both the physician's service and the provider's practice expense costs such as electricity in his/her own office.

When a patient is seen at a physician's office or receives care in a physician's clinic, the billing and coding process is as follows:

CODING/BILLING FOR HEALTHCARE SERVICES AT PHYSICIAN'S OFFICE

- Diagnosis Codes – ICD-10-CM
- Procedure Codes – CPT®

- Supply Codes – HCPCS (if applicable)
- Billing – CMS-1500 form

Physician offices can range from small, single physician offices to large, multiple physician clinics with laboratory, radiology, and minor surgery capabilities. The size of the office does not matter for the purposes of the medical coder. Care received in the physician office where the physician or physician group owns the facility is always coded with the diagnosis code from ICD-10-CM and procedures from the CPT® codebook.

We've placed a visual aid in the appendix on page 384.

We've placed a visual aid in the appendix on page 387.

I. **TRUE/FALSE.**
   Mark the following true or false.

   1. Physician's offices only use the CMS-1500 form for billing.

      ○ true
      ○ false

   2. The billing and coding process at a physician's clinic begins with procedure codes from CPT.

      ○ true
      ○ false

   3. A large physician's office will have a different billing procedure than a small one.

      ○ true
      ○ false

PHYSICIAN CARE AT OUTSIDE FACILITIES

In addition to physicians providing care in the office setting, medical coders who work for physicians or physician groups will also code the physician's services performed outside the physician's office. A physician who sees patients in the office also will have privileges at independent healthcare facilities, such as hospitals, nursing homes, or convalescent homes. When a physician sees a patient in one of those settings, the professional services are coded and billed by the physician's staff and not by the hospital, nursing home, or convalescent home. The medical coding specialist and medical biller for the physician will code and bill for the patient's care as follows:

Highlights

Occasionally a physician will take supplies when visiting patients at an outside facility to provide patient care. Those supplies are coded and billed by the physician's support staff.

CODING/BILLING FOR HEALTHCARE SERVICES AT AN INDEPENDENT FACILITY

- Diagnosis Codes – ICD-10-CM
- Procedure Codes – CPT®
- Supply Codes – HCPCS LEVEL II (if applicable)
- Billing – CMS-1500 form

Physicians will sometimes take supplies with them when visiting an outpatient facility to provide care. For example, a podiatrist doing a foot clinic in a nursing home may bring his own instruments and dressings for providing podiatric care. Or an orthopedist visiting a patient in a convalescent home may bring a supply of needles and medicines to perform joint injections or other orthopedic care services. In these cases, the supplies provided by the physician are coded and billed by the physician's healthcare support staff on the CMS-1500.

We've placed a visual aid in the appendix on page 388.

I. **TRUE/FALSE.**
   Mark the following true or false.

   1. A physician who sees patients in outside facilities will have the services coded by his or her own staff.
      - ⟲ true
      - ⟲ false

   2. The physician's staff will use only a CMS-1500 form when billing for his or her work at an outside facility.
      - ⟲ true
      - ⟲ false

   3. If a physician brings supplies with him when visiting an outpatient facility, it is billed on a UB-04.
      - ⟲ true
      - ⟲ false

HEALTHCARE PROVIDERS AT OUTSIDE FACILITIES

Medical coders and billers may also be employed by less "traditional" physicians or physicians' groups, such as radiologists or emergency room physicians. These professional healthcare providers don't generally have a physical office where they see patients; instead the physicians contract to provide professional services at independent healthcare providers (institutions).

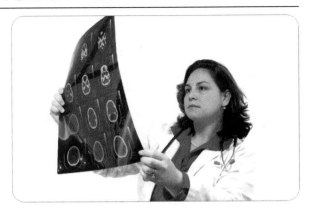

When a patient receives professional services at a standalone or independent healthcare facility, such as a hospital, radiology clinic, or independent laboratory, the professional services are coded and billed by the physician's staff and not by the hospital, radiology clinic, or independent facility. The medical coding specialist and medical biller for the physician/physicians' group will code and bill the professional services for the patient's healthcare.

We've placed a visual aid in the appendix on page 389.

CODING/BILLING FOR PHYSICIAN SERVICES AT INDEPENDENT FACILITY

- Diagnosis Codes – ICD-10-CM
- Procedure Codes – CPT®
- Supply Codes – HCPCS (if applicable)
- Billing – CMS-1500 form

The term "sees patient" may not actually mean that the physician examines the patient. A patient may receive professional services without ever being physically seen by the physician providing the services. Radiologists and pathologists are good examples of this type of professional care. Radiologists and pathologists rarely have an office where patients go to be seen. More often, radiologists and pathologists form a physician group that provides professional services—reading radiologic tests or examining tissue—for patients seen in an independent facility. In many cases, the radiologist or pathologist sees only the films or the tissue specimen and not the whole patient.

The medical coding and medical billing for radiology professional services falls under the same coding and billing pattern as other physician-based medical coding and billing. However, these types of professionals rarely, if ever, have supplies to be coded because the supplies are furnished by the facility.

We've placed a visual aid in the appendix on page 390.

OTHER NON-PHYSICIAN PROFESSIONALS

Individual healthcare service provider coding and billing does not always center around physician-based care. Other medical professionals provide services such as in mental health or other specialized areas where psychologists, physical therapists, counselors, or other provider professional services are coded and billed. Regardless of whether or not the provider is a licensed social worker, physical therapist, physician, nurse practitioner, or physician's assistant, the same rules apply to coding and billing for healthcare services. This applies even when the professional providers are providing services in their offices or at independent facilities.

We've placed a visual aid in the appendix on page 391.

CODING/BILLING FOR NON-PHYSICIAN PROFESSIONAL SERVICES AT INDEPENDENT FACILITY

- Diagnosis Codes – ICD-10-CM
- Procedure Codes – CPT®
- Supply Codes – HCPCS (if applicable)
- Billing – CMS-1500 form

Remember, non-physician professional service providers (with very few exceptions) provide services under the direction of a physician.

REVIEW: CODING AND BILLING FOR PHYSICIANS

I. **TRUE/FALSE.**
   Mark the following true or false.

   1. ICD-10-CM codes are used in the diagnosis coding and billing process for professional services.
      ○ true
      ○ false

   2. The professional services performed by a physician are billed on the CMS-1500 claim form.
      ○ true
      ○ false

3. Procedures performed at a physician's office are reported with CPT® codes.

   ○ true
   ○ false

4. The coding and billing of non-physician professional services are coded and billed differently than physician professional services.

   ○ true
   ○ false

5. When physicians provide their own supplies while visiting an outpatient facility to provide care, they can code and bill for these supplies.

   ○ true
   ○ false

CODING AND BILLING FOR FACILITIES

When the physician provides patient care in the office or clinic, the equipment, supplies, and facility charges are coded and billed on the CMS-1500 and coded and billed by healthcare support staff employed by the physician or physicians' group. Professional services (physician charges) for patients seen in independent or standalone healthcare facilities are also coded and billed by coders and billers employed by the physician or physicians' group.

For many years, facility (non-physician office) charges were billed on the UB-92. UB-04 replaced the UB-92 in July 2007.

The other coding and billing opportunity is coding and billing for facilities providing healthcare setting only, not owned by the physician or physicians' group. Hospitals, surgery centers, urgent care centers, standalone radiology clinics, nursing homes, convalescent homes, and other inpatient and outpatient facilities employ healthcare support staff to handle coding and billing for the use of facility, equipment, supplies, and other costs associated with providing outpatient healthcare services. These facility charges are billed on the UB-04.

Medical coding and billing for facilities providing institutional **outpatient** services is as follows:

CODING/BILLING FOR OUTPATIENT HEALTHCARE INSTITUTIONS

- Diagnosis Codes – ICD-10-CM
- Procedure Codes – CPT® (billing)
- Supply Codes – HCPCS (as appropriate)
- Billing – UB-04 form

Note: It is important to note that procedures are reported with CPT® and HCPCS codes in all outpatient hospital settings. The new procedure system ICD-10-PCS is ONLY used by hospital inpatient billing. While some facilities may assign ICD codes for data tracking purposes, these are not allowed to appear on the bill and will not be discussed in this course on billing.

We've placed a visual aid in the appendix on page 392.

THE MEDICARE EXCEPTION

When a medical coder is working for an ambulatory surgical center (also known as same-day surgery), the coding and billing requirements are different if the patient receiving care has third-party coverage through Medicare. Medicare requires all charges for same-day surgery to be billed on the CMS-1500. Medicare will still receive two separate bills; one bill for professional services from the physician on the CMS-1500 and the other for the facility, supply, and equipment charges from the ambulatory surgical center from the outpatient facility (also on the CMS-1500). Therefore, the coding and billing process for the ambulatory surgical center for Medicare patients is as follows:

We've placed a visual aid in the appendix on page 393.

CODING/BILLING FOR MEDICARE PATIENTS FOR OUTPATIENT SURGERY

- Diagnosis Codes – ICD-10
- Procedure Codes – CPT® (billing)
- Supply Codes – HCPCS (as appropriate)
- Billing – CMS-1500

CODING AND BILLING BY SERVICE PROVIDER

CMS-1500	UB-04

Physician Office
 	
Physician and Non-physician Professional Services
 	
Outpatient (Ambulatory/Same-Day) Surgery for Medicare Patients
	Healthcare Institutions (Non-Physician Office)
	
	    Hospital Outpatient
	    Radiology
	    Emergency Room
	    Nursing Home
	    Ambulatory Surgery
	    Urgent Care Clinics
	    Mental Health Clinics
	    Convalescent Homes
	    And all other OP providers

Coding Process	Coding Process
Diagnosis Codes:	Diagnosis Codes:
• ICD-10-CM	• ICD-10-CM
Procedures Codes:	Procedures Codes:
• CPT®	• CPT
Supply Codes:	Supply Codes:
• HCPCS	• HCPCS

Certain specialties may require additional codes for third-party payers and/or disease or procedure tracking. For example, mental health and oncology have specialty coding systems and resources: *Diagnostic and Statistical Manual of Mental Disorders – DSM-5-TR* and *ASTRO* or *ACR Guide to Radiation Oncology Coding 2012*. Instructions on using these resources would be given by the provider.

REVIEW: CODING AND BILLING FOR FACILITIES

I. **TRUE/FALSE.**
   Mark the following true or false.

1. Emergency room services are billed on the UB-04 claim form.
   ○ true
   ○ false

2. All facility charges are reported on the UB-04 claim form.
   ○ true
   ○ false

3. Facility charges are billed on the CMS-1500 claim form.
   ○ true
   ○ false

4. ICD-10-PCS codes are not reported for outpatient services.
   ○ true
   ○ false

5. The charges for Medicare patients seen in an ambulatory surgical center are billed on the CMS-1500 claim form.
   ○ true
   ○ false

UNIT 3

Healthcare Reimbursement

HEALTHCARE REIMBURSEMENT – INTRODUCTION

The United States has a first-party and third-party payer system; a patient directly reimburses the healthcare provider (first-party payer) for healthcare services or the patient has secured coverage from another source (third-party payer) that reimburses some or all of the cost of a patient's healthcare services.

Patient reimburses healthcare provider for services = first-party payer

Entity other than the patient reimburses provider for services = third-party payer

A list of third-party payers includes:

- Government (Medicare/Medicaid)
- Group/Individual Insurers
- Industrial/Workers' Compensation
- Automobile Insurers
- Liability Insurers

This unit will explore reimbursement methodologies used by payers in the healthcare reimbursement system.

Highlights

Healthcare costs may be covered by charitable organizations, donations, or other philanthropic endowments. Many thousands of patients benefit from the work of organizations such as The Shriners and St. Jude Children's Research Hospital.

REIMBURSEMENT IN THE HEALTHCARE ENVIRONMENT

In the previous unit, the healthcare providers' process for billing for services was presented; in this unit, reimbursement methodologies used by first and third-party payers to determine how much is *actually paid* for healthcare services are discussed.

Healthcare providers set fees for their services or their fees are set by the contract with their payer. Fees are based on a number of variables, including labor costs, professional credentials, malpractice insurance, competition, and the cost of office space and equipment. The cost of office expenses varies significantly based on geographic loaction, so these factors (and many not listed) are considerations for healthcare providers as they set charges/fees for services. However, healthcare providers usually don't collect the same amount they charge.

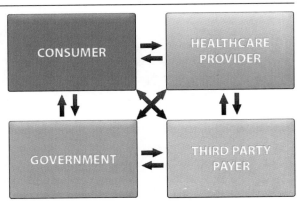

Complex contractual relationships exist between patient, government, third–party payers, and providers.

If healthcare operated like a large retail store, providers would set the prices based on costs and the competition in their area of service; patients would come in and choose whether to purchase goods and services. If they decided to purchase, a bill would be presented and paid (by the patient or third-party payer).

Why doesn't the healthcare industry operate like this?

There are four key reasons why healthcare reimbursement is different from other types of consumer purchases:

- The consumer of healthcare services (patient) is often not the person who pays for healthcare goods/ services.
- Complex contractual relationships exist between patient, government, third-party payers, and providers.
- The dollar amount actually collected by the provider for a service may vary widely depending on who pays for the service.
- The government is the largest single payer of healthcare services, and the amount they pay is not governed by the price charged but by reimbursement rules and regulations based on laws.

THE CONSUMER

☑ **The consumer of healthcare services (patient) is often not the person who pays for healthcare goods/services.**

Fee-for-service reimbursement is payment in which providers receive payment for each service provided, and is a common method of calculating reimbursement.

A fee is the set amount or price, and fee-for-service means a specific payment is made for each service by patients or insurance companies. These fees or prices are also known as charges. Examples of fee-for-service reimbursement are self-pay, traditional retrospective payment, and managed care. Patients with health insurance that reimburses on fee-for-service have some independence because they are free to make decisions about which provider to see. A disadvantage of fee-for-service is that the patient may have higher deductibles or copayments than other types of insurance plans. Self-pay is a type of fee-for-service because patients pay a set amount for services received.

Because of higher costs, many insurance plans establish fee schedules and contractual arrangements with facilities. A fee schedule is a predetermined list of fees that the third-party payer will allow for healthcare services. The allowable fee is the average or maximum amount the payer will reimburse providers for services.

The standard healthcare model operated on a fee-for-service model for many years until healthcare costs escalated out of control. The provider presented a bill to the insurance company who then paid the bill. The provider and the patient did not have much incentive to keep costs low or restrict the scope of services.

Eventually, government and private insurance providers rebelled. Third-party payers wanted more control over what the patient could choose and what the provider could provide if they were paying the bill. Third-party payers began to look seriously at ways of "managing" what services the patient could access and under what conditions they could access them. Third-party payers also began to look seriously at ways of incentivizing healthcare providers to work with them to control spiraling healthcare costs.

I. **TRUE/FALSE.**
   Mark the following true or false.

   1. Self-pay is an example of fee-for-service reimbursement.
      - ( ) true
      - ( ) false

   2. The consumer of healthcare services always pays directly for healthcare goods and services.
      - ( ) true
      - ( ) false

   3. Third-party payers eventually began to manage what services the patient could access and under what conditions they could access them.
      - ( ) true
      - ( ) false

GOVERNMENT CONTROLS

The third-party payer system began to undergo significant change. Healthcare providers could no longer set prices and expect to receive dollar for dollar payment. By changing insurance contracts with patients and entering into contractual relationships with providers, third-party payers began to restrict and "manage" healthcare relationships between providers and patients.

Today there are several managed-care models and strategies employed by third-party payers to manage healthcare costs.

Highlights

Medicare is the only government program considered to be health insurance. Medicare is defined as insurance because Medicare premiums are withheld from the paychecks of working Americans and used to fund the Medicare program.

The government doesn't sell insurance through employers or private policies. Government is the third-party payer for special demographic groups of Americans, such as veterans, indigenous people, the disabled, and the poor. Individuals who qualify for government-sponsored healthcare services prove they fit the requirements for the government-sponsored program and they receive healthcare benefits.

Government puts price and choice control pressure on healthcare providers through rules and regulations mandating reimbursement based on systems other than the traditional payment of provider-set rates.

In the future we will discuss government reimbursement methodologies in more detail.

CONTRACT RELATIONSHIPS

Healthcare reimbursement methodologies are different from traditional market systems:

> ☑ **Complex contractual relationships exist between patient, government, third-party payers, and providers.**

Healthcare purchases are not straight buy-the-goods, pay-the-bill two-party transactions. High healthcare costs add layers of complexity to the healthcare transaction, requiring the said contract relationships.

Prior to Blue Cross and Blue Shield in the 1920s and 1930s, virtually all reimbursement was between patient and provider. The most common form of payment was first-party payer. If individuals had insurance at all, it was "sickness" insurance and not health insurance. Sickness insurance paid the employee for work time lost from being sick so he/she could pay medical bills; this system did not involve direct payment to healthcare providers.

In the 1920s, Blue Cross and Blue Shield introduced the revolutionary concept of negotiated reimbursement rates for insured patients. Also there was no turning back. The 1920s and 1930s also marked a period of explosive advances in healthcare research with resulting leaps forward in advanced treatment options and (of course) costs.

The period between 1940 and 1960 saw explosive growth in the ranks of the insured patient, from 20 million in 1940 to 142 million in the 1950s. This ushered in the decades of spiraling healthcare costs and the desire of insurers to take a more active role in managing healthcare reimbursement.

I. TRUE/FALSE.
Mark the following true or false.

1. Blue Cross and Blue Shield began the healthcare reimbursement revolution.
   - ◯ true
   - ◯ false

2. All medical payments were between the patient and the provider until the healthcare reimbursement revolution in the 1920s and 1930s.
   - ◯ true
   - ◯ false

3. Healthcare purchases are usually very straightforward two-party transactions.
   - ◯ true
   - ◯ false

PAYMENT

Today, relationships between patient, provider, government, and private-third party payers range in complexity from uninsured patients paying as they access healthcare services to insurance companies owning healthcare provider networks where their insured are treated at vastly reduced rates.

The intricate relationships between payer, patient, and provider lead to the third reason healthcare reimbursement structures are complex.

> ☑ **The dollar amount actually collected by the provider for a service may vary widely depending on who pays for the service.**

When the patient pays, the transaction is often dollar for dollar. The patient pays the amount billed for the service with the use of cash, credit, or payment plans. The provider may offer discounts for payment at the time of service or assist the patient in setting up payment plans or applying for loans.

Self-pay example

Fred is a self-pay patient of Dr. Tony Gates. Fred was examined by Dr. Gates for fever, sore throat, and cough. Dr. Gates performed a rapid strep test.

DR. GATES'S CHARGES			PRIVATE PAY	
CODE	DESCRIPTION	CHARGE	CODE	REIMBURSEMENT
99213	EXAM	$85.00	99213	$85.00
87880	STREP TEST	$15.00	87880	$15.00

Fred pays $20 at the counter as he leaves the office. He pays the balance of $80 by check after he receives his statement in the mail.

On the other hand, third-party relationships may result in the healthcare provider collecting less than the billed amount for services.

Insurance example

Elaine had been seen by Dr. Tony Gates six weeks ago because she had a fever, sore throat, and cough. The office billed her insurance carrier, UnknownHealthcare, and received the following reimbursement:

DR. GATES'S CHARGES			UNKNOWNHEALTHCARE REIMBURSEMENT	
CODE	DESCRIPTION	CHARGE	CODE	REIMBURSEMENT
99213	EXAM	$85.00	99213	$75.75
87880	STREP TEST	$15.00	87880	$14.25

UnknownHealthcare has a contractual agreement with Dr. Gates' office. Dr. Gates accepts a negotiated lower rate as payment in full for UnknownHealthcare patients, and the balance of $10 is written off by Dr. Gates and not billed to the patient.

Government also uses reimbursement formulas that result in total payment being significantly less than the total bill.

Government example

Barb has Medicaid and was seen by Dr. Tony Gates five weeks ago for a fever, cough, and sore throat. The office billed Barb's insurance and received the following reimbursement:

DR. GATES'S CHARGES			MEDICAID REIMBURSEMENT	
CODE	DESCRIPTION	CHARGE	CODE	REIMBURSEMENT
99213	EXAM	$85.00	99213	$40.34
87880	STREP TEST	$15.00	87880	$8.74

In Barb's state, Medicaid regulations do not allow providers to collect copayment or balances from the patient. Dr. Gates writes off the balance of $50.92.

The net effect is healthcare providers are constantly working to maintain a healthy cost/profit to amount collected ratio.

Fee: $100	Patient 1: Patient pays $100
	Patient 2: Third party payer pays $90
	Patient 3: Government pays $49.08

Average amount collected for service: $79.69

Healthcare providers must balance fees, the cost of doing business, and the reimbursement received to continue to provide healthcare services.

I. TRUE/FALSE.
Mark the following true or false.

1. Healthcare transactions are always dollar-for-dollar.
   - ○ true
   - ○ false

2. Third-party relationships may mean the healthcare provider collects less than the billed amount for services
   - ○ true
   - ○ false

3. The government's reimbursement formulas result in total payments being significantly less than the total bill.
   - ○ true
   - ○ false

GOVERNMENT

☑ **The government is the largest single payer of healthcare services, and the amount they pay is not governed by the price charged but by reimbursement rules and regulations based on laws.**

The U.S. government pays for more healthcare services than any other single entity in the U.S. healthcare system. In more and more situations, the government does not base healthcare reimbursement on what is charged by healthcare providers. Reimbursement is driven by various laws and regulations from Congress and various rule making processes. The Centers for Medicare & Medicaid Services(CMS), Indian Health Services (IHS), the Department of Veterans' Affairs (VA), and other government-sponsored healthcare programs each follow the reimbursement methodology mandated by law and written by their governing agencies.

Medicare is the largest health insurance program, covering nearly 50 million Americans.

For example, IHS uses a per diem system for outpatient physician billing where, regardless of the cost for treatment and/or complexity of the patient's condition, reimbursement is based on a per diem or per encounter rate. IHS tracks average cost per patient per day or per patient per encounter over time and, based on this history, sets a daily reimbursement rate for patients who are qualified to receive IHS benefits. To learn more, click here.

If a provider charges $100 for a service and the government standard reimbursement is only $40 for the service, the provider receives $60 less than billed for each patient. Healthcare providers may respond by A) raising prices or B) by cancelling their contract with the government third-party payer who is reimbursing the physician the lowest.

I. TRUE/FALSE.
Mark the following true or false.

1. The largest health insurance program is Medicare.
   ○ true
   ○ false

2. The U.S. government bases healthcare reimbursement on what is charged by healthcare providers.
   ○ true
   ○ false

3. Healthcare providers may cancel their contract with the government third-party payer.
   ○ true
   ○ false

REVIEW: REIMBURSEMENT

I. MULTIPLE CHOICE.
Choose the best answer.

1. There are four reasons why healthcare reimbursement is different than other types of consumer purchases. Select the statement that is NOT one of those reasons.
    - ○ Government requires all payers to reimburse at the same rate for the same services.
    - ○ The patient is not always the person who pays for their healthcare services.
    - ○ Complex contractual agreements exist between patients, third-party payers, government payers and providers.
    - ○ Reimbursement/amount collected by the provider may vary greatly depending on who is paying for the service.

2. Who is the largest single payer of healthcare costs in the United States?
    - ○ Blue Cross Blue Shield
    - ○ United Healthcare
    - ○ private pay
    - ○ government

3. Today many third-party payers have turned to _____ to control healthcare costs.
    - ○ the government
    - ○ other third-party payers
    - ○ managed-care coverage
    - ○ discount insurance carriers

4. Healthcare providers bill for services from a chargemaster or list of charges. Prices for services are based on a variety of factors. Which of the following would NOT be a consideration for developing a list of charges?
    - ○ competition and labor costs
    - ○ price of malpractice insurance
    - ○ labor and office space costs
    - ○ patient ethnicity

5. Third-party payers make managed care more attractive to employers by offering _____ for selecting healthcare plans with more managed care features.
    - ○ lifetime coverage
    - ○ lower premiums (rates)
    - ○ extended payment plans
    - ○ minimized coding efforts

HEALTHCARE REIMBURSEMENT METHODOLOGIES

Specific types of healthcare reimbursement methodologies will be covered and examples provided in reimbursement methodologies charts. The various reimbursement methodologies presented do not represent a comprehensive list of all reimbursement methodologies; the most common methodologies are covered. Reimbursement terms, definitions, and examples are also covered.

FEE-FOR-SERVICE AND EPISODE-OF-CARE

Healthcare reimbursement methodologies breakdown into two primary types:

1. **Fee-For-Service**
2. **Episode-of-Care**

In a fee-for-service reimbursement system, the provider receives payment for each service provided to the patient. The amount of reimbursement is determined by reviewing the services received by the patient. In other words, determination is based on "what was done" for the patient and not "what was wrong" with the patient.

In a fee-for-service reimbursement system, reimbursement is based on what services are provided to the patient.

The physician's office sent in a claim to the insurance company for a patient's date of service six weeks ago for the following charges, and the office has received the following reimbursement:

PHYSICIAN'S CHARGES			INSURANCE REIMBURSEMENT	
CODE	DESCRIPTION	CHARGE	CODE	PAYMENT
99214	Exam	$110.00	99214	$95.68
71010	2-view chest x-ray	$95.00	71010	$81.73

Episode-of-care is a reimbursement system under which payment is based upon services provided for conditions for which the patient is treated. There are different situations this reimbursement method applies. Depending upon the specific method, the unit of time a patient is treated may affect the received reimbursement. An example of this is a global package. Reimbursement for services provided to patients who undergo a surgical procedure is typically a combined payment for the procedure a set time period afterwards when the patient returns for postoperative services. The global package is either 10 or 90 days of care after the surgery where the physician is not paid additionally for an office visit pertaining to the surgery.

Under an episode-of-care reimbursement system, reimbursement is based on the patient's particular condition/illness or a specified time period over which the patient receives care.

Lorraine, a 75-year-old woman, had a total hip replacement performed four weeks ago. She is in today to see the surgeon for a follow-up visit from her surgery. Medicare was billed $3,500.00. Medicare reimbursed

$1,216.49. Lorraine's office visit's charge for today is 0.00 because it is included in the charged amount for the hip replacement.

Fee-For-Service

> Reimbursement based on:
> * Services provided to the patient

Episode-of-Care

> Patient's condition/illness
> * A specified time period

Fee-For-Service	Episode-of-Care
1. Self-pay 2. Retrospective payment 3. Managed care	1. Managed care – capitation 2. Global payment 3. Prospective payment

I. **TRUE/FALSE.**
   Mark the following true or false.

1. Healthcare reimbursement methodologies are based on only one model.
   ○ true
   ○ false

2. Fee-for-service systems determine reimbursement based on what was done for the patient rather than what was wrong with the patient.
   ○ true
   ○ false

3. In episode-of-care, reimbursement is based on the patient's illness or an amount of time over which the patient is cared for.
   ○ true
   ○ false

SELF-PAY

Reimbursement based on:
Services provided to the patient

☑ **1. Self-pay**
2. Retrospective payment
3. Managed care

Patients without third-party payer coverage or with very restrictive third-party coverage pay for healthcare services on a fee-for-service basis. The patient seeks healthcare services, receives a bill itemizing services received, and makes payment directly to the provider. Payment options for self-pay patients vary depending on the policies of the healthcare provider. Some providers will not see patients who do not have insurance coverage without payment in full at the time of service. Other providers offer options for monthly payment plans.

Self-Pay Example 1

This self-pay patient came into the office with complaints of hives and itching. She was examined by the physician; she was given an injection of Benadryl 50 mg IM for the itching and hives. The patient went to the front desk to check out and pay her bill. Her charges were:

CHARGES			PAYMENT WITH DEBIT CARD	
CODE	DESCRIPTION	CHARGE	CODE	PAYMENT
99212	Exam	$65.00	99212	$65.00
J1200	Benadryl 50 mg	$15.00	J1200	$15.00

Self-Pay w/Discount Example 2

Patient came to physician office today for heart palpitations and dizziness. An exam and an EKG were performed. A discount of 5% was given to the patient for payment in full.

CHARGES			PAYMENT WITH DEBIT CARD		
CODE	DESCRIPTION	CHARGE	CODE	DISCOUNT	PAYMENT
99213	Exam	$75.00	99213	$3.75	$71.25
93000	EKG	$50.00	93000	$2.50	$47.50

Payer with Private Policy Reimbursement Example 3

This patient was seen eight weeks ago for a routine physical, EKG, and urinalysis. The patient is not technically a self-pay patient since she has insurance through a private policy she has purchased herself. However, her physician does not participate with her insurance. The patient paid her bill in full at the time of service and received an itemized statement to send to the insurance company for reimbursement. The charges submitted and the insurance reimbursement to the patient are listed.

CHARGES			REIMBURSEMENT TO PATIENT	
99396	Routine Physical	$115.00	99396	$100.00
93000	EKG	$50.00	93000	$45.00
81000	Urinalysis	$10.00	81000	$5.00

Patients without third-party health insurance who do not qualify for benefits under a government health program are on the rise in the United States. With the high cost of healthcare, many self-pay patients find their healthcare options limited when they cannot pay for the services they need. January 1, 2014 will be the start of new health insurance coverage for millions of Americans under the Affordable Care Act.

Important information can be found at the following websites:

www.healthcare.gov/news/factsheets/2012/11/market-reforms11202012a.html

I. **FILL IN THE BLANK.**

   Enter the correct word in the blank provided.

   1. Many_____ patients find their options for healthcare are limited when they are unable to pay for needed services.

   2. Patients without_____ coverage pay for healthcare on a fee-for-service basis.

   3. _____ for self-pay patients vary depending on the policies of the individual healthcare provider.

RETROSPECTIVE PAYMENT

Reimbursement based on:
Services provided to the patient

   1. Self-pay
   ☑ **2. Retrospective payment**
   3. Managed care

Self-pay is a form of retrospective payment, but traditionally retrospective payment systems are discussed in terms of third-party payers.

> ## RETROSPECTIVE PAYMENT: REVIEW OF PAST EVENTS
> Retrospective payment is described as a fee-for-service that is reimbursed to providers after health services have been given.

As with all fee-for-service reimbursement methodologies, retrospective payment systems make payment based on services rendered ("what was done" for the patient) and not based on "what was wrong" with the patient or "how long" the patient was treated. Retrospective payment systems are called retrospective because payment is based on costs or charges actually incurred for the care of the patient during his or her healthcare encounter. Payment decisions are made after the costs are incurred (retrospectively).

Self-pay patients usually pay the full amount for services rendered. Under traditional retrospective payment systems, third-party payers can pay the full amount of the services rendered, but more often they negotiate a discounted fee-for-service system. Under a discounted fee-for-service retrospective payment system, the third-party payer pays less than the full price charged for the service. Depending on the contractual agreement(s) between provider, third-party payer, and patient, the difference between the price charged and the amount paid by the third-party payer may or may not be passed on to the patient. In other words, the discount gained by the third-party payer doesn't necessarily have to be passed on to the patient.

I. FILL IN THE BLANK.

Enter the correct word in the blank provided.

1. Retrospective payment is based on _____ actually incurred for the care of the patient.

2. Payment decisions are made_____ the costs are incurred.

3. In retrospective payment, the third-party payer pays_____ the full price charged for the service.

FEE SCHEDULES

Third party fee schedules are a predetermined list of maximum allowable fees for specific healthcare services. Third-party payers establish a fee schedule that lists all services and the maximum allowable rate the insurer will pay. When the provider sends the claim to the third-party payer, reimbursement is based on the service provided but not at the provider's rate. The reimbursement rate is based on the third-party payer's fee schedule for that service. An explanation of benefits (EOB) is a document or report sent to the policyholder and to the provider by the insurer. This

document describes the healthcare services, the cost, the applicable cost sharing, and the amount that the particulate insurer will cover. Any amount not covered by the third-party payer, would be the responsibility of the patient.

CODE	DESCRIPTION	PROVIDER FEE	THIRD-PARTY FEE
99214	Exam	$110.00	$90.75
93000	EKG	$55.00	$48.39
81000	Urinalysis	$10.00	$8.10
71010	2-view chest x-ray	$90.00	$80.50

The provider sends a claim for an exam for $110.00 and the third-party (insurer) pays $90.75 based on their fee schedule. The balance of $19.25 may be billed to the patient by the provider or may be written off by the provider depending on the contractual relationships between the provider, the third-party payer, and the patient.

Sample explanation of benefits for reimbursement based on fee schedules:

Example 1

Patient Name: Adam Mitchell										Patient Acct #: 251761		
Member ID # 321657415												
Relation: Child										Member: Janet Mitchell		

Service Dates	CPT® Codes	PL	Num SVC	Submitted Charges	Copay Amount	Not Payable	See Remarks	Deduct	Co-Ins	Patient Responsible	Payable Amount
2/12/XX	22808	21	1	$2,500.00		$425.68	212				$2074.32
TOTALS				$2,500.00		$425.68					$2074.32

Remark codes 212 - Maximum allowable rate for service	
For Questions regarding this claim call 888-997-4188 for assistance. Please use ID number for reference to this claim	Total Patient Responsibility _____

An explanation of benefits shows the insurance company will pay charges up to their maximum allowable rate based on their fee schedule. The insurance company does not assign patient responsibility to the balance, so it is the provider's decision to bill or not bill the patient for the balance.

Example 2

Patient Name: John Doe										Patient Acct #: 197581		
Member ID # 992556630												
Relation: Self										Member: John Doe		

Service Dates	CPT Codes	PL	Num SVC	Submitted Charges	Copay Amount	Not Payable	See Remarks	Deduct	Co-Ins	Patient Responsible	Payable Amount
08/04/XX	99213	11	1	$65.00	$15.00					$15.00	$50.00
08/04/XX	89050	11	1	$15.00		$8.35	325				$6.65
TOTALS				$80.00	$15.00	$8.35				$15.00	$56.65

Remark codes 325 - This is a contractual adjustment for this CPT code; do not bill the patient for this amount.	
For Questions regarding this claim call 888-697-9356 for assistance. Please use ID number for reference to this claim	Total Patient Responsibility $15.00

The insurance company has a contract with the provider to pay a lesser amount than the provider's charged fee for the service. The provider cannot collect the difference between the charged amount and the discounted paid amount. The provider can only collect the patient's copay amount.

Example 3

Patient Name: Alan Jackson Jr.							Patient Acct #: 257141					

Member ID # 888569452

Relation: Child   Member: Alan Jackson

Service Dates	CPT Codes	PL	Num SVC	Submitted Charges	Copay Amount	Not Payable	See Remarks	Deduct	Co-Ins	Patient Responsible	Payable Amount
08/05/ XX	99213	11	1	$65.00	$20.00					$20.00	$45.00
08/05/ XX	71020	11	1	$95.00		$52.41	185				$42.59
TOTALS				$160.00	$20.00	$52.41				$20.00	$87.59

Remark codes 185 - Contractual adjustment; participating physician discount.

For Questions regarding this claim call 888-551-9689 for assistance. Please use ID number for reference to this claim	Total Patient Responsibility $20.00

Once again, the insurance company and provider have a contractual relationship where the provider agrees to accept the insurer's fee schedule payment as payment in full. The provider cannot collect the difference from the patient; the provider collects only the patient's copay (set by the insurance company).

Here is some additional information on EOBs:

http://www.anthem.com/provider/nv/f5/s1/t0/pw_002206.pdf

www.cms.gov/Outreach-and-Education/Outreach/Partnerships/Downloads/11234-P.pdf

www.aetna.com/provider/data/sample_provider_eob_numb.pdf

USUAL, CUSTOMARY, AND REASONABLE

The usual, customary, and reasonable (UCR) is the amount paid for a medical service in a geographic area based on what providers in the area usually charge for the same or similar medical service. The UCR amount sometimes is used to determine the allowed amount. UCR reimbursement methodology is an extension of the fee schedule retrospective reimbursement system. Fee schedules are set rates for services. Usual, customary, and reasonable takes the set rate concept one step further. Usual, customary, and reasonable reimbursement rates are set by the third-party payer based on historical data for a given geographical area or a given medical

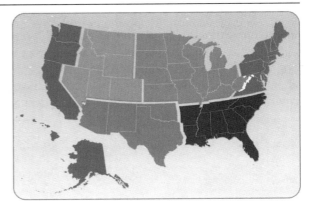

specialty. Third-party payers then pay claims at the "usual, customary, and reasonable" rate and not necessarily at the billed rate. Usual, customary, and reasonable term definitions are listed below.

Usual: Usual for the provider's practice

Customary: Customary for the community

Reasonable: Reasonable for the situation

Sample Third-Party Payer Usual, Customary, and Reasonable Fee Schedules Based on Costs by Geographic Area.

CODE	SERVICE DESCRIPTION/ NORTHWEST AREA	CHARGE	USUAL/CUSTOMARY REIMBURSEMENT NORTHWEST AREA
99213	Mid-level exam	$85.00	$61.21
99214	Detailed exam	$100.00	$92.07
99215	Comprehensive exam	$135.00	$124.16
58150	Total Abdominal Hysterectomy	$1,400.00	$910.06

CODE	SERVICE DESCRIPTION/ MIDWEST AREA	CHARGE	USUAL/CUSTOMARY REIMBURSEMENT MIDWEST AREA
99213	Mid-level exam	$75.00	$64.97
99214	Detailed exam	$125.00	$97.38
99215	Comprehensive exam	$140.00	$131.99
58150	Total Abdominal Hysterectomy	$1,200.00	$1,033.17

CODE	SERVICE DESCRIPTION/ SOUTHEAST AREA	CHARGE	USUAL/CUSTOMARY REIMBURSEMENT SOUTHEAST AREA
99213	Mid-level exam	$85.00	$65.52
99214	Detailed exam	$110.00	$98.95
99215	Comprehensive exam	$140.00	$134.48
58150	Total Abdominal Hysterectomy	$1,500.00	$1,102.59

With usual, customary, and reasonable fee-for-service reimbursement, the balance may or may not be billed to the patient. Usual, customary, and reasonable retrospective payment systems may be based on geographical areas, urban versus rural, medical specialty, or other factors. Explanation of benefits often describes the difference between the amount billed by the provider and the amount paid as "over usual, customary, and reasonable (UCR) are excluded as defined by the plan."

Above Usual, Customary, and Reasonable Example #1

Patient Name: Hilary Clifford							Patient Acct #: 358761					
Member ID # 996331887												
Relation: Self							Member: Hilary Clifford					

Service Dates	CPT® Codes	PL	Num SVC	Submitted Charges	Copay Amount	Not Payable	See Remarks	Deduct	Co-Ins	Patient Responsible	Payable Amount
08/10/ XX	99213		1	$65.00		$10.50	735			$10.50	$54.50
08/10/ XX	71020		1	$95.00		$62.35	735			$62.35	$32.65
08/10/ XX											
08/10/ XX											
TOTALS				**$160.00**		**$72.85**				**$72.85**	**$87.15**

Remark codes 735 - Above usual, customary, and reasonable

For Questions regarding this claim call 888-999-6868 for assistance. Please use ID number for reference to this claim	Total Patient Responsibility $72.85

Usual, customary, and reasonable reimbursement methodology is a common reimbursement model used by third-party insurers.

REVIEW: FEE-FOR-SERVICE REIMBURSEMENT

I. **MULTIPLE CHOICE.**
   Choose the best answer.

1. Retrospective payment is an example of what type of reimbursement methodology?
   - ○ fee-for-service
   - ○ episode-of-care

2. Which reimbursement methodology reimbursement rates are set by the third-party payer based on historical data for a given geographical area or a given medical specialty?
   - ○ self-pay
   - ○ managed care
   - ○ usual, customary, and reasonable
   - ○ capitation

3. Episode-of-care is a reimbursement system under which the provider receives payment based on what?
   - ○ each service provided to the patient
   - ○ patient's condition or illness
   - ○ the geographical area of the visit
   - ○ the length of time patient has been insured

4. Fee schedules are an example of what type of payment system?
   - ○ prospective
   - ○ retrospective

5. The _____ reimbursement system is based on the patient's condition/illness or a specified time period over which the patient receives care.
   - ○ episode-of-care
   - ○ fee-for-service
   - ○ fee-for-visit
   - ○ episode-of-service

RESOURCE-BASED RELATIVE VALUE SCALE

Particularly important in coding for physician-based care is the RBRVS method used by Medicare to reimburse physicians. RBRVS, or resource-based relative value scale, is the retrospective fee-for-service reimbursement methodology used by Medicare to determine reimbursement amounts for physician-based services.

Medicaid varies from state to state since Medicaid is a joint federal and state program. Medicaid reimbursement may be based on RBRVS or a modified RBRVS system or other state-specific reimbursement methodology.

Highlights

The secretary of CMS must make available to Medicare Payment Advisory Commission (MedPac) and the public by March 1st of every year the estimated conversion factor applicable for physician services for the following year and supply the underlying data for these estimates. So for 2013, the conversion factor is $34.0230.

Established in 1992, the RBRVS reimbursement system seeks to set reimbursement rates for physician services based on three primary factors:

- Physician work (effort)
- Practice expense (overhead)
- Professional liability (malpractice insurance)

Each of these factors is translated into a "relative value unit" and multiplied by a dollar amount supplied by CMS (Centers for Medicare and Medicaid Services). Payments are adjusted for geographical differences.

Procedure codes are defined in the CPT® codebook. The AMA and CMS work together to analyze these codes from the perspective of the physicians providing the services. They take into account how much physician work, technical skill, physical and mental effort, judgment, stress, and potential risk is involved in each procedure. Consideration is also given to the expense involved in setting up and managing various types of physician practices and the costs of professional liability insurance in different geographic areas.

Several informational websites provide details about RBRVS. AMA and CMS in particular can provide additional reading material and background information on physician reimbursement.

Based on the factors listed above, each code is assigned a relative value unit. When a claim is received from the provider, the relative value unit for each CPT code is multiplied by the current CMS multiplier and a reimbursement is calculated for each service.

Suppose the CMS conversion factor for 2014 multiplier is $38. Reimbursement is calculated by multiplying the CMS conversion factor by the relative value assigned to the CPT® (or HCPCS) code.

In a case where the patient had two physician procedures/services performed, one with a relative value of 3 and one with a relative value of 6. The reimbursement would be:

CMS conversion factor	Relative Value	Total Reimbursement
38	X 3	= $114
38	X 6	= $228
		= $342

Sample RBRVS Reimbursement Chart:

CPT CODE	DESCRIPTION	RVU	CMS CONVERSION FACTOR	CMS REIMBURSEMENT
99213	Exam	1.02	X 38.0870	$38.85
38745	Axillary, lymphadenectomy, complete	21.52	X 38.0870	$819.63
92997	Percutaneous transluminal artery balloon angioplasty, single vessel	17.31	X 38.0870	$659.29

Correct, complete, and accurate medical coding is critical to the healthcare reimbursement process. A breakdown anywhere along the chain of the healthcare documentation process can result in less than full reimbursement for provided services and can directly impact the financial wellbeing of a healthcare provider.

Also, notice RBRVS fits the fee-for-service and retrospective payment system categories because reimbursement is based on individual services provided to the patient. The reimbursement amounts are determined after the patient receives care and the claim is submitted.

I. MULTIPLE CHOICE.
Choose the best answer.

1. The primary entity using the RBRVS reimbursement methodology is _____.
   - ○ the military
   - ○ the teachers' union
   - ○ Medicare
   - ○ all of the above

2. What type of code is used to determine the relative value unit?
   - ○ ICD-10-CM diagnosis code
   - ○ CPT code
   - ○ ICD-10-PCS procedure code
   - ○ none of the above

3. The reimbursement amount for the RBRVS system is based on the relative value unit and the _____.
   - ○ CMS multiplier
   - ○ patient's geographical location
   - ○ type of specialty used
   - ○ age of the patient

4. The RBRVS reimbursement system sets reimbursement rates for physician services based on which of the following factors?
   - ○ practice expense
   - ○ professional liability
   - ○ physician work
   - ○ all of the above

5. The RBRVS reimbursement system is an example of what type of reimbursement methodology?
   - ○ fee-for-service
   - ○ episode-of-care

MANAGED CARE

Reimbursement based on:
   Services provided to the patient

   1. Self-pay
   2. Retrospective payment
   ☑ 3. Managed care

As learned earlier, in recent decades third-party and government payers have evolved from being the ones who paid the bills to taking an active part in influencing patient healthcare decisions and provider reimbursement.

Managed care can operate under a fee-for-service model or under an episode-of-care model. Managed care simply means the third-party payer takes an active role in influencing cost and quality through its policies and provisions.

A simple example of a managed care policy is pre-authorization. The third-party payer requires the patient to obtain approval from the insurance company prior to scheduling surgery as a condition for the third-party payer to reimburse the provider for the surgery claim. If the patient fails to get prior approval, the third-party payer may pay a significantly reduced amount or not pay at all. Pre-authorization allows the insurance company (third-party payer) to influence the patient's decision-making by requiring second opinions or conservative therapy first. The insurance company can review healthcare documentation prior to the surgery and educate providers and patients about length of stay limitations and so forth.

Managed care may operate under a fee-for-service model or an episode-of-care model. Let's take a look at a few fee-for-service managed care payment methodologies.

I. **MULTIPLE CHOICE.**
   Choose the best answer.

   1. Managed care means the third-party payer takes an (◯ active, ◯ inactive) role in influencing cost and quality.

   2. The requirement for the patient to obtain approval from the insurance company prior to scheduling a procedure is known as (◯ pre-authorization, ◯ managed care)

   3. Pre-authorization allows (◯ the patient, ◯ the third-party payer) to make decisions requiring second opinions or conservative therapy prior to surgery.

HEALTH MAINTENANCE ORGANIZATIONS (HMOS)

The primary factor in fee-for-service is that reimbursement is based on services provided to the patient. If a managed care payer is determining reimbursement on services provided, then it fits the fee-for-service category.

Although we haven't included managed care directly under the retrospective payment system category, fee-for-service HMOs and preferred provider organizations (PPOs) do use a retrospective payment model.

HMOs, or health maintenance organizations, exercise the most control over patient choice and provider treatment options. HMOs follow a set of care guidelines patients must follow in order to receive maximum benefits. A structure common to many HMOs is the requirement for a patient to choose a primary care physician. The primary care physician acts as a gateway to all medical services. The patient must obtain a referral by the primary care physician in order to see a specialist or authorize other types of treatment. Another structure seen in HMOs is case management. Patients with certain illnesses—cancer, diabetes, asthma—are assigned a case manager who coordinates patient care to reduce overlapping care, duplication of treatments, and so forth.

HMOs (third-party payers) contract with physicians, physician groups, hospitals, and clinics to provide care under the terms of the HMO. HMO patients are seen at steeply discounted rates and providers have a "pipeline" of patients through the HMO.

Under the fee-for-service HMO model, both the patient and the provider must follow the care guidelines set by the HMO in order to receive maximum reimbursement.

> We've placed a visual aid in the appendix on page 394.

The patient and provider receive the maximum contracted benefit when they follow the HMO guidelines.

> We've placed a visual aid in the appendix on page 395.

The patient and provider do not receive the maximum benefit (in this case a reduction of $35) when they do not follow the plan guidelines of the managed-care payer or HMO. The difference may or may not be billed to the patient based on the plan provision/provider policy.

I. **TRUE/FALSE.**
Mark the following true or false.

1. Many HMOs require a patient to choose a primary care physician.
   ○ true
   ○ false

2. Fee-for-service HMO's use a self-payment model.
   ○ true
   ○ false

3. HMOs contract with healthcare providers to provide care at discounted rates.
   ○ true
   ○ false

PREFERRED PROVIDER ORGANIZATIONS (PPOS)

Preferred provider organizations are a less restrictive type of managed care. Third-party payers contract with healthcare providers for discounted rates. If a covered patient elects to see a preferred provider in the preferred provider "network," the patient pays a smaller amount than if the patient elects to see a provider outside of the preferred provider network.

Highlights

Preferred providers are providers who have contracted with third-party payers to provide services at a discounted rate for insurance plan members.

> We've placed a visual aid in the appendix on page 396.

The patient visits a provider who is contracted with Sun Valley Group to provide services at a discounted rate (preferred provider rate).

We've placed a visual aid in the appendix on page 397.

The patient has the option to visit a physician who is not contracted to provide discounted services for Sun Valley Group participants. The patient has the option but the patient pays more for the services of the out-of-network provider.

FEE-FOR-SERVICE SUMMARY

Of course, this list of fee-for-service models is not exhaustive. In addition to those covered, a number of other fee-for-service models exist, including point-of-service plans, exclusive-provider-organizations, private policy (indemnity), and many others.

All fee-for-service reimbursement methodologies have a few common elements:

- Fee-for-service providers are reimbursed for each service they provide.
- The more services a fee-for-service provider renders, the more reimbursement the provider receives.
- Most fee-for-service reimbursement methodologies are based on a retrospective payment system. Reimbursement amounts are determined after the patient has already received the services.
- Discounted fee-for-service arrangements are common.
- The difference between the amount billed by the provider and the amount paid by a third-party payer in a fee-for-service environment may or may not be billed to the patient. Contractual agreements between patient, provider, and third-party payer determine whether or not the patient is billed some or all of the difference.
- Medicare pays physicians using the resource-based relative value system, a discounted fee-for-service system.
- Some states use the resource-based-relative-value-system multiplied by some form of a conversion factor for their Medicaid reimbursement, while others use a state mandated Medicaid fee schedule or a combination of both.

Reimbursement based on:
Services provided to the patient

1. Self-pay
2. Retrospective payment
   a. fee schedules
   b. usual, customary, and reasonable
   c. RBRVS (resource-based relative value scale)

3. Managed care
   a. HMOs
   b. PPOs

REVIEW: MANAGED CARE

I. TRUE/FALSE.
Mark the following true or false.

1. HMOs exercise control over patient choice and provider treatment options.
   - ○ true
   - ○ false

2. Members of an HMO may be required to obtain pre-authorization prior to scheduling surgery.
   - ○ true
   - ○ false

3. Patients that belong to an HMO may be required to obtain a referral from their primary care physician in order to see a specialist.
   - ○ true
   - ○ false

4. In HMOs the patients pay a smaller amount if they see physicians out of the "network."
   - ○ true
   - ○ false

5. Managed care organizations operate only under the fee-for-service model.
   - ○ true
   - ○ false

EPISODE-OF-CARE

Episode-of-care reimbursement models don't pay based on individual services rendered. Episode-of-care models determine payment based on one lump sum payment for all the care provided related to a disease or particular condition. Many times it is based on a time factor. An example is in home health all services delivered to the patient during a 60-day period is considered an episode of care. A unit of time may be a visit (encounter for care) or a daily, monthly, or other specified time period of care when a patient receives continuous care.

In the next several lessons, we'll take a closer look at some major types of episode-of-care reimbursement methodologies: managed care, global and prospective payment systems.

Let's start with the managed care episode-of-care reimbursement method.

MANAGED CARE – CAPITATION

Reimbursement based on:

Patient's condition/illness
A specified time period

☑ **1. Managed Care – Capitation**
2. Global payment
3. Prospective payment

Capitation is a reimbursement method used by some managed care plans. The third-party payer contracts with the healthcare provider(s) to pay a flat fee per individual enrolled in the healthcare plan. The actual services provided to the patient—few or numerous—don't affect the reimbursement to the provider.

Happy Health Wellness HMO, Inc. has contracted with Peter Benton, M.D., to be a participating primary care physician in their network. The contract, in part, states the following method of reimbursement: Dr. Peter Benton shall be reimbursed on a per-member per-month (PMPM) basis. Dr. Benton shall receive a check on the first of each month based on the number of patients who have signed up with him for care. The payment methodology is broken down as follows:

- Age 0–1 year: $17.88/PMPM–vaccinations will be paid separately
- Age 2–4 yrs: $17.88/PMPM–vaccinations will be paid separately
- Age 5–12 yrs: $11.54/PMPM
- Age 13–20 yrs: $9.82/PMPM
- Age 21–49 yrs: $ 8.94/PMPM
- Age 50–60 yrs: $10.72/PMPM
- Age 61–64 yrs: $11.53/PMPM

Additionally, Dr. Benton may collect the copays from the patient as determined by the patient's policy.

A phrase commonly heard in the industry to refer to capitation payments is PMPM or "per member per month." The provider receives a set amount "per member per month." If the rate is $17—the provider receives $17/PMPM.

Under capitation reimbursement, the provider is paid the same rate for a patient with complex medical needs who is seen frequently as for a healthy patient who rarely seeks treatment. Capitation allows for certainty for the third–party payer and the provider because rates are set. The third-party payer knows what the cost will be for each member. The provider knows they are responsible for providing care for a given number of patients and will have a set income for those patients. However, the provider absorbs a certain degree of risk because how many patients will need high levels of care in a given month is unknown. Providers need a high enough capitation rate to balance those risks and average a positive cash flow.

Capitation Chart

Month	# of Patients Enrolled	Capitation Rate	Capitation Reimbursement	Actual Cost
January	212	$12	$2544	$2300
February	233	$12	$2796	$2990

March	210	$12	$2520	$1860
April	194	$12	$2328	$2410
May	260	$12	$3120	$2207
June	251	$12	$3012	$2825
Average	227	$12	$2720	$2432

This simplified example shows an average cost over six months to treat the average of 227 patients of $2432. The provider is reimbursed the same amount per patient regardless of the cost of treatment: $12. The provider had an average profit margin of $288 per month for treating patients under this managed care capitation agreement.

I. **TRUE/FALSE.**
Mark the following true or false.

1. The abbreviation PMPM in reference to capitation payments means per member per month.
   ○ true
   ○ false

2. Under the capitation reimbursement method the number of services provided to the patient affects the reimbursement to the provider.
   ○ true
   ○ false

3. Capitation does not provide any risk of financial loss to the provider since the same rate is paid for each patient.
   ○ true
   ○ false

4. The episode-of-care reimbursement methodology determines payment based on the patient's condition, disease or unit of time.
   ○ true
   ○ false

5. The capitation reimbursement method is the best method of reimbursement for physicians whose patients have complex medical needs.
   ○ true
   ○ false

GLOBAL PAYMENT/PROSPECTIVE PAYMENT SYSTEMS

Reimbursement based on:
Patient's condition/illness
A specified time period

1. Managed Care – Capitation
☑ **2. Global payment**
3. Prospective payment

Global reimbursement is a fixed amount of money or a lump-sum payment designated to cover a related group of services.

Global payments and prospective payment are closely related.

PROSPECTIVE: THE ACT OF LOOKING FORWARD

When the costs of healthcare services are projected and allowable reimbursement amounts set for future healthcare services, this is called a **prospective payment system.**

Third-party payers have set up a number of prospective global payment systems, particularly government third-party payers.

An example of a **global prospective payment system** is the Medicare system used to reimburse home health services: HHPPS, or home health prospective payment system. The Balanced Budget Act (BBA) of 1997, as amended by the Omnibus Consolidated and Emergency Supplemental Appropriations Act (OCESAA) of 1999, called for the development and implementation of a prospective payment system (PPS) for Medicare home health services. The BBA put in place the interim payment system (IPS) until the PPS could be implemented. Effective October 1, 2000, the home health PPS (HHPPS) replaced the IPS for all home health agencies (HHAs). Under prospective payment, Medicare pays home health agencies (HHAs) a predetermined base payment. The payment is adjusted for the health condition and care needs of the beneficiary. The payment is also adjusted for the geographic differences in wages for HHAs across the country. Medicare pays for speech therapy, physical therapy, occupational therapy, nursing visits, home health aide visits, and other related home health costs with one payment to the Home Health Agency. The agency then distributes payment to all the professionals and agencies providing home health services.

Consider a patient receiving home healthcare services following a stroke:

Global payment means one payment is made to cover the multiple services.

EXAMPLE:

Annette receives a daily home health aide visit and twice-weekly physical and occupational therapy to assist her with grooming, dressing, and transfer skills. She has no speech difficulty so she does not receive any occupational therapy for speech. A skilled nurse comes in daily for the first two weeks, then twice weekly, and finally bi-weekly as Annette progresses and is able to prepare her own medication. She also receives oxygen and oxygen supplies from a local supplier.

Although Annette receives services from a physical therapist, occupational therapist, skilled nurse, medical supply company, and a nurses' aide, the third-party payer will send one payment to the Home Health Agency for 60 days of care. The lump-sum payment will be distributed to the other professionals by the Home Health Agency.

HHPPS is a global payment system.

I. FILL IN THE BLANK.

Enter the correct word in the blank provided.

1. A_____ is when allowable reimbursement amounts are set for future healthcare services.

2. _____ is a fixed amount of money designated to cover a related group of services by more than one provider.

3. An example of the global prospective payment system is the _____ used to reimburse home health services.

HOME HEALTH PROSPECTIVE PAYMENT SYSTEM (HHPPS)

HHPPS is also a prospective payment system because reimbursement rates are set in advance for home healthcare. Reimbursement rates are paid for 60-day blocks of time. The HHPPS system uses a multiplier, known as HHRG (home health resource group), and operates by setting a fixed rate for home health services based on historical data. Once this fixed rate is set, adjustments may be made for severely acute patients or for patients receiving care in more (or less) expensive geographic areas.

An adjustment to the basic rate for difference in health condition and other considerations is called the case-mix adjustment and is done with the use of an OASIS form (outcome and assessment information set).

The CMS website describes the HHPPS global payment system as follows:

Medicare pays home health agencies (HHAs) a predetermined base payment. The payment is adjusted for the health condition and care needs of the beneficiary. The payment is also adjusted for the geographic differences in wages for HHAs across the country. The adjustment for the health condition, or clinical characteristics, and service needs of the beneficiary is referred to as the case-mix adjustment. A nurse or therapist from the HHA uses the Outcome and Assessment Information Set (OASIS) instrument to assess the patient's condition. (All HHAs have been using OASIS since July 19, 1999.) The home health PPS (Prospective Payment System) will provide HHAs with payments for each 60-day episode of care for each beneficiary. If a beneficiary is still eligible for care after the end of the first episode, a second episode can begin; there are no limits to the number of episodes a beneficiary who remains eligible for the home health benefit can receive. http://www.cms.gov/Medicare/Medicare-Fee-for-Service-Payment/HomeHealthPPS/index.html

Government sets reimbursement rate based on historical data for home healthcare costs.

Patient receives home healthcare services coordinated by a home health agency.

Documentation is coded.

Home health agent completes a patient assessment (called an OASIS) to adjust for variables like critical care versus low–level rehabilitative care.

Claim is sent to Medicare/Medicaid.

Claim is reimbursed in one lump sum using OASIS*, predetermined based payment amount (HHRG).

Check is sent to home health agency and dispersed to professionals and providers who provided home health services.

*Outcome and Assessment Information Set is the assessment tool used to adjust for differences in health conditions, geographic differences etc.

HHPPS is both a global payment system and a prospective payment system.

REVIEW: PAYMENT/PROSPECTIVE PAYMENT SYSTEMS

I. **TRUE/FALSE.**
   Mark the following true or false.

   1. The home health prospective payment system is an example of a global prospective payment system.
      ◯ true
      ◯ false

   2. HHPPS, a prospective payment system, projects the cost of home healthcare services and sets the allowable reimbursement amounts for future home healthcare services.
      ◯ true
      ◯ false

   3. Under the HHPPS system, each provider receives a separate payment for the services provided.
      ◯ true
      ◯ false

   4. Global reimbursement is a fixed payment amount designated to cover a related group of services by multiple providers.
      ◯ true
      ◯ false

   5. Reimbursement rates under the HHPPS are paid for 30-day blocks of time.
      ◯ true
      ◯ false

PROSPECTIVE PAYMENT SYSTEMS

Reimbursement based on:
Patient's condition/illness
A specified time period

   1. Managed Care – Capitation
   2. Global payment
   ☑ **3. Prospective payment**

Under a prospective payment system, the third-party payer is interested in looking at averages over time and paying the average cost for each patient instead of the actual cost for each patient. Prospective payment systems establish payment amounts in advance for future healthcare services.

Highlights

Not all prospective payment systems are global payment systems. Global payment means multiple services share a single payment. Prospective payment systems can be set up so that different payments are made to different providers—although the payment amount is not based on what was actually done but on historical averages.

The HHPPS system is a prospective payment systems based on a unit of time (60 days) with adjustments for healthcare considerations. However, prospective payment systems may be based on time units or based on services for specific conditions or diseases.

Another example of a time unit-based reimbursement system is the Indian Health Services (IHS) reimbursement system. IHS sets a per-diem (daily) rate. Reimbursement rates are set based on historical daily costs of providing healthcare services and then reimbursed on a per-day basis or per-encounter basis. To learn more about IHS, click here.

GOVERNMENT PROSPECTIVE PAYMENT SYSTEMS

HHPPS was covered in some detail, and now other prospective payment systems will be presented.

Provider	System	Calculation Unit
Home Health Care	HHPPS – Home Health Prospective Payment System	HRG w/case-mix adjustment
Ambulatory Surgical Centers	ASCPPS – Ambulatory Surgical Center Prospective Payment System	ASC (Ambulatory Surgical Center) Group
Skilled Nursing Facilities (Nursing Homes)	SNFPPS – Skilled Nursing Facility Prospective Payment System	RUG – Resource Utilization Group
Outpatient Hospital Services	OPPS – Outpatient Prospective Payment Systems	APC – Ambulatory Payment Classification
Inpatient Hospital Services	IPPS – Inpatient Prospective Payment System	MS-DRG – Medicare Severity Diagnosis-related Groups

HHPPS is a prospective payment system based on a unit of time. Let's take a look at a prospective payment system based on disease or condition. The basics of prospective payment systems:

- Payment is not made on individual services provided but on predetermined calculated rates.
- Predetermined calculated rates are based on historical information/data and set for future healthcare costs.
- Prospective payment systems are based on averages of actual data and projections, not on individual services provided.

If you would like more information on prospective payment systems, click the link below:

http://www.cms.gov/Medicare/Medicare-Fee-for-Service-Payment/ProspMedicareFeeSvcPmtGen/index.html

OUTPATIENT PROSPECTIVE PAYMENT SYSTEM

Hospitals provide both inpatient and outpatient services. Outpatient services are reimbursed by Medicare and Medicaid through a prospective payment system known as the outpatient prospective payment system.

Services listed in the CPT® procedure coding book and the HCPCS book are analyzed by CMS (Centers for Medicaid and Medicare Services). CMS looks at what resources are required to provide the services. Clinical services that require similar resources are grouped into payment classifications called Ambulatory Payment Classifications (APCs).

Reimbursement rates are set for each Ambulatory Payment Classification and reimbursement is based on the Ambulatory Payment Classifications listed on the patient's claim. Keep in mind the claim also lists the patient's diagnosis (ICD-10-CM codes), and the procedures performed.

CMS sets reimbursement rates for each APC (ambulatory payment classification).

Patient receives outpatient services at a hospital.

Documentation is coded.

Codes are transferred to claim.

Claim sent to third-party payer.

CPT and HCPCS codes are grouped to the appropriate APC (Ambulatory Payment Classification) by third-party payer.

Claim is reimbursed based on pre-set APC rates.

Note: Hospitals may be paid for more than one APC per encounter. Adjustments may be calculated for geographic area.

The following link provides additional information about outpatient prospective payment systems: http://www.cms.gov/Outreach-and-Education/Medicare-Learning-Network-MLN/ Hospital_Outpatient_Payment_System_Factsheet.pdf.

I. MATCHING.
Match the following steps to the number which represents the order in which they happen.

1. ___	1	A. Patient receives outpatient services at a hospital.
2. ___	2	B. CPT and HCPCS codes are grouped to the appropriate APC (Ambulatory Payment Classification) by third-party payer.
3. ___	3	C. Codes are transferred to claim.
4. ___	4	D. CMS sets reimbursement rates for each APC (ambulatory payment classification).
5. ___	5	E. Claim is reimbursed based on pre-set APC rates.
6. ___	6	F. Documentation is coded.
7. ___	7	G. Claim sent to third-party payer.

CMS DESCRIPTIONS – AMBULATORY PAYMENT CLASSIFICATION SYSTEM

The Centers for Medicaid and Medicare Services describes the Outpatient Prospective Payment Systems for outpatient hospital services (APC) and outpatient surgical center services (ASC) as follows:

Ambulatory payment classification (APC) system – A coding and reimbursement hierarchy for outpatient services that organizes CPT® and HCPCS codes into several hundred groups. Each code of Level I and II HCPCS are assigned a payment status indicator, identifying how it will be paid. These service bundles are the basis for Medicare reimbursement for many outpatient hospital services. Some hospital services such as anesthesia, recovery room, and many drugs and supplies are considered bundled into the APC payment and, therefore, reimbursement is minimized. Other procedures are not bundled or packaged such as ancillary services like x-rays, and MRI, and other minor procedures such as injections. These all have separate APC groups. Each CPT code is assigned to only one APC. The APC assignment does NOT change based on the diagnosis or condition of the patient. So in other words, it is only the CPT/HCPCS codes that drive the reimbursement.

There are 10 types of APCs and can be identified by the payment status indicator. A list of these indicators follows.

Payment Status Indicator	Value
Clinic or emergency department visit	V
Significant procedures, multiple reduction applies	T
Significant procedure, not discounted when multiple	S
Ancillary service	X
Non-pass-through drugs and nonimplantable biological agents including therapeutic radiopharmaceuticals	K
Pass-through drugs or biological agents	G
Pass-through device categories	H
Partial hospitalization	P

Blood and blood products	R
Brachytherapy sources	U

I. MULTIPLE CHOICE.
Choose the best answer.

1. The APC system does which of the following?
   ○ determines who gets charged for bundled Medicare services
   ○ bundles CPT and HCPCS codes into a hierarchy of groups to minimize reimbursement
   ○ separates bundled CPT and HCPCS codes in order to minimize reimbursement
   ○ all of the above

2. What services are considered bundled into the APC payment?
   ○ drugs and supplies
   ○ recovery room
   ○ anesthesia
   ○ all of the above

OPPS EXAMPLE

Patient was brought to County General Hospital's E.R. for a gunshot wound to the upper-right arm and left upper chest. Dr. Tony Gates examined him and ordered x-rays of the right upper arm and a 2-view chest x-ray to determine the amount of damage. Dr. Gates performed an exploration of a penetrating wound to the chest and right upper arm and was able to remove two bullets. He also performed a complex wound closure—7 cm to the chest and 8 cm to the right arm.

Listed below are the codes and charges:

APC	CPT® CODES	DESCRIPTION	CHARGES	REIMBURSEMENT
0137	20101-59	Exploration of penetrating wound chest	$1,800.00	$1,510.07
0007	20103-59-RT	Exploration of penetrating wound of right arm	$850.00	$725.58
0134	13121	Complex wound repair right arm 7.5 cm	$350.00	$251.48
0133	13122	Complex wound repair right arm add'l .5 cm	$300.00	$85.75
0135	13101	Complex wound repair of chest 7.5 cm	$500.00	$393.38
0628	G0382	Medicare's emergency room level 3 exam	$175.00	$89.89

0260	71020	X-ray of chest, 2 view	$100.00	$45.95
0260	73060-RT	X-ray of right upper arm, 2-view	$125.00	$45.95
TOTALS			CHARGES $4,200.00	REIMBURSEMENT $3,148.05

CPT codes are grouped into APC classifications. Notice, for example, two different x-rays with two different CPT codes (71020 and 73060-RT) are both grouped into APC classification surgical 0260 (Level I plain film except teeth).

A reimbursement rate is set for APC classification 0260 (Level I plain film except teeth) of $45.95 by CMS, and all x-rays in this classification are reimbursed at the same level. The billed charges were different for each x-ray.

APC payment rates are maximum reimbursement rates. For surgical claims, only the highest APC (highest dollar value) is paid at the maximum rate; all other surgical charges are paid at 50% of the maximum rate. X-rays/radiology are not considered surgical procedures, so they are paid at the maximum rate.

Excerpt from 2013 APC Group List, published by CMS:

APC	Group Title	SI*	Relative Weight**	Payment Rate
0137	Level V Skin Repair	T	21.1752	$1,510.07
0007	Level II Incision & Drainage	T	10.1746	$725.58
0134	Level II Skin Repair	T	3.5264	$251.48
0133	Level I Skin Repair	T	1.2024	$85.75
0135	Level III Skin Repair	T	5.5162	$393.38
0628	Level 3 Type B Emergency Visits	V	1.2605	$89.89
0260	Level I Plain Film Except Teeth	X	0.6443	$45.95

*SI is the APC Status Indicator. **Relative weights are assigned based on complexity of procedure, cost to provide procedure, degree of skill required, and other factors.

Medical coding specialists do not need to understand every nuance of relative weight payment. However, medical coding specialists do need to understand the general principles involved in outpatient prospective payment systems. Accurate medical coding, accurate medical billing, accurate auditing, and accurate reimbursement all depend on the teamwork of medical coders, medical billers, healthcare auditors, and the reimbursement specialists they work with.

CMS DESCRIPTIONS – AMBULATORY SURGICAL CENTER

The Centers for Medicaid and Medicare describes the Outpatient Prospective Payment Systems for outpatient hospital services (APC) and outpatient surgical center services (ASC) as follows:

Ambulatory surgical center (ASC) system – The ASC is a freestanding outpatient facility that provides outpatient surgeries to patients. Previously the payment system consisted of an ASC list with procedure codes grouped into the different payment rates. Inpatient procedures were also shifted into the outpatient setting. This trend identified a need to change the ASC list to APCs. It took many years for this transition to become a reality, and finally in 2008, the final rule established that the components of the ASC PPS would be updated every year as part of the annual OPPS rule-making process CMS uses the ambulatory payment classifications (APCs) established in the hospital OPPS as the mechanism for grouping ASC procedures. The APC relative payment weights for hospitals become the basis for calculating ASC payment rates under the new payment system.

1. Managed Care – Capitation
   a. Capitation HMO

2. Global payment/Prospective payment
   a. HHPPS

3. Prospective payment
   a. IHS
   b. OPPS
   c. **ASC**
   d. APC
   e. SNF PP
   f. IPPS

I. **TRUE/FALSE.**
   Mark the following true or false.

   1. The new ASC facility payment system links ASC facility payments to Medicare payments to hospital outpatient departments for the same procedure.
      ◯ true
      ◯ false

   2. The mechanism for groups ASC procedures is determined by the HHPPS.
      ◯ true
      ◯ false

   3. ASC payment rates are calculated using APC relative payment weights.
      ◯ true
      ◯ false

OTHER POSTACUTE PPS

In addition to Home Health there are other postacute care PPS such as for Skilled nursing facilities (SNFs), Long-term care hospitals (LTCHs, and Inpatient rehabilitation facilities (IRFs). Each will be briefly covered.

Skilled Nursing Facilities (SNFs)

A nursing home provides 24-hour skilled care and personal care services to residents. Medicare beneficiaries are eligible for SNF services immediately after acute-care inpatient stays that are three days or more in length. The SNF PPS pays a daily rate and mandates consolidated billing. To participate, the SNF must complete the Minimum Data Set (MDS) that provides clinical documentation about the resident's care. The MDS consists of an extensive database containing all of this clinical data. This becomes part of the resident's health record. Part of the data of the MDS is comprehensive assessment information. Assessments must be prepared for the start of therapy; the change of therapy; the end of therapy and any significant change in status. In addition, treatment plans are also part of the clinical data on the MDS.

As stated, the PPS payment starts with the daily rate (per diem rate) and then adjustments are made for geographic factors and inflation, other adjustments mandated by statute or regulation and the patient case mix. The case mix of a resident means the complexity and resource intensity of the residents' condition.

The part of the reimbursement that adjusts for the case mix is called the resident's resource utilization group (RUG). There are three components to each RUG: The nursing component, the therapy component and the non-case-mix-adjusted component.

The SNF is reimbursed based on the all-inclusive Perdiem rate and the RUGs. The payment system rewards those that efficiently and effectively treat complex cases.

Long-Term Care Hospital (LTCH)

After acute care is finished, those patients that have serious long-term conditions may require extended stays. These patients may have multiple acute and chronic diseases and certainly can require complex care. Part A of Medicare provides services for this long-term care hospitalization for its beneficiaries. Services consist of 90-days in this setting. LTCH PPS was implemented in 2002. Many of these patients have chronic diseases such as cancer, tuberculosis, respiratory conditions and head trauma. Many of these patients are ventilator-dependent or require extensive rehabilitative services. Because these lengths-of-stay (LOS) are so much longer than an acute inpatient stay, there is a special reimbursement. The average LOS may be about 25 days or longer. The system is very similar to the MS-DRG system, but the calculations are different to account for this special circumstance. The PPS is based on MS-LTC-DRGs. They actually have the same groups as the MS-DRGs that are in effect for acute-care hospitals. The main difference is that the MS-LTC-DRGs have different relative weights and so therefore different payments.

Inpatient Rehabilitation Facility (IRF)

An inpatient rehabilitation facility provides intense rehabilitation services to patients in an inpatient setting. These services are multidisciplinary services that require a team of healthcare professionals providing care to the patient. Physicians, nurses, physical therapists, occupational therapists, and speech therapists may all be involved. The type of injuries can be severe, and the goal of this care is to help the patient to restore or enhance functions after an injury or illness. The classification of patients into special groups involves similar characteristics, and there are specific conditions that qualify such as strokes, major brain and spinal cord injuries.

There is a special data collection tool called the Inpatient rehabilitation facility patient assessment instrument (IRF PAI). This is an 85-item tool to collect specific data about the patient so that the PPS rate can be calculated. This data is electronically submitted and the case-mix grouping drives the reimbursement for the inpatient rehabilitation PPS.

I. **MULTIPLE CHOICE.**
   Choose the best answer.

   1. Medicare covers_____days in the LTCH.
      ○ 30
      ○ 45
      ○ 60
      ○ 90

   2. The clinical documentation tool called the Minimum Data Set is used in:
      ○ skilled nursing facilities
      ○ Home Health
      ○ inpatient rehabilitation facility
      ○ hospital outpatient facility

   3. The data collection tool called the IRF PAI is used in:
      ○ long-term care hospital
      ○ inpatient rehabilitation facility
      ○ skilled nursing facility
      ○ hospital acute care

II. **TRUE/FALSE.**
   Mark the following true or false.

   1. The average LOS in the LTCH is 15 days.
      ○ true
      ○ false

   2. The part of reimbursement that adjusts for case mix in the SNF is the RUG.
      ○ true
      ○ false

   3. A full healthcare team is involved in the care of the IRF patient.
      ○ true
      ○ false

INPATIENT PROSPECTIVE PAYMENT SYSTEM

Medicare, Medicaid, Blue Cross, TRICARE, and many other third-party payers use a prospective payment system to reimburse for inpatient healthcare. Hospital inpatient visits vary from the routine to the most extended, complex cases. The inpatient prospective payment system (IPPS) looks at the historical costs for providing inpatient services for a given diagnosis and sets a payment amount for treatment of the diagnosis in patients fitting a certain profile (age, sex, complications, etc).

In 1983, Medicare used the historical information to introduce an inpatient prospective payment system based on DRGs (diagnosis related groups). Diagnosis related groups list groups based on diagnoses and procedures, treatments, and supplies hospitals used to treat those diagnoses for patients fitting a specific profile (age, sex, weight, complications, etc.). Medicare Severity DRGs (MS-DRGs), which on Oct. 1, 2007 replaced the version 24 Centers for Medicare and Medicaid Services (CMS) DRGs. CMS implemented the new MS-DRG system to better account for differences in patient severity.

When the inpatient facility submits a claim to a third-party payer under PPS, the claim is categorized into a diagnosis related group. The diagnosis related group determines the amount the hospital will receive.

CMS sets MS-DRGs (Medicare severity diagnosis related groups) for classifying hospital services for a given diagnosis.

Patient receives inpatient services at a hospital.

Documentation is coded.

Codes are transferred to claim.

Claim sent to third-party payer.

Third-party payers assign itemized charges to appropriate DRG classification based on diagnosis and patient profile.

Claim is reimbursed at DRG rate.*

DRG reimbursement may be adjusted for special factors such as hospitals serving high indigent population, teaching facilities, etc.

Please go online to download the document that appears here.

STEPS IN DETERMINING AN IPPS PAYMENT

Step 1 – Hospitals submit a bill for each Medicare patient they treat to Medicare administrative contractor (MAC) (a private insurance company that contracts with Medicare to carry out the operational functions of the Medicare program—Part A and B). The MAC administers the funds and replaces the previous Medicare

Carriers and Fiscal Intermediaries. Based on the information provided on the bill, the case is categorized into a Medicare severity diagnosis related group (MS-DRG), which determines how much payment the hospital receives.

Step 2 – The base payment rate is comprised of a standardized amount, which is divided into a labor-related and nonlabor share. The labor-related share is adjusted by the wage index applicable to the area where the hospital is located and if the hospital is located in Alaska or Hawaii, the nonlabor share is adjusted by a cost of living adjustment factor. This base payment rate is multiplied by the MS-DRG relative weight.

Step 3 – If the hospital is recognized as serving a disproportionate share of low-income patients, it receives a percentage add-on for each case paid through the PPS. This percentage varies depending on several factors, including the percentage of low-income patients served. It is applied to the MS-DRG-adjusted base payment rate, plus any outlier payments received.

Step 4 – If the hospital is an approved teaching hospital it receives a percentage add-on payment for each case paid through the PPS. This percentage varies depending on the ratio of residents-to-beds.

Step 5 – Next, the costs incurred by the hospital for the case are evaluated to determine whether it is eligible for additional payments as an outlier case. This additional payment is designed to protect the hospital from large financial losses due to unusually expensive cases. Any outlier payment due is added onto the MS-DRG-adjusted base payment rate.

REVIEW: PROSPECTIVE PAYMENT SYSTEMS

I. **TRUE/FALSE.**
   Mark the following true or false.

1. All third-party payers use the outpatient prospective payment system as the basis for reimbursement.
   ○ true
   ○ false

2. Discounted fee-for-service arrangements are common in prospective payment systems.
   ○ true
   ○ false

3. Reimbursement under the outpatient prospective payment system is based on Ambulatory Payment Classifications.
   ○ true
   ○ false

4. All prospective payment systems are considered global payment systems.
   ○ true
   ○ false

5. The ambulatory surgical center payment system uses the ambulatory payment classifications as the mechanism for grouping ASC procedures.
   ○ true
   ○ false

QUALITY IMPROVEMENT ORGANIZATIONS

In order to help Medicare beneficiaries with quality-of-care complaints and to help implement healthcare improvement, CMS has established Quality Improvement Organizations (QIO)'s. In each state, Medicare contracts with a QIO organization to take care of quality improvement in their state. These organizations are always staffed by healthcare professionals. Contracts with QIO organizations are granted for a period of 3 years at a time.

According to the CMS webpage about QIO's, www.cms.gov/QualityImprovementOrgs, "the mission of the QIO Program is to improve the effectiveness, efficiency, economy, and quality of services delivered to Medicare beneficiaries." Important duties include addressing Medicare beneficiary's complaints, handling provider-based notice appeals, watching for violations of the Emergency Medical Treatment and Labor Act (EMTALA), ensuring Medicare pays only for reasonable and necessary care, and improving quality of care in general.

I. **MULTIPLE CHOICE.**
   Choose the best answer.

1. QIO contracts are granted for _____ years at a time.
   ○ 2
   ○ 3
   ○ 4
   ○ 5

2. The main purpose of the QIO program is to _____.
   ○ ensure that effective, efficient, and quality care is delivered to Medicare beneficiaries
   ○ evaluate Medicare reimbursements in each state
   ○ investigate Medicare fraud
   ○ all of the above

CONCLUDING THOUGHTS

Medical coding and billing specialists work to create an accurate claim. Accuracy is important not only to assure proper payment for each individual patient, but also because encoded medical record documentation (and, subsequently, healthcare claims) are the raw data used to track trends and determine future reimbursement rates.

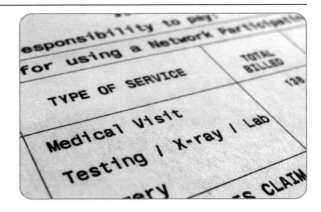

As a medical coder, you will work with elements of prospective and retrospective payment systems. Depending on your work environment, software may be used that automatically assigns APCs or MS-DRGs when ICD-10-CM, ICD-10-PCS, CPT®, or HCPCS codes are input. The revenue codes, other billing elements or some CPT, or HCPCS codes may automatically be entered via the chargemaster. Or the process may be totally manual input. Regardless, accurate claims are expected and claims reviewers may request additional information from you to justify code choices.

The Healthcare Reimbursement module isn't designed to teach every detail of preparing or calculating reimbursements. The objective is to understand the basic reimbursement systems and the important ways all of the pieces of documentation, coding, billing, and reimbursement interconnect.

UNIT 4

Life Cycle of a Claim

LIFE CYCLE OF A CLAIM – INTRODUCTION

Insurance companies have policies and procedures in place to process received claims based on the rule and regulations of insurance coverage. Considering all the claims to be processes each year, the system must be efficient. In an effort to simplify this, the industry has created its own terminology to identify the claim information.

In this unit, terminology and the typical medical claim process is discussed. Understanding the information and the role of the biller is necessary to be successful.

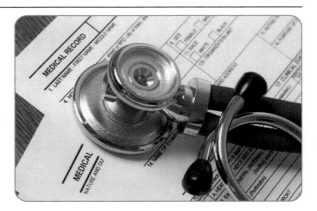

THE FIVE STEPS IN A MEDICAL CLAIM

All medical claims going through third-party payers follow the same cycle. The cycle begins when a patient with medical benefits receives medical services and a medical insurance claim is created. The cycle ends when the claim is paid. What happens in between is pretty universal, with minor exceptions depending upon the third-party payer.

In its most basic form, the life cycle of a claim looks like this:

| Submission | Processing | Adjudication | Payment |

Submission – The healthcare provider sends the claim to the third-party payer requesting payment. Submissions are made electronically (or occasionally by paper bill).

Processing – The third-party payer receives the claim and gathers information related to the case (specifics about the patient, the case, and the coverage).

Adjudication – The third-party payer's process of checking the details of the claim against the information they have on the patient and his/her insurance benefits. This process also checks for completeness of the claim, bundling issues for CPT® codes, medical necessity, and recent claims (to avoid unnecessary service or duplicate claims).

Payment – A financial payment is made by the third party payer and received by the provider. The payment may be a lump sum for multiple claims or a single payment for one claim. The third-party payer also submits a remittance advice to the healthcare provider and an explanation of benefits (EOB) is sent to the patient. These forms explain what was covered by the third-party payer, what was not, and why. These forms contain patient and facility information, types and dates of services, charges, type of bill, and reason and remark codes, which will be discussed later.

Reconciliation – The process the healthcare provider analyzes received payment information compared to submitted claim information for accuracy. If the provider believes a claim was inappropriately denied by the payer, the dispute process begins until satisfactory reconciliation is achieved by the provider and the third party payer.

I. **TRUE/FALSE.**
    Mark the following true or false.

1. All medical visits produce a third-party medical claim.
    ○ true
    ○ false

2. Medical claims are always printed on paper.
    ○ true
    ○ false

3. The submission of a claim begins with the healthcare provider.
    ○ true
    ○ false

4. Explanations of payments or non-payments are sent to both the healthcare provider and the patient.
    ○ true
    ○ false

5. All third-party payers use the exact same methods of processing claims.
    ○ true
    ○ false

CLAIM SUBMISSION – DOCUMENTATION PREPARATION

Accurate documentation facilitates an efficient reimbursement process. For a claim to be submitted properly, all information must be accurate, up-to-date, and clearly documented. Documentation is the foundation for tracking patient treatment, proving appropriateness of medical care, compliance with regulations imposed by various agencies, and supports the billed services. For document accuracy, pre-billing software scrubbers pre-edit the content prior to reaching the biller. This is discussed later.

Every outpatient visit, from a complicated trip to the emergency room to a routine physician office follow-up, is tied to a specific patient and documented in a paper or electronic record (or some combination of both called a hybrid record). Healthcare documentation is extensively covered in other modules, but it comes up as an important factor in healthcare reimbursement. When the patient comes in for treatment, demographic information is collected and the details of the patient's visit are documented to form the patient's medical record.

Information is collected from the patient regarding financial responsibility for the administered healthcare services. In many cases, the financially responsible person is the patient; however, a parent or legal guardian would be responsible for a minor or ward. Even when third-party payer information is provided, most healthcare providers require the patient or legal guardian to accept financial responsibility in the event the third-party payer only pays a portion of the charges or denies the claim.

Highlights

Each patient record has two components that may or may not be stored together:

1. The medical record documentation component records the details of the healthcare visit.
2. The financial record component includes the patient's contact information, billing information, payment history, insurance cards, and financial liability form.

Keep in mind that the patient's registration form needs to be updated at a minimum annually. Before releasing private patient information to insurance carriers, patients must give signed authorization as to not violate HIPAA regulations for patient confidentiality. In addition, a photocopy of both sides of the patients' insurance identification cards needs to be part of the financial records. Each provider must have a system in place to maintain all documentation related to the patient's financial responsibility.

We've placed a multi-page visual aid in the appendix on pages 398-399.

ADVANCE BENEFICIARY NOTICE OF NONCOVERAGE (ABN)

If the patient is a Medicare patient an Advance Beneficiary Notice of Noncoverage (ABN) form may be needed. Medicare provides coverage for many services, but not for all. The execution of the form allows the beneficiary the option to make an informed decision about whether to get services and accept financial responsibility for the services if Medicare does not pay. The form is issued when:

- The organization believes Medicare may not pay for an item or service.
- Medicare usually covers the item or service and Medicare may not consider it medically reasonable and necessary for this patient in this particular instance.

If the organization does not issue a valid ABN to the beneficiary when Medicare requires, they cannot bill the beneficiary for the service and the organization will be financially liable. The ABN form serves as proof that the beneficiary knew prior to getting the service that Medicare might not pay. It also serves as an optional (voluntary) notice used to forewarn beneficiaries of their financial liability prior to providing care that Medicare never covers. Medicare does not require an ABN to be issued in order to bill a beneficiary for an item or service that is not a Medicare benefit and never covered.

Go to http://www.cms.gov/Outreach-and-Education/Medicare-Learning-Network-MLN/MLNProducts/downloads/abn_booklet_icn006266.pdf

Review the booklet and then answer the questions related to the content of the ABN. Be sure to review the sample ABN form on page 12. It is important that all of the components are completed. For example there are three various options for the beneficiary to select.

I. MULTIPLE CHOICE.
Choose the best answer.

1. What is a Medicare coverage policy?
   - ○ NCD
   - ○ LCD
   - ○ ABN
   - ○ both a and b
   - ○ all of the above

2. Where are the NCDs and LCDs located?
   - ○ American Medical Association
   - ○ National Center for Health Statistics
   - ○ Medicare Coverage Database
   - ○ Beneficiary Notices Initiative

3. Medicare denies claims as not medically reasonable and necessary for:
   - ○ experimental procedures
   - ○ a procedure that is not indicated for a particular diagnosis
   - ○ a procedure not considered safe
   - ○ all of the above

4. An ABN should normally be retained for:
   - ○ 5 years
   - ○ 3 years
   - ○ 10 years
   - ○ permanently

II. TRUE/FALSE.
Mark the following true or false.

1. Medicare has frequency limitations on certain services.
   - ○ true
   - ○ false

2. Organizations may issue an ABN to all beneficiaries to protect themselves.
   - ○ true
   - ○ false

3. An ABN may be completed by e-mail if needed.
   - ○ true
   - ○ false

NATIONAL AND LOCAL COVERAGE DETERMINATIONS

The National Coverage Determinations (NCDs) or Local Coverage Determinations (LCDs) are available to provide guidance on Medicare coverage. The NCDs describe whether Medicare pays for specific medical items, services, treatment procedures or technologies. In the absence of an NCD, the LCDs indicate which items and services Medicare considers reasonable, medically necessary, and appropriate. In most cases, the availability of this information indicates that the organization knew, or should have known, that Medicare would deny the item or service as not medically necessary.

In order to practice the ability to identify Medicare covered services, click on the link below and locate the National Coverage Determination (NCD) for Mammograms (220.4) and answer the following coverage determination question:

> Please go online to download the document that appears here.

Keep in mind that the patient's registration form needs to be updated at a minimum annually. Before releasing private patient information to insurance carriers, patients must give signed authorization as to not violate HIPAA regulations for patient confidentiality. In addition, a photocopy of both sides of the patients' insurance identification cards needs to be part of the financial records. Each provider must have a system in place to maintain all documentation related to the patient's financial responsibility.

I. **MULTIPLE CHOICE.**
   Choose the best answer.

1. A radiological mammogram is a covered diagnostic test under which of the following?
   ○ A patient has distinct signs and symptoms for which a mammogram is indicated.
   ○ A patient has a history of breast cancer.
   ○ A patient is asymptomatic but, on the basis of the patient's history and other factors the physician considers significant, the physician's judgment is that a mammogram is appropriate.
   ○ all of the above

CLAIM SUBMISSION – 3RD-PARTY PAYER INFORMATION

A medical claim cannot begin correctly if the correct health insurance and billing information is not collected and kept up to date. Billing information (along with other demographic information) is usually collected when the patient comes in for treatment. Patient information is re-verified at each visit to ensure records are up to date. This information allows the submission to go to the correct place with the correct identifiers.

Front Side of Insurance Card:

I.D. Number – This identifies the patient and the patient's family members to the third-party payer.

Name – The subscriber name (employee) is typically shown here.

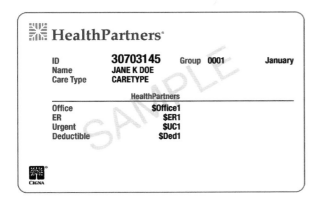

Claims Submission – Indicates where paper claims are to be mailed (if permitted) and how electronic claims are to be processed. There is other important information on this side of the card that pertains to verification of benefits, prior approval for services, and prescription coverage.

Care Type – Indicates the type of plan the patient has with the third-party payer.

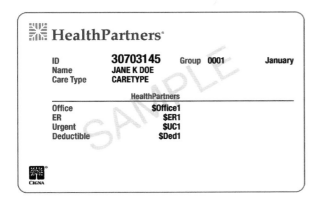

I. TRUE/FALSE.
Mark the following true or false.

1. It is the patient's responsibility to make sure all up-to-date demographic and insurance information is on file at the healthcare provider.
   - ○ true
   - ○ false

2. A financial responsibility form signed by the patient assigns the patient or guardian responsibility of any part of a claim that is unpaid by the third-party payer.
   - ○ true
   - ○ false

3. It is illegal for healthcare providers to copy or duplicate patients' insurance cards.
   ○ true
   ○ false

4. An insurance policy indicated on a single insurance card can cover more than one person.
   ○ true
   ○ false

CLAIM FORMS

Two different claim forms, UB-04 and CMS-1500, are used to bill healthcare services regardless of the third party payer. The UB-04 is the claim form used to bill inpatient and outpatient facility charges: surgery centers, freestanding radiology clinics, laboratories, hospitals, skilled nursing, and emergency rooms. The CMS-1500 is the claim form used to bill professional services: surgeon's fees for a surgery performed at an outpatient surgery center or an emergency physician's fee for professional services provided in the emergency room.

Let's look at a couple of examples:

> Dorothy cuts her finger preparing Sunday dinner and goes to the Valley Emergency Room. The ER doctor, Dr. Ross, examines her and requests an x-ray of the finger. An x-ray is performed and read by the radiologist, Dr. Greene. Dr. Ross stitches the laceration and discharges Dorothy.

UB-04: Hospital Emergency Room facility charges, suture kit, x-ray, bandages, anesthetic, and other supplies are billed on the UB-04 as outpatient charges by Valley Hospital. The hospital bills for the facility, equipment, and supplies.

CMS-1500: Emergency room physician charges, professional services for emergency care and suturing by Dr. Ross are billed on CMS-1500. Radiologist professional charges for Dr. Greene's reading of the x-ray are billed on CMS-1500. The professional services are billed by the professional provider who provides services at the outpatient facility.

> Henry's orthopedist, Dr. Lewis, recommends rotator cuff surgery since all of the conservative treatments for shoulder pain and immobility have failed. Dr. Lewis schedules Henry's surgery at the Chugach Surgery Clinic. Henry undergoes successful same-day surgery rotator cuff repair at the Chugach Surgery Clinic.

UB-04: Chugach Surgery Clinic bills the surgery and recovery room care charges, supplies, drugs, and surgical equipment because Chugach Surgery Clinic owns the facility and the equipment and supplies used to perform the surgery.

CMS-1500: Dr. Lewis bills professional services for performance of the rotator cuff surgery. The anesthesiologist for the surgery also bills his professional services separately on CMS-1500.

> We've placed a visual aid in the appendix on page 400.

I. **MULTIPLE CHOICE.**
   Choose the claim form that would be used in each situation.

   1. Jim falls on his wrist while skateboarding and goes to the emergency room where he has an x-ray. What form would be used for the x-ray charges?
      ○ UB-04
      ○ CMS-1500

   2. What form would be used for the reading of the x-ray charges?
      ○ UB-04
      ○ CMS-1500

   3. Jim's wrist is put in a cast. Which form would be used to charge for the casting materials?
      ○ UB-04
      ○ CMS-1500

   4. What form would be used to charge for the doctor's professional services for casting Jim's wrist?
      ○ UB-04
      ○ CMS-1500

SUBMITTING A CLAIM

Claims are prepared for submission after healthcare services are rendered. Care is then documented and charges are entered according to the provider's process. All claims must contain diagnosis and procedure codes that are assigned based on the provider's documentation. Code assignment process varies according to the provider. Diagnoses and procedures may be selected by a physician in an electronic health record system. Inpatient admissions have codes assigned after discharge by a certified medical coder. Other settings have their own processes. Regardless of the process, all the diagnosis and procedure codes are selected based on the physician's documentation. Audits are performed to make sure that all billable services are appropriately coded. Audits will be covered in a future unit of this module.

In order for claims to be reimbursed efficiently and accurately, the submission process must be completed in an exacting manner. There have been some excellent advances in this process in recent years that have made the entire claims process much simpler, quicker, and more accurate.

Here is an example of an outpatient physician visit submission. The following should be produced and maintained for each patient upon each visit:

- Patient registration
- Receipted copayment from patient
- Correctly coded encounter form. Charges will be totaled for all services performed. These same codes should be verified against the patient's medical record before the claim is filed.
- Charges should be entered into patient's account
- Claim form should be completed
- Supporting documentation (as needed) should be attached to the claim. (This is needed for certain codes that require further information or to review and verify past payments.)
- A copy of the claim should be made and stored in the facility
- Claim form to be submitted to third-party payer

The manner of the claim submission will depend upon the medical provider's system—most commonly for electronic submissions, though some may be paper-based. Claims submitted electronically (via the Internet or a private network) have the advantage of being received quickly, making the entire processing time quicker.

CLAIMS PROCESSING

The way a claim is processed depends very much upon the way the submission was made. In the past claims were traditionally submitted by mail. When working in an office that still uses a paper-based system, careful review of the CMS-1500 for errors or omissions is indicated. Approximately 1/3 of all paper-based submissions are initially rejected due to incorrect or incomplete claim forms. These rejections will result in resubmissions that will take up valuable time and delay payment. The CMS-1500 form is described in great detail in the next unit.

We've placed a visual aid in the appendix on page 384.

Paper-based claims processing looks like this:

Third-party payers receive mailed claims forms and date them (date received).

They are organized by the payer or they are scanned electronically.

Third-party payers enter the information into their own claims software.

Claim is reviewed by claims examiner for validation of information.

Recently, however, electronic submissions have become the standard of many healthcare providers and a requirement of many third-party payers. Because of new Medicare regulations, a reduced operating cost, and updated HIPAA mandates, electronic submissions are used by nearly all healthcare providers. There are several ways that electronic submissions can be made:

- A provider may complete the claim using specialized software and submit it to the third-party payer
- A provider may enter essential data into a database and have a clearinghouse (see below) complete and submit the claim
- A provider may hire a company to complete and file the claim based on the information gathered at the office

There are many advantages to the electronic claims submission. Using software to complete a claim form allows for an electronic review of the claim prior to submission. This eliminates many of the small errors that would otherwise create a rejection of the claim (and a delay in payment). These electronic claims can then be filed over the Internet or a similar network), cutting down on time in transit.

With the advent of the electronic claim filing came several new needs: a way to make the format of claims coming from many different types of software more universal; a need to pre-screen the electronic submissions for errors; a need to distribute the submissions to the correct third-party payers; and a need to handle data. This is where the clearinghouse comes in. A **clearinghouse** is a company contracted by the third-party payers to handle and format submissions, screen claims, and make data available to providers. The clearinghouse has pre-edits built in so claims that do not meet the clean claim requirements are sent back to the providers to be reviewed, to have errors corrected, and to be resubmitted once they are correct. The goal is to submit a clean claim. A **clean claim** is a complete and accurate claim form that includes all provider and member information, as well as records, additional information, or documents needed from the member or provider to enable the payer to process the claim. The clean claim date is the date on which all such necessary information has been received. Only clean claims are then submitted from the clearinghouse to the third-party payer; however, this does not mean the provider will still not receive rejections on the claims that were sent on by the clearinghouse.

The clearinghouses actually save the insurance companies money because they reduce the amount of time spent reviewing claims, altering formats, and sending and receiving information to and from the providers. The electronic files are easily stored and recalled when needed. And, as with all parties involved in medical information transference, clearinghouses must meet HIPAA guidelines.

All of this electronic billing is made possible by electronic data interchange (EDI). The EDI allows data to be transferred between different computer systems or computer networks. These networks allow for electronic data interchange (EDI). An example of EDI is the electronic transmission of health insurance claims rather than paper-based claims. It is important that there are standards and procedures in place so that the receiving computer can interpret the data transmitted. In 1996, the National Institute of Standards and Technology defined electronic data interchange as "the computer-to-computer interchange of strictly formatted messages that represent documents other than monetary instruments." In the EDI there of course are two parties, and either one can serve as the originator or recipient. "The documents may be sent via telecommunications or physically transported on electronic storage media." The U.S. standard ANSI ASC X12 is used in North America. The ANSI is the American National Standards Institute and the ASC X12 stands for the Accredited Standards Committee X12. This committee is made of government and industry members from North America. This committee was chartered in 1979 by ANSI to create uniform standards for all electronic data interchange documents. This committee meets three times each year to develop and maintain standards. The U.S. Federal Government has endorsed the use of the ANSI X12 standards for EDI with the government. The previous version 4010 has been updated with version 5010 which allows for the billing of ICD-10-CM/PCS code sets.

So in the end, whether filing via mail or electronically, the processing steps get the claim to the right party in the right format so payment decisions can be made quickly and accurately.

I. **MULTIPLE CHOICE.**
   Choose the best answer.

   1. Most claims today are filed _____.
      ○ late
      ○ on paper
      ○ electronically
      ○ by the coder

   2. The claim itself must be filed on the _____.
      ○ CMS-1500
      ○ AHIMA-100
      ○ CMV
      ○ PPO-E

   3. An advantage of the electronic claim is _____.
      ○ increased speed
      ○ decreased errors
      ○ decreased cost
      ○ all of the above

4. A clearinghouse acts as a liaison between _____.
   ○ the coder and the biller
   ○ the patient and the healthcare provider
   ○ the healthcare provider and the third-party payer
   ○ the insurance company and the third-party payer

5. One of the duties of the clearinghouse is to _____.
   ○ contact the patient about errors in the claim
   ○ pre-edit claims for errors
   ○ bill patients for unpaid claims
   ○ provide superbills to providers

CLAIMS ADJUDICATION

The detailed work by the payer begins in the **claims adjudication** process. By definition, *adjudication* means rendering a decision or making a judgment. While this may sound like claims are judged subjectively, the process is very objective and follows a very strict protocol.

In general, the adjudication process is as follows:

Step 1 – The adjudication process begins by comparing the patient information and demographics on the claim to the information and demographics on the policy. This verifies that the correct person is identified on the claim and that person is eligible for benefits. If the identifying information is not the same, the claim is rejected.

> ### Highlights
>
> Medical claims are not judged or evaluated subjectively. There are very strict guidelines payers follow when determining payment of a claim. This does not mean, however, that a payer and a physician may not have different opinions on how a claim is or is not paid.

Step 2 – The next step in the process is a check of the diagnostic and procedure codes. The codes listed on the claim are compared against those on the list of covered codes for that particular policy. The procedure codes are checked to make sure they correspond to the diagnosis codes and represent a necessary medical procedure. At this point in the process, the claim is also checked to ensure proper authorization (or preauthorization) was obtained for any procedure that the policy states requires such. The claim may be rejected if there are codes on the claim that are not covered by the policy, if a procedure is deemed medically unnecessary, or if proper authorization was not obtained.

Step 3 – The adjudication process continues with a check of the **common data file**. The common data file is an overview of claims recently filed on the patient. It is reviewed to make sure there are no duplicate claims and to check to see if the claim is related to other procedures performed recently.

Step 4 – Next, the payer determines what the allowed charges are for each service on the claim. The **allowed charge** is simply the amount the policy states is payable for a particular procedure. Using this payment figure, the payer can then determine the **deductible** (the amount the insured must pay yearly before benefits begin) and the **coinsurance** (the percentage of the bill the patient pays once the deductible is met).

Step 5 – The adjudication process is now complete. All payment determinations have been made regarding third-party payer obligations and policyholder obligations. The next step is to inform the medical service provider and the policyholder of the determinations made.

I. MATCHING.
Match the correct term to the definition.

1. ___ adjudication
2. ___ coinsurance
3. ___ allowed charge
4. ___ deductible
5. ___ common data file

A. an overview of claims recently filed on the patient
B. the amount the insured must pay yearly before benefits begin
C. the amount the policy states is payable for a particular procedure
D. the percentage of the bill the patient pays once the deductible is met
E. the process of reviewing a claim and deciding what claims are to be paid

CLAIM INFORMATION

Hard Copy Notices

It is important that there is a free flow of information between the policyholder, the healthcare provider, and the third-party payer. Because there are so many millions of claims made each year, it is impossible for payers to spend an exorbitant amount of time explaining each claim. Payers have a system of explaining the claim payment to the healthcare provider (so they will know what payments to expect and they will know how to bill the policyholder) and to the policyholder (so he/she will know what was covered and what will need to be paid).

Upon completion of the adjudication process, the third-party payer will send out a **remittance advice** (RA) or an **explanation of benefits** (EOB) to the healthcare provider, though they differ. A remittance advice contains information of multiple claims to one provider; whereas the EOB is one patient's explanation of the paid services. The provider will review the document for consistency and check it against the claim they filed. These are often sent electronically to expedite the process. Explanations of benefits don't all look identical although they generally contain the same types of information. The look and the details of the explanation of benefits vary from third-party payer to third-party payer. When a check or other form of payment accompanies the explanation of benefits, it is often referred to as the remittance advice. Government third-party payers' notifications to providers are also often called remittance advices. Either an Electronic Remit Advice (ERA) or a Standard Paper Remit (SPR) is sent including payment information and final claim adjudication once a claim is processed.

We've placed a visual aid in the appendix on page 401.

We've placed a visual aid in the appendix on page 402.

The third-party payer will also send out an EOB to the policyholder. This contains information about the patient, the services, and the claim so the patient can review it for accuracy and completeness.

Following are examples of EOBs and how they are used to explain benefits and payments:

The patient, is the 6-year-old daughter of an employee with insurance through work. The insurance company receives a claim for the visit to the family physician. Because this is a first claim, the Insurance contacts the employer to make sure that the child has been added as a dependent to the employee's policy prior to processing the claim. If the employer verifies that the child has been added as a dependent, the insurance company will continue processing the claim. **If the employer does not show the child has been added to her parent's policy, the claim will not be processed.**

In the instance where the insurance company checked with the employer and found the child was not added to the employee's policy, an explanation of benefits would be sent to the family physician showing the insurance determination that no payment is made because the child is not covered by the policy.

An insurance company has received a claim for a routine office visit. It was determined that patient is covered and the claim is medically appropriate. The reviewer looks up the details of Patient's policy. The policy states patient must pay the first $200 in medical expenses each calendar year, and then the charges are paid 80% by the insurance company and 20% by the patient. The reviewer determines the patient has already paid $200 this year, so the insurance company pays 80% of the allowed amount to the doctor's office. The patient receives a statement from the insurance company showing their benefit determination and a bill from the physician for the remaining 20%.

An explanation of benefits would be sent to the patient's physician's office and to the patient. The explanation of benefits would show the date of visit, the provider, the total charge, the amount covered by the insurance, and the amount the patient is responsible to pay based on the insurance company's 80/20 determination of benefits.

There are some EOB terms and categories common to all carriers. Insurance carriers often use codes on the EOB to refer to these terms or situations. These codes are called reason codes and remark codes. Usually these codes are explained on the face or back of the EOB. If one line is read at a time, the descriptions and calculations for each patient are easily understood. An EOB statement has three sections that explain how a claim was processed:

1. Service Information. Identifies the provider (hospital or other facility, doctor, specialist, or clinic), dates of service, and charges from the provider.
2. Coverage Determination. Summarizes the total deductions, charges not covered by the plan, and the amount the patient may owe the provider.
3. Benefit Payment Information. Indicates who was paid, how much, and when.

Posting Payments

After posting the payment to the specific date and procedure, an adjustment may be needed. An adjustment is a positive or negative change to a patient's account balance. Corrections, changes, and write-offs to patients' accounts are made by means of adjustments to the existing transaction. A **write-off** is the difference between total charge and the allowable amount by the insurance. The patient's bill might also be adjusted as a result of any discounts given. If the provider is a PAR (participating) provider, the difference between the billed amount and the allowed amount is adjusted from the amount the patient owes. Also note whether a balance is due from the patient, or whether a refund is due the patient or insurance carrier.

Inquiries

A patient or provider need not wait until the EOB is received to find out what is happening with a claim. The status of a claim can be accessed any time during or after the claim process by making an **inquiry**. An inquiry can be made via a written request, but technology has made inquiries quicker and more up-to-date. Most healthcare providers will have electronic access to a claim's status, allowing them to see where in the process that particular claim is.

Reconciling a Claim

Providers may make inquiries via mail, computer, or phone for several reasons. Perhaps the payer has not responded to a claim in a timely manner (it usually takes 4 to 6 weeks for paper-based submissions, less for electronic submissions). Or maybe the claim was completed but payment was not made. Maybe there was a discrepancy in the amount paid and the amount indicated on the completed claim. It could be that there is a difference in the codes that were submitted and the codes that were listed on the Remittance advice. This happens when an insurance company's coverage policies exclude coverage for an appropriately submitted procedure code. The remittance advice sent by the insurance company may list the code for the procedure that they will cover in lieu of the originally submitted code. It is important to remember to submit the appropriate code for the actual procedure performed and not the code that the provider knows the insurance company will cover. Coding based on insurance company coverage policy is inappropriate reporting and may be viewed as fraud.

MANAGING CLAIMS

A medical coder/biller will be obligated legally and professionally to maintain medical claims in an organized, easily accessible system. According to the CMS, any claims filed to Medicare, Medicaid, or any other government entity must be kept for at least 5 years. If the claim was made electronically, the superbill, abstract, or encounter form used to create the claim and the remittance advice must be kept for the same amount of time.

Claims will be kept in two files: open claims and closed claims.

>   **Open/Pending claims** – claims that have not yet completed the claims processing cycle. Open claims may have been recently submitted, re-submitted, or appealed; whatever the case, they have not been completed.

>   **Closed/Paid claims** – claims for which the entire process has been completed. Open and closed claims may be organized and filed by date and/or the third-party payer to whom they were submitted.

A billing clerk or billing specialist in the provider's office will be responsible for keeping track of paid and unpaid claims and remainders. There are several ways that this can be done. Most offices will run an **aging report** that reconciles claims by date (current, 30 days unpaid, 60 days unpaid, etc.). The biller can then look into the unpaid claims and take appropriate action. Some offices may use a **claims log** or **claims register** into which all claims are entered. They are first put into the log when the claims are filed and all applicable information is included in the log. When payments are received, they are reviewed for accuracy and entered into the log. Any notes needed regarding the payment, patient billing, or status of the claim may be entered.

We've placed a visual aid in the appendix on page 403.

We've placed a visual aid in the appendix on page 404.

The medical biller will reconcile the closed claims and bill the first-party payer (policyholder) for any remaining charges. Statements that show date of service, service provider, and itemized charges are standard for billing first-party payers.

We've placed a visual aid in the appendix on page 405.

As a medical biller, financial duties are common at the end of each month. All charges and deposits are posted and aging reports checked to ensure that they are up to date and all invoices have been sent. The exact way in which this is done will depend upon the type of office, your individual duties in regard to billing, your employer's preferences, and the billing software/system used.

Of course, one of the most time-consuming parts of medical billing will be following up on claims that have been denied, rejected, or paid at a reduced rate. The physician and his/her staff may question the validity of the rejection or reduced payment and decide to follow up on the claim. In this case, before filing an appeal, a polite phone call should be made to see if the issue can be resolved. If it cannot, a letter should be sent to the payer stating that, in the physician's judgment, there has been an incorrect payment of the claim.

Organizations are continuously looking at ways to decrease payment delays and lost revenue through their revenue cycle management (RCM) process. Just like maintaining the chargemaster, the RCM is a team approach and involves all those involved in the billing cycle. Each part of the revenue cycle is important to an efficient and compliant reimbursement of healthcare claims. The process is consistent across different types of facilities, although the terminology may change somewhat depending on the size of the organization.

There are four major steps in the RCM and they are:

1. Preclaims submission
2. Claims processing
3. Accounts receivable
4. Claims reconcilation and collections

Each of these steps requires all members of the team working together. The process is involved and includes the data entry clerks, coding professionals, billing professionals, and all involved in finance, and certainly others on the team. The importance of the CDM update process was previously discussed, and how it impacts correct code assignment. Even members of the clinical team are involved in the CDM maintenance process.

Following is an example showing how the CPT® codes in the chargemaster might be updated. In 2012, CPT code 90791, psychiatric diagnostic interview has changed to code 90801 in 2013. The chargemaster must reflect current codes, so the chargemaster maintenance team would identify any changed codes, and make necessary changes to the database. Another example is that 2012 CPT identified gastrointestinal tract transit and pressure measurement, stomach through colon, wireless capsule, with interpretation and report as Category III code 0242T. In 2013, this same procedure became CPT code 91112. The chargemaster team would make the changes in the database to reflect this change.

The coders are responsible for the coding which then affects the billing. Many organizations have a standard coding turnaround time. Discharges that have not been billed are often called discharged not final billed (DNFB) and of course delays impact potential revenue. For this reason, the financial and billing services are closely involved in the revenue cycle management. Many large facilities, such as acute care hospitals find that the HIM department reports directly to the Chief Financial Officer (CFO) for these reasons.

I. MULTIPLE CHOICE.
Choose the best answer.

1. Who typically needs to review EOBs and RAs sent by the third- party payers?
   - ○ the policyholder
   - ○ the healthcare provider
   - ○ both A and B
   - ○ neither A nor B

2. To maintain an accurate record of claims and payments, many healthcare providers will use what?
   - ○ a common data file
   - ○ an aging report
   - ○ coinsurance
   - ○ secondary insurance

3. In a physician's office who is ultimately the person in charge of deciding whether or not to follow up on a denied claim?
   - ○ the coder
   - ○ the biller
   - ○ the patient
   - ○ the physician

4. How can inquiries pertaining to a claim can be made?
   - ○ by mail
   - ○ electronically
   - ○ by phone
   - ○ all of the above

5. Which of the following is NOT a reason to make an inquiry about a claim?
   - ○ A payment is made but not for the correct amount.
   - ○ A claim is not processed on time.
   - ○ A remittance advice is sent to the healthcare provider.
   - ○ The codes on the RA do not match those on the claim.

APPEALING CLAIMS

The fact of the matter is that claims are not always paid. Throughout this unit, many reasons have been mentioned on why a claim may not be paid. When a claim is denied, you will gather all of the information relevant to the claim and review it: the claim form, the remittance advice or EOB, the remark codes by each claim line explaining why this claim was rejected, the patient's medical record documentation, and the 3rd-party payer's fee schedule (if one is provided). If a review of these forms seems to support a payment of the claim—and if that support is well documented—the physician may wish to appeal the claim.

Appeals are often made if:

A claim is denied for lack of pre-authorization but there were evident reasons why pre-authorization could not be obtained.

A claim is denied because the payer deems a procedure not medically necessary, yet the physician believes it was medically necessary.

The third-party payer denies a claim based on a pre-existing condition that the physician does not believe falls under the terms of pre-existing conditions.

Payment is denied without reason or a lower payment is made without adequate explanation.

Services are bundled and only one of the bundled codes will be reimbursed.

No modifiers are used (however, the third-party payer will not directly state this is missing).

The appeal process may vary slightly depending upon the third-party payer, but most of the steps are very similar. The appeal must be made in writing and must state the reason for the appeal (some carriers, like Medicare and Tricare, have forms to be filled out that will act as the written request). Since most carriers have a set time in which an appeal must be made, timeliness is important. There is a window in which appeals must be started they must be dated and make copies of all documents used in appeals process. Attached to this written appeal will be all supporting documents and records.

Following Up on Appeals

The third-party payer will review the appeal. (They usually have internal time limits on their review process, as well—typically 30 days.) They will inform the provider of their decision through a phone call or a letter. If unsatisfied with the decision, the payer may allow for one or more followup "levels" of appeal. At this point, if the payer's decision is still unsatisfactory, there are steps that can be taken. Some payers will use an objective peer review. The **peer review** is a group of physicians who can review the claim as well as the supporting documentation and arbitrate the differences between the payer and the provider. They can decide, based on the medical care, the necessity of the procedures performed or services provided, and the payments made, whether the healthcare provider is entitled to a payment or partial payment.

Government insurers, such as Medicare and Tricare, have more prescribed steps in the appeal and review process. These should be followed exactly and within the time limits set forth by their guidelines. For more information on Medicare appeals, visit their website:www.medicare.gov/Pubs/pdf/11525.pdf.

For Tricare appeals information, visit their website: http://www.mccshh.com/pdf/tricare_claims_process.pdf.

I. TRUE/FALSE.
Mark the following true or false.

1. Documentation is important to making an appeal.
   - ○ true
   - ○ false

2. If a physician believes a treatment was medically necessary but the insurance company does not, the provider can appeal the claim.
   - ○ true
   - ○ false

3. Once an appeal is denied, the appeals process has ended.
   - ○ true
   - ○ false

4. Peer reviews are done by adjudicators from insurance companies.
   - ○ true
   - ○ false

5. Appeals processes vary from one third-party payer to the next.
   - ○ true
   - ○ false

UNIT 5

Completing the CMS-1500 Claim Form

COMPLETING THE CMS-1500 CLAIM FORM – INTRODUCTION

In the second half of the twentieth century the healthcare industry recognized a need to organize and centralize the medical claims process. At the time, there were several different types of claim forms being used for the many available private and government carriers. The American Medical Association teamed up with the Centers for Medicare & Medicaid Services (CMS) and the result was a uniform claim document that nearly all providers and payers could use—the CMS-1500 Claim Form.

While a government committee continues to standardize and adapt the form to be efficient and safe in the electronic age, the CMS-1500 that is used is not very different from the original form. The CMS-1500 form is approved by the National Uniform Claim Committee (NUCC). For more information, click here.

We've placed a visual aid in the appendix on page 384.

Because the components of this form are so important to the medical claim reimbursement system, time will be spent reviewing the process of completing the form for a claim. The standards for the CMS-1500 Claim Form are very exacting, and not being precise and consistent in filling out the form can lead to a claim's rejection. Each rejection and its consequential resubmission wastes valuable time for the billing/coding professional (which equates to money) and a delay in the payment of the claim.

Today, nearly all claims submissions are electronic. There are very few healthcare providers that are eligible to submit paper claims (they can petition to submit paper claims if hardware/software requirements impose an insurmountable financial burden). Even while using electronic submissions it is imperative to understand the CMS-1500 Claim Form in its entirety. When questions, problems, or rejections arise, the form is used to identify particular questions and what the requirements for that part of the form are. The paper process will be covered, along with comments and tips for filling out the form for different payers (mainly Medicare) and when using software.

The CMS 1500 is used by non-institutional healthcare organizations, including physicians and the UB-04 claim form is used in hospitals. The electronic version of the CMS 1500 paper claim is the 837P and the electronic version of the UB-04 is the 837I.

PREPARING DOCUMENTATION

Accurate and complete documentation of patients and encounters is vital. When completing the CMS-1500, all of the information gathered will be used and verified by the clearinghouse and carrier, so this information must be current, accurate, and complete. Remember, the CMS-1500 form is used to request payment from health insurance payers, like Medicare, after a patient has been treated for professional services.

In order to fill out the CMS-1500 Claim Form, several types of documentation are needed:

The patient registration form: This contains the patient's demographic information and health insurance payer information. This information must be up to date, and most practices will institute a policy of verifying the information upon each visit. This form is usually accompanied by photocopies of the insurance card(s) to ensure accurate spelling, group numbers, and contact information.

The patient health record documentation: The health record is comprised of all of the information pertaining to the assessment and treatment of the patient. Generally, these will be separated by encounter.

The superbill/encounter form: This preprinted form is filled out on each visit and contains the codes that are used in the particular healthcare setting. This form will have the diagnosis codes and procedure codes designated by the physician at the completion of the encounter.

We've placed a visual aid in the appendix on page 382.

Of course codebooks are required to assign the diagnosis and procedure codes for the visit. You will need:

ICD-10-CM codebook

CPT® codebook

HCPCS codebook

An encoder (software) may be used instead of codebooks

I. **TRUE/FALSE.**
   Mark the following true or false.

   1. The CMS-1500 was created to unify a scattered system of healthcare reimbursement claim styles.
      ○ true
      ○ false

   2. Most coders/billers will fill out their claim forms by hand.
      ○ true
      ○ false

   3. The encounter form/superbill is vital because it contains all of the patient's demographic information.
      ○ true
      ○ false

   4. You will use your codebooks to verify the codes that appear on the documentation from the patient's visit.
      ○ true
      ○ false

   5. Demographic information for a patient can change from one visit to the next.
      ○ true
      ○ false

THE PAPER CLAIM

A claim can be made in one of two ways: on paper or in electronic format. Paper claims will be discussed first. Even though much of the healthcare industry's information transfer has become electronic, there are still CMS-1500 paper claims made for small physician offices. Understanding the process as well as understanding all the field locators is crucial to efficient and accurate claims submissions.

The term **paper claim** refers to any form that is submitted to the third-party payer on paper, whether it is typed or completed on a computer and printed on the computer's printer.

CMS-1500 forms completed in paper form are usually done using computer software that allows the biller to enter the information into the program and print it out on the CMS-1500 form. Because many third-party payers will use an optical scanner to convert a paper claim to an electronic format, the paper claim must be filled out following some very strict guidelines (otherwise, the scanner cannot read it). The CMS-1500 Claim Form has three boxes in both the upper-left and upper-right margins with the word *PICA* beside them. This is there so the biller can check the alignment and type size of the typewriter or printer. A **pica** is a measurement of text that is used in design and print. In a hand submission, a size 10 print will fit into those boxes correctly. Misalignment resulting in an error in scanning is a viable reason for claim rejection. In an electronic submission, those boxes are not used.

> ## Highlights
>
> Today, nearly all CMS-1500 forms are filed electronically as mandated by the Administrative Simplification Compliance Act. Some practices may apply for a waiver and be granted permission to use the paper form for submissions if:
>
> 1. They have fewer than 10 full-time employees
> 2. The submissions are for vaccinations given in a place where use of a computer would not be hygienic or possible (senior center)
> 3. The submissions are to Medicare and have more than one primary payer

> We've placed a multi-page visual aid in the appendix on pages 406-411.

CMS-1500: ITEMS 1–3

When looking at the CMS-1500, you see that the form is broken into sections by dark dividing lines and each section is broken into smaller **fields**, or boxes. The sections are labeled on the right side and arrows are used to show the demarcation of the individual sections.

Carrier Information

The first section is marked "CARRIER" just to the right of the right-hand PICA boxes. Although there are no individual smaller fields in this large blank area, this is where the name and address of the third-party payer handling the claim will go. This will be typed in its entirety *in all capital letters with no periods or commas*. The only punctuation allowed in the carrier block is a hyphen in a zip code that has a 4-digit suffix. This may look strange because it is not standard in proper addresses, but it is necessary for the claim to be clean. Throughout the CMS-1500, all letters will be capitalized and limited punctuation will be used (this will be addressed individually).

```
┌──────────────────────────────────────────────────────────────────────────────────────┐
│                                           CHAMPION INSURANCE                            │
│  ┌──────┐                                 CLAIMS DEPARTMENT                             │
│  │ 1500 │                                 1463 ELM DRIVE                                │ CARRIER
│  └──────┘                                 LINCOLN TN 12345                              │
│  HEALTH INSURANCE CLAIM FORM                                                            │
│  APPROVED BY NATIONAL UNIFORM CLAIM COMMITTEE 08/05                                     │
│     PICA                                                                      PICA      │
│  1. MEDICARE    MEDICAID    TRICARE      CHAMPVA    GROUP      FECA    OTHER  1a. INSURED'S I.D. NUMBER         (For Program in Item 1) │
│                             CHAMPUS                 HEALTH PLAN BLK LUNG                                                               │
│   (Medicare #)  (Medicaid #) (Sponsor's SSN) (Member ID#) X (SSN or ID)  (SSN)   (ID)   YTH8568477882                                 │
│  2. PATIENT'S NAME (Last Name, First Name, Middle Initial)  3. PATIENT'S BIRTH DATE   SEX   4. INSURED'S NAME (Last Name, First Name, Middle Initial) │
│                                                               MM   DD   YY                                                            │
│  JOHNSON     MELANIE     J                                   04  18  1972 M    F        JOHNSON     MELANIE     J                      │
│  5. PATIENT'S ADDRESS (No., Street)          6. PATIENT RELATIONSHIP TO INSURED   7. INSURED'S ADDRESS (No., Street)                  │
└──────────────────────────────────────────────────────────────────────────────────────┘
```

The next section of the Claim Form is marked "PATIENT AND INSURED INFORMATION."

Item 1 will require identification of the type of health insurance held by the patient. The correct insurance type will be marked with a capital X

Item 1a is the identifying number of the person who is insured by the policy. This is found on the insurance identification card.

Item 2 will include the patient's full name—last name, first name, middle initial. Do not use punctuation or suffixes (e.g. Jr., III) unless it appears that way on the patient's insurance card.

Item 3 contains two fields. The first piece of information in this field is the patient's date of birth. This must be entered in the MM DD YYYY format (e.g. 09 22 20XX). There is also a place to indicate whether the patient is male or female in this field.

I. **MULTIPLE CHOICE.**
   Choose the best answer.

1. Which of the following is a correct entry line in the CARRIER section?
   ○ 220 N. LAKE DR.
   ○ 220 North Lake Drive
   ○ 220 NORTH LAKE DRIVE
   ○ 220 North Lake Drive

2. When "checking" a box in a field, what mark should you use?
   ○ Ã
   ○ x
   ○ *
   ○ X

3. Which of the following would be a correct entry for Item 2?
   - ○ Jack Smith Jr.
   - ○ Jonathon A Smith
   - ○ SMITH JONATHON A
   - ○ SMITH, JONATHON A

4. All patients will need to provide what information?
   - ○ insurance carrier
   - ○ insurance identification number
   - ○ type of insurance held
   - ○ all of the above

5. Which of the following would be a correct entry for Item 3?
   - ○ 08 10 1996
   - ○ 8 10 1996
   - ○ 08-10-1996
   - ○ 08 10-'96

PATIENT AND INSURED INFORMATION: ITEMS 4–9

Item 4 requires the insured's name. This is the name of the insurance policyholder (which may be the same as the patient). The name should be entered last name, first name, middle initial. Do not use suffixes (e.g. Jr., III) unless it appears that way on the patient's insurance card.

Item 5 will contain the patient's full address. It is broken into spaces for the street address, city, state, zip and telephone number. Enter these without any punctuation. The exception will be if the zip code contains a 4 digit suffix, it will be separated from the first five digits by a hyphen. Use no spaces or hyphens in the telephone number (the parentheses for the area code are provided).

Item 6 indicates what the relationship the patient is to the policyholder. If the patient is the policyholder, then self would be marked with an X.

Item 7 requires the full address of the insured to be entered. This should follow the same format as item 5.

Item 8 is required by some third-party payers. It asks for the marriage and employment status of the patient, and this may change from visit to visit, causing incorrect or out-of-date demographic information.

Item 9 asks for the other insured's name. This will be used if the patient is covered by secondary health coverage. The name of the policyholder of this secondary coverage will be entered in the same manner as the name in item 4.

The next few items all hinge upon whether there is a secondary insurer entered into Item 9:

Item 9a will include the group number of the secondary insurance. This will be written with no space and no punctuation.

Item 9b will include the birthdate (mm dd yyyy) and sex of the policyholder of the other insurance.

Item 9c asks for the employer or school attended by the policyholder of the secondary insurance.

Item 9d requires the name of the company or plan that was referenced in item 9.

1. MEDICARE MEDICAID TRICARE CHAMPUS CHAMPVA GROUP HEALTH PLAN FECA BLK LUNG OTHER ☐(Medicare #) ☐(Medicaid #) ☐(Sponsor's SSN) ☐(Member ID#) ☒(SSN or ID) ☐(SSN) ☐(ID)	1a. INSURED'S I.D. NUMBER (For Program in Item 1) YTH8568477882		

2. PATIENT'S NAME (Last Name, First Name, Middle Initial) JOHNSON MELANIE	3. PATIENT'S BIRTH DATE SEX MM 04 DD 18 YY 1972 M ☐ F ☐	4. INSURED'S NAME (Last Name, First Name, Middle Initial) JOHNSON MELANIE
5. PATIENT'S ADDRESS (No., Street) 13 MATTELL LN	6. PATIENT RELATIONSHIP TO INSURED Self ☒ Spouse ☐ Child ☐ Other ☐	7. INSURED'S ADDRESS (No., Street) 13 MATTELL LN
CITY MIDDLETON STATE WI	8. PATIENT STATUS Single ☐ Married ☒ Other ☐	CITY MIDDLETON STATE WI
ZIP CODE 53562 TELEPHONE (Include Area Code) (842) 7790450	Employed ☐ Full-Time Student ☐ Part-Time Student ☐	ZIP CODE 53562 TELEPHONE (Include Area Code) (842) 7790450
9. OTHER INSURED'S NAME (Last Name, First Name, Middle Initial) JOHNSON KEN D	10. IS PATIENT'S CONDITION RELATED TO:	11. INSURED'S POLICY GROUP OR FECA NUMBER 14980
a. OTHER INSURED'S POLICY OR GROUP NUMBER 568405	a. EMPLOYMENT? (Current or Previous) ☐ YES ☒ NO	a. INSURED'S DATE OF BIRTH SEX MM 04 DD 18 YY 1972 M ☒ F ☐
b. OTHER INSURED'S DATE OF BIRTH SEX MM 02 DD 25 YY 1978 M ☐ F ☒	b. AUTO ACCIDENT? PLACE (State) ☐ YES ☒ NO	b. EMPLOYER'S NAME OR SCHOOL NAME BUNYAN UNIVERSITY
c. EMPLOYER'S NAME OR SCHOOL NAME BUNYAN UNIVERSITY	c. OTHER ACCIDENT? ☐ YES ☒ NO	c. INSURANCE PLAN NAME OR PROGRAM NAME CHAMPION INSURANCE
d. INSURANCE PLAN NAME OR PROGRAM NAME CHAMPION INSURANCE	10d. RESERVED FOR LOCAL USE	d. IS THERE ANOTHER HEALTH BENEFIT PLAN? ☒ YES ☐ NO If yes, return to and complete item 9 a-d.
READ BACK OF FORM BEFORE COMPLETING & SIGNING THIS FORM. 12. PATIENT'S OR AUTHORIZED PERSON'S SIGNATURE I authorize the release of any medical or other information necessary to process this claim. I also request payment of government benefits either to myself or to the party who accepts assignment below. SIGNED SIGNATURE ON FILE DATE 01 20 2009		13. INSURED'S OR AUTHORIZED PERSON'S SIGNATURE I authorize payment of medical benefits to the undersigned physician or supplier for services described below. SIGNED SIGNATURE ON FILE

PATIENT AND INSURED INFORMATION

I. MATCHING.
Match the correct term to the definition.

1. ____ Person who was seen by the healthcare provider.

2. ____ Person or persons covered by an insurance policy.

3. ____ Plan responsible for paying any allowable charges not covered by the primary insurance.

4. ____ The subscriber who pays the premiums and in whose name the policy is written.

5. ____ The payer that pays expenses before any other coverage.

A. patient
B. secondary coverage
C. primary coverage
D. insured
E. policyholder

PATIENT AND INSURED INFORMATION: ITEMS 10–13

Item 10 is an important item. Mark "yes" or "no" for each of the questions regarding the patient's condition. Automobile, work, or possible liability claims are handled differently from other visits.

> **Item 10d** is reserved for local use. Some payers will request certain information be filled in here.

The next several items deal with the insured referenced in Item 1a and Item 4.

> **Item 11** this item is asking for the policy number of the *primary* policy as it appears on the insured's card (the insured listed in Item 4). Do not use spaces or hyphens in this field.

> **Item 11a** again refers to the primary policy. It asks for the insured's birth date (mm dd yyyy) and the insured's sex.

> **Item 11b** asks for the employer or school attended by the person insured by the primary insurance.

> **Item 11c** requires the name of the company or plan that was referenced in Item 1a.

Item 12 is a very important item. As with all medical documentation, the use and transmission of the CMS-1500 must meet HIPAA regulations. Because third-party payers require access to each patient's medical record, a signed release of medical information is required from each patient. While Item 12 has a place for patients to sign for the release of their medical records, nearly all healthcare providers today use a form specific to their facility that patients will sign giving permission to release medical information to their insurance company. If there is a signed and dated release of information on file (and it is not out of date), fill in "Signature on File" or "SOF." If an authorization is not on file, leave this space blank or enter "No Signature on File."

Item 13 is different from Item 12. While the information on the back of the CMS-1500 regarding Item 12 directs the reader to obtain permission to release medical records, Item 13 is asking for the reader to obtain permission to authorize payment from the third-party payer to the healthcare provider. Again, if there is a signed and dated release of information on file (and is not out of date), this should also contain an authorization of payment permission. If this is the case, fill in "Signature on File" or "SOF." If there is no authorization on file, leave this space blank or enter "No Signature on File."

With the completion of Item 13, the PATIENT AND INSURED INFORMATION section is complete.

Remember that these instructions are not specific to any one payer. Medicare, Tricare, Medicaid and certain commercial payers may have slightly different requirements for the different fields in the CMS-1500. For example, here are some detailed instructions from a BlueCross payer:

We've placed a multi-page visual aid in the appendix on pages 412-418.

To verify or find further instruction and examples, check the National Uniform Claim Committee's instructions found here: http://www.nucc.org/images/stories/PDF/claim_form_manual_v5-0_7-09.pdf.

I. **TRUE/FALSE.**
   Mark the following true or false.

   1. The policyholder and the patient are always the same person.
      ○ true
      ○ false

   2. Since most claim forms today are completed electronically, it is not necessary to have signed permission to release patient records.
      ○ true
      ○ false

   3. Authorization is needed by the patient to have the insurance company make payments to the healthcare provider that submitted the claim.
      ○ true
      ○ false

4. The insured's birth date must match the policyholder's birth date.

   ◯ true
   ◯ false

5. In Item 10, three fields must be "checked."

   ◯ true
   ◯ false

BEGINNING THE PATIENT OR SUPPLIER INFORMATION: ITEMS 14–18

Physician or Supplier Information

The next section on the right margin of the form is titled "PHYSICIAN OR SUPPLIER INFORMATION." This information will describe the story of when, why, what and where of the specific patient listed on this claim (the when—box 14, the why—box 21, the what—box 24-D, the where—box 24-B and box 32). Accuracy in all of these boxes is critical to properly inform the third-party payer of the details of the encounter. One wrong digit in the wrong box or numbers in a code transposed and the claim would be sent back as unprocessable due to invalid information.

Item 14 asks for the date of the current illness, accident, or pregnancy. Since there are really three options here as to the nature of the encounter, it is important to understand what they are requesting for each. Again, dates will be given in the mm dd yyyy format.

- If the claim is for an **illness**, the date of the first symptom recorded in the health record documentation should be used. If no date is given, the date of service (Item 24) will be used.
- If the claim is for an **injury,** the date of the accident or injury will be entered. This is absolutely required for Worker's Compensation claims and automobile accident claims.
- If the claim is for a **pregnancy**, the date of the last menstrual cycle is used.

Item 15 seems a bit odd after filling out the previous item. It asks for dates of similar illnesses. This item is not often used. It would be used if the documentation clearly indicates the patient had a similar illness at a prior date that is also documented. Medicare and many private insurers do not require this information so this item is often left blank.

Item 16 really deals solely with worker's compensation claims. These fields will have the beginning and ending dates the patient was unable to work (mm dd yyyy). Check with individual payers as to the requirements for this item because most do not require this to be filled in.

Item 17 requires the full name and the professional credentials of the physician who referred the service/supplies or who ordered the service/supplies. Even if a service was referred or ordered by a physician and was completed by a technician, the ordering physician's name goes in this space. The name is written first name *space* middle initial *space* last name *space* professional credentials. Do not use any punctuation.

Item 17a is no longer used as it was replaced by the National Provider Identifier number (Item 17b).

Item 17b is where the NPI number will go. HIPAA required all physicians and anyone else who will be reimbursed by insurance companies to apply for one of these numbers. The main purpose was to ease medical information transference. These numbers can be found on the National Plan and Provider Enumeration System <u>here</u>.

Item 18 is used when a physician admits a patient to a hospital for any length of stay. The coder/biller would enter the date of admission in the "from" box and the date the patient is discharged from the hospital in the "to" box. Note: The UB-04 form would be utilized by the hospital for inpatient encounters. The CMS-1500 form is utilized by the physician.

14. DATE OF CURRENT: MM DD YY ◄ ILLNESS (First symptom) OR INJURY (Accident) OR PREGNANCY(LMP)	15. IF PATIENT HAS HAD SAME OR SIMILAR ILLNESS. GIVE FIRST DATE MM DD YY	16. DATES PATIENT UNABLE TO WORK IN CURRENT OCCUPATION MM DD YY MM DD YY
02 13 2009		FROM 02 13 2009 TO 04 19 2009
17. NAME OF REFERRING PROVIDER OR OTHER SOURCE	17a.	18. HOSPITALIZATION DATES RELATED TO CURRENT SERVICES MM DD YY MM DD YY
DARLENE BROWN MD	17b. NPI 9371048686	FROM 02 13 2009 TO 02 20 2009

I. MULTIPLE CHOICE.
Choose the best answer.

1. When filling out item 14 for an injury, the date entered would be _____.
   - ⭕ the date of the visit to the healthcare provider
   - ⭕ the date of the claim
   - ⭕ the date of the injury
   - ⭕ the date of the first treatment

2. Item #18 deals with inpatient hospital length of stay. A patient was in the hospital on February 13, 2014–February 20, 2014. How would the dates appear in item #18?
   - ⭕ 021314 021314
   - ⭕ 02132014 02202014
   - ⭕ 2132014 2132014
   - ⭕ 21314 21314

3. The dates in item 16 deal with _____.
   - ⭕ dates that the patient was seen
   - ⭕ dates the patient was injured
   - ⭕ dates the patient could not work
   - ⭕ "from" and "to" dates the patient was ill

4. NPI numbers are required for _____.
   ○ all clearinghouses
   ○ any healthcare provider seeking reimbursement
   ○ patients injured in a work-related accident
   ○ physicians only

5. An accurate entry for item 17 would be _____.
   ○ Wilson, Allen A MD
   ○ ALLEN WILSON, MD
   ○ ALLEN A WILSON
   ○ ALLEN A WILSON MD

PATIENT OR SUPPLIER INFORMATION: ITEMS 19–23

Item 19 states that it is "reserved for local use." As the description says, some third-party payers want this box left blank, while others will provide instructions to put various information in here based on different circumstances. All third-party payers will want information in this box when billing an unlisted procedure CPT® code drug. Please refer to the individual payer for requirements for Item 19.

14. DATE OF CURRENT: MM DD YY 02 13 2009	ILLNESS (First symptom) OR INJURY (Accident) OR PREGNANCY(LMP)	15. IF PATIENT HAS HAD SAME OR SIMILAR ILLNESS. GIVE FIRST DATE MM DD YY	16. DATES PATIENT UNABLE TO WORK IN CURRENT OCCUPATION MM DD YY MM DD YY FROM 02 13 2009 TO 04 19 2009
17. NAME OF REFERRING PROVIDER OR OTHER SOURCE **DARLENE BROWN MD**	17a. 17b. NPI 9371048686		18. HOSPITALIZATION DATES RELATED TO CURRENT SERVICES MM DD YY MM DD YY FROM 02 13 2009 TO 02 20 2009
19. RESERVED FOR LOCAL USE			20. OUTSIDE LAB? $ CHARGES [X] YES [ ] NO 1353
21. DIAGNOSIS OR NATURE OF ILLNESS OR INJURY (Relate Items 1, 2, 3 or 4 to Item 24E by Line) 1. 719 46 2. 715 96		3. 4.	22. MEDICAID RESUBMISSION CODE ORIGINAL REF. NO. 23. PRIOR AUTHORIZATION NUMBER 9812375923

This box is used for many different situations. Sometimes compiling a simple excel spreadsheet may be useful to keep track of what a third-party payer requires in some of these boxes, especially when just getting started.

Item 20 is used for Medicare only. It is used when a physician pays an outside entity to perform a service. If the physician has an agreement to pay for the service himself and he wants to be reimbursed for the service, he will mark "yes" and enter the amount he paid for it. Payment is entered with no dollar sign and no decimal point and will all be entered to the left of the vertical dividing line.

Item 21 contains spaces for ICD-10-CM diagnosis codes to be entered. A maximum of four codes can be entered. Depending on the medical billing software the ICD-10-CM diagnosis codes are entered with or without the period.

Item 22 pertains to Medicaid only. You only use it when you are resubmitting a rejected claim for additional money or if there was a coding error that has been corrected. The code is typically the rejection code for that particular claim line and the original reference number is a number that has been assigned by Medicaid for that particular claim line. Verify with the state what they expect when resubmitting a corrected claim in that particular state.

Item 23 will be used if the third-party payer requires a preauthorization or precertification of a service. Usually these are reserved for inpatient services, but there are some outpatient services that require these. Medicare does not require preauthorization for services. Preauthorization/precertification numbers should be written with no spaces or punctuation.

PATIENT OF SUPPLIER INFORMATION: ITEM 24

Item 24 is the most detailed item concerning the encounter that there is on the CMS-1500. Item 24 is broken down into many parts, allowing one to give details of exactly *what* happened and *when* it happened.

Item 24A requests the dates of service in a "from___ to___" format. Report the dates of service in a mmddyyyy format (no spaces) because there are dividing lines embedded in the form. If reporting one day of service only, fill in the "from" column and put in the same date in the "to" column. Do not leave this column blank (or it may cause a rejection). However, if the physician saw a patient in the hospital for subsequent daily visits, enter in the "from" column the first date of the "subsequent visits" for that one code and in the "to" column enter the last day the physician visited for the same CPT® code.

Item 24B requires coding the place of service (POS) for each of the corresponding service dates. The POS codes are standard for every third-party payer. Every physician's office can create an internal code for the different place of services to distinguish one hospital from another if the physician(s) goes to multiple hospitals. The following is a sample chart of the standard POS codes recognized by all third-party payers.

POS CODE	PLACE OF SERVICE NAME
11	Physician Office
12	Patient's Home
13	Assisted Living
21	Inpatient Hospital
22	Outpatient Hospital
23	Emergency Room - Hospital
31	Skilled Nursing Facility
20	Urgent Care

Item 24C is generally only used for Medicaid. Indicate whether or not the patient's treatment was an emergency by marking Y (yes) or N (no).

Item 24D is broken into one large box with four small boxes. These allow for complete procedure, service, or supply codes. In the first box enter the CPT or HCPCS code. The remaining four boxes are used for up to four modifiers (a two-digit modifier per box). There is a note to explain unusual circumstances (which would apply to a modifier 99—unlisted code). In this instance, it is required to attach the patient's medical record and/or a written explanation of the service or procedure.

Item 24E asks for the diagnosis pointer. The pointer is the corresponding number(s) from Item 21 (the diagnosis codes). Adding the single-digit number next to a procedure code informs the payer of "why" the procedure was performed. This is also known as "linking" the diagnosis and procedure together. Payers use the information to verify the medical necessity of the procedure according to their guidelines. Make sure to enter the single-digit list number in this box and not the actual diagnosis code number.

Item 24F requires careful attention. Enter the charges in dollars and cents, which are separated by the embedded vertical line, for each procedure. Use no dollar signs or commas.

Item 24G requests the days or units for each service. Most services/procedures that are billed will have a unit of 1 since most services/procedures can only be billed once per 24 hours. However, there are always exceptions: if a medication comes in 15mg and the physician wants the patient to have 30mg, then the units would be 2 because 2 15mg units were given to the patient. Another example of billing multiple units would be billing subsequent hospital days. Remember, box 24A has "from" and "to" columns for the dates of service. The number of units counted would be the number of days starting with the date in the "from" column, all the days in between and including the date in the "to" column. The calculation is entered in the "units" column.

Item 24H pertains to Medicaid patients only. There is a special exam and form that needs to be filled out when performing this special exam. ESPDT- Early Screening Periodic Diagnosis and Treatment for children from birth to age 21. If the physician participates in this program, he must indicate if he has performed this evaluation on the claim form for appropriate reimbursement.

Item 24I may not be used. It is where the modifier explaining the type of identification number that will go in Item 24J belongs. If the payer requires an identification number in addition to the NPI number, that number will go in the shaded area of Item 24J and the modifier will be entered in the shaded area of Item 24I.

Item 24J will require the provider's NPI number in the unshaded blank and the additional identification number (if required) in the shaded area.

19. RESERVED FOR LOCAL USE			20. OUTSIDE LAB? YES ☐ NO ☒	$ CHARGES **1353**

21. DIAGNOSIS OR NATURE OF ILLNESS OR INJURY (Relate Items 1, 2, 3 or 4 to Item 24E by Line)	22. MEDICAID RESUBMISSION CODE ____ ORIGINAL REF. NO.
1. **M25 . 561** 3. ___ . ___	23. PRIOR AUTHORIZATION NUMBER **9812375923**
2. **M17 . 11** 4. ___ . ___	

24. A. DATE(S) OF SERVICE From MM DD YY	To MM DD YY	B. PLACE OF SERVICE	C. EMG	D. PROCEDURES, SERVICES, OR SUPPLIES (Explain Unusual Circumstances) CPT/HCPCS | MODIFIER	E. DIAGNOSIS POINTER	F. $ CHARGES	G. DAYS OR UNITS	H. EPSDT Family Plan	I. ID. QUAL.	J. RENDERING PROVIDER ID. #
1	01 19 2009	01 19 2009	11		99214 | 25	12	110 00	1		NPI	56446408112
2	01 19 2009	01 19 2009	11		20610 | RT	2	125 00	1		NPI	56446408112
3	01 19 2009	01 19 2009	11		J7321 |	2	300 00	1		NPI	56446408112
4					|					NPI	
5					|					NPI	
6					|					NPI	

PHYSICIAN OR SUPPLIER INFORMATION

I. MATCHING.
Match the correct term to the definition.

1. ____ A number used to correspond to the ICD-10 code listed earlier in the form.

2. ____ Unique identifier required by providers.

3. ____ Refers to the number of days, dosages, or number of injections administered.

4. ____ Allows dates to be shown with a beginning and ending date.

5. ____ Identifies where a service was administered.

A. From ____ To ____ format

B. units of service

C. diagnosis pointer

D. POS

E. NPI number

PATIENT OR SUPPLIER INFORMATION: ITEMS 25–33

Item 25 is for the provider's SSN or EIN. Every physician practice files a business name with the IRS when they apply for a Federal Tax ID number, which is also known as the Employer Identification Number (EIN). This identifies to the third-party payer which physician or physician practice rendered the services and to whom to make the check payable. It is also a verification method for the third party payer to see if this physician or physician group has reported services to them before. Another important fact is that this number is how the revenue that the practice receives is reported to the IRS. Whether entering the EIN or the SSN, no hyphens or spaces are used in this field.

Item 26 is where the patient's account number is entered. This number is assigned by the provider and should be entered with no spaces or hyphens.

Item 27 gives the third-party payer consent to mail the payment to the physician's office. For government plans such as Medicare, Medicaid and TRICARE and those third-party payers where the physician has a "signed contract," marking "yes" in box 27 means that the medical biller cannot bill the patient the difference between the charge amount and the allowed amount.

Item 28 indicates the total amount billed on the claim form. This is gathered by adding lines 1–6 together in Item 24F. Do not enter dollar signs, decimals, or commas.

Item 29 asks for the amount already paid and will generally be left blank when making submission to the primary insurer. If sending the claim to the secondary insurer, fill in the amount of the claim paid by the primary insurer. Do not use dollar signs, decimals, or commas.

Item 30 follows up on the previous two boxes. Generally this will be blank if the claim is going to the primary insurer. If the primary insurer has paid on the claim and the remainder is going to a secondary insurer, the difference would go in this box.

Item 31 requires the physician's signature, credentials, and date. If filling this out by hand, he/she would sign here or "SOF" would be entered. Software will complete this by inserting the physician's name and the date the claim is printed in the correct spaces.

Item 32 has a large space for the name and location where the service was provided. The instructions are pretty specific. Remember, no commas, periods, dashes or other forms of punctuations. These will throw off the spacing in electronic transmission of information. Most third-party payers require the following:

> Line 1: Name of facility (hospital name, physician office name, physical therapist clinic name to name a few)
>
> Line 2: Street address of facility (PO Box is not acceptable)
>
> Line 3: City, state postal code, zip code
>
> **Item 32a** is reserved for the NPI number of the service facility which is entered here with no dashes, hyphens, or spaces.
>
> **Item 32b** will be left blank.

Item 33 requires entering the healthcare provider clinic name that is filing the claim for payment. Keep in mind that the name that appears in this box must match the name that owns the EIN/Federal Tax ID number in box 25. Enter the full address (remember no punctuation is to be used unless a hyphen is needed in a 9-digit zip code), and telephone number (no parentheses, dashes, or spaces).

> **Item 33a** is reserved for the NPI number of the facility requesting payment which is entered here with no dashes, hyphens, or spaces.
>
> **Item 33b** will be left blank.

While some of the information may seem excessive or redundant, the goal of all of the information is to make information transfer accurate, safe, and efficient.

25. FEDERAL TAX I.D. NUMBER	SSN EIN	26. PATIENT'S ACCOUNT NO.	27. ACCEPT ASSIGNMENT? (For govt. claims, see back)	28. TOTAL CHARGE	29. AMOUNT PAID	30. BALANCE DUE
237654321	☐ ☒	836135	☒ YES ☐ NO	$ 535 | 00	$ 0 | 00	$

31. SIGNATURE OF PHYSICIAN OR SUPPLIER INCLUDING DEGREES OR CREDENTIALS (I certify that the statements on the reverse apply to this bill and are made a part thereof.)	32. SERVICE FACILITY LOCATION INFORMATION	33. BILLING PROVIDER INFO & PH # (842) 7790450
DARLENE BROWN 01202009	GARAGE FAMILY PHYSICIANS 1472 FAIRWAY RD MIDDLETON WI 53562	GARAGE FAMILY PHYSICIANS 1472 FAIRWAY RD MIDDLETON WI 53562
SIGNED DATE	a. 3030314711 b.	a. 3030314711 b.

I. **TRUE/FALSE.**
    Mark the following true or false.

1. The physician's SSN or EIN number should be entered exactly how they appear on their SSN or EIN card.

    ◯ true
    ◯ false

2. The SSN or EIN must match that filed for the clinic name in Item 33.

    ◯ true
    ◯ false

3. The physician must sign item 31 on all claims submitted.

    ◯ true
    ◯ false

4. If item 29 is left blank, that means no payment has yet been made on the claim.

    ◯ true
    ◯ false

5. Patient account numbers are universal and are assigned by insurance companies.

    ◯ true
    ◯ false

UNIT 6

Completing the UB-04 Claim Form

COMPLETING THE UB-04 CLAIM FORM – INTRODUCTION

The standard documents for seeking reimbursement in the healthcare industry are the CMS-1500 claim form and the UB-04 claim form. The claim forms were created specifically for different types of medical encounters. The CMS-1500 claim form is used specifically by physicians' offices. The UB-04 form is to be used by medical facilities.

Completing the form properly is critical to ensuring reimbursements are paid in a timely manner. The UB-04, like the CMS-1500, is typically submitted electronically and isoften completed with the aid of software specifically designed for the form. However, the software requires the proper information be gathered and entered and failing to do so can result in claim denials.

This unit discusses the UB-04 form and how to accurately complete it. Because the form is complex and an array of information is required, images of the various parts of the form will be used to illustrate correct format and documentation.

THE UB-04 CLAIM FORM

The History of the UB-04

For many years hospitals were forced to use different claim forms for all of the different payers they were billing. Because each payer required a different form, and because each form required different information (hospital codes were not standardized), reimbursement was not guaranteed to be quick or complete. In an effort to unify and streamline the hospital billing process, the National Uniform Billing Committee (NUBC) was created in the mid-1970s. The goal of this committee was to improve the hospital billing process by creating a uniform bill that required standardized information and presented it in a standardized format.

After many drafts and trials, the first form—the UB-82—was adopted in 1982. After a period of national adoption and a continued evolution of the form, the latest revision was implemented in 2007. This version was called the Uniform Bill-04 (UB-04) and is used today for filing for reimbursement by medical facilities. The UB-04 (also known as CMS-1450) is a red ink on white paper form, and at first glance it looks similar to the CMS-1500. Closer inspection, however, reveals a completely different document requiring a very different set of information. The UB-04 allows for compliance with all HIPAA standards and the electronic documentation transfer standards and addresses the issues of the evolving billing process, which are constantly changing in health information management.

Who Uses the UB-04?

Because facilities are required to use some different codes than physicians, and because facilities provide different accommodations and supplies for patients, a different billing format is required for these facilities. The UB-04 allows for the specific charges for procedures and care supplied by facilities. Common facilities that use the UB-04 are:

- Hospitals
- Nursing homes
- Ambulatory surgery centers
- Hospices
- Rehabilitation centers

A couple of examples of billing scenarios are presented.

An established patient went to see his family physician with a chief complaint of a sore throat and cough. The physician performed a problem focused history and exam. The physician also performed a strep test in the office, which was positive for strep. The medical decision making was low.

This visit would be coded for the strep throat diagnosis, the evaluation and management, and the strep test service. The encounter would then be recorded using the CMS-1500 form and submitted to the third-party payer.

A second patient was brought to the emergency room last night by his father. His chief complaint was right upper quadrant abdominal pain, nausea, and a high fever. The emergency room physician performed a level 3 hospital emergency department visit. During the evaluation, the presence of Rovsing's sign was indicated. The physician spoke with the father and explained the patient needed an appendectomy and explained all the risks to him. The decision to perform a laparoscopic appendectomy early in the morning was made. After the appendectomy, the patient was admitted to the hospital.

This visit would be coded for the diagnosis (acute appendicitis), the ER visit, and an ICD-10-PCS procedure code for the appendectomy. Also included on the UB-04 form would be the operating room charge, laboratory CPT codes, x-ray CPT codes (which are then also assigned revenue codes). The entire encounter (hospital stay) would then be coded with either a code book, encoder (a software program), or a computer-assisted coding software. All of the codes would be entered into the UB-04 claim form and submitted to the third-party payer from whom the patient receives coverage.

The UB-04 claim form will be reviewed item by item.

PATIENT INFORMATION – LESSON 1

We've placed a visual aid in the appendix on page 419.

The UB-04 is a single-page form containing 81 numbered items on the front side and some additional information printed on the back of the form. The numbered items on the form are referred to as *form locators* (since they will locate items on the form). These are typically shortened to *FLs*. There are variations in the size and number of boxes within the FLs, with many of the FLs containing multiple numbered or lettered items. Another thing to notice is that unlike the CMS-1500, the information is not grouped by the type of information requested. The items will presented in the order of the form locators.

There is an electronic handbook created by the National Uniform Billing Committee called the *Official UB-04 Data Specifications Manual* that explains and defines each form locator and explains how to properly complete the form. Because many of the codes needed to complete this form will come from this manual (or from the software program used in the medical billing department), this manual will be referenced often in this unit. It is not necessary at this time to have the manual, but when actually performing billing for a facility, it is important to follow this manual. Information about this manual and the NUBC is available at the NUBC website.

Other good references are located on the CMS website. Click here to view the UB-04 factsheet and the Medicare Claims Processing Manual Chapter 25:

www.cms.gov/Regulations-and-Guidance/Guidance/Manuals/downloads/clm104c25.pdf

Patient Information

Most of the patient information will come from the demographic information received at the time of registration at the facility. The fields related to patient information begin with FL 3.

FL 3a is the first item designated for patient information. This FL asks for the patient's control number, which many facilities will call the account number. This number is assigned by the facility. Inpatient account numbers are usually tied to each encounter. Since payers are billed for each encounter, this patient control number will be unique for each visit and will be tied to the billing of that visit. This number allows payment and correspondence to be designated for each particular encounter.

FL 3b is where a permanent patient medical record number goes. This number is tied to the patient's history and information that does not change from one visit to the next. This number is also assigned by the facility.

FL 4 is titled "Type of Bill." The NUBC Data Specifications Manual has a list of the types of bills that are submitted and the corresponding codes for these types of bills (TOBs). These numbers are 4 digits in length and the first digit is always a zero. However, the zero is not used when filing the UB-04 electronically. The other digits refer to the type of facility, the classification of the bill, and the frequency of the bill.

> A common TOB number is 0131 (for hospital outpatient services).
>
> The 0 is just a leading 0
>
> The first 1 stands for the type of facility – hospital
>
> The 3 stands for the classification of the bill – outpatient
>
> The final 1 stands for the frequency of the bill – it covers admittance through discharge
>
> Another common TOB number is 0111 (for hospital inpatient encounters)

FL 6 is the next patient information field. In this field, enter the dates of admittance ("from" date) and the date of discharge ("to" date). These will be entered in the MMDDYY format. The UB-04 requires no punctuation in most of the form locators (e.g., From 101412 To 101712).

FL 8 is titled "Patient Name" and is broken into two fields (8a and 8b). 8a is a patient identifier and is assigned by the third-party payer. If there is a patient identifier assigned that is not the same as the insurance subscriber number in FL 60, the payer may require this form locator to be filled in. Otherwise, the payer may allow it to remain blank.

FL 8b is the name of the patient and is entered in the LAST NAME   FIRST NAME   MIDDLE INITIAL format. Do not use punctuation between names.

FL 9 has spaces for FL 9a–FL9e.

> **FL 9a** is the patient's mailing address. Again, all letters should be capitalized and no punctuation should be used.

FL 9b is the city.

FL 9c is the two-letter state abbreviation.

FL 9d is the zip code and may contain as many as 9 numbers.

FL 9e is the country code and is used if the services were performed outside of the United States. Country codes can be found at www.ansi.org.

PATIENT INFORMATION – LESSON 2

FL 10 is for the patient's date of birth. This field is unique in that it requires a MMDDYYYY format for the date of birth (rather than a two-digit year). Ex. 12231981

FL 11 is for patient sex and should be designated M or F.

FL 12 is used for inpatient services and home healthcare services. Here the date of the service being billed is entered in the MMDDYY format.

FL 13 is used to report the hour of admission. This is required for inpatient services, but it may not be required by the third-party payer for other types of services. The time is recorded in two-digit format using a 24-hour clock format:

Time	Hour Code
3:00–3:59 AM	03
4:00–4:59 AM	04
5:00–5:59 AM	05

The rest of the hour codes follow this same pattern.

FL 14 is used to indicate the priority of the visit based on a single-digit code assignment. These code assignments are designated by the National Uniform Bill Committee and are as follows:

Code	Priority
1	Emergency visit in which medical treatment must be immediately administered to prevent disabling, severe, or life-threatening harm.
2	Urgent visit for immediate medical treatment.
3	Planned elective services.
4	Newborns born on the same date as their admittance date, which was recorded in FL 6. This code requires a subsequent code in FL 15.
5	For trauma patients treated at a trauma center or hospital that is verified by the American College of Surgeons (ACS) or designated by state or local authority.
9	There is no information concerning priority of visit.

FL 15 requires the use of the NUBC Data Specifications Manual. This FL is where the source of the referral for the encounter is coded. Each code in the manual has a detailed description of the source of the referral. There is also a section of special codes for newborns who were born on the admittance date.

FL 16 is used to record the hour of the patient's discharge. This FL uses the same manner of recording hours that was used in FL 13.

FL 17 can be a difficult field. This is where the patient's discharge status is recorded. The status is coded by using the NUBC Data Specifications Manual to match a detailed description of the patient's discharge status to a two-digit code. These codes are often updated so using the most recent online UB-04 manual is required.

FL 18–FL 28 There are 10 numbered boxes of equal proportion here that are for recording condition codes. The NUBC Official Data Specifications Manual lists many pages of condition codes that are used for indicating conditions of the claim that will ultimately give direction or information pertaining to the payment of the claim. These codes can apply to specific procedures listed on the claim form, the coverage status of a patient, details of the patient's treatment, or many of the dozens of other condition codes.

There certainly may be more than one code that applies to a claim and **all that apply must be listed**. This will take some familiarity with the different condition codes, some double checking of the NUBC Official Data Specifications Manual, and clear communication with the payers about their requirements. When listing multiple codes in these numbered boxes, they are listed from smallest number to largest number, with codes containing letters listed alphabetically after the numeric codes (e.g 01 68 AK C5).

FL 29 is used when a payer requires the state in which an automobile accident occurred be reported. Checking with the third-party payer concerning requirements will clarify when this is used.

¹ Faith United Hospital	2		3a PAT. CNTL # 525252				4 TYPE OF BILL
700 LaCross Ave			b. MED. REC. # 555999				135
City XX 12345			5 FED. TAX NO.	6 STATEMENT COVERS PERIOD FROM THROUGH		7	
9892223333			12-3456789	011907	012007		
8 PATIENT NAME a		9 PATIENT ADDRESS a 2014 ANNIE ST					
b STRONG WENDY		b DETROIT				c MI d 48234	e
10 BIRTHDATE	11 SEX	12 DATE	ADMISSION 13 HR 14 TYPE 15 SRC	16 DHR	17 STAT	18 19 20 21 CONDITION CODES 22 23 24 25 26 27 28	29 ACDT STATE 30
07241951	F	011907	22 2 1	04	01		

I. MULTIPLE CHOICE.
Choose the best answer.

1. FL 3b differs from FL 3a because _____.

   ○ FL 3b is always longer

   ○ FL 3b is only for inpatient billing

   ○ FL 3b will not change from one bill to the next

   ○ Fl 3b is only used if a patient is seen in an emergency room.

2. Code 0135 in FL 4 would indicate _____.

   ○ an outpatient encounter

   ○ an inpatient encounter

   ○ an emergency room encounter

   ○ a nursing facility charge

3. A proper entry in FL 9a would be _____.
   ○ 117 Marsh Harbour Dr.
   ○ 117 MARSH HARBOUR DR.
   ○ 117 Marsh Harbour Drive
   ○ 117 MARSH HARBOUR DR

4. A correct entry in FL 13 for an admission that occurred at 4:20 P.M. would be _____.
   ○ 06
   ○ 16
   ○ 04
   ○ 14

5. Codes for FL 17 can be found _____.
   ○ by looking at FLs 11 and 12
   ○ in the NUBC Official Data Specifications Manual
   ○ in the chart on the front of the UB-04
   ○ by contacting the patient

PATIENT INFORMATION – LESSON 3

The UB-04 is a complex form in which much of the information in a patient's medical record is condensed to a three-dimensional description of a patient's treatment. The challenge of a form like this is to say as much as possible without using a narrative format. The information contained in a narrative format is converted into an alphanumeric code language that tells the third-party payers everything they need to know about the encounter.

Continuing with the form locators dealing with patient information.

FL 30 is to be left blank at this time. It may be used in the future for recording information.

FLs 31–34 comprise four identical fields that each contain two lines for occurrence codes and two lines for occurrence dates. An occurrence is anything that happens during a patient's treatment that may affect the billing/payment of the claim is an occurrence. A change in healthcare coverage during a patient's inpatient stay would require an occurrence code and the exact date of the change. The NUBC Official Data Specifications Manual lists these codes and their detailed descriptions. Again, care must be taken to make sure that these codes are as accurate and detailed as they can possibly be. The codes should be listed alphanumerically from left to right, beginning with FL31a → FL32a → FL33a → FL34a → FL31b → FL32b, etc.

FL 35 and 36 are set up just like the previous FLs except the dates have a beginning and an ending date requirement. Because of this, these are referred to as occurrence **span** codes and dates. These are for events that would affect the billing/payment of a claim for which there are a "to" and a "from" date associated with the event. These are filled out in the same order and manner as FLs 31–34 and are also listed in the NUBC Official Data Specifications Manual.

FL 37 is to be left blank at this time. It may be used in the future for recording information.

FL 38 may be required by some third-party payers. This space is used to record the name and address of the person who is responsible for the bill.

FLs 39–41 are identical boxes, each with four lettered spaces, where value codes are reported. Value codes, like occurrence codes, must be listed if they apply to the bill. Unlike occurrence codes, these codes are listed in the NUBC Official Data Specifications Manual with a monetary amount. Value codes are used to assign a dollar value to specific pieces of medical encounters. Again, this list of codes is extensive and great care must be taken in making sure the documentation matches the chosen codes. These are also listed left to right and then down the columns as needed, organizing them in numeric—alpha sequence.

At this point, the FLs related to the patient information skip several of the large boxes in the center of the form.

PATIENT INFORMATION – LESSON 4

Skipping down toward the bottom of the UB-04 and starting with patient information FL 50:

FL 50 is broken down into three lines—line A, B, and C. Line A is mandatory and will contain the third-party payer responsible for the claim. Many people, however, have coverage through more than one payer. The subsequent lines are available for multiple payers.

FL 51 is used to report the number that the payer uses to identify the health plan it has provided to the insured. Because FL 50 allows for multiple health plans in rows A, B, and C, a separate entry will be made for each health plan listed in item 50.

FL 52 is where the biller indicates whether the patient or the patient's guardian signed a release of information supplied by the provider. The release of information is needed so the third-party payer can use the medical information to accurately process the claim. If the provider has a signed release, this box will be filled in with a Y. Because FL 50 allows for multiple health plans in rows A, B, and C, a separate entry will be made for each health plan listed in item 50. Row A will always be entered first.

FL 53 is used to indicate whether the patient has signed a statement that assigns the benefits paid by the third-party payer to the healthcare provider. This is indicated with a Y for yes or an N for no. Like FL 52, a separate entry is required for each third-party payer listed in FL 50.

FL 54 may be required by some third-party payers. This where an amount can be entered to specify how much money has already been paid by the third-party payer.

At this point, skip down to FL 58.

FL 58 is a required field. The name of the insured person is entered here in the LAST NAME   FIRST NAME   MIDDLE INITIAL format. There will be a name listed for each third-party payer listed in FL 50.

FL 59 indicates the relationship of the patient to the insured person. There are nine possible codes that cover the possible relationships listed in the NUBC Official Data Specifications Manual. They are as follows:

Code	Relationship
01	Spouse
18	Self

19	Child
20	Employee
21	Unknown
39	Organ donor
40	Cadaver donor
53	Life partner
G8	Other relationship

Since FL 50 may have multiple entries if there are multiple third-party payers, there may be different codes for different payers, depending upon who the insured person listed in FL 58 may be.

FL 60 is used to record the subscriber's unique identification number. This number is assigned by the insurance company.

FL 61 requires the group name of the insured person if a group name is available. Again, this is entered in capital letters without punctuation.

FL 62 requires the group number if one is available.

FL 63 is used for services requiring authorization or preauthorization. When authorization is sought, a number is assigned by the third-party payer to the patient for that treatment. That number will need to match the treatment reported on the UB-04 in order for reimbursement to be paid.

FL 64 is used if a claim has already been processed and is now being sent as a voided claim or as a claim to replace the original. When a third-party payer reimburses a provider, they will provide a document control number. If re-sending a claim to them as a voided claim or as a replacement claim, one would need to include this number to indicate what encounter the new UB-04 is referring to.

FL 65 is used to enter the name of the employer providing coverage to the insured listed in FL 58. This form locator is not always required.

50 PAYER NAME		51 HEALTH PLAN ID	52 REL INFO	53 ASG BEN.	54 PRIOR PAYMENTS	55 EST. AMOUNT DUE	56 NPI	1234512345	
A	MEDICARE	XXX	Y	Y			57	999888	A
B							OTHER		B
C							PRV ID		C

58 INSURED'S NAME		59 P.REL	60 INSURED'S UNIQUE ID	61 GROUP NAME	62 INSURANCE GROUP NO.	
A	STRONG WENDY	18	333222555		782153	A
B						B
C						C

63 TREATMENT AUTHORIZATION CODES	64 DOCUMENT CONTROL NUMBER	65 EMPLOYER NAME	
A			A
B			B
C			C

Form locator 65 completes the Patient Information section of the UB-04.

The importance of documentation has been emphasized and it is clear how vital it is. Proper, accurate documentation would be needed for the extremely detailed information provided about the patient. All of this information has been "compressed" to a series of codes, dates, and names that a payer can decipher and use to adjudicate the claim.

PATENT INFORMATION – EXERCISES

I. TRUE/FALSE.
Mark the following true or false.

1. The number of payers listed in FL 50 may affect the number of entries in FLs 51, 52, 53, 54, 58 and 59.

    ◯ true
    ◯ false

2. Codes in FL 34 only require one date to be entered with each code.

    ◯ true
    ◯ false

3. When listing codes in FLs 39–41, codes that begin with letters come first.

    ◯ true
    ◯ false

4. 2:21 A.M. would be coded as 02 for FLs 13 and 16.

    ◯ true
    ◯ false

5. Condition codes are reported in a two-digit format.

    ◯ true
    ◯ false

6. 12191977 is a proper date entry for FL 6.

    ◯ true
    ◯ false

7. 12191977 is a proper date entry for FL 10.

    ◯ true
    ◯ false

8. Code 3 would be used to indicate an emergency in FL 14.

    ◯ true
    ◯ false

9. FLs 31–34 are to be filled out left to right before moving on to the second row.
   ○ true
   ○ false

10. FL 29 is required for all submissions.
    ○ true
    ○ false

II. MATCHING.
Match the correct term to the definition.

1. ___ FL 10
2. ___ FL 15
3. ___ NUBC
4. ___ FL
5. ___ FL 59
6. ___ UB-82
7. ___ FL 8b
8. ___ FL 14
9. ___ UB-04
10. ___ Official UB-04 Data Specifications Manual

A. Form locator
B. Used for referral source code
C. Used to code the priority of the encounter
D. The first adopted Uniform Bill
E. Used to enter the name of the patient
F. Used by facilities to bill payers today
G. National Uniform Billing Committee
H. Used to enter the patient date of birth
I. Electronic guide explaining how to complete the UB-04
J. Used to show the relationship of patient to the insured

HEALTHCARE PROVIDER INFORMATION – LESSON 1

For third-party payers to have a complete picture of the services they are being billed for, they must also have some detailed information about the healthcare providers who delivered the services.

There are several form locators devoted to reporting the details of the healthcare provider.

FL 1 is one of the most conspicuous locators on the entire UB-04 form. It is a large box divided into 4 equal lines and it contains no heading. This is the space for the healthcare provider submitting the claim form to the payer to enter their name, address, and telephone number. These are to be entered without punctuation, and no punctuation or spaces are used in the telephone number, as seen below:

1 Shady Oak Nursing Home	2	3a PAT. CNTL #	2345179612		
117 Elm Ave		b. MED. REC. #	151236		
Lincoln WV 7772		5 FED. TAX NO.		6 STATEMENT COVERS PERIOD FROM	THROUGH
1115552389		17-6145178		101206	101206

FL 2 is used if the healthcare provider needs payment to be sent to an address other than that listed in item 1. If this is not used, it should be left blank.

FLs 3 and 4 have already been covered.

FL 5 is reserved for the employer's identification number (often referred to as the EIN). This is the tax identification number that the IRS assigns to nearly all businesses. When this number is being entered electronically, the hyphen used in the number should not be entered.

FL 56 is another unique identifier assigned to the healthcare provider. When the HIPAA rule was enacted, one of the provisions was the creation of the National Plan and Provider Enumeration System to assign unique identifying numbers to all healthcare providers. The purpose was to use the numbers to more accurately and efficiently transfer healthcare information (like all of the information on the UB-04) electronically.

HEALTHCARE PROVIDER INFORMATION – LESSON 2

FL 57 is used for identifying numbers that third-party payers assign to the providers for their own use. There are three available lines in this form locator. The numbers should align with the proper third-party payer from FL 50.

FL 76 is used to identify the attending physician (inpatient) or the ordering physician (outpatient). There is a place for the physician's NPI number. The space to the right of the National Provider Identifier (NPI) is used for entering the physician's qualifying codes. The first box has room for two characters. These are used to identify what type of secondary identifier will follow (1G=Provider Unique Physician Identification Number; G2=Provider's commercial number; 0B=Physician's license number from licensing state). The number that follows in the box to the right can then be matched to the proper type of identifier.

The line below the identifying numbers is for the physician's last name and first name (all caps).

FL 77 is used to identify the physician who performed a surgical procedure (if one was performed). The format is the same as FL 76.

FLs 78 and 79 are used to identify any other physicians who had roles in the care provided. The NUBC Official Data Specifications Manual has codes listed that are used to identify the type or role of individual physicians listed in these FLs. That code is entered into the first blank next to the word *other*. The remaining spaces are to be completed in the same manner as FLs 76 and 77.

50 PAYER NAME		51 HEALTH PLAN ID	52 REL INFO	53 ASG. BEN.	54 PRIOR PAYMENTS	55 EST. AMOUNT DUE	56 NPI	7811654831	
A	IHC	678	Y	Y			57	678143	A
B							OTHER		B
C							PRV ID		C

58 INSURED'S NAME		59 P.REL	60 INSURED'S UNIQUE ID	61 GROUP NAME	62 INSURANCE GROUP NO.	
A	Jackson John	18	AAAA123666173		782153	A
B						B
C						C

63 TREATMENT AUTHORIZATION CODES	64 DOCUMENT CONTROL NUMBER	65 EMPLOYER NAME	
A			A
B			B
C			C

66 DX	N40.0	R30.0	B	C	D	E	F	G	H	68
	I	J	K	L	M	N	O	P	Q	

69 ADMIT DX	N40.0	70 PATIENT REASON DX	a	b	c	71 PPS CODE	72 ECI	a	b	c	73

74 PRINCIPAL PROCEDURE CODE / DATE	a. OTHER PROCEDURE CODE / DATE	b. OTHER PROCEDURE CODE / DATE	75	76 ATTENDING	NPI 6137251732	QUAL G2
c. OTHER PROCEDURE CODE / DATE	d. OTHER PROCEDURE CODE / DATE	e. OTHER PROCEDURE CODE / DATE		LAST Jones		FIRST John
				77 OPERATING	NPI	QUAL
80 REMARKS	81CC a			LAST		FIRST
	b			78 OTHER	NPI	QUAL
	c			LAST		FIRST
	d			79 OTHER	NPI	QUAL
				LAST		FIRST

UB-04 CMS-1450   APPROVED OMB NO. 0938-0997   NUBC National Uniform Billing Committee   THE CERTIFICATIONS ON THE REVERSE APPLY TO THIS BILL AND ARE MADE A PART HEREOF.

I. MULTIPLE CHOICE.
Choose the best answer.

1. FL 2 is completed _____.
   ○ always
   ○ only if the provider needs payments to be sent to an alternate address
   ○ for providers to duplicate their business address
   ○ only if the provider has international offices

2. FL 5 has a space for the EIN. This number is _____.
   ○ assigned by the IRS
   ○ optional
   ○ always hyphenated
   ○ used to provide information about the provider's history

3. FL 57 is used for identifying numbers _____.
   ○ for each physician
   ○ that indicate providers' physical locations
   ○ assigned by the third-party payer
   ○ for outpatient providers only

4. FL 1 requires _____.
   ○ no punctuation
   ○ an identifying number
   ○ an attached document
   ○ all of the above

5. FL 56 is _____.
   ○ the same as the number entered in FL 57
   ○ is used for a number assigned by the National Plan and Provider Enumeration System
   ○ filled in if the provider being used is based outside of the United States
   ○ optional

HEALTHCARE SERVICES INFORMATION – LESSON 1

The last group of form locators are those dealing with the encounter and the services provided. These will detail to the third-party payer exactly what the diagnoses were and what care was given. With this information, the payer will have a complete picture of the who, what, where, when, why, and how of the entire encounter all provided on one page. It's pretty impressive how much information is contained in this one small form.

FLs 42 and 43 need to be addressed together because they are both doing the same thing—documenting the revenue codes.

Revenue codes are extensive and are listed in full in the NUBC Official Data Specifications Manual.

> Please go online to download the document that appears here.

Revenue codes are used to describe services rendered during treatment. They are different for inpatient and outpatient encounters. Inpatient revenue codes will bundled under an umbrella that covers all associated services. Outpatient revenue codes are itemized and listed separately for each service. FL 42 is used to record the four-digit code itself. The codes are divided into categories by the first three digits, and the last digit is a variable that gives specific details of the service. Let's look at the revenue codes for renal dialysis services:

800	Inpatient Renal Dialysis – General Classification
801	Inpatient Renal Dialysis – Inpatient Hemodialysis
801	Inpatient Renal Dialysis – Inpatient Peritoneal (Non-CAPD)
803	Inpatient Renal Dialysis – Inpatient Continuous Ambulatory Peritoneal Dialysis
804	Inpatient Renal Dialysis – Inpatient Continuous Cycling Peritoneal Dialysis
809	Inpatient Renal Dialysis – Other

The revenue code 0800 is used for renal dialysis, with the final zero denoting a "general" code. Many payers require a more detailed 4th code. The fourth digit is the only part of the code that differs and each fourth digit provides more information about the renal dialysis.

Revenue codes are vast and varied, ranging from room and board codes to anesthesia codes to pharmacy codes.

Line 22 of this locator must be filled in with revenue code 0001, total charge. This line will be used to calculate the total charge once FLs 42–49 are entered.

FL 43 is used to give a shortened description of the revenue code (notice the descriptions in the example above). Most software programs used for entering revenue codes will populate FL 43 automatically when the numeric code is entered in FL 42.

There are 22 total spaces in FLs 42 and 43 and the codes listed should be entered numerically, beginning with the smallest number and working to the greatest number.

FL 44 has three distinct headers: "HCPCS/Accommodation Rates/HIPPS." The type of revenue code listed will determine which of these codes will be used. If the bill is for an outpatient procedure, the appropriate CPT®/HCPCS code must be listed. For outpatient services, procedures done more than once will be listed in FL 42 as many times as they were performed. The corresponding CPT/HCPCS code will be listed by each entry. If a CPT/HCPCS code is available for an inpatient service, it must be listed here.

Health Insurance Prospective Payment System (HIPPS) rate codes represent specific sets of patient characteristics (or case-mix groups) on which payment determinations are made under several prospective payment systems. Examples include Skilled Nursing Facilities, Inpatient Rehabilitation Facilities, and Home Health Agencies. Case-mix groups are developed based on research into utilization patterns among various provider types. For the payment systems that use HIPPS codes, clinical assessment data is the basic input used to determine which case-mix group applies to a particular patient. A standard patient assessment instrument is interpreted by case-mix grouping software algorithms, which assign the case mix group. For payment purposes, at least one HIPPS code is defined to represent each case-mix group. These HIPPS codes are reported on claims to insurers. To learn more about HIPPS codes, visit http://www.cms.gov/Medicare/Medicare-Fee-for-Service-Payment/ProspMedicareFeeSvcPmtGen/HIPPSCodes.html.

FL 45 is used for outpatient services. The date the service was rendered is entered for each of the revenue codes and is listed in the MMDDYY format. These are generally not required for inpatient services.

At the bottom of this column, a space is available for "Creation date." Enter the date the bill is created in this space using the same format for the date.

FL 46 is used to denote the units "used" in the revenue code. Revenue codes represent a wide variety of services so the units represented can mean many things. The number of days may be entered for an accommodation code, but for different codes, the unit number could represent the number of times a patient was treated or a metric measurement of fluids.

FL 47 is used to record the total charge for the revenue code. If the service units are more than one, the charge would be multiplied by that number. For instance, if an inpatient bill states that a pediatric patient remained for 5 nights, the charge for revenue code 0123 would be multiplied by five to get the total reported in FL 47.

At the bottom of this column, the total charges will be entered into line 22 and the box below titled "Totals."

FL 48 is titled "Non-covered charges." This is used to record monetary amounts of charges that are not covered by the third-party payer or those that are not deemed reasonable for the type of care being given.

FL 49 is not used at this time and may be used in the future for additional codes.

FL 55 is not required by all third-party payers. This is where the total charges the provider is expecting to be paid is recorded.

I. **TRUE/FALSE.**
   Mark the following true or false.

1. Since FL 49 is not used "N/A" should be entered in this space.
   ○ true
   ○ false

2. A proper FL 45 entry would be 091971.
   ○ true
   ○ false

3. The units recorded in FL 46 always represent days.
   ○ true
   ○ false

4. FL 44 may contain a HCPCS code.
   ○ true
   ○ false

5. FL 48 is used only for elective surgeries.
   ○ true
   ○ false

HEALTHCARE SERVICES INFORMATION – LESSON 2

Continuing on with form locators:

FL 66 is used to report the version of the International Classification of Diseases codeset being used to report the diagnosis codes. When the U.S. has transitioned to ICD-10 (Oct 1, 2014), 10 is entered in this space.

FL 67 is unique in appearance and use. The number 67 is watermarked in the background of the first space and then there are consecutive spaces lettered A–Q. The locator marked 67 is used to record the principal ICD-10-CM diagnosis code and a different code used for denoting the status of the diagnosis at the time of admission (referred to as present on admission or POA). All diagnosis codes have a POA indicator assigned to the code for inpatient admission claims. The POA codes are as follows:

Indicator	Description
Y	Diagnosis was present at time of inpatient admission.
N	Diagnosis was not present at time of inpatient admission.
U	Documentation insufficient to determine if condition was present at the time of inpatient admission.
W	Clinically undetermined. Provider was unable to clinically determine whether the condition was present at the time of inpatient admission.
1	Exempt from POA reporting. This code is the equivalent of a blank on the UB-04; however, it was determined that blanks were undesirable on Medicare claims when submitting this data via the 004010/00410A1. **NOTE:** The number "1" is no longer valid on the claims submitted under the version 5010 format, effective January 1, 2011. The POA field will instead be left blank for codes exempt from POA reporting.

The subsequent A–Q spaces are used to report codes for any additional conditions that the patient may have had on admission or may have acquired during treatment.

FL 68 is to be left blank at this time. It may be used in the future for recording information.

FL 69 is used to report the ICD-10-CM diagnosis code that is the reason for admission (for inpatient treatment). The reason for admission/condition is determined by the official ICD-10-CM coding guidelines.

FL 70 has 3 lettered spaces (a–c) for reporting the codes for the diagnoses responsible for the patient's initial visit. This FL is used to code ICD-10-CM codes for outpatient visits only. These codes will give the payer the reason for the patient's visit, which can affect payment.

FL 71, while small, is important to reimbursement and can be complicated. Many providers have contracts with third-party payers that outline payment of procedures through a prospective payment system. These codes, known as Medicare Severity-Diagnosis Related Groups (MS-DRGs), encompass a variety of resources and compile them into a single code with a single charge. The last unit of this module will explain in detail how to arrive at the proper MS-DRG assignment.

FL 72 has spaces for 3 codes. Report the external cause of injury codes (if there are any). These codes may be mandatory in some states when a patient has been injured, poisoned, or suffered an adverse effect. These codes also use the present on admission modifiers that were used in FL 67.

FL 73 is to be left blank at this time. It may be used in the future for recording information.

FL 74 is used to report the principal ICD-10-CM procedure code. The box beside the code is reserved for the date the procedure was performed. There are also duplicate spaces A–E that are used for other procedures that may have been performed.

FL 75 is to be left blank at this time. It may be used in the future for recording information.

FL 80 is the last remaining form locator. FL 80 allows for a provider to enter comments that they feel were not represented in the codes or that will make the claim form more accurate and complete when the payer is evaluating it. This is not mandatory.

4. Type of Bill (TOB)   4 digits w. first digit 0 (UB-04 not used 0)

Permanent Patient medical number.   0 1 3 1
                                     ↓ ↓ → admittance through discharge.
                                ↓ outpatient
                            hospital

* account #
* assign by the facility

                                     0 1 1 1
                                        ↓
                                     inpatient

Cer. no
Con't #
Med.
Pol. #

1. Healthcare provider info w/o punctuation & space

2.

5. Fed Tax No.

6. Statement cover period

FROM	THROUGH
	mmddyy

8 PATIENT NAME	a	9 PATIENT ADDRESS	a		c	d
	Assigned by Third-party see 60		All capitalized / NO Punctuation			
b	LAST FIRST MIDDLE	b				

10 BIRTHDATE	11 SEX	ADMISSION 12 DATE	13 HR	14 TYPE	15 SRC	16 DHR	17 STAT	CONDITION CODES 18	19	20	21	22	23	24	25	26	27	28	29 ACDT STATE	30
MMDDYYYY	M or F	MMDDYY																	auto	

date service being billed

	31 OCCURRENCE CODE	DATE	32 OCCURRENCE CODE	DATE	33 OCCURRENCE CODE	DATE	34 OCCURRENCE CODE	DATE	35 OCCURRENCE SPAN CODE	FROM	THROUGH	36 OCCURRENCE SPAN CODE	FROM	THROUGH	37
a															
b															

38

	39 VALUE CODES CODE	AMOUNT	40 VALUE CODES CODE	AMOUNT	41 VALUE CODES CODE	AMOUNT
a						
b						
c						
d						

	42 REV. CD.	43 DESCRIPTION	44 HCPCS / RATE / HIPPS CODE	45 SERV. DATE	46 SERV. UNITS	47 TOTAL CHARGES	48 NON-COVERED CHARGES
1			Health Insurance Prospective Payment System	Outpatient MMDDYY	e.g. number of days.		
2							
3							
4							
5							
6							
7							
8							
9							
10							
11							
12							
13							
14							
15							
16							
17							

UB-04 CMS-1450 Claim Form

PAGE ___ OF ___

CREATION DATE _____

TOTALS →

50 PAYER NAME	51 HEALTH PLAN ID	52 REL INFO	53 ASG BEN.	54 PRIOR PAYMENTS	55 EST. AMOUNT DUE	56 NPI
A						57
B						OTHER
C						PRV ID

58 INSURED'S NAME	59 P.REL	60 INSURED'S UNIQUE ID	61 GROUP NAME	62 INSURANCE GROUP NO.
A				
B				
C				

If different from 8a. 8a need to fill in.

63 TREATMENT AUTHORIZATION CODES	64 DOCUMENT CONTROL NUMBER	65 EMPLOYER NAME
A		
B		
C		

66 DX	67	A	B	C	D	E	F	G	H	I	J	K	L	M	N	O	P	Q	68
	69 ADMIT DX	70 PATIENT REASON DX	a	b	c	71 PPS CODE	72 ECI	a	b	c	73							

74 PRINCIPAL PROCEDURE CODE / DATE	a. OTHER PROCEDURE CODE / DATE	b. OTHER PROCEDURE CODE / DATE	75	76 ATTENDING	NPI		QUAL
c. OTHER PROCEDURE CODE / DATE	d. OTHER PROCEDURE CODE / DATE	e. OTHER PROCEDURE CODE / DATE		LAST		FIRST	

77 OPERATING	NPI		QUAL
LAST		FIRST	

80 REMARKS	81CC	78 OTHER	NPI		QUAL
	a	LAST		FIRST	
	b	79 OTHER	NPI		QUAL
	c	LAST		FIRST	
	d				

UB-04 CMS-1450   APPROVED OMB NO. 0938-0997

NUBC™ National Uniform Billing Committee

THE CERTIFICATIONS ON THE REVERSE APPLY TO THIS BILL AND ARE MADE A

42 REV. CD.	43 DESCRIPTION	44 HCPCS / RATE / HIPPS CODE	45 SERV. DATE	46 SERV. UNITS	47 TOTAL CHARGES	48 NON-COVERED CHARGES	49
1 0300	Lab	84153		1	75 : 00	:	1
2 0300	Lab	84086		1	20 : 00	:	2
3					:	:	3
4					:	:	4

66 DX	N40.0		R30.0		B		C		D		E		F		G		H		68
	I		J		K		L		M		N		O		P		Q		

69 ADMIT DX	N40.0	70 PATIENT REASON DX	a	b	c	71 PPS CODE	72 ECI	a	b	c	73

74 PRINCIPAL PROCEDURE CODE / DATE	a. OTHER PROCEDURE CODE / DATE	b. OTHER PROCEDURE CODE / DATE	75	76 ATTENDING	NPI 6137251732	QUAL G2
				LAST Jones	FIRST John	
c. OTHER PROCEDURE CODE / DATE	d. OTHER PROCEDURE CODE / DATE	e. OTHER PROCEDURE CODE / DATE		77 OPERATING	NPI	QUAL
				LAST	FIRST	
80 REMARKS		81CC a		78 OTHER	NPI	QUAL
		b		LAST	FIRST	
		c		79 OTHER	NPI	QUAL
		d		LAST	FIRST	

UB-04 CMS-1450   APPROVED OMB NO. 0938-0997   **NUBC** National Uniform Billing Committee   THE CERTIFICATIONS ON THE REVERSE APPLY TO THIS BILL AND ARE MADE A PART HEREOF.

UNIT 7

Quality Assurance Practices and Regulatory Compliance

QUALITY ASSURANCE PRACTICES AND REGULATORY COMPLIANCE – INTRODUCTION

The efforts of companies, corporations, and public agencies to comply with and verify compliance with laws and regulations pertinent to operating within an industry(ies) is regulatory compliance. Regulatory compliance is achieved by setting up processes and systems such as training personnel, implementing Quality Assurance (QA) processes, auditing, or designating departments and/or individuals to direct compliance efforts.

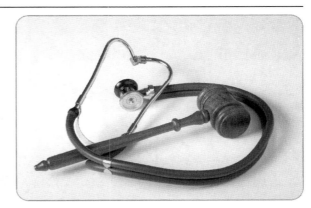

Healthcare is a highly regulated industry because of four important factors:

1. Healthcare involves quality of life and death issues.
2. Healthcare is expensive.
3. People and companies want to be protected from fraud and abuse.
4. Government subsidizes billions of dollars for healthcare.

Regulatory compliance is an important issue in healthcare. *Healthcare personnel are expected to know and apply the relevant rules and regulations in the treatment of patients, in the documentation of healthcare, and in healthcare billing.* The government takes seriously issues of fraud and abuse.

REGULATORY AGENCIES

The Department of Health and Human Services (HHS) is tasked with governing and regulating healthcare in the United States.

The Centers for Medicare and Medicaid (CMS) develop many of the rules and regulations for the healthcare industry, but the Office of Inspector General (OIG) is tasked with "protect[ing] the integrity of DHHS programs…through a nationwide network of audits, investigations, inspections, and other mission-related functions."

When the Office of Inspector General finds issues of fraud, abuse, or illegal activity, the complaints are directed to the Department of Justice (DOJ) for criminal prosecution. The DOJ is an independent law enforcement agency and is not under the DHHS umbrella. The OIG is outside of DHHS and is part of the DOJ. This is another way to ensure checks and balances.

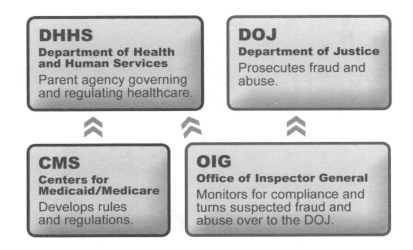

DHHS
Department of Health and Human Services
Parent agency governing and regulating healthcare.

DOJ
Department of Justice
Prosecutes fraud and abuse.

CMS
Centers for Medicaid/Medicare
Develops rules and regulations.

OIG
Office of Inspector General
Monitors for compliance and turns suspected fraud and abuse over to the DOJ.

Although there are rare circumstances when a few healthcare providers are dishonest and engage in fraudulent practices, it is the goal of the vast majority of healthcare providers to understand and achieve regulatory compliance through education and adoption of quality assurance practices.

AUDITS

The tool used by regulatory agencies and healthcare providers to educate, check for regulatory compliance, and update policies and procedures is an audit.

An **audit** is an evaluation of provided healthcare services to ensure all aspects are in compliance with industry rules and regulations.

Healthcare documentation audits review some or all of the following:

- The patient's medical record documentation
- Copies of the charge slip(s) or superbill(s) for the specified date(s) of service
- Diagnosis, procedural, and supply code assignments
- Claims sent to patient and third-party payer
- EOBs/remittance advice received from third-party payers to verify payment posting and rejection management

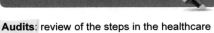

Highlights

Audits: review of the steps in the healthcare documentation process.

Concurrent review: review done while the patient is actively receiving care.

Retrospective review: review done after the patient has received care.

Audits may reveal several things and can be of great importance to a medical facility. HIM (health information management) audits may uncover:

- Lack of documentation in the medical record to support charges and fees
- Undercoding
- Upcoding
- Unbundling
- Not coding to the highest specificity
- Diagnoses not properly matched to procedure codes
- Duplicate billing
- Lost or missing charge slips or visits not billed or coded

- Medical necessity issues
- Billing for services not provided

When one or more of these issues are identified, a plan or procedure must be implemented to correct past problems and prevent future problems.

When an audit is performed by personnel within a healthcare provider organization, it is called an **internal audit**. Internal audits should be performed at a minimum on an annual basis. But actually waiting an entire year to find errors is not even a viable option. Coding and billing must be continuously reviewed to ensure accuracy. When an audit is performed by personnel or agencies outside of the healthcare provider organization, it is called an **external audit**. External audits may be conducted at the request of the healthcare provider or at the request of an outside party or agency.

I. **MULTIPLE CHOICE.**
    Choose the best answer.

1. A review done while a patient is actively receiving care is called a(n) _____.
   ○ retrospective review
   ○ concurrent review
   ○ audit
   ○ check up

2. A review of the steps in the healthcare documentation process is called a(n) _____.
   ○ retrospective review
   ○ concurrent review
   ○ audit
   ○ external audit

3. A review done after the patient has received care is called a(n) _____.
   ○ retrospective review
   ○ concurrent review
   ○ audit
   ○ internal audit

4. An audit performed by personnel within a healthcare organization is called a(n) _____.
   ○ retrospective review
   ○ concurrent review
   ○ internal audit
   ○ external audit

INTERNAL AUDITS

Internal audits are performed by personnel within the healthcare provider organization. The Office of the Inspector General (OIG) recommends all healthcare providers institute an ongoing regulatory compliance program that includes an ongoing internal auditing program. The OIG offers compliance guidance and compliance resource material to assist healthcare providers in setting up and maintaining a regulatory compliance program.

An internal audit is an audit performed by personnel within the healthcare provider organization.

The OIG offers a 7—step basic guide for individual and small group practices to create and maintain a voluntary regulatory compliance program:

1. Conduct internal monitoring and auditing through the performance of periodic audits.
2. Implement compliance and practice standards through the development of written standards and procedures.
3. Designate a compliance officer or contact(s) to monitor compliance efforts and to enforce practice standards.
4. Conduct appropriate training and education on practice standards and procedures.
5. Respond appropriately to detected violations through the investigation of allegations and the disclosure of incidents to appropriate government entities.
6. Develop open lines of communication, such as discussions at staff meetings, regarding how to avoid erroneous or fraudulent conduct to keep employees updated regarding compliance activities.
7. Enforce disciplinary standards through well-publicized guidelines.

The OIG also offers compliance plans for hospitals as well as several other provider types. These can be found by going to www.oig.hhs.gov and selecting Compliance and then Compliance Guidance.

Healthcare providers range in size from a single physician working out of a small office to a group of radiology physicians providing contracted services to entire outpatient departments within large acute-care hospitals.

Highlights

The key to a successful internal auditing program for regulatory compliance is ensuring that the facility or provider makes changes when problems or issues are discovered.

Every healthcare provider, large or small, should have an ongoing internal auditing program in place to monitor regulatory compliance. Whether the provider is a single physician office operating with a single staff member or a large outpatient facility, staff should include internal review and auditing as part of an ongoing healthcare documentation integrity and regulatory compliance program.

The key to a successful internal auditing program for regulatory compliance is ensuring that the facility or provider makes changes when problems or issues are discovered.

SAMPLE CODING AUDITOR JOB DESCRIPTION

The Coding Audit and Education Specialist is responsible for auditing/analyzing the coding/ documentation for accuracy and completeness of coded medical records. This person works closely with the staff in education and auditing functions as it pertains to coding. This person will also assist the supervisor with QA on each provider and with audits requested by other departments. The person in this position works independently under the supervision of the Coding Supervisor. Work situations require extensive knowledge, experience, and training in coding and coding guidelines, and the ability to effectively teach others. A high degree of diplomacy, tact, and excellent customer service and communications skills are required.

Conducting Internal Audits

The American Academy of Neurology provides good information on how to prepare for an internal audit. This resource is available at:
http://www.aan.com/globals/axon/assets/2539.pdf

The American College of Physicians also has information on how to prepare for an internal audit. This resource is available at:
http://www.acponline.org/running_practice/payment_coding/coding/coding_audit.htm

The suggested audit form by the American College of Physicians is available at:
http://www.scribd.com/doc/24737506/Trailblazer-Medicare-Audit-Tool

I. **TRUE/FALSE.**
   Mark the following true or false.

1. Healthcare institutions do not have a need for internal audits except when potential problems arise.
   - ○ true
   - ○ false

2. The OIG recommends that all healthcare providers institute an ongoing regulatory compliance program, including an internal auditing program.
   - ○ true
   - ○ false

3. Smaller healthcare operations have little need for internal audits-- only large operations need to worry about them.
   - ○ true
   - ○ false

4. Facilities or providers should make changes when problems or issues are discovered in an internal audit.
   - ○ true
   - ○ false

REASONS FOR AUDITS

The purpose of internal audits is to proactively address non-compliance issues and to work to bring the healthcare provider into compliance and keep the healthcare provider in compliance.

Some potential problems that might be uncovered during an audit:

- missed charges
- not properly linking diagnoses with procedures or services
- unbundling services that are usually billed under one code
- inadequate documentation in the medical record
- illegible or missing documentation in the medical record
- documentation that is spread out and not centralized for easy review in the medical record
- upcoding to gain higher reimbursement
- unnecessary medical services
- undercoding for services that require higher level of service codes
- inappropriate billing of physician services during patient's postoperative global surgery period
- locating errors on the charge slip, superbill, or chargemaster (old codes, deleted codes, etc.)
- failure to write off insurance discounts
- duplicate billing

If an audit uncovered an error, the first step is to correct the error, followed by investigating how the error occurred. An error can occur at any point in the people process or technology phases. Questions to ask during the review of the cause include: Is the staff adequately trained? Is there a software problem? Once answers to these questions are found, education, training, new policies, processes, procedures, or other appropriate measures can be taken to reduce the chances of future duplicate billing errors occurring.

Internal audits help the facility to achieve and maintain regulatory compliance.

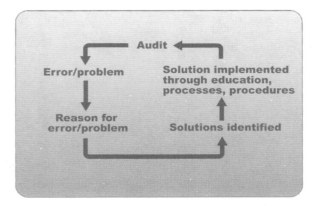

Auditing is an ongoing process to assure quality care and avoid non-compliance.

I. TERMINOLOGY.
Enter each term in the space provided. Read the definition and description for each term.

1. **undercoding** _____

Selecting codes at a lower level than the service documented.

2. **upcoding** _____

Selecting codes at a higher level than the service documented.

3. **unbundling** _____

Billing two or three procedures when the services are typically covered by a single comprehensive code.

SAMPLE CODING AND BILLING AUDIT FORM

The Office of Inspector General offers many tools for performing internal audits. Review the samples: Coding and Billing Audit, Documentation Audit, and Medicare/Medicaid Complaint and Resolution Form.

We've placed a visual aid in the appendix on page 420.

We've placed a visual aid in the appendix on page 421.

We've placed a visual aid in the appendix on page 422.

We've placed a visual aid in the appendix on page 423.

REVIEW: INTERNAL AUDITS

I. MATCHING.
Match the correct term to the definition.

1. ____ A provider requests the coding specialist to review documentation in patients' medical records, superbills, verify diagnosis codes, support procedure code assignments, and review third-party payer EOBs.

2. ____ This regulatory agency governs and regulates healthcare in the United States.

3. ____ Claims filed with the knowledge of falsity on the claim.

4. ____ When fraudulent claims are discovered during an external audit, these are turned over to this government organization for investigation.

5. ____ This regulatory agency protects the integrity of the Department of Human and Health Services through audits and investigations.

A. DHHS
B. fraudulent claims
C. OIG
D. internal audit
E. DOJ

EXTERNAL AUDITS

The government has an interest in making sure healthcare providers are compliant with all the rules and regulations appropriate for their beneficiaries. As one of the largest payers, in addition to provider of healthcare services, the government has moral, financial, and legal responsibilities to ensure the healthcare provided is of high quality and accurately reimbursed. Many others have a vested interest in monitoring healthcare and healthcare practices. Ultimately, employers, payers, and consumers of healthcare want to know the provided services are in compliance with industry standards in all aspects from treatments to payments rendered.

> **Highlights**
>
> When an audit is performed by a regulatory agency or by an independent auditor outside of the healthcare provider organization—at the request of the healthcare provider or at the request of an individual, company, or agency outside of the healthcare provider—it is an external audit.

Any external audits of the healthcare documentation process are a way to validate the healthcare providers's compliance with rules, regulations, and standards of care. An audit may be conducted at the request of the provider or at the request of an outside individual, company, or agency. External audits are conducted by individuals outside of the healthcare provider organization.

External audits fall under two categories: reactive and proactive.

PROACTIVE EXTERNAL AUDITS

A proactive audit is a routine or random audit to check the healthcare provider's compliance with rules and regulations for:

- providing services
- documenting healthcare services
- billing healthcare services

The auditing team(s) would meet with various departments or individuals to review healthcare practices—including coding and billing practices—by reviewing healthcare record documentation, codes, and bills (claims).

Auditors would identify deficiencies and the provider would submit a corrective plan of action to address any deficiencies. In most cases the audit team would work with the facility team to assist in addressing issues and implementing best practices and improved procedures.

Proactive audits may be conducted by an accounting firm, an independent consulting firm, or third-party payers (only on the records for their insured). Facilities may also choose to participate in a voluntary overall third-party audit program, such as the Joint Commission.

If routine issues are uncovered and are appropriately addressed, healthcare providers can benefit from a proactive external audit. If, however, an external proactive audit uncovers a pattern of noncompliance, grossly inadequate healthcare documentation practices, or suspected fraud or abuse, the findings will be turned over to an investigating agency.

I. FILL IN THE BLANK.

Enter the correct word in the blank provided.

1. Auditors identify _____ and the provider submits a corrective plan of action to address them.

2. A proactive audit is a _____ audit to check the healthcare provider's compliance with rules and regulations.

3. Facilities may choose to participate in a voluntary third-party audit program such as the

   _____.

4. If issues are uncovered and appropriately addressed, healthcare providers can benefit from a

   _____.

II. MULTIPLE CHOICE.
Read the article and answer the following questions.

1. What step is necessary to prepare for the external coding audit?
   - ○ define goals
   - ○ secure executive support and prepare coders
   - ○ identify cases
   - ○ all of the above

2. The final step in the audit process is:
   - ○ preparing for the audit
   - ○ managing the audit
   - ○ implementing recommendations
   - ○ preparing the coders

III. TRUE/FALSE.
Read the article and answer the following questions.

1. External audits require significant time, effort, and money.
   - ○ true
   - ○ false

2. Once the audit is complete and the recommendations received, HIM departments are finished.
   - ○ true
   - ○ false

3. Most external coding audtis are conducted off-site.
   - ○ true
   - ○ false

4. Random samples with adequate sample size validate current performance across the board and expose unknown problems.
   - ○ true
   - ○ false

REACTIVE EXTERNAL AUDITS

External audits conducted as the result of a complaint, concern, or suspicion of wrongdoing are reactive external audits.

Reactive audits may be prompted by any one of a number of things: an individual patient complaint, a pattern of unusual billing activity reported by one or more third-party payers, or a complaint by another healthcare provider.

The audit may be restricted to the specific circumstances that prompted the audit or the audit may be expanded to a full-scale healthcare audit. Government regulatory agencies, third-party payers, and others with contractual relationships with the healthcare provider may conduct reactive audits.

If evidence of deliberate wrongdoing/fraudulent activity is found, the information will be turned over to an investigating agency for review (most commonly the Department of Justice).

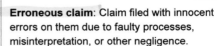

Erroneous claim: Claim filed with innocent errors on them due to faulty processes, misinterpretation, or other negligence.

Fraudulent claim: Claim filed with knowledge of falsity of the claim.

> The Department of Justice has made fighting fraud and abuse in the healthcare industry one of the Department's top priorities. Healthcare fraud and abuse drains billions of dollars from Medicare and Medicaid, which provide essential healthcare services to millions of elderly, low income, and disabled Americans. The impact of healthcare fraud and abuse cannot be measured in terms of dollars alone. While healthcare fraud burdens our nation with enormous financial costs, it also threatens the quality of healthcare.*
>
> (*http://www.justice.gov/opa/pr/2012/February/12-ag-213.html).

If a healthcare provider is found to be making fraudulent claims instead of simply erroneous claims, legal action may be pursued against those participating in the fraud.

In many cases, reactive external audits find no evidence of deliberate wrongdoing and serve to help the healthcare facility address deficiencies in their healthcare documentation practices. Be aware that stiff fines/penalties are most likely the result of any errors, regardless of deliberate or not.

> The Department [of Justice] continues to prevent fraud and abuse in a number of ways: by encouraging providers to police their own activities through compliance programs; and by sponsoring consumer outreach initiatives, such as the consumer's fraud hotlines, to involve patients with first-hand knowledge in the detection of fraudulent practices. Settlement agreements with providers also emphasize future prevention efforts.*
>
> (*Department of Justice. www.usdoj.gov/dag/pubdoc/health98.htm)

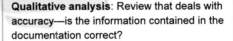

Qualitative analysis: Review that deals with accuracy—is the information contained in the documentation correct?

Quantitative analysis: Review that deals with completeness—is the documentation thorough and complete?

Medical coding specialists occupy a central role in the healthcare documentation process. Often it is the medical coding specialist who first becomes aware of problems with insufficient, incomplete, or inaccurate documentation.

Even if a medical coding specialist is not directly assigned the role of "auditor," the medical coder has a responsibility to look for acceptable documentation through ongoing qualitative and quantitative analysis of the medical record.

Click on the link below to download the HHS Fraud and Abuse fact sheet:
http://www.cms.gov/Outreach-and-Education/Medicare-Learning-Network-MLN/Fraud_and_Abuse.pdf

I. **FILL IN THE BLANK.**

   Enter the correct word in the blank provided.

   1. A review that deals with accuracy is called a _____.

   2. A claim filed with knowledge of falsity of the claim is called a _____.

   3. Reactive external audits are the result of _____ concern, or suspicion of wrongdoing.

   4. A review that deals with completeness is called a _____.

   5. A claim filed with innocent errors due to faulty processes, misinterpretation, or other negligence is called an _____.

RAC: THE RECOVERY AUDIT CONTRACTOR

Medicare receives over 1.2 billion claims every year, equivalent to 9,579 claims received per minute. In 2006, Medicare began a three-year demonstration project with contracted auditors in several states across the country to find out if Medicare's coverage, coding, and medical necessities are met.

Some of the payment errors identified included some of the following:

- incorrect payment amounts
- non-covered services
- incorrectly coded services
- duplicate services/claims

The Recovery Audit Contractor program (RAC), as it is called, has now been implemented all around the country. The Centers for Medicare & Medicaid Services (CMS) have contracted several auditing companies to be their eyes and ears, performing audits to determine these improper payments.

For additional information on RAC and Medocaid Integrity Program, click on the links below:

http://www.cms.gov/Research-Statistics-Data-and-Systems/Monitoring-Programs/recovery-audit-program/index.html

https://www.cms.gov/Medicare-Medicaid-Coordination/Fraud-Prevention/MedicaidIntegrityProgram/index.html

REVIEW: EXTERNAL AUDITS

Medical coding specialists have a responsibility to understand and adhere to the coding guidelines outlined in the ICD-10-CM/PCS codebooks, the CPT® codebook and the HCPCS codebook. Medical coders have a responsibility to know the guidelines and apply the guidelines correctly and thoroughly.

Keeping up to date on coding changes and updates, actively participating in quality assurance programs designed to assure regulatory compliance, and maintaining quality healthcare services to all patients should be the coder's focus as part of the healthcare support services team.

I. **TRUE/FALSE.**
   Mark the following true or false.

1. A proactive external audit is typically performed by either an independent consulting firm or by the staff in the provider's office.

   ○ true
   ○ false

2. If evidence of deliberate fraudulent billing is found during an audit process, this information is turned over by the OIG to the DOJ for further investigation.

   ○ true
   ○ false

3. The Office of Inspector General offers tools to perform internal audits.

   ○ true
   ○ false

4. A reactive audit is performed after a complaint has been filed or a third-party payer suspects fraudulent billing.

   ○ true
   ○ false

5. Coding specialists are very busy with their day-to-day jobs so if they do not keep up with the rules and regulations, the Office of the Inspector General will overlook this during an audit.

   ○ true
   ○ false

UNIT 8

Medicare Severity Diagnosis Related Groups

MEDICARE SEVERITY DIAGNOSIS RELATED GROUPS – INTRODUCTION

This module will further explore Medicare's acute care prospective payment system. Acute care hospitals typically receive Medicare payments as governed by the inpatient prospective payment system (IPPS) using Medicare severity diagnosis groups (MS-DRGs).

In 1983, the government enacted the system using diagnosis related groups (DRGs) as the payment methodology. The theory is based upon patients with similar characteristics consuming similar resources. Determining how patients are similar is a key factor for the system, which defines the similarities by the DRGs. More details regarding how the system determines a DRG is discussed later.

One of the biggest criticisms of the DRG system was its lack of addressing patient severity of illness. Originally, for select DRGs a patient may have one condition which is considered a complication or comorbid condition (CC), or five conditions considered a complication or comorbid condition, and payments would be similar for the same DRG.

In response to this concern, Medicare revised the system to better reflect patient severity. The revision was one of the most significant revisions since the inception of DRGs and is known as the **Medicare Severity Diagnosis Related Group** (MS-DRG) system. While the details are discussed on other pages, the system was created to further account for similar patients with different severity of illness as defined by Medicare.

The system was created by Medicare; however many other larger payers have implemented a DRG system, such as Tricare, Medicaid, and Blue Cross. The other commercial payers are not required by regulation to follow Medicare's system exactly but many choose to follow their system. A billing professional working in a hospital should learn if their payers are using a DRG system in addition to knowing if they follow Medicare's logic. Knowing more details about one of hospital's largest third party payer's (Medicare) reimbursement method will help billing professionals in their work to ensure claims are processed and paid accurately.

MS-DRG TERMINOLOGY – LESSON 1

Knowing the terminology surrounding the MS-DRG is vital to understanding how the system works.

against medical advice: A type of discharge status in which a patient chooses to leave the facility even though all medical personnel recommend the patient stays for treatment.

discharge status: When patients who were considered inpatients at healthcare facilities leave the facility to go to another location. The status indicates the new location of the patient. For example, a patient returns home to his/her house after being treated at their local community hospital.

case mix index (CMI): The sum of all MS-DRG weights, divided by the total number of Medicare discharges for the same time period. Slight increases or decreases impact a hospitals overall reimbursement amount. Facilities routinely monitor the CMI.

CC: Abbreviation for complications and comorbid conditions.

comorbid condition: A pre-existing condition which, because of its presence, causes an increase in length of stay by at least one day in approximately 75% of the cases.

complication: A condition that arises during the hospital stay which prolongs the length of stay by at least one day in approximately 75% of the cases.

grouper: A software program designed to determine MS-DRGs and typically contains Medicare code edits.

hospital wage index: A numeric factor defined by Medicare that considers the geographic location of hospitals. This factor is used in the reimbursement calculations for facilities to account for geographic differences.

major complication/comorbid condition (MCC): Complications and comorbid conditions defined by Medicare to have a higher severity of illness impact on a patient.

major diagnostic category (MDC): A broad classification of conditions typically grouped by body systems diseases.

medicare code edits: A method to identify various situations based upon assigned ICD-10-CM codes. For example, the sex conflict edit identifies situations when a female only diagnosis code is on a claim indicating the patient is a male.

I. MATCHING.
Match the correct term to the definition.

1. ____ discharge status
2. ____ hospital wage index
3. ____ CC
4. ____ comorbid condition
5. ____ grouper
6. ____ major complication/comorbid condition (MCC)
7. ____ case mix index (CMI)
8. ____ complication
9. ____ major diagnostic category (MDC)
10. ____ medicare code edits
11. ____ against medical advice

A. A pre-existing condition which, because of its presence, causes an increase in length of stay by at least one day in approximately 75% of the cases.

B. A software program designed to determine MS-DRGs and typically contains Medicare code edits.

C. A method to identify various situations based upon assigned ICD-10-CM codes.

D. Complications and comorbid conditions defined by Medicare to have a higher severity of illness impact on a patient.

E. A broad classification of conditions typically grouped by body systems diseases.

F. When patients who were considered inpatients at healthcare facilities leave the facility to go to another location. The status indicates the new location of the patient.

G. The sum of all MS-DRG weights, divided by the total number of Medicare discharges for the same time period.

H. A numeric factor defined by Medicare that considers the geographic location of hospitals. This factor is used in the reimbursement calculations for facilities to account for geographic differences.

I. A type of discharge status in which a patient chooses to leave the facility even though all medical personnel recommend the patient stays for treatment.

J. Abbreviation for complications and comorbid conditions.

K. A condition that arises during the hospital stay which prolongs the length of stay by at least one day in approximately 75% of the cases.

MS-DRG TERMINOLOGY – LESSON 2

non-operating room procedure: Procedures which may or may NOT be performed in a surgical operating suite; however, the procedure codes affect MS-DRG assignment.

operating room procedure: Procedures identified as requiring the use of an operating room suite. The identified codes influence MS-DRG assignment.

outliers: Hospital cases with specific circumstances that place the admission extremely outside the normal or average admission. For example, high cost outlier is when the patient&rsqho;s hospital charges are high and above the average charge for a similar case. Additional payment may be received for such outliers.

per diem rate: A set payment amount to a facility for each day the patient stayed at the facility. For MS-DRG purposes, the amount is paid to the facility that transferred the patient.

pre-MDC Categories established by Medicare where cases are automatically assigned without applying all the MS-DRG logic. These cases are usually high-risk, lower volume admissions, such as organ transplants.

principal diagnosis: Condition established after study to be chiefly responsible for occasioning the admission of the patient to the hospital for care.

principal procedure: Procedure performed for definitive treatment rather than diagnostic or exploratory; or to treat a complication. This procedure is typically related to the principal diagnosis.

relative weight (RW): A number assigned to each MS-DRG reflecting an average patientÕs resource consumption. The higher the number value represents greater resources used to care for the patient. This number is used in calculating the MS-DRG reimbursement amount a facility receives. The higher the RW, the higher the reimbursement amount received.

surgical heirarchy: Ordering of surgical cases from the most to least resource intensive.

transfer: A type of discharge status where a patient is moved from one facility to another facility. A patient may be moved to many different types of facilities, such as to skilled nursing facility, or another acute care facility. There are different discharge status codes to assign depending upon the type of facility.

volume: The number of patients in each MS-DRG. The volume of patients in specific DRGs is important when reviewing the case mix index.

I. MATCHING.
Match the correct term to the definition.

1. ___ volume
2. ___ surgical hierarchy
3. ___ relative weight (RW)
4. ___ principal procedure
5. ___ principal diagnosis
6. ___ pre-MDC
7. ___ per diem rate
8. ___ outliers
9. ___ operating room procedure
10. ___ non-operating room procedure
11. ___ transfer

A. Ordering of surgical cases from the most to least resource intensive.

B. A number assigned to each MS-DRG reflecting an average patient's resource consumption.

C. Hospital cases with specific circumstances that place the admission extremely outside the normal or average admission.

D. Condition established after study to be chiefly responsible for occasioning the admission of the patient to the hospital for care.

E. Procedures identified as requiring the use of an operating room suite.

F. A set payment amount to a facility for each day the patient stayed at the facility.

G. Categories established by Medicare where cases are automatically assigned without applying all the MS-DRG logic.

H. Procedure performed for definitive treatment rather than diagnostic or exploratory; or to treat a complication.

I. A type of discharge status where a patient is moved from one facility to another facility.

J. The number of patients in each MS-DRG.

K. Procedures which may or may NOT be performed in a surgical operating suite; however, the procedure codes affect MS-DRG assignment.

FACTORS INFLUENCING MS-DRGS

Hospital inpatient services fall into one of the over 750 MS-DRG classifications for Medicare. Other payers may have their own version of a DRG system; regardless of the specifics only one DRG is assigned per each inpatient admission. The **inpatient prospective payment system** (IPPS) is based upon figures and data from past patients and procedures. The prospective payment system utilizes this data to determine a single resource consumption value for the various hospital services provided to patients. This figure determines the relative weight of a single MS-DRG.

Hospital inpatients are placed into the proper groupsin several ways. The first question to answer is: *What information is used to place an inpatient in a particular MS-DRG?*

Prior to grouping an admission into a specific MS-DRG using all the logic, the admission is testing against the pre-MDC factors to determine a MS-DRG assignment. If the admission does not group to a MS-DRG based upon the pre-MDC criteria then the remaining logic is applied to the admission.

Before applying the remaining logic there are six factors that influence the assignment of DRGs:

1. principal and secondary diagnosis and procedure codes
2. sex
3. age
4. discharge status
5. presence or absence of major complications and comorbidities (MCCs)
6. presence or absence of complications and comorbidities (CCs)

It is essential to understand how each of these factors influences the assignment of MS-DRGs. As a coder/biller, it is required to reconcile the MS-DRG on a remittance advice with the one billed.

MS-DRG ASSIGNMENT

Remember the factors influencing MS-DRG assignment:

1. principal and secondary diagnosis and procedure codes
2. sex
3. age
4. discharge status
5. presence or absence of major complications and comorbidities (MCCs)
6. presence or absence of complications and comorbidities (CCs)

Today, most MS-DRGs are calculated using software tools known as **groupers**. Early on, they were determined using a flow-chart book. The book contains a series of decision tree diagrams. The same information would have been necessary to determine the correct DRG (as MS-DRGs were not implemented).

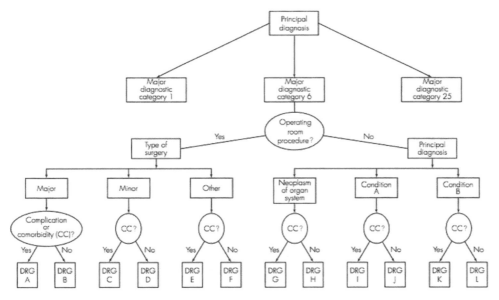

Example Decision Tree. Source: http://www.medpac.gov/publications/congressional_reports/mar02_ch1.pdf

318

Let's look at each of these factors individually.

1. **Principal and Secondary Diagnosis and Procedure Codes**

   Does the logic look for a principal procedure code first?

   - If *no*, then a principal diagnosis code is reviewed for appropriate placement in an MDC (major diagnostic category).
   - If *yes*, then logic follows the surgical MS-DRGs pathways for the admission.
   - Next question: "Does the procedure code fall into the pre MDC MS-DRG?" If *yes*, a MS-DRG is assigned.
     - Currently, there are 17 pre-MDC groups.
     - Examples include:
       —MS-DRG 01 (MDC PRE) HEART TRANSPLANT OR IMPLANT OF HEART ASSIST SYSTEM W MCC
       —MS-DRG 014 (MDC PRE) ALLOGENIC BONE MARROW TRANSPLANT
   - If *no*, pre MDC the remaining grouper logic is followed.

   Secondary diagnosis codes are reviewed after the principal diagnosis for the selection of the correct MS-DRG.

   The medical coder identifies all the principal and secondary diagnosis and procedure codes. This will lead to the assignment of the correct DRG.

2. **Sex of the Patient**

   There are specific codes and MS-DRGs that are gender specific. Certain diagnoses and procedures can only be assigned to males or females.

   Examples of these include the following:

   Male Diagnoses

   - prostate cancer
   - hydrocele
   - torsion of testicle

   Male Procedures

   - orchiectomy
   - prostatectomy
   - vasectomy

   Female Diagnoses

   - endometriosis of ovary
   - dysmenorrhea
   - tubal pregnancy

   Female Procedures

   - salpingo-oophorectomy
   - hysterectomy
   - dilation and curettage (D&C)

3. **Age of Patient**

If a patient in one age group tends to use more resources than patients in another age group, then the MS-DRGs are split according to age.

4. **DRG Assignment—Discharge Status**

When a patient is transferred from one acute care hospital to another or from one acute care hospital to a certain postacute care provider (e.g., skilled nursing facility), the payment for some MS-DRGs is reduced.

The MS-DRGs affected by being transferred to specific post-acute care facilities is known as Post-Acute DRG. Medicare identifies those MS-DRGs with an indicator of "Yes." An example would be MS-DRG 031 Ventricular Shunt Procedure w MCC.

5. **DRG Assignment—Presence or Absence of Major Complications and Comorbidities (MCCs) and Complications and Comorbidities (CCs)**

The presence of a major complication or comorbidity diagnosis can cause the patient's case to be grouped into the higher-weighted MS-DRG. After determining if a MCC is present or not, the logic reviews for complications and comorbidities (CCs).

MS-DRG EXAMPLES

193 (MDC 04) SIMPLE PNEUMONIA & PLEURISY W MCC

194 (MDC 04) SIMPLE PNEUMONIA & PLEURISY W CC

195 (MDC 04) SIMPLE PNEUMONIA & PLEURISY W/O CC/MCC

Please go online to download the document that appears here.

It should be noted that hospital acquired conditions (HAC) also factor into the assignment of MS-DRGs. Basically, these are codes that identify conditions that are high cost, high volume, or both; they may also be CCs or MCCs. Most importantly, they could have been reasonably prevented through the application of evidence-based guidelines. The point of this notification is that if the condition IS NOT PRESENT ON ADMISSION, it will NOT be grouped to that higher-paying MS-DRG. Review any code assignments that are designated as HAC. Accurate and complete documentation is essential. Most facilities have a physician-led review committee to investigate and develop additional preventative measures.

Click on the link below to review more information regard HAC:
http://www.cms.gov/Medicare/Medicare-Fee-for-Service-Payment/HospitalAcqCond/downloads/hacfactsheet.pdf

CALCULATING A FACILITY PAYMENT

Once the MS-DRG has been determined, the relative weight associated with the MS-DRG is known. The **relative weight** is used in the mathematical calculation to determine an actual dollar amount. The final dollar amount received is affected by other factors; however, the basic mathematical formula is:

> MS-DRG relative weight x facility base rate = dollar reimbursement

Each year a facility receives a base rate which is an actual dollar amount specific to each facility. While the exact amount varies, for our purposes the average is $3,500.

Example calculation using the relative weights and average base rate:

> MS-DRG 102 HEADACHES W MCC has a relative weight of 1.0209
>
> $\quad$ 1.0209 x $3,500 = $3,573.15
>
> MS-DRG 103 HEADACHES W/O MCC has a relative weight of 0.6893
>
> $\quad$ 0.6893 x $3,500 = $2,412.55

Keep in mind there are other factors influencing the actual dollar amount as listed below:

- wage index
- new technology add-on payment
- outlier

The **wage index** is the method used to account for geographical cost of living differences. Outliers were defined earlier in this module; however the payment is an additional payment to account for the admission being statistically significant away from the average.

New technology add-on payments are additional payments for specific technology Medicare has identified as new. The additional payment is to account for the increased cost associated with obtaining the technology.

Medicare reviews all the information annually and posts updated files to their website. Please refer to the Centers for Medicare and Medicaid website at www.cms.gov for individual location details.

Answer Key

1. Health Information Management

2. Healthcare Delivery Systems

3. Legal and Compliance

4. Reimbursement Methodologies

Structure of Healthcare Data

PATIENT INFORMATION

I. TRUE/FALSE.

1. true
2. false
3. false
4. true

SUBJECTIVE/OBJECTIVE DATA

I. MULTIPLE CHOICE.

1. subjective
2. objective
3. objective
4. subjective

II. TRUE/FALSE.

1. true
2. false
3. false

Outpatient Medical Reports

FACE SHEET

I. MULTIPLE CHOICE.

1. penicillin
2. renal disease
3. jogging
4. rotator cuff tear
5. frequent headaches

PHYSICIAN'S ORDERS

I. MULTIPLE CHOICE.

1. regular
2. PAR
3. right
4. crutch train
5. crutches

NURSE'S NOTES

I. MULTIPLE CHOICE.

1. Glucophage
2. ORIF left ankle
3. gemfibrozil
4. opiate analgesic
5. 600 mg

HISTORY AND PHYSICAL REPORTS

I. MULTIPLE CHOICE.

1. ptosis of the upper eyelids
2. no significant medical problems
3. blepharoplasty
4. all of the above
5. tomorrow morning

EMERGENCY ROOM (ER) REPORTS

I. MULTIPLE CHOICE.

1. cough
2. antibiotic
3. bronchitis
4. expectorant
5. COPD

OPERATIVE REPORTS

I. MULTIPLE CHOICE.

1. trigger finger
2. A1 pulley release
3. Bier block
4. recovery room

ANCILLARY REPORTS – LABORATORY

I. MULTIPLE CHOICE.

1. 5
2. Band % and Lymph %
3. 2
4. Creatinine

ANCILLARY REPORTS – PATHOLOGY

I. MULTIPLE CHOICE.

1. 2
2. infiltrating ductal carcinoma
3. pathology report
4. dermal fibrosis

ANCILLARY REPORTS – RADIOLOGY

I. MULTIPLE CHOICE.

1. left
2. rule out medial meniscus tear
3. collateral ligaments
4. joint

DISCHARGE SUMMARY – EXERCISES

I. MULTIPLE CHOICE.

1. 1
2. home
3. failed total knee arthroplasty
4. opiate analgesic
5. revision left tibial knee arthroplasty

HISTORY AND PHYSICAL – EXERCISES

I. MULTIPLE CHOICE.

1. atrial flutter
2. chest pain
3. 5
4. propafenone

CONSULTATION – EXERCISES

I. MULTIPLE CHOICE.

1. right foot pain
2. hospital
3. acute CVA
4. albuterol
5. cam walker

PHYSICIAN PROGRESS NOTE – EXERCISES

I. MULTIPLE CHOICE.

1. heroin drug addiction
2. no
3. mild blood pressure elevation
4. occasionally
5. Subutex and detoxification

II. MULTIPLE CHOICE.

1. renal transplant
2. brother
3. end-stage renal disease due to IgA nephropathy
4. two weeks
5. peritoneal dialysis

DEATH SUMMARY – EXERCISES

I. MULTIPLE CHOICE.

1. emergency room
2. ventricular fibrillation
3. yes
4. pneumonia
5. yes

AUTOPSY – EXERCISES

I. MULTIPLE CHOICE.

1. perforating brain injury
2. self-inflicted gunshot wound
3. cerebral artery berry aneurysm
4. county morgue
5. 30 minutes

Medical Record Organization

REVIEW: SUBJECTIVE

I. MULTIPLE CHOICE.

1. Cranial nerves were intact.
2. HISTORY OF PRESENT ILLNESS
3. His last fall was difficult as he got stuck in the bathroom.
4. Some notes indicate that the wife was having some difficulties managing him at home.

II. MULTIPLE CHOICE.

1. A triple arthrodesis with possible harvest of iliac bone graft, left foot.
2. PHYSICAL EXAMINATION
3. ...relates continued pain with ambulation and shoe gear and limitation of activities.
4. Patient asks for surgical intervention at this time.

REVIEW: OBJECTIVE

I. MULTIPLE CHOICE.

1. Total bilirubin is 0.5.
2. PAST MEDICAL HISTORY
3. objective
4. subjective
5. objective

DESCRIPTIVE INFORMATION HEADINGS

I. MULTIPLE CHOICE.

1. objective
2. subjective
3. other information
4. objective
5. subjective

REVIEW: ASSESSMENT

I. MULTIPLE CHOICE.

1. Plan
2. Exacerbation of patellar subluxation.
3. She reports that four days ago, after going to the Steeler exhibition game, she walked to her car.
4. The quadriceps and patellar tendons are nontender with palpation.
5. Left Achilles tendinopathy, hip abductor strain with trochanteric bursitis and external oblique strain.

REVIEW: PLAN

I. MULTIPLE CHOICE.

1. discontinue Naprosyn
2. true
3. false
4. consider resuming chemotherapy
5. yes
6. return for followup

Health Information Processes

MASTER PATIENT INDEX

I. TRUE/FALSE.

1. true
2. false
3. true

FILING SYSTEMS

I. MULTIPLE CHOICE.

1. Defined by state law
2. 30 years
3. 10 years
4. Permanently
5. 5 years after age of majority

Data Quality and Integrity

QUALITATIVE AND QUANTITATIVE ANALYSES

CHALLENGE BOX.

1. **Qualitative analysis**
2. **Quantitative analysis**

REVIEW: CONSISTENCY AND AUDITING

I. MATCHING.

1. C. Review of the medical record while the patient is still a patient.
2. D. Review of medical record to ensure that documentation standards are met.
3. B. Review of the medical record to identify potential medical errors.
4. A. Medical record review performed after the patient has been discharged.
5. E. Medical record review for completeness.

II. FILL IN THE BLANK.

1. concurrent review
2. occurrence screening
3. qualitative analysis
4. quantitative analysis
5. retrospective review

COMMON DOCUMENTATION ERRORS

I. FILL IN THE BLANK.

1. deficiency slip
2. medical coder
3. incomplete record file
4. signature

COMMON ERRORS – SCENARIO 1

I. MULTIPLE CHOICE.
1. patient name

COMMON ERRORS – SCENARIO 2

I. MULTIPLE CHOICE.
1. gender inconsistency

COMMON ERRORS – SCENARIO 3

I. MULTIPLE CHOICE.
1. date inconsistency

COMMON ERRORS – SCENARIO 4

I. MULTIPLE CHOICE.
1. location discrepancy

COMMON ERRORS – SCENARIO 5

I. MULTIPLE CHOICE.
1. diagnosis discrepancy

PRIMARY AND SECONDARY DATA USE

I. TRUE/FALSE.
1. true
2. false
3. false

SECONDARY DATA SOURCE TYPES

I. TRUE/FALSE.
1. true
2. false
3. false
4. true
5. false

Technology and the Health Record

COMPUTER NETWORKS

I. MULTIPLE CHOICE.
1. WAN
2. EDI
3. both a. and b.

THE ADVENT OF EHR

I. FILL IN THE BLANK.
1. EHR
2. access
3. information

II. TRUE/FALSE.
1. true
2. false
3. true

HEALTH INFORMATION SPECIALTY SYSTEMS (CODING)

I. TRUE/FALSE.
1. true
2. false
3. true
4. false

EHR BENEFITS — LESSON 1

I. MATCHING.
1. C. An EHR benefit that helps save space when storing records.
2. F. An EHR benefit that offers easy and immediate access to information.
3. E. An EHR benefit wherein information is accessible the moment it is entered to whoever needs it.
4. B. An EHR benefit that expedites the time it takes to search for an item and makes it easier to find.
5. D. Medical record data printed and stored on paper in hard copy format.
6. A. Medical record data stored in an electronic format in a computer system or systems.

PERSONAL HEALTH RECORD

I. TRUE/FALSE.
1. false
2. true
3. true
4. false
5. false
6. true

II. MULTIPLE CHOICE.
1. patient
2. all of the above

Healthcare Delivery Systems

Licensure, Certification, and Accreditation

CONDITIONS OF PARTICIPATION FOR HOSPITALS

I. MULTIPLE CHOICE.

1. for 5 years

2. August 1st

II. TRUE/FALSE.

1. true

2. false

Ethics, Compliance, and Risk Management

OVERVIEW OF CODE OF ETHICS

I. MULTIPLE CHOICE.

1. Query the physician for clarification.

2. Assign the code for surgical complication.

3. Research the appropriate generic name/ classification of the drug.

Medical Billing Basics

CHARGE DESCRIPTION MASTER

I. MULTIPLE CHOICE.

1. all of the above
2. CDM
3. vary from provider to provider
4. every year (at a minimum)

CDM MAINTENANCE

I. Matching.

1. C. also known as item description
2. D. identifies the specific service or procedure
3. G. four-digit code identifying accommodation, ancillary service, or billing calculation required for Medicare
4. B. fee for the service
5. E. used for accounting purposes to distribute revenue to appropriate location
6. F. internally assigned unique number identifying each item listed
7. A. activity date element

REVIEW: OUTPATIENT BILLING PROCESS

I. TRUE/FALSE.

1. false
2. false
3. true
4. true
5. false

CODING AND BILLING AT THE PHYSICIAN'S OFFICE

I. TRUE/FALSE.

1. true
2. false
3. false

PHYSICIAN CARE AT OUTSIDE FACILITIES

I. TRUE/FALSE.

1. true
2. true
3. false

REVIEW: CODING AND BILLING FOR PHYSICIANS

I. TRUE/FALSE.

1. true
2. true
3. true
4. false
5. true

REVIEW: CODING AND BILLING FOR FACILITIES

I. TRUE/FALSE.

1. true
2. false
3. false
4. true
5. true

Healthcare Reimbursement

THE CONSUMER

I. TRUE/FALSE.

1. true
2. false
3. true

CONTRACT RELATIONSHIPS

I. TRUE/FALSE.

1. true
2. true
3. false

PAYMENT

I. TRUE/FALSE.

1. false
2. true
3. true

GOVERNMENT

I. TRUE/FALSE.

1. true
2. false
3. true

REVIEW: REIMBURSEMENT

I. MULTIPLE CHOICE.

1. Government requires all payers to reimburse at the same rate for the same services.
2. government
3. managed-care coverage
4. patient ethnicity
5. lower premiums (rates)

FEE-FOR-SERVICE AND EPISODE-OF-CARE

I. TRUE/FALSE.

1. false
2. true
3. true

SELF-PAY

I. FILL IN THE BLANK.

1. self-pay
2. third-party payer
3. Payment options

RETROSPECTIVE PAYMENT

I. FILL IN THE BLANK.

1. costs or charges
2. after
3. less than

REVIEW: FEE-FOR-SERVICE REIMBURSEMENT

I. MULTIPLE CHOICE.

1. fee-for-service
2. usual, customary, and reasonable
3. patient's condition or illness
4. retrospective
5. episode-of-care

RESOURCE-BASED RELATIVE VALUE SCALE

I. MULTIPLE CHOICE.

1. Medicare
2. CPT code
3. CMS multiplier
4. all of the above
5. fee-for-service

MANAGED CARE

I. MULTIPLE CHOICE.

1. active
2. pre-authorization
3. the third-party payer

HEALTH MAINTENANCE ORGANIZATIONS (HMOS)

I. TRUE/FALSE.

1. true
2. false
3. true

REVIEW: MANAGED CARE

I. TRUE/FALSE.
1. true
2. true
3. true
4. false
5. false

MANAGED CARE – CAPITATION

I. TRUE/FALSE.
1. true
2. false
3. false
4. true
5. false

GLOBAL PAYMENT/PROSPECTIVE PAYMENT SYSTEMS

I. FILL IN THE BLANK.
1. prospective payment system
2. global reimbursement
3. Medicare system

REVIEW: PAYMENT/PROSPECTIVE PAYMENT SYSTEMS

I. TRUE/FALSE.
1. true
2. true
3. false
4. true
5. false

OUTPATIENT PROSPECTIVE PAYMENT SYSTEM

I. MATCHING.
1. D. CMS sets reimbursement rates for each APC (ambulatory payment classification).
2. A. Patient receives outpatient services at a hospital.
3. F. Documentation is coded.
4. C. Codes are transferred to claim.
5. G. Claim sent to third-party payer.
6. B. CPT and HCPCS codes are grouped to the appropriate APC (Ambulatory Payment Classification) by third-party payer.
7. E. Claim is reimbursed based on pre-set APC rates.

CMS DESCRIPTIONS – AMBULATORY PAYMENT CLASSIFICATION SYSTEM

I. MULTIPLE CHOICE.
1. bundles CPT and HCPCS codes into a hierarchy of groups to minimize reimbursement
2. all of the above

CMS DESCRIPTIONS – AMBULATORY SURGICAL CENTER

I. TRUE/FALSE.

1. true
2. false
3. true

OTHER POSTACUTE PPS

I. MULTIPLE CHOICE.

1. 90
2. skilled nursing facilities
3. inpatient rehabilitation facility

II. TRUE/FALSE.

1. false
2. true
3. true

REVIEW: PROSPECTIVE PAYMENT SYSTEMS

I. TRUE/FALSE.

1. false
2. false
3. true
4. false
5. true

QUALITY IMPROVEMENT ORGANIZATIONS

I. MULTIPLE CHOICE.

1. 3
2. ensure that effective, efficient, and quality care is delivered to Medicare beneficiaries

Life Cycle of a Claim

THE FIVE STEPS IN A MEDICAL CLAIM

I. TRUE/FALSE.

1. false
2. false
3. true
4. true
5. false

ADVANCE BENEFICIARY NOTICE OF NONCOVERAGE (ABN)

I. MULTIPLE CHOICE.

1. both a and b
2. Medicare Coverage Database
3. all of the above
4. 5 years

II. TRUE/FALSE.

1. true
2. false
3. true

NATIONAL AND LOCAL COVERAGE DETERMINATIONS

I. MULTIPLE CHOICE.
1. all of the above

CLAIM SUBMISSION – 3RD-PARTY PAYER INFORMATION

I. TRUE/FALSE.
1. false
3. false

2. true
4. true

CLAIM FORMS

I. MULTIPLE CHOICE.
1. UB-04
3. UB-04

2. CMS-1500
4. CMS-1500

CLAIMS PROCESSING

I. MULTIPLE CHOICE.
1. electronically
3. all of the above

2. CMS-1500
4. the healthcare provider and the third-party payer

5. pre-edit claims for errors

CLAIMS ADJUDICATION

I. MATCHING.
1. E. the process of reviewing a claim and deciding what claims are to be paid
3. C. the amount the policy states is payable for a particular procedure
5. A. an overview of claims recently filed on the patient

2. D. the percentage of the bill the patient pays once the deductible is met
4. B. the amount the insured must pay yearly before benefits begin

MANAGING CLAIMS

I. MULTIPLE CHOICE.
1. both A and B
3. the physician
5. A remittance advice is sent to the healthcare provider.

2. an aging report
4. all of the above

APPEALING CLAIMS

I. TRUE/FALSE.
1. true
3. false
5. true

2. true
4. false

Completing the CMS-1500 Claim Form

PREPARING DOCUMENTATION

I. TRUE/FALSE.

1. true
2. false
3. false
4. true
5. true

CMS-1500: ITEMS 1–3

I. MULTIPLE CHOICE.

1. 220 NORTH LAKE DRIVE
2. X
3. SMITH JONATHON A
4. all of the above
5. 08 10 1996

PATIENT AND INSURED INFORMATION: ITEMS 4–9

I. MATCHING.

1. A. patient
2. D. insured
3. B. secondary coverage
4. E. policyholder
5. C. primary coverage

PATIENT AND INSURED INFORMATION: ITEMS 10–13

I. TRUE/FALSE.

1. false
2. false
3. true
4. true
5. true

BEGINNING THE PATIENT OR SUPPLIER INFORMATION: ITEMS 14–18

I. MULTIPLE CHOICE.

1. the date of the injury
2. 02132014 02202014
3. dates the patient could not work
4. any healthcare provider seeking reimbursement
5. ALLEN A WILSON MD

PATIENT OF SUPPLIER INFORMATION: ITEM 24

I. MATCHING.

1. C. diagnosis pointer
2. E. NPI number
3. B. units of service
4. A. From _____ To _____ format
5. D. POS

PATIENT OR SUPPLIER INFORMATION: ITEMS 25–33

I. TRUE/FALSE.

1. false
2. true
3. false
4. true
5. false

Completing the UB-04 Claim Form

PATIENT INFORMATION – LESSON 2

I. MULTIPLE CHOICE.

1. FL 3b will not change from one bill to the next
2. an outpatient encounter
3. 117 MARSH HARBOUR DR
4. 16
5. in the NUBC Official Data Specifications Manual

PATIENT INFORMATION – EXERCISES

I. TRUE/FALSE.

1. true
2. true
3. false
4. true
5. true
6. false
7. true
8. false
9. true
10. false

II. MATCHING.

1. H. Used to enter the patient date of birth
2. B. Used for referral source code
3. G. National Uniform Billing Committee
4. A. Form locator
5. J. Used to show the relationship of patient to the insured
6. D. The first adopted Uniform Bill
7. E. Used to enter the name of the patient
8. C. Used to code the priority of the encounter
9. F. Used by facilities to bill payers today
10. I. Electronic guide explaining how to complete the UB-04

HEALTHCARE PROVIDER INFORMATION – LESSON 2

I. MULTIPLE CHOICE.

1. only if the provider needs payments to be sent to an alternate address
2. assigned by the IRS
3. assigned by the third-party payer
4. no punctuation
5. is used for a number assigned by the National Plan and Provider Enumeration System

HEALTHCARE SERVICES INFORMATION – LESSON 1

I. TRUE/FALSE.

1. false
2. true
3. false
4. true
5. false

Quality Assurance Practices and Regulatory Compliance

AUDITS

I. MULTIPLE CHOICE.

1. concurrent review
2. audit
3. retrospective review
4. internal audit

INTERNAL AUDITS

I. TRUE/FALSE.

1. false
2. true
3. false
4. true

REVIEW: INTERNAL AUDITS

I. MATCHING.

1. D. internal audit
2. A. DHHS
3. B. fraudulent claims
4. E. DOJ
5. C. OIG

PROACTIVE EXTERNAL AUDITS

I. FILL IN THE BLANK.

1. deficiencies
2. routine or random
3. Joint Commission
4. proactive external audit

II. MULTIPLE CHOICE.

1. all of the above
2. implementing recommendations

III. TRUE/FALSE.

1. true
2. false
3. false
4. true

REACTIVE EXTERNAL AUDITS

I. FILL IN THE BLANK.

1. qualitative analysis
2. fraudulent claim
3. complaint
4. quantitative analysis
5. erroneous claim

REVIEW: EXTERNAL AUDITS

I. TRUE/FALSE.
1. false
2. true
3. true
4. true
5. false

Medicare Severity Diagnosis Related Groups

MS-DRG TERMINOLOGY – LESSON 1

I. MATCHING.
1. F. When patients who were considered inpatients at healthcare facilities leave the facility to go to another location. The status indicates the new location of the patient.

2. H. A numeric factor defined by Medicare that considers the geographic location of hospitals. This factor is used in the reimbursement calculations for facilities to account for geographic differences.

3. J. Abbreviation for complications and comorbid conditions.

4. A. A pre-existing condition which, because of its presence, causes an increase in length of stay by at least one day in approximately 75% of the cases.

5. B. A software program designed to determine MS-DRGs and typically contains Medicare code edits.

6. D. Complications and comorbid conditions defined by Medicare to have a higher severity of illness impact on a patient.

7. G. The sum of all MS-DRG weights, divided by the total number of Medicare discharges for the same time period.

8. K. A condition that arises during the hospital stay which prolongs the length of stay by at least one day in approximately 75% of the cases.

9. E. A broad classification of conditions typically grouped by body systems diseases.

10. C. A method to identify various situations based upon assigned ICD-10-CM codes.

11. I. A type of discharge status in which a patient chooses to leave the facility even though all medical personnel recommend the patient stays for treatment.

MS-DRG TERMINOLOGY – LESSON 2

I. MATCHING.
1. J. The number of patients in each MS-DRG.

2. A. Ordering of surgical cases from the most to least resource intensive.

3. B. A number assigned to each MS-DRG reflecting an average patient's resource consumption.

4. H. Procedure performed for definitive treatment rather than diagnostic or exploratory; or to treat a complication.

5. D. Condition established after study to be chiefly responsible for occasioning the admission of the patient to the hospital for care.

6. G. Categories established by Medicare where cases are automatically assigned without applying all the MS-DRG logic.

7. F. A set payment amount to a facility for each day the patient stayed at the facility.

8. C. Hospital cases with specific circumstances that place the admission extremely outside the normal or average admission.

9. E. Procedures identified as requiring the use of an operating room suite.

10. K. Procedures which may or may NOT be performed in a surgical operating suite; however, the procedure codes affect MS-DRG assignment.

11. I. A type of discharge status where a patient is moved from one facility to another facility.

APPENDIX

PATIENT HISTORY

NAME: LAST	FIRST		MIDDLE	DOB		AGE	SEX
							M___ F
EMERGENCY CONTACT PERSON			RELATIONSHIP			HOME PHONE: ( )	
PHARMACY PHONE #:		HEIGHT	WEIGHT	OCCUPATION			

CURRENT MEDICAL PROBLEMS

IF YOU ARE BEING TREATED FOR ANY OTHER ILLNESSES OR MEDICAL PROBLEMS BY ANOTHER PHYSICIAN, PLEASE DESCRIBE THE PROBLEMS & INDICATE THE NAME OF THE PHYSICIAN TREATING YOU.

ILLNESS OR MEDICAL PROBLEMS	PHYSICIANS TREATING YOU

ILLNESS AND MEDICAL PROBLEMS

PLEASE MARK WITH A (X) ANY OF THE FOLLOWING ILLNESSES & MEDICAL PROBLEMS YOU HAVE OR HAVE HAD. ALSO INDICATE THE YEAR WHEN EACH STARTED. IF YOU ARE NOT CERTAIN WHEN THE ILLNESS STARTED, WRITE DOWN AN APPROXIMATE YEAR.

ILLNESS	X	YEAR	ILLNESS	X	YEAR	ILLNESS	X	YEAR
MIGRAINE HEADACHES			HIGH BLOOD PRESSURE			JAUNDICE		
HEADACHES			HEART ATTACK			LIVER TROUBLE		
HEAD INJURY			HIGH CHOLESTEROL			GALLBLADDER PROBLEMS		
STROKE			POOR CIRCULATION			HERNIA		
SEIZURE			HEART MURMUR			HEMORRHOIDS		
GLAUCOMA			BLEEDING TENDENCY			KIDNEY DISEASE		
OTHER EYE PROBLEMS			ANEMIA			BLADDER DISEASE		
DEAFNESS			OTHER HEART COND.			PROSTATE PROBLEMS		
BRONCHITIS			BREAST CANCER			KIDNEY STONES		
EMPHYSEMA			COLON CANCER			ARTHRITIS		
PNEUMONIA			PROSTATE CANCER			CHICKEN POX		
ALLERGIES			OTHER CANCER			DIABETES		
ASTHMA			ULCER			HEPATITIS		
TUBERCULOSIS			DIVERTICULITIS			MEASLES		
MENTAL ILLNESS			SUBSTANCE ABUSE			PSORIASIS		

ALCOHOLISM			AIDS/HIV			VENEREAL DISEASE		
THYROID DISEASE			RHEUMATIC FEVER					

IMMUNIZATIONS

DATE OF LAST TETANUS SHOT	INFLUENZA VACCINE	GERMAN MEASLES VACCINE

MEDICATIONS

PLEASE LIST ALL MEDICATIONS YOU ARE NOW TAKING, INCLUDING THOSE YOU TAKE WITHOUT A DOCTOR'S PRESCRIPTION (SUCH AS ASPIRIN OR COLD TABLETS).

1.	2.	3.
4.	5.	6.
7.	8.	9.
10.	11.	12.
13.	14.	15.

ALLERGIES AND SENSITIVITIES

LIST ANYTHING THAT YOU ARE ALLERGIC TO, SUCH AS CERTAIN FOODS, MEDICATIONS, DUST, CHEMICALS OR SOAPS, HOUSEHOLD ITEMS, POLLEN, BEE STINGS, ETC. INDICATE HOW EACH AFFECTS YOU.

ALLERGIC TO:	REACTION:	ALLERGIC TO:	REACTION:
1.		5.	
2.		6.	
3.		7.	
4.		8.	

SOCIAL/PERSONAL HISTORY

DO YOU SMOKE? ___YES ___NO   IF YES, HOW MANY PACKS PER DAY? _____
ARE YOU A FORMER SMOKER? ___YES ___NO   IF YES HOW MANY MONTHS/YEARS SINCE YOU QUIT?
_____

DO YOU DRINK ALCOHOLIC BEVERAGES? ___YES ___NO   HOW MANY OUNCES PER DAY? _____
IF YES WHAT TYPE OF ALCOHOL, (I.E. BEER, WINE, LIQUOR)?
_____
HOW MANY BEERS DO YOU DRINK PER DAY?

DO YOU DRINK COLA, COFFEE OR TEA? ___YES ___NO	DO YOU WEAR A SEAT BELT? ___YES ___NO DO YOU WEAR SUNBLOCK? ___YES ___NO

DO YOU USE RECREATIONAL DRUGS/NOT PURCHASED AT A DRUG STORE?   ___YES ___NO

ARE THERE ANY RELIGIOUS OR CULTURE ISSUES THAT MAY AFFECT YOUR MEDICAL CARE?

FAMILY HISTORY

PLEASE GIVE THE FOLLOWING INFORMATION ABOUT YOUR IMMEDIATE FAMILY:				HAVE ANY BLOOD RELATIVES HAD ANY OF THE FOLLOWING ILLNESSES? IF SO, INDICATE RELATIONSHIP BY PLACING AN "X" IN THE APPROPRIATE BOX:				
RELATIONSHIP:	AGE IF LIVING	AGE AT DEATH	STATE OF HEALTH OR CAUSE OF DEATH	ILLNESS	FATHER	MOTHER	BROTHER	SISTER
FATHER				HEART DISEASE				
MOTHER				HIGH BLOOD PRESSURE				
BROTHER (S)				CANCER				
SISTER (S)				DIABETES				
SPOUSE				BLOOD DISEASE				
CHILDREN				EPILEPSY				
				RHEUMATOID ARTHRITIS				
				GOUT				
				GLAUCOMA				
				TUBERCULOSIS				

MEN ONLY – ANY PROBLEMS WITH THE FOLLOWING

HERNIA ___ YES ___ NO	PAIN IN TESTICLES ___ YES ___ NO	SEXUAL DIFFIC. ___ YES ___ NO
DISCHARGE FROM PENIS ___ YES ___ NO	SEXUALLY TRANSMITTED DISEASE ___ YES ___ NO	

WOMEN ONLY – ANY PROBLEMS WITH THE FOLLOWING

VAGINAL ITCHING/BURNING _____
VAGINAL DISCHARGE _____
PROBLEM WITH MENSTRUAL PERIODS _____
FIRST MENSTRUAL PERIOD _____
DATE OF LAST MENSTRUAL PERIOD _____
DATE OF LAST PAP SMEAR _____
METHOD OF CONTRACEPTION _____
SEXUALLY TRANSMITTED DISEASE _____

SEXUAL DIFFICULTIES _____
NUMBER OF PREGNANCIES _____
NUMBER OF MISCARRIAGES/ABORTIONS _____
NUMBER OF LIVE BIRTHS _____
PROBLEMS WITH PREGNANCIES _____
LUMPS IN BREAST _____
DISCHARGE FROM NIPPLE(S) _____
DATE OF LAST MAMMOGRAM _____

DID YOU MISS MORE THAN (10) DAYS OF YOUR USUAL ACTIVITY LAST YEAR DUE TO ILLNESS OR INJURY? IF YES, PLEASE EXPLAIN:
_____
_____
_____

_____   _____   _____
PATIENT SIGNATURE   DATE   PHYSICIAN INITALS/DATE

347

Family Practice

Progress Notes

Name	Jennifer Winkle		DOB	6/15/20XX

Date	Notes
08/10/20XX	Jennifer is a well known patient to our office. She is here for an earache. T99.6 orally P-82-R-16. She is in moderate distress sitting in her mother's lap. Pt. made no eye contact. However, when asked which ear she pointed to her R. ear. Sue. Everett M.A. 8/10/20XX 10:15AM
08/10/20XX	Jennifer 4 y/o white female is here with her mother. Patient is complaining of Right ear pain for 2 days. She had an elevated temp, which mom has treated with children's Advil which has also controlled the ear pain somewhat. Right ear tympanic membrane is bulging with ear wax. Threat minimal to date. Cloudy post nasal drip. Lungs clear. Impression: Right acute perousotitis media. Will start on Augmenten today for 7 days. Return in 2 wks. for a recheck or sooner if symptoms do not improve. Steve Harvey MD 10:45AM
08/10/20XX	Prescription for Augmentin, 250mg T10 x 7 days. Mother was given instruction for administering the medication, earcare, sign 9 symptoms to watch for & monitor for temperature. Mom is to call the office if symptoms worsen. Schedule return appt. in 2 weeks for a recheck. Sue. Everett M.A. 8/10/20XX 10:15AM

Oakland Medical Center

Patient Name: DOB: MRN#

Date	ER Physician Notes
9/21/20XX	CC abdominal pain, nausea, vomiting & diarrheah of sudden onset. No precipitating factors indicated. Last meal 5 hours ago. Exam: lungs clear to auscul taken q percussion hear, RRR no murmur. Abdomen: tenderness in RUQ, no masses or hernias palpated. Assessment plan: Routine labs will be drawn, X Rays acute abdominal r/o appendicitis, gallbladder disease. Await test results. John Carter, MD 20:30

Oakland
MEDICAL CENTERS
Clinical Reference Studies

DR#1205
DR#2
DR#3
DR#4

DOCTOR NAME CODE	DOCTOR SIGNATURE		AAP #176295
1205	John Carter MD		

PATIENT LAST NAME (PRINT)	FIRST	M.I.	DATE OF BIRTH	SEX	MARITAL ST	DATE OF INJURY
Jones	William	R	10/10/1960	☒M ☐F	☒M ☐D ☐S ☐W	N/A

PATIENT ADDRESS	CITY	STATE	ZIP CODE	REG. NO.
5632 Cass Lk. Rd	Keego Harbor	MI	58329	

PATIENT HOME PHONE	SOCIAL SECURITY NO.	PLEASE (✓) BILLING TYPE:	MEDICAL RECORD NO.
(999)5559696	899-10-9090	☐ CLIENT ☐ PATIENT ☒ INSURANCE	7891235

RESPONSIBLE PARTY'S LAST NAME	FIRST	M.I.	SEX	PT. MEDICARE NO.	PT. MEDICAID NO.	DATE COLLECTED
Jones	William	R	☒M ☐F	N/A	N/A	9/21/20xx

ADDRESS	CITY	STATE	ZIP CODE	PHONE NO.	TIME COLLECTED
				( )	2100 ☐AM ☐PM

INSURED / SUBSCRIBER NAME	INSURANCE CO. NAME & ADDRESS	COPY RESULTS TO
William Jones	BCBS of MI	John Carter

SUBSCRIBER'S EMPLOYER	RELATIONSHIP TO PATIENT	CONTRACT NO. / S.S. NO.	GRP./POL. NO.	SERVICE CODES
GM	☒ SELF ☐ SPOUSE ☐ DEP	GMC899109090		ER

☒NON-FASTING	LAST DOSE	URINE	PHONE RESULTS TO
☐FASTING ___ HRS	TIME ___ DATE ___	VOL ___ ML ___ HRS ☒ STAT ☐ PHONE	( )

ICD-9-CM DIAGNOSIS CODES (A DIAGNOSIS IS NECESSARY FOR ALL INSURANCE CLAIMS)

DIAGNOSIS: Abdominal Pain RUQ	ICD-9 CODE: 789.01
DIAGNOSIS:	ICD-9 CODE:
DIAGNOSIS:	ICD-9 CODE:

PHYSICIAN ICD-9 DIAGNOSIS — When ordering any test and/or any disease oriented panel, please remember: In order for the lab to bill, each and every test must be medically necessary for treatment or diagnosis of the patient. The ordering physician is required to submit ICD-9 diagnosis information supported by the patient medical record. Limited coverage tests are indicated by a solid triangle (▲). Advanced Beneficiary Notice (ABN) is required.

NOMC REFERENCE LABORATORY DIAGNOSTIC GROUPS

☐ BASIC METABOLIC PANEL SST	☒ COMPREHENSIVE METABOLIC PANEL SST	☐ GENERAL HEALTH PROFILE SST, L	☐ HEPATITIS PROFILE SST	☐ OBSTETRIC PROFILE SST, L, R
	☒ ELECTROLYTES PROFILE SST	☐ HEPATIC PROFILE SST	☐ LIPID PANEL ▲ SST	

INDIVIDUAL TESTS

☐ ABO / RH R	☐ CEA ▲ L	☐ GGTP SST	☐ LH SST	☐ PTT B
☐ AFP - TUMOR MARKER ● SST	☐ CHOLESTEROL ▲ SST	☐ GLUCOSE ▲ G	☐ LIPASE SST	☐ RA FACTOR SST
☐ ALT (SGPT) SST	☐ CK SST	☐ GLYCOHEMOGLOBIN ▲ L	☐ LITHIUM SST	☐ RUBELLA SST
☐ AMYLASE SST	☐ CK - MB SST	☐ HEP A AB, IGM R	☐ MAGNESIUM SST	☐ SED. RATE L
☐ ANTIBODY SCREEN R	☐ CORTISOL SST	☐ HCG, QUAL. (URINE) U	☐ MONONUCLEOSIS SST	☐ T3 BY RIA ● SST
☐ ANA SST	☐ CRP SST	☐ HDL CHOLESTEROL ▲ SST	MS - AFP (SEE BELOW)	☐ T3U SST
☐ AST (SGOT) SST	☐ CREATININE SST	☐ HEP B SURFACE AG SST	☐ PHENOBARBITAL R	☐ T4 (THYROXINE) SST
☐ BETA HCG QUANT. SST	☐ DIGOXIN R	☐ HEP B SURFACE AB SST	☐ POTASSIUM SST	☐ TESTOSTERONE SST
☐ BILIRUBIN, TOTAL SST	☐ DILANTIN R	☐ HEP B CORE AB SST	☐ PROGESTERONE ● SST	☐ THEOPHYLLINE R
☐ BUN SST	☐ ESTRADIOL ● SST	☐ HEP C AB ● SST	☐ PROT. ELECTROPH SST	☐ TRIGLYCERIDES ▲ SST
☐ CALCIUM SST	☐ FERRITIN ▲ SST	☐ HIV ANTIBODY SST	☐ PROTIME B	☐ TSH SST
☒ CBC W/DIFF. L	☐ FOLATE ☐ VIT. B12 SST	☐ IRON - TIBC SST	☐ PSA ▲ (DIAGNOSTIC) SST	☐ VDRL ▲ SST
☐ CBC W/O DIFF. (PBC) L	☐ FSH SST	☐ LDH SST	☐ PSA ▲ (SCREENING) SST	☒ URINALYSIS U
OTHER TEST		☐ LDL SST	☐ PTH ● SST	☐ VALPROIC ACID R
		OTHER TEST		

INDIVIDUAL TESTS

☐ OB QUAD SCREEN ● R	REPEAT SAMPLE ☐N ☐Y	FAMILY HX OF OPEN NTD ☐N ☐Y
MS-AFP	☐ CAUCASIAN ☐ BLACK ☐ OTHER	DESCRIBE ___
UNC. ESTRIOL	DIABETES MELLITUS ☐N ☐Y	LMP DATE ___
HCG	INSULIN DEP. DIABETIC ☐N ☐Y	GEST. ___ WKS. ___ DAYS
INHIBIN A	MAT. WEIGHT ___ LBS.	ULTRASOUND DATE ___
☐ MS - AFP SCREEN ● SST	MULTIPLE GEST. ☐N ☐Y ___	GEST. ___ WKS. ___ DAYS

MICROBIOLOGY
SOURCE:

CURRENT MEDICATION:

☐ CULTURE & SENS. C	☐ FUNGUS CULTURE ST	☐ HERPES CULTURE VT
☐ ACID FAST CULTURE/SMEAR ST	☐ GC - GEN PROBE GP	☐ O & P PVA
☐ ANAEROBIC CULTURE AC	☐ GC CULTURE GC	☐ STOOL CULTURE SC
☐ CHLAMYDIA-GEN PROBE GP	☐ GRAM STAIN C	☐ STREP SCREEN C
		☐ THROAT CULTURE C
☐ CHLAMYDIA and GC-GEN PROBE GP	☐ GROUP B STREP CULTURE C	☐ URINE CULTURE UC

SPECIMEN CODES

SST Ser. Sep. Tube	U Urinalysis Vial	GC GC Transp.	UC Urine Cult. Transp.
G Gray V. Tube	AC Anaerobic Cult. Transp.	PVA O&P Transp.	VT Viral Transp.
L Lavender Tube	C Routine Cult. Transp.	SC Stool Cult. Transp.	B Blue Tube
R Red V. Tube	CT Chlamydia Transp.	ST Sterile Transp.	GP Gen Probe

AAP #176295   AAP #176295

AAP #176295   AAP #176295

AAP #176295   AAP #176295

4100444 (10-04)   (WHITE & CANARY - SEND TO NOMC LABORATORY   PINK - CLIENT RETAIN FOR YOUR RECORDS)   ● TEST SENT TO REFERENCE LAB   ▲ ADVANCED BENEFICIARY NOTICE REQUIRED

OAKLAND MEDICAL CENTER

Name: *William Jones*   Room # *Bed 07*

Age: *46*   Sex: *M*   Race: *White*   Service Clinic: *ER*   Date: *10/10/2000*

CLINICAL DIAGNOSIS: *RUQ abdominal pain*

Summary of Chief Clinical Symptoms and Findings: *Nausea, vomiting, diarrhea (acute onset)*

Operation and date: *n/a*

Type of Patient: Ambulatory ( ) Wheelchair( ) Roller (X) Portable ( )

Previous Radiographs: Yes ( ) No (X)   Date:

May Dressing be Removed? *n/a*

EXAMINATION DESIRED: *Abdominal X-Ray A.P. oblique*

PHYSICIAN'S SIGNATURE: *John Carter MD*   Date: *10/10/2000*

PATIENT NAME: Roland Smith   **DOB:** 5/10/1992 **MRN#:** 978643214

DATE	TRIAGE / NURSES NOTES
7/10/20xx	Roland a 15 y/o male arrives in the E.R. c̄ his parents c/o of ® ankle pain. Apparently he slid into 1st base when he heard a popping sound from his ankle. His ankle is swollen according to his mom. He is unable to bear any weight. Vitals: T-99 orally, B/p 126/70, P-84, R-21. Roland's mom provides insurance information & signs the authorization forms for treatment. Roland will be taken back to the E.R. treatment area for further evaluation.
	7/10/20xx Jan Brady RN 19:30, Triage Nurse
7/10/20xx	Roland is a 15 y/o male who suffered an injury to his ® ankle playing softball c̄ his family. His family is with him tonight. Vitals: T-99 orally, B/p 128/78, P-88, R-22. He is alert, oriented & in no acute distress. Past hx was review c̄ the patient & his mother - unremarkable. There are no known allergies, no previous surgies, no previous fx's. ® ankle is swollen c̄ point tenderness along the lateral aspect of the ankle joint. He is able to move his toes. No open wound noted. Patient will be seen by E.R physician for further assessment.
7/10/20xx	20:45 Rachel Green RN - ER Nurse

SEATTLE GRACE HOSPITAL
E.R. DEPARTMENT

5683 GREYS AVE.
SEATTLE WA 89623

PATIENT NAME: Roland Smith **DOB:** 5/10/1992 **MRN#** 9786 43214

DATE	E.R. PHYSICIAN NOTES
7/10/20xx	Roland is a 15 y/o male who has sustained an injury to his ® ankle while playing softball. He was sliding into 1st base + heard a popping sound. He is unable to bear weight on the ® foot. Exam reveals: Swelling + bruising to ® ankle along the lateral aspect of the malleolus. He is able to move his toes. He is able to discriminate light touch on either side of the ankle. There is no overt distortion of the ankle. Will order X-Ray of the ® ankle to assess for fx + will see him again when x-ray results are available.
7/10/20xx	Derek Shepherd MD 21:30
7/10/20xx	21:45 taken to X-Ray Cindy Brady x-ray tech
7/10/20xx	22:15 brought back to E.R. Cindy Brady x-ray tech
7/10/20xx	Post radiographs revealed a nondisplaced fx of the lateral malleolus. The patient + parents were advised of the findings. The patient will be placed in a non-wt bearing splint to allow swelling to decrease. Will refer to an orthopedic surgeon for further care. Discharge instructions will be provided by the nurse.
7/10/20xx	D Shepherd MD 23:15

SEATTLE GRACE HOSPITAL

NPI # 1892367540

5683 GREYS AVE.

SEATTLE WA 89623

Name: _Koland Smith_   ROOM # _Bed 3B -ER_

Age: _15_ Sex: _m_ Race: _____ Service Clinic: _ER_   Date: _7/10/20xx_

CLINICAL DIAGNOSIS: _© ankle pain R/o ankle fx_

Summary of Chief Clinical Symptoms and Findings (Specify Duration): _lateral malleolus_
© side pain, injury occurred today

Operation and date: _N/A_

Type of Patient: Ambulatory ( ) Wheelchair (X) Roller ( ) Portable ( )

Previous Radiographs: Yes ( ) No (X) Date: _____.

May Dressing Be Removed?

EXAMINATION DESIRED: _2 view ankle xray ®_

PHYSICIAN'S SIGNATURE: _D. Shepherd MD_   DATE: _7/10/20xx_

PATIENT NAME: Roland Smith   DOB: 5/10/1992 MRN#: 978643214

DATE	TRIAGE / NURSES NOTES
7/10/20xx	Roland Smith is being discharged from the E.R. He was diagnosed c̄ a non-displaced lateral malleolus fx confirmed by x-ray. He has been splinted & his parents were given the names & phone numbers of 3 orthopedic surgeons. Both the patient & his parents were advised to make an appt. c̄ an orthopedic surgeon in the next 2 days. to have the fx further evaluated. The patient is to take ibuprofen 2 tabs, q 4-6hr for pain and to remain non-weight bearing ℞ He is not to remove the splint. All questions regarding the fx & care were answered. The patient & his parents understood the need for continued care of the fx.
7/10/20xx	Rachel Green RN 23:45

Name Jennifer Winkler   DOB: 6/15/2003   Page # ____

DATE	NOTES
8/26/20xx	Jennifer returns today c̄ her mom for a follow-up visit for her ® otitis media. She has completed her 7 day course of Augmentin. Her ear pain & temp subsided after 3 days. Vitals: T-98.4 orally, P-72, R-24. She is alert & sitting in her mom's lap. She indicates her ear no longer hurts by shaking her head no. She will be seen by the doctor.
8/26/20xx	Carol Hathaway PA-C 9:45 AM
8/26/20xx	Jennifer who is 4 y/o returns today c̄ her mom for an ear check. She completed her 7 day course of antibiotics; symptoms subsided after 3 days. Exam of ® ear reveals pearly gray tympanic membrane. No bulging, no pain. left ear WNL. Throat is s̄ exudate or redness. Neck is supple. Lungs are clear. Heart has regular rate & rhythm. Impression: ® serous otitis media resolved. Patient to return on a PRN basis
8/26/20xx	Abbey Lockhart MD 10:30 AM

356

PATIENT INFORMATION

DATE: 2/10/20xx

YOUR NAME: FRANK   N   STEIN
FIRST   MIDDLE   LAST

BIRTH DATE: 11/06/1968   SEX: X MALE ___ FEMALE   S.S.#: 991-88-9988

MARITAL STATUS: ___ S X M ___ D ___ W   HOME PHONE #: (994) 555-6169

HOME ADDRESS: 1313 Mockingbird Ln CITY: Blissfield   STATE: MT ZIP CODE: 87438

EMPLOYER: Masters Metalshop WK PHONE: 994-555-5656

SPOUSE NAME: MARY A STEIN   DOB: 4/11/1967 WK #: 994 555 5355

COMPLETE THIS SECTION IF THE **PATIENT IS** A CHILD, (WE BILL THE CUSTODIAL PARENT):

RESPONSIBLE PARTY: _____ DOB: _____
(FULL NAME)
RELATIONSHIP TO PATIENT: _____ PHONE NO: (____) _____

ADDRESS: _____ CITY: _____

STATE: ___ ZIP CODE: _____ SOCIAL SECURITY NUMBER: _____

EMPLOYER: _____ EMPLOYER NUMBER: _____

In Case of Emergency, Contact (Name): Mary Stein

RELATIONSHIP TO PATIENT: Spouse   HOME PHONE: 994 555 6169

WORK PHONE: 994 555 5355

INSURANCE AND AUTHORIZATION INFORMATION

[PRIMARY COVERAGE]

Insurance Co. Name: Cigna   EFFECT. DATE: _____

Insured Name: FRANK N. STEIN   DOB: 11/06/1968

CONTRACT / ID NO: 991889988   GROUP /POLICY # 1CB43

EMPLOYER NAME: Masters Metalshop   Employer Phone Number: 994 555 5656

Employer Address: Dixie Hwy Blissfield MT 87438

PLEASE SEE OTHER SIDE

357

INSURANCE AND AUTHORIZATION INFORMATION (CONT)

[SECONDARY COVERAGE (IF APPLICABLE)]

Name of Insurance Co.: N/A   **EFFECTIVE DATE:**

Insured Name: **D.O.B:**   **S.S.#:**

CONTRACT/ID#   **GROUP/POLICY#**

EMPLOYER NAME: **Employer Phone Number:**

Employer Address:

****

- I consent to any medical, diagnostic, therapeutic, or minor surgical procedure rendered to the patient under the supervision of the physicians. I hereby recognize that the practice of medicine & surgery is not an exact science & I acknowledge that no one has made any representation, guarantee, or warranty to me regarding the results to be achieved by any treatments or examination that I (or the patient) will receive as a result of services.

- The information authorized for release also may include drug/alcohol abuse treatment records. This category of medical information/records is protected by **Federal confidentiality rules (42 CFR Part 2).** The Federal rules prohibit anyone receiving this information or records from making further release unless further release is expressly permitted by the written permitted by the written authorization of the person to whom it pertains or as otherwise permitted by 42 CFR Part 2. A general authorization for the release of medical or other information is not sufficient for this purpose. The Federal rules restrict any use of the information to criminally investigate or prosecute any alcohol or drug abuse patient. As a result, by signing below I specifically authorize any such records included in my health information to be releases.

- The information authorized for release also may include protected health information related to mental health.

- I authorize & request my insurance company to pay directly to the provider the amount due for medical care. In addition, I understand that I will be responsible for any amounts that are not covered by insurance.

- I understand that if any employee, physician, of _MountainView Family Practice_ sustain a percutaneous (through the skin), mucous membrane (through the mouth or eye), or open wound exposure to my blood or other bodily fluids, I may be tested for human immunodeficiency virus (HIV) that causes acquired immune deficiency syndrome (AIDS).

- Information used or disclosed under this authorization may be subject to re-disclosure by the recipient and no longer protected by federal privacy regulations.

I hereby certify that the contents of this form are understood by me. Paragraphs or lines that I choose not to pertain to me, if any, were stricken & initialed by me, before I signed:

I attest that the information that I have provided on this form is complete and accurate to the best of my knowledge

Name (Please Print): Frank N Stein

FrankNStein   **Date:** 2/10/20xx
Patient's Signature (Parent/Guardian if patient is under the age of 18 years)

DATE: 2/10/20xx

PATIENT NAME: FRANK N. STEIN   **DOB:** 11/6/1968 **S.S.#:** 991-88-9988

DRUG ALLERGIES		FAMILY HISTORY						
PENCILLIN			Father	Mother	Father's Parents	Mother's Parents	Siblings	Children
		Heart Disease	Deceased				Brother	
		High BP		X			Sister	
		Stroke						
		Glaucoma						
CURRENT MEDICATIONS (INCLUDING DOSAGE / FREQUENCY)		Diabetes		X			Brother	
1. Crestor		Epilepsy / conv.						
		Bleeding Disorder						
2		Kidney Disease						
3		Thyroid Disease						
4		Mental Illness						
5		Osteoporosis		X			Sister	
6								

HOSPITAL OR SURGERY:	REASON Rotater cuff DATE winter 1996		REASON pneumonia DATE @ 1978
REASON/DATE	REASON DATE		REASON DATE

HEADACHE frequently	LACTOSE INTOL	DEPRESSION
SOB	GALLBLADDER	GOUT
HEART PALPITATIONS	PROSTATE DIS	SCARLET FEVER
HEART MURMUR	BOWEL IRREG	CHRONIC RASH
CHEST PAIN	INCONTINENCE	RHEUMATIC FEVER
DIZZINESS/	SEXUAL DYSFUNCTION	MUMPS as a child
FAINTING	MENSTRUAL PROBLEM	MEASLES as a child
PERIPHERAL VASCULAR DIS	VENERAL DISEASE	RUBELLA
ALLERGIES/HAY FEVER Yes	FREQUENT INFECTIONS	POLIO
ASTHMA	HEPATITIS	DIPHTHERIA
BRONCHITIS	ANEMIA	TETANUS
PNEUMONIA Yes 1978	ARTHRITIS joint stiffness	OTHER
ULCER	OSTEOPOROSIS	
GI BLEED	NERVOUSNESS	OTHER

HABITS:		WOMEN ONLY
☑SMOKE: PACKS DAILY: 1 HOW LONG? 20yrs INTERESTED IN STOPPING? yes	☐ SLEEP: DIFFICULTY FALLING ASLEEP _____ CONTINUITY DISTURBANCES _____ SNORING: _____	PREGNANT? ☐ YES ☐ NO PLANNING PREGNANCY? ☐ YES ☐ NO
☑COFFEE: CUPS DAILY: 2 ☑OTHER CAFFEINE DRINKS: coke ☑ALCOHOL: TYPE: Beer AMOUNT: 2/day	EARLY MORNING AWAKENING: _____ DAYTIME DROWSINESS: _____ OTHER: _____	**MEN ONLY** ☒ - LAST PROSTATE EXAM Never ☒ - PROBLEMS URINATING? NO

DR. / P.A. SIGNATURE: _____   **DATE:** _____

DATE LAST REVIEWED: _____

DATE: 4-14-20xx	PATIENT NAME: Jones, Alex	DOB: 36 yrs.	S.S.# 888-11-9999

HT: 5'10"	WT: 276 #	TEMP 979/8	RESP	PULSE 78	BP (SIT OR STAND) 124/80	BP (SUPINE) /

CHIEF COMPLAINT?
Lump on Right side of face, also needs fasting blood draw.
venipuncture (4) (MM)

HOW LONG HAS PATIENT FELT LIKE THIS?
FASTING!

WOMEN: LMP: — LAST PAP — LAST MAMMO: —	MEN LAST PROSTATE EXAM	M.A. INITIALS 2 (MM)

ROS – DESCRIPTION FROM THE PT DESCRIBING HOW THEY FEEL: CONSTITUITIONAL (FEVER) CHILLS:

ENT:	NECK	HEART	RESPIRATORY	SKIN Lasia	ENDOCRINE Fasedu

MUSCULOSKELTAL	G.I.	GENITOURINARY	NEUROS	PSYCH good

PHYSICAL EXAM:
√ = NORMAL   X = ABNORMAL FINDINGS

ALLERGIES: Vicodin   Bee Stings

☒ HEAD	SHAPE, SIZE, DEFECTS, HAIR
☒ FACE	APPEARANCE, SCARS, DEFECTS, TENDERNESS
☒ NECK	APPEARANCE, SYMMETRY, MASSES, THYROID, TRACHEA skin lesion ? nodes
☐ EYES	LIDS, CONJUNCTIVA SCLERA, PUPILS, LIDS, IRISES FUNDI, VISION
☐ EARS	AUD. CANALS, TYMP. MEMB. HEARING DEFECTS, PINNEA
☐ NOSE	NASAL MUCOSA, CONGESTION SEPTUM, TURBINATES
☐ MOUTH	LIPS, MUCOSA, TEETH, GUMS, MASSES
☐ THROAT	PALATE, TONGUE, UVULA, TONSILS, PHARYNX
☐ CHEST (BREAST)	NIPPLE DISCHARGE, SIZE, SHAPE, SYMMETRY TENDER, MASSES
☐ RESPIRATORY	↑EFFORT, WHEEZES, RALES, ↓BREATH SOUNDS
☐ CARDIOVASCULAR	P.M.I. RATE, RHYTHM, MURMURS, PULSE EDEMA, BRUITS
☐ ABDOMEN	SCARS, TENDERNESS, BOWEL SOUNDS MASSES, LIVER, SPLEEN
☐ GASTROINTESTINAL	HERNIAS, ANUS: HEMORRHOIDS; RECTUM: MASSES, BLOOD
☐ GENITALIA FEMALE:	LABIA, VAGINA DISCHARGE, WARTS, LESIONS, MASSES

☐ GENITALIA MALE	DISCHARGE, WARTS, LESIONS MASSES
☐ GROIN	TENDERNESS, HERNIAS, MASSES
☐ GENITOURINARY	URETHRA, BLADDER, CERVIX, UTERUS, DISCHARGE, MASSES
☐ HEMATOLOGIC	PETECHIAE, BRUISES
☐ LYMPHATIC	ENLARGED LYMPNODES: NECK, AXILLA, GROIN
☒ INTEGUMENTARY	HAIR, NAILS, SKIN: JAUNDICE, CYANOSIS, RASHES, ULCERS, DEFECTS neck
☐ BACK (SPINE)	TENDERNESS, SWELLING MASSES, SCOLIOSIS KYPHOSIS, LORDOSIS
☐ MUSCULOSKELETAL (LOWER EXTERMITIES, HIPS, PELVIS, KNEES, ANKLES)	
A. MUSCLES	TENDERNESS, SWELLING, WEAKNESS, MASSES ATROPHY
B. BONES/JOINTS	ROM, STABILITY, TENDER, SWELLING FLUIDS
☐ MUSCULOSKELTAL (UPPER EXTERMITIES NECK SHOULDERS, ELBOWS, WRISTS, HANDS)	
A. MUSCLES	TENDERNESS, SWELLING, WEAKNESS, MASSES, ATROPHY
B. BONES/JOINTS	ROM, STABILITY, TENDER, SWELLING FLUIDS
☒ NEUROLOGIC	CRANIAL NERVES, DTR'S PATH. REFLEXES, GAIT SENSATION fasting x 1 month
☐ PSYCHIATRIC	ORIENTATION, MEMORY, DEPRESSION, ANXIETY

4-14-20xx   Jones Alex

ANY CHANGES IN PAST MEDICAL/FAMILY HISTORY?	PLAN/ASSESSMENT & TEST ORDERED (WHY)
R/o DM.	F/S 6/07

ABNORMAL FINDINGS:

(1) Pt o profound fatigue. Worse for a month + pt can work.	→ T3 /T4, TgA CBC, LFT, CMP, LIP, SS.
(2) (R) near mass is related an internal hair on a sebaceous cyst.	→ monitor cyst.
(4) Possible hypo glycemia	→ consider 5 hour LTT if labs ⊖.
(5) Recommend mammo	

_____   4/13/
Physician Signature   Date

Name ████████████████   SS# ████████████   Page #_____   Name

DATE	NOTES

9-14-20XX

ht: 5'4"   Wt: 122#   Temp: 98.6°   P-84 reg   B/p- 132/84   RM#1

C/c: injury to left knee, pt states that   10:36am
while jogging she fell and injured   ⒮M
her left knee this morning

S: Ⓛ KNEE PAIN DUE TO A FALL.

O: PT IS ATHLETIC & HAS A
SWOLLEN Ⓛ KNEE. MILD ABRASION.
⊕ ECCHYMOSIS. KNEE EXAM DONE
AND SHOWS GOOD RANGE OF MOTION,
NO CREPITUS, NEGATIVE DRAWER
SIGN, NEGATIVE LACHMANS SIGN.
PT IS ABLE TO BEAR WEIGHT.

A: CONTUSION Ⓛ KNEE

P: IF NOT IMPROVED, CONSIDER
X-RAYS.
REST Ⓛ KNEE. IBUPROFEN 600
PO QID #40 1RF.
CALL IF WORSE

<u>**Post-Operative Orders**</u>

1.   ☒ Patient to PAR   ☐ Admit Patient to Hospital Floor

2.   Dx: _CLOSED REDUCTION (R) 2ND AND 3RD METS._

3.   Vitals: ☒ Per Routine
             ☐ Other: _____

4.   ☒ NKDA   ☐ Allergy to: _____

5.   ☒ Elevate [Right/Left] Foot
     ☒ Circulation check to [Right/Left] foot Q 10 minutes until stable. If not stable at 30
        minutes, call Dr. Hoyal.
     ☐ Check Blood Glucose x1
     ☐ X-Ray [Right/Left] [Foot/Ankle] [2/3 Views]
     ☐ Other: _____

6.   Diet: ☒ Regular   ☐ ADA 2000

7.   ☐ Toradol 30 mg IV x1
     ☐ Vicodin ES 1-2 Tabs po Q 4 H for pain
     ☐ Codiene #3 1-2 Tabs po Q 4 H for pain
     ☐ Demerol 50 mg IV or 1-2 Tabs po Q 4 H for severe pain

8.   ☐ Post-Op Shoe   ☐ Cast Shoe to [Right/Left]
     ☐ Weightbearing   ☒ Non-weightbearing [Right/Left]
     ☒ Crutch Train
        DISPENSE CRUTCHES

9.   Discharge to home when discharge criteria met.

Noted 6-4-4 @ 1145 m Parley

363

MEDICATION ADMINISTRATION RECORD

CHECKED BY _____

DIAGNOSIS: ORIF LEFT ANKLE

ADMIT: 11/07/01 WT: 197 LBS. HT: 5FT 9IN BSA: 2.11X9

AGE: 61 SEX:F Est. CREATINE CL: LAB RESULT: N/A

NOTES:

ALLERGIES: No Report

UNIT #: _____

ACCT #: _____

ADMINISTRATION PERIOD 1530 11/07/01 TO 1529 11/08/01	START/STOP	1530-2319	2320-0729	0730-1529
********** PRN MEDS **********				
OXYCODONE HCl/ACETAMINOPHEN (PERCOCET) RX #: 00560682 1 TABLET ORAL PRN PAIN COMMENTS: MAX. ACETAMINOPHEN DOSE IS 4 G/24 HOURS	11/07/01 11/10/01			
OXYCODONE HCl/ACETAMINOPHEN (PERCOCET) RX #: 00560682 1 TABLET ORAL PRN PAIN COMMENTS: MAX. ACETAMINOPHEN DOSE IS 4 G/24 HOURS	11/07/01 11/10/01	1900	0300	0800
DROPERIDOL RX #: 00560684 0.5ML INTRAVEN. PRN NAUSEA	11/07/01 11/21/01			
Humulin N 25u g AM				0800
12 u R AM				
Humulin N 20u 8 PM				
12 u R PM				
Glucophage 1000mg bid			2200	0800
Synthroid 0.015mg 8AM				0800
Gemfibrozil 600mg 8AM				0800
Evista 60mg 8AM				0800

****************** FINAL MAR PAGE FOR THIS PATIENT ******************

PAIN SCALE 0-10 0-NO PAIN 10 WORST POSSIBLE PAIN	MED EFFECTIVENESS A - EFFECTIVE B - MED EFFECTIVE C - NOT EFFECTIVE	INITIALS	SIGNATURE	INITIALS	SIGNATURE

COMMENTS:

| SUMMARY REPORT | DATE / TIME | | ADMIT DATE |
| 08/26/98 | 02:27 | | 08/19/98 |

| ATIENT NAME: | | BIRTH DATE | PATIENT ACCOUNT NUMBER | | DISCHARGE DATE |
| | | 08/19/1998 | | | 08/21/98 |

| ATIENT I.D. NUMBER: | MEDICAL RECORD NUMBER: | ROOM / BED | SEX | DOCTOR: |
| | | NICU / ICN | M | |

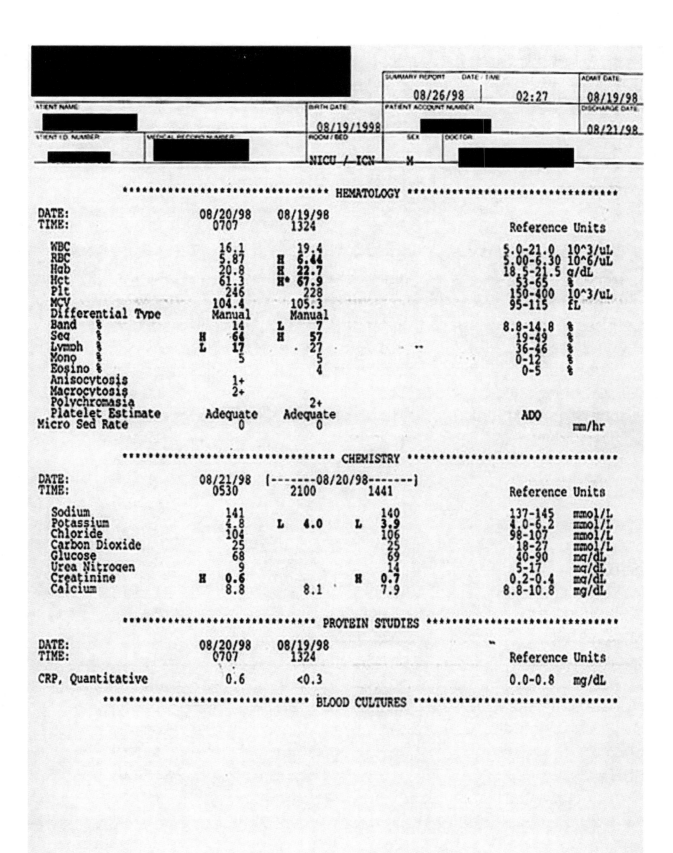

**************************** HEMATOLOGY ****************************

DATE:	08/20/98	08/19/98		
TIME:	0707	1324		Reference Units
WBC	16.1	19.4		5.0-21.0	10^3/uL
RBC	5.87	H 6.44		5.00-6.30	10^6/uL
Hgb	20.8	H 22.7		18.5-21.5	g/dL
Hct	61.3	H* 67.9		53-65	%
Plt	246	228		150-400	10^3/uL
MCV	104.4	105.3		95-115	fL
Differential Type	Manual	Manual			
Band %	14	L 7		8.8-14.8	%
Seg %	H 64	H 57		19-49	%
Lymph %	L 17	27	**	36-46	%
Mono %	5	5		0-12	%
Eosino %		4		0-5	%
Anisocytosis	1+				
Macrocytosis	2+				
Polychromasia		2+			
Platelet Estimate	Adequate	Adequate		ADQ	
Micro Sed Rate	0	0			mm/hr

**************************** CHEMISTRY ****************************

DATE:	08/21/98	[-------08/20/98-------]		
TIME:	0530	2100	1441	Reference Units
Sodium	141		140	137-145	mmol/L
Potassium	4.8	L 4.0	L 3.9	4.0-6.2	mmol/L
Chloride	104		106	98-107	mmol/L
Carbon Dioxide	25		25	18-27	mmol/L
Glucose	68		69	40-90	mg/dL
Urea Nitrogen	9		14	5-17	mg/dL
Creatinine	H 0.6		H 0.7	0.2-0.4	mg/dL
Calcium	8.8	8.1	7.9	8.8-10.8	mg/dL

**************************** PROTEIN STUDIES ****************************

DATE:	08/20/98	08/19/98		
TIME:	0707	1324		Reference Units
CRP, Quantitative	0.6	<0.3		0.0-0.8	mg/dL

**************************** BLOOD CULTURES ****************************

NAME: INPATIENT MEDICAL RECORDS COPY
PAGE 1   CONTINUED

Clinical Laboratory Report

Patient Name	Date Drawn	Date Received	Date of Report
Dwyer, John	12/20/XX	12/20/XX	12/22/XX

Sex	Age	Client Name / Address	ID Number	Account Number
M	31	Grace Medical Center	78987654	86574

Ordering Physician
Shepherd, D.
123094567

Client Name / Address
Grace Medical Center
Derek Shepherd, M.D.
5874 West Street
Seattle, WA 80023

Specimen Number	Time Drawn
918273	11:00

Patient ID / Soc. Sec. #

TEST NAME	RESULT		UNITS	REFERENCE RANGE
COMPLETE BLOOD COUNT W/DIFF				
WBC	5.2		Thous/cu.mm	3.9-11.1
RBC	3.51	L	Mil/cu.mm	4.20-5.70
HGB(HEMOGLOBIN)	14.5		g/dL	13.2-16.9
HCT(HEMATOCRIT)	41.2		Percent	28.6-49.0
MCV	117	H	fl	80-97
MCH	41.4	H	pg	27.5-33.5
MCHC	35.3		Percent	32.0-36.0
RDW	11.8		Percent	11.0-15.0
PLATELET COUNT	172		Thous/cu.mm	140-390
MPV	7.6		fl	7.5-11.5
DIFFERENTIAL				
TOTAL NEUTROPHILS, %	40.1		Percent	38.0-80.0
TOTAL LYMPHOCYTES, %	46.1		Percent	15.0-49.0
MONOCYTES, %	12.9		Percent	0.0-13.0
EOSINOPHILS, %	0.6		Percent	0.0-8.0
BASOPHILS, %	0.3		Percent	0.0-2.0
TOTAL NEUTROPHILS, ABSOLUTE	2085		Cells/cu.mm	1650-8000
TOTAL LYMPHOCYTES, ABSOLUTE	2397		Cells/cu.mm	1000-3500
MONOCYTES, ABSOLUTE	671		Cells/cu.mm	40-900
EOSINOPHILS, ABSOLUTE	31		Cells/cu.mm	30-600
BASOPHILS, ABSOLUTE	16		Cells/cu.mm	0-125

SEATTLE GRACE HOSPITAL 2975658874

Name: Hector Martinez   **Date:** 04/18/20XX   **MRN No.:** 5187935

DOB: 06/24/19XX   **Sex:** Male   **Race:** Hispanic

Ordering Physician: Meredith Grey, MD

EXAMINATION DESIRED: Metastatic series

REASON FOR EXAM: Carcinoma of lung

REPORT:

Calcified opacity is noted in the left femoral head and left ilium; also in the skull;
these are probably Osteoblastic metastatic lesions.

Date: 4/19/20XX   Exam: Metastatic   Radiologist: Miranda Bailey, MD

X-RAY REPORT

Patient Name: Daniel Hayes   **DOB: 8/10/19XX**   **MRN# 6358719**

Attending Physician: John Carter, MD

Date of Surgery: 5/20/20XX

Operative Report

PREOPERATIVE DIAGNOSIS: Internal and external hemorrhoids.

POSTOPERATIVE DIAGNOSIS: Internal and external hemorrhoids.

PROCEDURE PERFORMED: Internal and external hemorrhoidectomy.

ATTENDING SURGEON: Dr. J. Carter

FIRST ASSISTANT: Dr. Mark Green

SECOND ASSISTANT: _____[NAME].

ANESTHESIA: General endotracheal.

INDICATIONS FOR PROCEDURE: Mr. Hayes is a 53-year-old male with a history of internal and external hemorrhoids which had continued to bleed despite normal conservative measures including sitz baths and increased fiber. He had undergone one attempt at banding without success. For this reason, it was decided that he would be best served with elective hemorrhoidectomy.

DETAILS OF PROCEDURE: Having obtained informed consent, the patient was taken to the operating room and placed on the operating table in the supine position. Following induction of general endotracheal anesthesia without complications, the patient was positioned in the dorsal lithotomy position, and his perirectal and perineal area were prepped and draped in the usual sterile fashion.

The patient's anus and rectum were dilated until they could admit 3 fingers easily. Next, an anal retractor was placed in the anal canal. Three large clusters of combined internal and external hemorrhoids were noted at the 12 o'clock, 3 o'clock, and 6 o'clock positions. Each cluster was first grasped using a set of Allis forceps. They were then divided and removed using a GIA stapler. Hemostasis was ensured using Bovie electrocautery. The rectum was then packed using Gelfoam which had been soaked in Marcaine containing epinephrine

The patient was awakened, extubated, and taken to the postanesthesia care unit in satisfactory condition. He tolerated the procedure well, and there were no complications. Dr. Green was present and scrubbed throughout the duration of this procedure.

§ 482.24 Condition of participation: Medical record services.

The hospital must have a medical record service that has administrative responsibility for medical records. A medical record must be maintained for every individual evaluated or treated in the hospital.

(a) *Standard: Organization and staffing.* The organization of the medical record service must be appropriate to the scope and complexity of the services performed. The hospital must employ adequate personnel to ensure prompt completion, filing, and retrieval of records.

(b) *Standard: Form and retention of record.* The hospital must maintain a medical record for each inpatient and outpatient. Medical records must be accurately written, promptly completed, properly filed and retained, and accessible. The hospital must use a system of author identification and record maintenance that ensures the integrity of the authentification and protects the security of all record entries.

(1) Medical records must be retained in their original or legally reproduced form for a period of at least 5 years.

(2) The hospital must have a system of coding and indexing medical records. The system must allow for timely retrieval by diagnosis and procedure, in order to support medical care evaluation studies.

(3) The hospital must have a procedure for ensuring the confidentiality of patient records. In-formation from or copies of records may be released only to authorized individuals, and the hospital must ensure that unauthorized individuals cannot gain access to or alter patient records. Original medical records must be released by the hospital only in accordance with Federal or State laws, court orders, or subpoenas.

(c) *Standard: Content of record.* The medical record must contain information to justify admission and continued hospitalization, support the diagnosis, and describe the patient's progress and response to medications and services.

(1) All entries must be legible and complete, and must be authenticated and dated promptly by the person (identified by name and discipline) who is responsible for ordering, providing, or evaluating the service furnished.

(i) The author of each entry must be identifed and must authenticate his or her entry.

(ii) Authentication may include signatures, written initials or computer entry.

(2) All records must document the following, as appropriate:

(i) Evidence of a physical examination, including a health history, performed no more than 7 days prior to admission or within 48 hours after admission.

(ii) Admitting diagnosis.

(iii) Results of all consultative evaluations of the patient and appropriate findings by clinical and other staff involved in the care of the patient.

(iv) Documentation of complications, hospital acquired infections, and unfavorable reactions to drugs and anesthesia.

(v) Properly executed informed consent forms for procedures and treatments specified by the medical staff, or by Federal or State law if applicable, to require written patient consent.

(vi) All practitioners' orders, nursing notes, reports of treatment, medication records, radiology, and laboratory reports, and vital signs and other information necessary to monitor the patient's condition.

(vii) Discharge summary with outcome of hospitalization, disposition of case, and provisions for follow-up care.

(viii) Final diagnosis with completion of medical records within 30 days following discharge.

OMB 0938 - 0930

Medicare Authorization To Disclose Personal Health Information

Use this form to ask Medicare to give out (disclose) your personal health information.

1. Print Your Name   Your Medicare Number   Your Date of Birth

2. **Check <u>one or more boxes</u> to tell Medicare the specific personal health information you want disclosed. Medicare will only disclose the personal health information you check below.**

   ❑ Information about a medical service or medical services you received. Fill in A, B, and/or C below:

       A. One medical service on this date: _____
       From this doctor or supplier: _____

       B. All medical services on the following date(s): _____

       C. All medical services from these doctor(s) or supplier(s): _____

   ❑ Information about your Medicare eligibility

   ❑ Information on your other health coverage

   ❑ Information on your deductible for the year(s) of: _____

   ❑ Copy of your Medicare Summary Notice for

       Date of Medical Service   Doctor or Supplier   Hospital or Facility
       _____   _____   _____
       _____   _____   _____

   ❑ Other personal health information:
   _____

3. **Check only <u>one</u> for how long Medicare can use this authorization to disclose your personal health information** (subject to applicable law—for example, your State may limit how long Medicare may give out your personal health information):

   ❑ Disclose my personal health information this one time only.

   ❑ Start disclosing my personal health information on this date: _____
       Stop disclosing my personal health information on this date: _____

   ❑ Disclose my personal health information for the duration of an event (for example, while you are enrolled in a Medicare health plan or while you are in a hospital).

       What is the event: _____

CMS – 10106 (11/04)

4. **Fill in the reason for the disclosure** (you may write "at my request"):

_____

5. **Fill in the name and address of the person(s) or organization(s) to whom you want Medicare to disclose your personal health information:**

_____
_____
_____
_____

6.

I authorize Medicare to disclose my personal health information listed above to the person(s) or organization(s) I have named on this form. I understand that my personal health information may be re-disclosed by the person(s) or organization(s) and may no longer be protected by law.

_____   _____ _____
Sign Your Name   **Your Telephone Number**   **Date**

☐ Check here if you are signing as a personal representative. Please attach the appropriate documentation (for example, Power of Attorney).

7. **Send your completed, signed authorization to:**

8. **Note:**

You have the right to take back ("revoke") your authorization at any time, in writing, except to the extent that Medicare has already acted based on your permission. If you would like to revoke your authorization, send a written request to the address shown above.

Your refusal to authorize this disclosure of your personal health information will have no effect on your enrollment, eligibility for benefits, or the amount Medicare pays for the health services you receive.

If you need help with this form, call 1-800-MEDICARE (1-800-633-4227).

Form CMS 10106 (11/04)

American Health Information Management Association Standards of Ethical Coding

Introduction

The Standards of Ethical Coding are based on the American Health Information Management Association's (AHIMA's) Code of Ethics. Both sets of principles reflect expectations of professional conduct for coding professionals involved in diagnostic and/or procedural coding or other health record data abstraction.

A Code of Ethics sets forth professional values and ethical principles and offers ethical guidelines to which professionals aspire and by which their actions can be judged. Health information management (HIM) professionals are expected to demonstrate professional values by their actions to patients, employers, members of the healthcare team, the public, and the many stakeholders they serve. A Code of Ethics is important in helping to guide the decision-making process and can be referenced by individuals, agencies, organizations, and bodies (such as licensing and regulatory boards, insurance providers, courts of law, government agencies, and other professional groups).

The AHIMA Code of Ethics (available on the AHIMA web site) is relevant to all AHIMA members and credentialed HIM professionals and students, regardless of their professional functions, the settings in which they work, or the populations they serve. Coding is one of the core HIM functions, and due to the complex regulatory requirements affecting the health information coding process, coding professionals are frequently faced with ethical challenges. The AHIMA Standards of Ethical Coding are intended to assist coding professionals and managers in decision-making processes and actions, outline expectations for making ethical decisions in the workplace, and demonstrate coding professionals' commitment to integrity during the coding process, regardless of the purpose for which the codes are being reported. They are relevant to all coding professionals and those who manage the coding function, regardless of the healthcare setting in which they work or whether they are AHIMA members or nonmembers.

These Standards of Ethical Coding have been revised in order to reflect the current healthcare environment and modern coding practices. The previous revision was published in 1999.

Standards of Ethical Coding

Coding professionals should:
1.   Apply accurate, complete, and consistent coding practices for the production of high-quality healthcare data.

2.   Report all healthcare data elements (e.g. diagnosis and procedure codes, present on admission indicator, discharge status) required for external reporting purposes (e.g. reimbursement and other administrative uses, population health, quality and patient safety measurement, and research) completely and accurately, in accordance with regulatory and documentation standards and requirements and applicable official coding conventions, rules, and guidelines.

3.   Assign and report only the codes and data that are clearly and consistently supported by health record documentation in accordance with applicable code set and abstraction conventions, rules, and guidelines.

4.   Query provider (physician or other qualified healthcare practitioner) for clarification and additional documentation prior to code assignment when there is conflicting, incomplete, or ambiguous information in the health record regarding a significant reportable condition or procedure or other reportable data element dependent on health record documentation (e.g. present on admission indicator).

5.   Refuse to change reported codes or the narratives of codes so that meanings are misrepresented.

6.   Refuse to participate in or support coding or documentation practices intended to inappropriately increase payment, qualify for insurance policy coverage, or skew data by means that do not comply with federal and state statutes, regulations and official rules and guidelines.

7.   Facilitate interdisciplinary collaboration in situations supporting proper coding practices.

8.   Advance coding knowledge and practice through continuing education.

9.   Refuse to participate in or conceal unethical coding or abstraction practices or procedures.

10.   Protect the confidentiality of the health record at all times and refuse to access protected health information not required for coding-related activities (examples of coding-related activities include completion of code assignment, other health record data abstraction, coding audits, and educational purposes).

11.   Demonstrate behavior that reflects integrity, shows a commitment to ethical and legal coding practices, and fosters trust in professional activities.

Revised and approved by the House of Delegates 09/08

Resources

(updated April 2013)
AHIMA Code of Ethics

ICD-9-CM Official Guidelines for Coding and Reporting

AHIMA's position statement on Quality Health Data and Information

AHIMA's position statement on Consistency of Healthcare Diagnostic and Procedural Coding

AHIMA Practice Brief titled "Managing an Effective Query Process

How to Interpret the Standards of Ethical Coding

The following ethical principles are based on the core values of the American Health Information Management Association and the AHIMA Code of Ethics and apply to all coding professionals. Guidelines for each ethical principle include examples of behaviors and situations that can help to clarify the principle. They are not meant as a comprehensive list of all situations that can occur.

1. *Apply accurate, complete, and consistent coding practices for the production of high-quality healthcare data.*
Coding professionals and those who manage coded data shall:

1.1. Support selection of appropriate diagnostic, procedure and other types of health service related codes (e.g. present on admission indicator, discharge status). Example:Policies and procedures are developed and used as a framework for the work process, and education and training is provided on their use.

1.2. Develop and comply with comprehensive internal coding policies and procedures that are consistent with official coding rules and guidelines, reimbursement regulations and policies and prohibit coding practices that misrepresent the patient's medical conditions and treatment provided or are not supported by the health record documentation. Example:Code assignment resulting in misrepresentation of facts carries significant consequences.

1.3. Participate in the development of institutional coding policies and ensure that coding policies complement, and do not conflict with, official coding rules and guidelines.

1.4. Foster an environment that supports honest and ethical coding practices resulting in accurate and reliable data. Coding professionals **shall not**:

1.5. Participate in improper preparation, alteration, or suppression of coded information.

2. *Report all healthcare data elements (e.g. diagnosis and procedure codes, present on admission indicator, discharge status) required for external reporting purposes (e.g. reimbursement and other administrative uses, population health, public data reporting, quality and patient safety measurement, research) completely and accurately, in accordance with regulatory and documentation standards and requirements and applicable official coding conventions, rules, and guidelines.*

Coding professionals **shall**:

2.1. Adhere to the ICD coding conventions, official coding guidelines approved by the Cooperating Parties,[1] the CPT rules established by the American Medical Association, and any other official coding rules and guidelines established for use with mandated standard code sets. Example:Appropriate resource tools that assist coding professionals with proper sequencing and reporting to stay in compliance with existing reporting requirements are available and used.

2.2. Select and sequence diagnosis and procedure codes in accordance with the definitions of required data sets for applicable healthcare settings.

2.3. Comply with AHIMA's standards governing data reporting practices, including health record documentation and clinician query standards.

3.   *Assign and report only the codes that are clearly and consistently supported by health record documentation in accordance with applicable code set conventions, rules, and guidelines.*

Coding professionals **shall**:

3.1. Apply skills, knowledge of currently mandated coding and classification systems, and official resources to select the appropriate diagnostic and procedural codes (including applicable modifiers), and other codes representing healthcare services (including substances, equipment, supplies, or other items used in the provision of healthcare services). Example:Failure to research or confirm the appropriate code for a clinical condition not indexed in the classification, or reporting a code for the sake of convenience or to affect reporting for a desired effect on the results, is considered unethical.

4.   *Query provider (physician or other qualified healthcare practitioner) for clarification and additional documentation prior to code assignment when there is conflicting, incomplete, or ambiguous information in the health record regarding a significant reportable condition or procedure or other reportable data element dependent on health record documentation (e.g. present on admission indicator).*
Coding professionals **shall**:

4.1. Participate in the development of query policies that support documentation improvement and meet regulatory, legal, and ethical standards for coding and reporting.

4.2. Query the provider for clarification when documentation in the health record that impacts an externally reportable data element is illegible, incomplete, unclear, inconsistent, or imprecise.

4.3. Use queries as a communication tool to improve the accuracy of code assignment and the quality of health record documentation, not to inappropriately increase reimbursement or misrepresent quality of care. Example: Policies regarding the circumstances when clinicians should be queried are designed to promote complete and accurate coding and complete documentation, regardless of whether reimbursement will be affected.

Coding professionals **shall not**:

4.4. Query the provider when there is no clinical information in the health record prompting the need for a query. Example:Query the provider regarding the presence of gram-negative pneumonia on every pneumonia case, regardless of whether there are any clinical indications of gram-negative pneumonia documented in the record.

5.   *Refuse to change reported codes or the narratives of codes so that meanings are misrepresented.*

Coding professionals **shall not**:

5.1. Change the description for a diagnosis or procedure code or other reported data element so that it does not accurately reflect the official definition of that code. Example:The description of a code is altered in the encoding software, resulting in incorrect reporting of this code.

6.   *Refuse to participate in or support coding or documentation practices intended to inappropriately increase payment, qualify for insurance policy coverage, or skew data by means that do not comply with federal and state statutes, regulations and official rules and guidelines.*

Coding professionals **shall**:

6.1. Select and sequence the codes such that the organization receives the optimal payment to which the facility is legally entitled, remembering that it is unethical and illegal to increase payment by means that contradict regulatory guidelines.

Coding professionals **shall not**:

6.2. Misrepresent the patient's clinical picture through intentional incorrect coding or omission of diagnosis or procedure codes, or the addition of diagnosis or procedure codes unsupported by health record documentation, to inappropriately increase reimbursement, justify medical necessity, improve publicly reported data, or qualify for insurance policy coverage benefits. Examples:A patient has a health plan that excludes reimbursement for reproductive management or contraception; so rather than report the correct code for admission for tubal ligation, it is reported as a medically necessary condition with performance of a salpingectomy. The narrative descriptions of both the diagnosis and procedures reflect an admission for tubal ligation and the procedure (tubal ligation) is displayed on the record. A code is changed at the patient's request so that the service will be covered by the patient's insurance.

Coding professionals **shall not**:

6.3. Inappropriately exclude diagnosis or procedure codes in order to misrepresent the quality of care provided. Examples:Following a surgical procedure, a patient acquired an infection due to a break in sterile procedure; the appropriate code for the surgical complication is omitted from the claims submission to avoid any adverse outcome to the institution. Quality outcomes are reported inaccurately in order to improve a healthcare organization's quality profile or pay-for-performance results.

7.   ***Facilitate interdisciplinary collaboration in situations supporting proper coding practices.***

Coding professionals **shall**:

7.1. Assist and educate physicians and other clinicians by advocating proper documentation practices, further specificity, and re-sequence or include diagnoses or procedures when needed to more accurately reflect the acuity, severity, and the occurrence of events. Example:Failure to advocate for ethical practices that seek to represent the truth in events as expressed by the associated code sets when needed is considered an intentional disregard of these standards.

8.   ***Advance coding knowledge and practice through continuing education.***

Coding professionals **shall**:

8.1. Maintain and continually enhance coding competency (e.g., through participation in educational programs, reading official coding publications such as the Coding Clinic for ICD-9-CM, and maintaining professional certifications) in order to stay abreast of changes in codes, coding guidelines, and regulatory and other requirements.

9.   ***Refuse to participate in or conceal unethical coding practices or procedures.***

Coding professionals **shall**:

9.1. Act in a professional and ethical manner at all times.

9.2. Take adequate measures to discourage, prevent, expose, and correct the unethical conduct of colleagues.

9.3. Be knowledgeable about established policies and procedures for handling concerns about colleagues' unethical behavior. These include policies and procedures created by AHIMA, licensing and regulatory bodies, employers, supervisors, agencies, and other professional organizations.

9.4. Seek resolution if there is a belief that a colleague has acted unethically or if there is a belief of incompetence or impairment by discussing their concerns with the colleague when feasible and when such discussion is likely to be productive. Take action through appropriate formal channels, such as contacting an accreditation or regulatory body and/or the AHIMA Professional Ethics Committee.

9.5. Consult with a colleague when feasible and assist the colleague in taking remedial action when there is direct knowledge of a health information management colleague's incompetence or impairment.

Coding professionals **shall not**:

9.6. Participate in, condone, or be associated with dishonesty, fraud and abuse, or deception. A non-exhaustive list of examples includes:

○ Allowing inappropriate patterns of retrospective documentation to avoid suspension or increase reimbursement
○ Assigning codes without supporting provider (physician or other qualified healthcare practitioner) documentation
○ Coding when documentation does not justify the diagnoses and/or procedures that have been billed
○ Coding an inappropriate level of service
○ Miscoding to avoid conflict with others
○ Adding, deleting, and altering health record documentation
○ Copying and pasting another clinician's documentation without identification of the original author and date
○ Knowingly reporting incorrect present on admission indicator
○ Knowingly reporting incorrect patient discharge status code
○ Engaging in negligent coding practices

10.   *Protect the confidentiality of the health record at all times and refuse to access protected health information not required for coding-related activities (examples of coding-related activities include completion of code assignment, other health record data abstraction, coding audits, and educational purposes).*

Coding professionals **shall**:

10.1. Protect all confidential information obtained in the course of professional service, including personal, health, financial, genetic, and outcome information.

10.2. Access only that information necessary to perform their duties.

11.   *Demonstrate behavior that reflects integrity, shows a commitment to ethical and legal coding practices, and fosters trust in professional activities.*

Coding professionals **shall**:

11.1. Act in an honest manner and bring honor to self, peers, and the profession.

11.2. Truthfully and accurately represent their credentials, professional education, and experience.

11.3. Demonstrate ethical principles and professional values in their actions to patients, employers, other members of the healthcare team, consumers, and other stakeholders served by the healthcare data they collect and report.

[1] The Cooperating Parties are the American Health Information Management Association, American Hospital Association, Centers for Medicare & Medicaid Services, and National Center for Health Statistics.

Source:
AHIMA House of Delegates. "AHIMA Standards of Ethical Coding." (September 2008).

Fee Schedule

Department	CPT Code	Description	Price
Evaluation and Management	99201	New Patient Office Visit - Level 1	$100.00
	99202	New Patient Office Visit - Level 2	$120.00
	99203	New Patient Office Visit - Level 3	$140.00
	99204	New Patient Office Visit - Level 4	$150.00
	99205	New Patient Office Visit - Level 5	$160.00
	99211	Est. Patient Office Visit - Level 1	$75.00
	99212	Est. Patient Office Visit - Level 2	$95.00
	99213	Est. Patient Office Visit - Level 3	$115.00
	99214	Est. Patient Office Visit - Level 4	$135.00
	99215	Est. Patient Office Visit - Level 5	$155.00
Surgery - Integumentary	10060	Incision and drainage of abscess	$195.00
	10080	Incision and drainage of pilonidal cyst	$250.00
	10120	Incision and drainage of hematoma, seroma, or fluid collection	$275.00
	10140	Puncture aspiration of abscess	$150.00
	11200	Removal of skin tags; up to 15	$70.00
	+11201	Each additional 10 skin tags	$30.00
Surgery - Respiratory	30100	Biopsy, intranasal	$185.00
	30110	Excision, nasal polyp(s)	$135.00
	32035	Thoracostomy with rib resection for empyema	$542.00
	32200	Pneumonostomy with drainage of abscess	$1,300.00
	32440	Total pneumonectomy	$1,750.00
Surgery - Cardiovascular	33206	Insertion or replacement of permanent pacemaker	$750.00
	33210	Insertion or replacement of temporary pacemaker	$550.00
	33500	Repair of coronary arteriovenous chamber	$975.00
	33510	Coronary artery bypass, vein only	$2,500.00
Surgery - Digestive	40500	Vermilionectomy	$375.00
	40650	Repair lip, full thickness, vermilion only	$250.00
	40830	Closure of laceration 2.5 cm- on vestibule	$95.00
	40831	Closure of laceration 2.6 cm+ on vestibule	$130.00
	43500	Gastromy; with exploration	$375.00
Radiology	73500	Hip; single unilateral x-ray	$45.00
	73510	Hip; minimum two complete view x-ray	$55.00
	74000	Abdominal; single anterposterior x-ray	$45.00
	74150	Abdominal; Tomography w/out contrast	$125.00
Pathology	80048	Basic metabolic panel (Calcium, total)	$65.00
	80051	Electrolyte panel	$45.00
	80100	Drug screen; qualitative	$20.00
	81000	Urinalysis	$20.00
	85025	Complete Blood Count	$20.00

Harris & Associates

Superbill #294659823

6489 Mannet Drive St.23
Hickory, IO, 56478

563-789-2198

CPT	DESCRIPTION	DX	FEE
NEW PATIENT			
99201	Minimal Office Visit		65
99202	Focused Office Visit		85
99203	Expanded Office Visit		125
99204	Detailed Office Visit		165
99205	Comp. Office Visit		215
ESTABLISHED PATIENT			
99211	Minimal Office Visit		30
99212	Focused Office Visit		55
99213	Expanded Office Visit		80
99214	Detailed Office Visit		110
99215	Comp. Office Visit		175
NEW PATIENT			
99381	Prevent., Under Age		130
99382	Preventative, Age 1-4		150
99383	Preventative, Age 5-11		150
99384	Prevent., Age 12-17		165
ESTABLISHED PATIENT			
99391	Prevent., Under Age		115
99392	Preventative, Age 1-4		130
99393	Preventative, Age 5-11		130
99394	Prevent., Age 12-17		150
OFFICE CONSULTS			
99241	Focused		83
99242	Expanded		114
99243	Detailed		141
99244	Comprehensive		174
99245	Complex		242

CPT	DESCRIPTION	DX	FEE
INJECTIONS			
90471	Admin., First Injection		17
90472	Admin., Subsequent		17
90633	Hepatitis A	V06.1	80
90647	HiB	V03.81	40
90657	Influenza, 6-35 Mos.	V04.81	15
90658	Influenza, 3-21 Years	V04.81	15
90669	Pneumococcal	V03.82	100
90700	DTaP	V06.1	35
90707	MMR	V06.4	60
90710	Pro Quad	V06.8	155
90713	Poliovirus	V04.0	40
90716	Varicella Virus	V05.4	95
90714	TD Over Age 7	V06.5	20
90715	Tdap - Boostrix	V06.1	70
90744	Hep B. Pediatric/Adoles.	V05.3	40
90734	Menactra	V03.89	160
90733	Menomune	V03.89	100
90723	Pediarix	V06.8	100
86580	TB Intradermal	V74.1	25
96372	Antibiotic Injection		26
95115	Allergy - Single Injection		20
95117	Allergy - Two +		45
J0696	Rocephin 250 mg		35

CPT	DESCRIPTION	DX	FEE
LAB SERVICES			
82270	Hemocult		10
81002	Urinalysis, w/o		15
85025	Hemogram, CBC		25
86403	Rapid Strep		25
86308	Monospot		15
82948	Glucometer Strip		10
81025	Pregnancy Test, Urine		25
36415	Venipuncture		15
OTHER SERVICES			
94760	Blood Oxygen Level		25
94761	Blood Oxygen Level		45
12001	Repair Superficial Wound		155
12011	Repair Superficial Face		180
16000	Initial, 1st Degree Burn		108
17250	Chem. Cauterization		75
69200	Remove Foreign Body		105
69210	Impacted Cerumen		70
92567	Tympanometry		35
94640	Inhal. Treatment		40
94640-76	Subs. Inhal. Treatment		40
99173	Vision		25
92551	Pure Tone Hearing, Air		35
99429	Sports Physical		35
10060	Incision & Drainage		125
17110	Cryotherapy/Wart Destruction		100
99050	Services After Hours		30
99051	Services on Sunday/Holiday		45
99078	Physician Educational Service		65

#	Diagnosis	ICD-9	Modifier
1			
2			
3			
4			
5			
6			

NEXT VISIT: _____ Days _____ Weeks _____ Months   M.D. _____ Vaccine _____

Today's Date		New Patient? ☐ Yes ☐ No		Today's Charges $
Patient's Name		DOB / /		Today's Payments $
Primary Ins	Secondary Ins	Sex		Cash
Primary Ins #	Secondary Ins #	Co-Pay		Check No. / Charge

Revised 9-26-6

Attachment C – Valid Revenue Codes

Revcode	Description
258	Pharmacy – IV Solutions
259	Pharmacy – Other Pharmacy
260	IV Therapy – General classification
261	IV Therapy – Infusion Pump
262	IV Therapy – Pharmacy Svcs
263	IV Therapy – Drug/Supply Delivery
264	IV Therapy – Supplies
269	IV Therapy – Other
270	Medical/Surgical Supplies and Devices – General Classification
271	Medical/Surgical Supplies and Devices – Non Sterile
272	Medical/Surgical Supplies and Devices – Sterile
273	Medical/Surgical Supplies and Devices – Take Home
274	Medical/Surgical Supplies and Devices – Prosthetic/Orthotic Devices
275	Medical/Surgical Supplies and Devices – Pace Maker
276	Medical/Surgical Supplies and Devices – Intraocular Lens
277	Medical/Surgical Supplies and Devices – Oxygen – Take Home
278	Medical/Surgical Supplies and Devices – Other Implants
279	Medical/Surgical Supplies and Devices – Other Supplies/Devices
280	Oncology – General Classification
289	Oncology – Other
290	Durable Medical Equipment – General Classification
291	Durable Medical Equipment – Rental
292	Durable Medical Equipment – Purchase of new DME
293	Durable Medical Equipment – Purchase of used DME
294	Durable Medical Equipment – Supplies/Drugs for DME Effectiveness
299	Durable Medical Equipment – Other Equipment
300	Laboratory – General Classification
301	Laboratory – Chemistry
302	Laboratory – Immunologu
303	Laboratory – Renal Patient (Home)
304	Laboratory – Non-Routine Dialysis
305	Laboratory – Hematology
306	Laboratory – Bacteriology and Microbiology
307	Laboratory – Urology
309	Laboratory – Other
310	Laboratory Pathological – General Classification
311	Laboratory Pathological – Cytology
312	Laboratory Pathological – Histology
314	Laboratory Pathological – Biopsy
319	Laboratory Pathological – Other
320	Radiology Diagnostic – General Classification
321	Radiology Diagnostic – Angiocardiography
322	Radiology Diagnostic – Arthography
323	Radiology Diagnostic – Arteriography
324	Radiology Diagnostic – Chest X-Ray
329	Radiology Diagnostic – Other
330	Radiology Therapeutic – General Classification
331	Radiology Therapeutic – Chemotherapy – Injected
332	Radiology Therapeutic – Chemotherapy – Oral
333	Radiology Therapeutic – Radiation Therapy
335	Radiology Therapeutic – Chemotherapy – IV
339	Radiology Therapeutic – Other
340	Nuclear Medicine – General Classification
341	Nuclear Medicine – Diagnostic
342	Nuclear Medicine - Therapeutic

1500

HEALTH INSURANCE CLAIM FORM

APPROVED BY NATIONAL UNIFORM CLAIM COMMITTEE 08/05

| | PICA | | | | | | | | | PICA | | |

1. MEDICARE (Medicare #) **MEDICAID** (Medicaid #) **TRICARE CHAMPUS** (Sponsor's SSN) **CHAMPVA** (Member ID#) **GROUP HEALTH PLAN** (SSN or ID) **FECA BLK LUNG** (SSN) **OTHER** (ID)   **1a. INSURED'S I.D. NUMBER** (For Program in Item 1)

2. PATIENT'S NAME (Last Name, First Name, Middle Initial)   **3. PATIENT'S BIRTH DATE** MM DD YY **SEX** M F   **4. INSURED'S NAME** (Last Name, First Name, Middle Initial)

5. PATIENT'S ADDRESS (No., Street)   **6. PATIENT RELATIONSHIP TO INSURED** Self Spouse Child Other   **7. INSURED'S ADDRESS** (No., Street)

CITY **STATE**   **8. PATIENT STATUS** Single Married Other   **CITY** **STATE**

ZIP CODE **TELEPHONE (Include Area Code)** ( )   Employed Full-Time Student Part-Time Student   **ZIP CODE** **TELEPHONE (Include Area Code)** ( )

9. OTHER INSURED'S NAME (Last Name, First Name, Middle Initial)   **10. IS PATIENT'S CONDITION RELATED TO:**   **11. INSURED'S POLICY GROUP OR FECA NUMBER**

a. OTHER INSURED'S POLICY OR GROUP NUMBER   **a. EMPLOYMENT?** (Current or Previous) YES NO   **a. INSURED'S DATE OF BIRTH** MM DD YY **SEX** M F

b. OTHER INSURED'S DATE OF BIRTH MM DD YY **SEX** M F   **b. AUTO ACCIDENT?** **PLACE (State)** YES NO   **b. EMPLOYER'S NAME OR SCHOOL NAME**

c. EMPLOYER'S NAME OR SCHOOL NAME   **c. OTHER ACCIDENT?** YES NO   **c. INSURANCE PLAN NAME OR PROGRAM NAME**

d. INSURANCE PLAN NAME OR PROGRAM NAME   **10d. RESERVED FOR LOCAL USE**   **d. IS THERE ANOTHER HEALTH BENEFIT PLAN?** YES NO *If yes*, return to and complete item 9 a-d.

READ BACK OF FORM BEFORE COMPLETING & SIGNING THIS FORM.
12. PATIENT'S OR AUTHORIZED PERSON'S SIGNATURE I authorize the release of any medical or other information necessary to process this claim. I also request payment of government benefits either to myself or to the party who accepts assignment below.

SIGNED _____ DATE _____

13. INSURED'S OR AUTHORIZED PERSON'S SIGNATURE I authorize payment of medical benefits to the undersigned physician or supplier for services described below.

SIGNED _____

14. DATE OF CURRENT: MM DD YY **ILLNESS (First symptom) OR INJURY (Accident) OR PREGNANCY(LMP)**   **15. IF PATIENT HAS HAD SAME OR SIMILAR ILLNESS. GIVE FIRST DATE** MM DD YY   **16. DATES PATIENT UNABLE TO WORK IN CURRENT OCCUPATION** FROM MM DD YY TO MM DD YY

17. NAME OF REFERRING PROVIDER OR OTHER SOURCE   **17a.** **17b. NPI**   **18. HOSPITALIZATION DATES RELATED TO CURRENT SERVICES** FROM MM DD YY TO MM DD YY

19. RESERVED FOR LOCAL USE   **20. OUTSIDE LAB?** YES NO **$ CHARGES**

21. DIAGNOSIS OR NATURE OF ILLNESS OR INJURY (Relate Items 1, 2, 3 or 4 to Item 24E by Line)
1. L____ . ____
2. L____ . ____
3. L____ . ____
4. L____ . ____

22. MEDICAID RESUBMISSION CODE **ORIGINAL REF. NO.**

23. PRIOR AUTHORIZATION NUMBER

24. A. DATE(S) OF SERVICE From MM DD YY	To MM DD YY	B. PLACE OF SERVICE	C. EMG	D. PROCEDURES, SERVICES, OR SUPPLIES (Explain Unusual Circumstances) CPT/HCPCS | MODIFIER	E. DIAGNOSIS POINTER	F. $ CHARGES	G. DAYS OR UNITS	H. EPSDT Family Plan	I. ID. QUAL.	J. RENDERING PROVIDER ID. #
1										NPI
2										NPI
3										NPI
4										NPI
5										NPI
6										NPI

25. FEDERAL TAX I.D. NUMBER SSN EIN   **26. PATIENT'S ACCOUNT NO.**   **27. ACCEPT ASSIGNMENT?** (For govt. claims, see back) YES NO   **28. TOTAL CHARGE** $ **29. AMOUNT PAID** $ **30. BALANCE DUE** $

31. SIGNATURE OF PHYSICIAN OR SUPPLIER INCLUDING DEGREES OR CREDENTIALS (I certify that the statements on the reverse apply to this bill and are made a part thereof.)

SIGNED _____ DATE _____

32. SERVICE FACILITY LOCATION INFORMATION
a. NPI b.

33. BILLING PROVIDER INFO & PH # ( )
a. NPI b.

NUCC Instruction Manual available at: www.nucc.org   APPROVED OMB-0938-0999 FORM CMS-1500 (08-05)

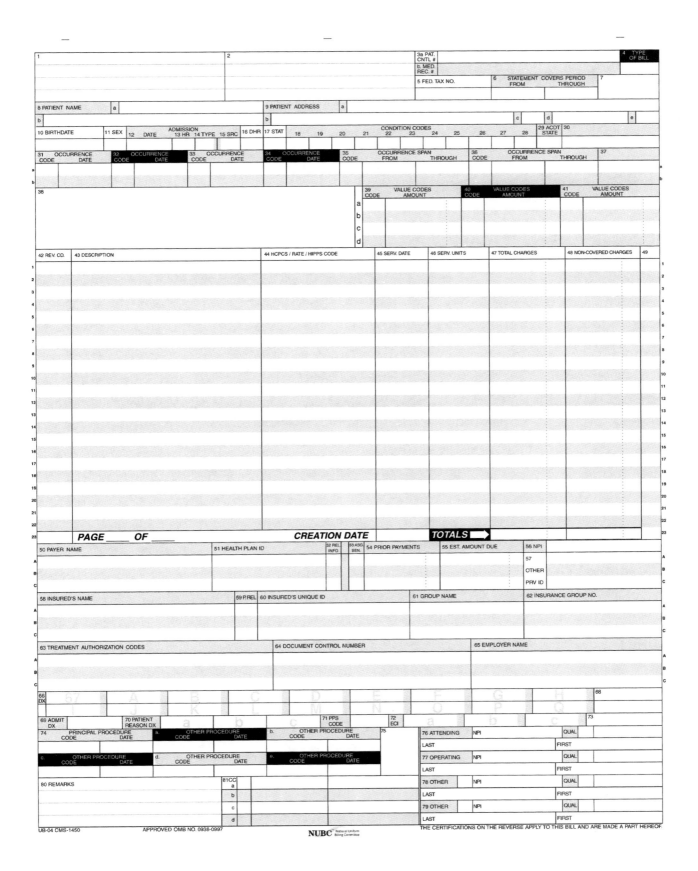

018500   HOSP09715

STATEMENT

PAYMENTS MADE AFTER 04/08/2012 WILL APPEAR ON
NEXT STATEMENT. QUESTIONS REGARDING THIS
INVOICE CATN BE DIRECTED TO THE OFFICE BETWEEN
1:00PM AND 4:00PM DAILY

ADDRESS SERVICE REQUESTED

SHOW AMOUNT
PAID HERE $ _____

168.12
PATIENT BALANCE

05/04/12   01

OFFICE PHONE   CLOSING DATE   YOUR ACCOUNT   PAGE NO.

NOTE: Charges and payments not appearing on this
statement will appear on next month's statement.

PLEASE RETURN THIS PORTION WITH PAYMENT

CHARGES APPEARING ON THIS STATEMENT ARE NOT INCLUDED ON ANY HOSPITAL BILL OR STATEMENT

DATE	PROVIDER	EXPLANATION OF ACTIVITY	PATIENT NAME	CHARGES AND DEBTS	PAYMENTS & CREDITS
072911		INITIAL INPTH COMP HISTORY		365.00	
073011		FOLLOW CONSULT		250.00	
060211		MEDICARE #11545 FILED			
092611		PAYMENT MEDICARE C# 115451			-291.17
092611		WRITE-OFF MEDICARE C# 115451			-251.04
092611		CO-INS 72.79			
080111		FOLLOW UP CONSULATATION		720.00	
060211		MEDICARE #11546 FILED			
092411		PAYMENT MEDICARE C# 115461			-319.68
092411		PAYMENT MEDICARE C# 115461			-320.40
092411		CO-INS 79.92			
080911		HOSPITAL DISCHARGE MGMT.		100.00	
060211		MEDICARE #11547 FILED			-61.64
092611		PAYMENT MEDICARE C# 115471			-22.95
092611		WRITE-OFF MEDICARE C#115471			
092611		CO-INS 15.41			

STATEMENT CLOSING DATE	05/04/12	PLEASE INDICATE YOUR ACCOUNT NUMBER WHEN CALLING OUR OFFICE.

CURRENT	30-60 DAYS	60-90 DAYS	> 90 DAYS	TOTAL	INS. PENDING	PATIENT BALANCE FOR THIS AMOUNT
			168.12	168.12	0.00	168.12

SEND INQUIRIES TO:

386

1500

HEALTH INSURANCE CLAIM FORM

APPROVED BY NATIONAL UNIFORM CLAIM COMMITTEE 08/05

1463 ELM DRIVE
LINCOLN TN 12345

☐ PICA

1.	MEDICARE (Medicare #)	MEDICAID (Medicaid #)	TRICARE CHAMPUS (Sponsor's SSN)	CHAMPVA (Member ID#)	GROUP HEALTH PLAN (SSN or ID) ☒	FECA BLK LUNG (SSN)	OTHER (ID)	1a. INSURED'S I.D. NUMBER (For Program in Item 1)

1a. INSURED'S I.D. NUMBER: **YTH8568477882**

2. PATIENT'S NAME (Last Name, First Name, Middle Initial)	3. PATIENT'S BIRTH DATE: MM 04 DD 18 YY 1972 — SEX M ☐ F ☐	4. INSURED'S NAME (Last Name, First Name, Middle Initial)
JOHNSON MELANIE J		**JOHNSON MELANIE J**

5. PATIENT'S ADDRESS (No., Street)	6. PATIENT RELATIONSHIP TO INSURED	7. INSURED'S ADDRESS (No., Street)
13 MATTELL LN	Self ☒ Spouse ☐ Child ☐ Other ☐	**13 MATTELL LN**
CITY **MIDDLETON** STATE **WI**	8. PATIENT STATUS	CITY **MIDDLETON** STATE **WI**
ZIP CODE **53562** TELEPHONE **(842)7790450**	Single ☐ Married ☒ Other ☐ / Employed ☐ Full-Time Student ☐ Part-Time Student ☐	ZIP CODE **53562** TELEPHONE **(842)7790450**

9. OTHER INSURED'S NAME (Last Name, First Name, Middle Initial)	10. IS PATIENT'S CONDITION RELATED TO:	11. INSURED'S POLICY GROUP OR FECA NUMBER
Johnson Ken D		**14980**
a. OTHER INSURED'S POLICY OR GROUP NUMBER **568405**	a. EMPLOYMENT? (Current or Previous) YES ☐ ☒ NO	a. INSURED'S DATE OF BIRTH MM 04 DD 18 YY 1972 — SEX M ☒ F ☐
b. OTHER INSURED'S DATE OF BIRTH MM 02 DD 25 YY 1978 SEX M ☐ F ☒	b. AUTO ACCIDENT? YES ☐ ☒ NO PLACE (State)	b. EMPLOYER'S NAME OR SCHOOL NAME **BUNYAN UNIVERSITY**
c. EMPLOYER'S NAME OR SCHOOL NAME **BUNYAN UNIVERSITY**	c. OTHER ACCIDENT? YES ☐ ☒ NO	c. INSURANCE PLAN NAME OR PROGRAM NAME **CHAMPION INSURANCE**
d. INSURANCE PLAN NAME OR PROGRAM NAME **CHAMPION INSURANCE**	10d. RESERVED FOR LOCAL USE	d. IS THERE ANOTHER HEALTH BENEFIT PLAN? ☒ YES ☐ NO *If yes*, return to and complete item 9 a-d.

READ BACK OF FORM BEFORE COMPLETING & SIGNING THIS FORM.

12. PATIENT'S OR AUTHORIZED PERSON'S SIGNATURE I authorize the release of any medical or other information necessary to process this claim. I also request payment of government benefits either to myself or to the party who accepts assignment below.

SIGNED **SIGNATURE ON FILE** DATE **01 20 2012**

13. INSURED'S OR AUTHORIZED PERSON'S SIGNATURE I authorize payment of medical benefits to the undersigned physician or supplier for services described below.

SIGNED **SIGNATURE ON FILE**

14. DATE OF CURRENT: MM 02 DD 13 YY 2012 ☐ ILLNESS (First symptom) OR INJURY (Accident) OR PREGNANCY(LMP)	15. IF PATIENT HAS HAD SAME OR SIMILAR ILLNESS. GIVE FIRST DATE MM DD YY	16. DATES PATIENT UNABLE TO WORK IN CURRENT OCCUPATION FROM 02 13 2012 TO 04 19 2012
17. NAME OF REFERRING PROVIDER OR OTHER SOURCE **ANNETTE HUFF MD**	17a. / 17b. NPI **9371048686**	18. HOSPITALIZATION DATES RELATED TO CURRENT SERVICES FROM 02 13 2012 TO 02 20 2012
19. RESERVED FOR LOCAL USE		20. OUTSIDE LAB? YES ☐ ☒ NO $ CHARGES **1353**

21. DIAGNOSIS OR NATURE OF ILLNESS OR INJURY (Relate Items 1, 2, 3 or 4 to Item 24E by Line)

1. **M25 561**
2. **M17 11**
3. ____
4. ____

22. MEDICAID RESUBMISSION CODE ____ ORIGINAL REF. NO. ____

23. PRIOR AUTHORIZATION NUMBER **9812375923**

24. A. DATE(S) OF SERVICE From MM DD YY / To MM DD YY	B. PLACE OF SERVICE	C. EMG	D. PROCEDURES, SERVICES, OR SUPPLIES CPT/HCPCS	MODIFIER	E. DIAGNOSIS POINTER	F. $ CHARGES	G. DAYS OR UNITS	H. EPSDT Family Plan	I. ID. QUAL	J. RENDERING PROVIDER ID. #
1	01 19 2012 01 19 2012	11		99214	25	1	110 00	1		NPI	56446408112
2	01 19 2012 01 19 2012	11		20610	RT	2	125 00	1		NPI	56446408112
3	01 19 2012 01 19 2012	11		J7321		2	300 00	1		NPI	56446408112
4										NPI	
5										NPI	
6										NPI	

25. FEDERAL TAX I.D. NUMBER SSN ☐ EIN ☒	26. PATIENT'S ACCOUNT NO. **836135**	27. ACCEPT ASSIGNMENT? ☒ YES ☐ NO	28. TOTAL CHARGE $ **535 00**	29. AMOUNT PAID $ **0 00**	30. BALANCE DUE $ **0 00**
31. SIGNATURE OF PHYSICIAN OR SUPPLIER INCLUDING DEGREES OR CREDENTIALS (I certify that the statements on the reverse apply to this bill and are made a part thereof.) **ANNETTE HUFF MD** 01202012 SIGNED DATE	32. SERVICE FACILITY LOCATION INFORMATION **GARAGE FAMILY PHYSICIANS 1472 FAIRWAY RD MIDDLETON WI 53562** a. 3030314711 b.		33. BILLING PROVIDER INFO & PH # **(842)7790450** **GARAGE FAMILY PHYSICIANS 1472 FAIRWAY RD MIDDLETON WI 53562** a. 3030314711 b.		

NUCC Instruction Manual available at: www.nucc.org

APPROVED OMB-0938-0999 FORM CMS-1500 (08-05)

387

1500

HEALTH INSURANCE CLAIM FORM

APPROVED BY NATIONAL UNIFORM CLAIM COMMITTEE 08/05

PO BOX 6704
FARGO, ND 58108-6704

☐☐ PICA   PICA ☐☐☐

1. MEDICARE	MEDICAID	TRICARE CHAMPUS	CHAMPVA	GROUP HEALTH PLAN	FECA BLK LUNG	OTHER	1a. INSURED'S I.D. NUMBER (For Program in Item 1)
☐ (Medicare #)	☐ (Medicaid #)	☐ (Sponsor's SSN)	☐ (Member ID#)	☐ (SSN or ID)	☐ (SSN)	☐ (ID)	094364987D

2. PATIENT'S NAME (Last Name, First Name, Middle Initial)	3. PATIENT'S BIRTH DATE	SEX	4. INSURED'S NAME (Last Name, First Name, Middle Initial)
ROBINSON BETTY	MM 02 DD 14 YY 1940	M☐ F☐	**ROBINSON BETTY**

5. PATIENT'S ADDRESS (No., Street)	6. PATIENT RELATIONSHIP TO INSURED	7. INSURED'S ADDRESS (No., Street)
2468 SUNSET LANE	Self☐ Spouse☐ Child☐ Other☐	**2468 SUNSET LANE**

CITY	STATE	8. PATIENT STATUS	CITY	STATE
PHOENIX	**AZ**	Single☐ Married☐ Other☐	**PHOENIX**	**AZ**

ZIP CODE	TELEPHONE (Include Area Code)		ZIP CODE	TELEPHONE (Include Area Code)
85001	**(854)9915151**	Employed☐ Full-Time Student☐ Part-Time Student☐	**85001**	**(854)9915151**

9. OTHER INSURED'S NAME (Last Name, First Name, Middle Initial)	10. IS PATIENT'S CONDITION RELATED TO:	11. INSURED'S POLICY GROUP OR FECA NUMBER
a. OTHER INSURED'S POLICY OR GROUP NUMBER	a. EMPLOYMENT? (Current or Previous) ☐ YES ☐ NO	a. INSURED'S DATE OF BIRTH MM 02 DD 14 YY 1940 SEX M☐ F☐
b. OTHER INSURED'S DATE OF BIRTH MM DD YY SEX M☐ F☐	b. AUTO ACCIDENT? PLACE (State) ☐ YES ☐ NO	b. EMPLOYER'S NAME OR SCHOOL NAME
c. EMPLOYER'S NAME OR SCHOOL NAME	c. OTHER ACCIDENT? ☐ YES ☐ NO	c. INSURANCE PLAN NAME OR PROGRAM NAME **NONE**
d. INSURANCE PLAN NAME OR PROGRAM NAME	10d. RESERVED FOR LOCAL USE	d. IS THERE ANOTHER HEALTH BENEFIT PLAN? ☐ YES ☐ NO If yes, return to and complete item 9 a-d.

READ BACK OF FORM BEFORE COMPLETING & SIGNING THIS FORM.

12. PATIENT'S OR AUTHORIZED PERSON'S SIGNATURE I authorize the release of any medical or other information necessary to process this claim. I also request payment of government benefits either to myself or to the party who accepts assignment below.

SIGNED **SIGNATURE ON FILE**   DATE **0318XXXX**

13. INSURED'S OR AUTHORIZED PERSON'S SIGNATURE I authorize payment of medical benefits to the undersigned physician or supplier for services described below.

SIGNED **SIGNATURE ON FILE**

14. DATE OF CURRENT: ILLNESS (First symptom) OR INJURY (Accident) OR PREGNANCY(LMP) MM 03 DD 18 YY XXXX	15. IF PATIENT HAS HAD SAME OR SIMILAR ILLNESS. GIVE FIRST DATE MM DD YY	16. DATES PATIENT UNABLE TO WORK IN CURRENT OCCUPATION MM DD YY FROM TO MM DD YY
17. NAME OF REFERRING PROVIDER OR OTHER SOURCE	17a. ___ 17b. NPI	18. HOSPITALIZATION DATES RELATED TO CURRENT SERVICES MM DD YY FROM TO MM DD YY
19. RESERVED FOR LOCAL USE		20. OUTSIDE LAB? ☐ YES ☐ NO $ CHARGES **NONE**

21. DIAGNOSIS OR NATURE OF ILLNESS OR INJURY (Relate Items 1, 2, 3 or 4 to Item 24E by Line)

1. **F0151**   3. **E11 9**
2. **I69 91**   4. ___

22. MEDICAID RESUBMISSION CODE	ORIGINAL REF. NO.
23. PRIOR AUTHORIZATION NUMBER	

24. A. DATE(S) OF SERVICE From MM DD YY	To MM DD YY	B. PLACE OF SERVICE	C. EMG	D. PROCEDURES, SERVICES, OR SUPPLIES (Explain Unusual Circumstances) CPT/HCPCS	MODIFIER	E. DIAGNOSIS POINTER	F. $ CHARGES	G. DAYS OR UNITS	H. EPSDT Family Plan	I. ID. QUAL.	J. RENDERING PROVIDER ID. #
1	03 18 XXXX	03 18 XXXX	13		99308		123	125 00	1		NPI	8415637029
2											NPI	
3											NPI	
4											NPI	
5											NPI	
6											NPI	

25. FEDERAL TAX I.D. NUMBER SSN EIN ☐☐	26. PATIENT'S ACCOUNT NO. **25641**	27. ACCEPT ASSIGNMENT? (For govt. claims, see back) ☐ YES ☐ NO	28. TOTAL CHARGE $ **125 00**	29. AMOUNT PAID $	30. BALANCE DUE $ **125 00**

31. SIGNATURE OF PHYSICIAN OR SUPPLIER INCLUDING DEGREES OR CREDENTIALS (I certify that the statements on the reverse apply to this bill and are made a part thereof.) **KEVIN THOMSON MD** SIGNED **0318XXXX** DATE	32. SERVICE FACILITY LOCATION INFORMATION **SUN VALLEY NURSING CENTER** **2468 SUNSET LANE** **PHOENIZ AZ 85001** a. 943628384 b.	33. BILLING PROVIDER INFO & PH # (854)9991212 **RED ROCK CLINIC** **4657 MESA DR** **PHOENIX AZ 85002** a. 8415637029 b.

NUCC Instruction Manual available at: www.nucc.org

APPROVED OMB-0938-0999 FORM CMS-1500 (08-05)

1500

HEALTH INSURANCE CLAIM FORM

APPROVED BY NATIONAL UNIFORM CLAIM COMMITTEE 08/05

BLUE CROSS BLUE SHIELD OF MICHIGAN
600 LAFAYETTE E
DETROIT MI 48226

☐☐ PICA

PICA ☐☐

1. MEDICARE (Medicare #)	MEDICAID (Medicaid #)	TRICARE CHAMPUS (Sponsor's SSN)	CHAMPVA (Member ID#)	GROUP HEALTH PLAN (SSN or ID) ☒	FECA BLK LUNG (SSN)	OTHER (ID)	1a. INSURED'S I.D. NUMBER (For Program in Item 1)

1a. INSURED'S I.D. NUMBER (For Program in Item 1): **XYZ941275638**

2. PATIENT'S NAME (Last Name, First Name, Middle Initial)
RICHARDSON DANIEL

3. PATIENT'S BIRTH DATE MM **11** DD **04** YY **1950** SEX M ☒ F ☐

4. INSURED'S NAME (Last Name, First Name, Middle Initial)
RICHARDSON DANIEL

5. PATIENT'S ADDRESS (No., Street)
265 MEADOWBROOK LN

6. PATIENT RELATIONSHIP TO INSURED
Self ☒ Spouse ☐ Child ☐ Other ☐

7. INSURED'S ADDRESS (No., Street)
265 MEADOWBROOK LANE

CITY **TROY** STATE **MI**

8. PATIENT STATUS
Single ☐ Married ☐ Other ☐
Employed ☐ Full-Time Student ☐ Part-Time Student ☐

CITY **TROY** STATE **MI**

ZIP CODE **48098** TELEPHONE (Include Area Code) **(213) 8881415**

ZIP CODE **48098** TELEPHONE (Include Area Code) **(213) 8881415**

9. OTHER INSURED'S NAME (Last Name, First Name, Middle Initial)

10. IS PATIENT'S CONDITION RELATED TO:

11. INSURED'S POLICY GROUP OR FECA NUMBER
81450

a. OTHER INSURED'S POLICY OR GROUP NUMBER

a. EMPLOYMENT? (Current or Previous) YES ☐ NO ☒

a. INSURED'S DATE OF BIRTH MM **11** DD **04** YY **1950** SEX M ☒ F ☐

b. OTHER INSURED'S DATE OF BIRTH MM DD YY SEX M ☐ F ☐

b. AUTO ACCIDENT? YES ☐ NO ☒ PLACE (State)

b. EMPLOYER'S NAME OR SCHOOL NAME

c. EMPLOYER'S NAME OR SCHOOL NAME

c. OTHER ACCIDENT? YES ☐ NO ☒

c. INSURANCE PLAN NAME OR PROGRAM NAME
NONE

d. INSURANCE PLAN NAME OR PROGRAM NAME

10d. RESERVED FOR LOCAL USE

d. IS THERE ANOTHER HEALTH BENEFIT PLAN?
YES ☐ NO ☒ If yes, return to and complete item 9 a-d.

READ BACK OF FORM BEFORE COMPLETING & SIGNING THIS FORM.
12. PATIENT'S OR AUTHORIZED PERSON'S SIGNATURE I authorize the release of any medical or other information necessary to process this claim. I also request payment of government benefits either to myself or to the party who accepts assignment below.

SIGNED **SIGNATURE ON FILE** DATE **0525XXXX**

13. INSURED'S OR AUTHORIZED PERSON'S SIGNATURE I authorize payment of medical benefits to the undersigned physician or supplier for services described below.

SIGNED **SIGNATURE ON FILE**

14. DATE OF CURRENT: ILLNESS (First symptom) OR INJURY (Accident) OR PREGNANCY(LMP) MM **02** DD **25** YY **XXXX**

15. IF PATIENT HAS HAD SAME OR SIMILAR ILLNESS. GIVE FIRST DATE MM DD YY

16. DATES PATIENT UNABLE TO WORK IN CURRENT OCCUPATION FROM TO

17. NAME OF REFERRING PROVIDER OR OTHER SOURCE
GREG PETERSON MD

17a. **GP04768**
17b. NPI

18. HOSPITALIZATION DATES RELATED TO CURRENT SERVICES FROM TO

19. RESERVED FOR LOCAL USE

20. OUTSIDE LAB? YES ☐ NO ☐ $ CHARGES **NONE**

21. DIAGNOSIS OR NATURE OF ILLNESS OR INJURY (Relate Items 1, 2, 3 or 4 to Item 24E by Line)
1. **J18 . 0**
2. ____
3. ____
4. ____

22. MEDICAID RESUBMISSION CODE ORIGINAL REF. NO.

23. PRIOR AUTHORIZATION NUMBER

24. A. DATE(S) OF SERVICE From MM DD YY To MM DD YY	B. PLACE OF SERVICE	C. EMG	D. PROCEDURES, SERVICES, OR SUPPLIES CPT/HCPCS	MODIFIER	E. DIAGNOSIS POINTER	F. $ CHARGES	G. DAYS OR UNITS	H. EPSDT Family Plan	I. ID. QUAL	J. RENDERING PROVIDER ID. #
1	05 25 xxxx 05 25 xxxx	23	Y	85025		1	75 00	1		NPI	753914269
2	05 25 xxxx 05 25 xxxx	23	Y	99282		1	150 00	1		NPI	753914269
3										NPI	
4										NPI	
5										NPI	
6										NPI	

25. FEDERAL TAX I.D. NUMBER **71 3912748** SSN ☐ EIN ☒

26. PATIENT'S ACCOUNT NO. **90244825**

27. ACCEPT ASSIGNMENT? (For govt. claims, see back) YES ☒ NO ☐

28. TOTAL CHARGE $ **225**

29. AMOUNT PAID $ **0**

30. BALANCE DUE $ **225**

31. SIGNATURE OF PHYSICIAN OR SUPPLIER INCLUDING DEGREES OR CREDENTIALS (I certify that the statements on the reverse apply to this bill and are made a part thereof.)
SIGNED **BILL MORRIS MD** DATE

32. SERVICE FACILITY LOCATION INFORMATION
**NORTH OAKLAND MEDICAL CENTER
461 W HURON ST
PONTIAC MI 48341**
a. 9760385412 b.

33. BILLING PROVIDER INFO & PH # **(284) 9991212**
**ARCHIE MORRIS MD PATHOLOGY ASSOCIATES
17564 TELEGRAPH
WEST BLOOMFIELD MI 48378**
a. 753914269 b.

NUCC Instruction Manual available at: www.nucc.org

APPROVED OMB-0938-0999 FORM CMS-1500 (08-05)

1500

HEALTH INSURANCE CLAIM FORM

APPROVED BY NATIONAL UNIFORM CLAIM COMMITTEE 08/05

BLUE CROSS BLUE SHIELD OF FLORIDA
PO BOX 1798
JACKSONVILLE FL 322310014

| | PICA | | | | | | | PICA | |

1. MEDICARE	MEDICAID	TRICARE CHAMPUS	CHAMPVA	GROUP HEALTH PLAN	FECA BLK LUNG	OTHER	1a. INSURED'S I.D. NUMBER	(For Program in Item 1)
(Medicare #)	(Medicaid #)	(Sponsor's SSN)	(Member ID#)	[X] (SSN or ID)	(SSN)	(ID)	694712853	

2. PATIENT'S NAME (Last Name, First Name, Middle Initial)
THOMAS MICHAEL

3. PATIENT'S BIRTH DATE MM DD YY
08 07 1950 **SEX** M [X] F [ ]

4. INSURED'S NAME (Last Name, First Name, Middle Initial)
THOMAS MICHAEL

5. PATIENT'S ADDRESS (No., Street)
61 MOONRAKER RD

6. PATIENT RELATIONSHIP TO INSURED
Self [X] Spouse [ ] Child [ ] Other [ ]

7. INSURED'S ADDRESS (No., Street)
61 MOONRAKER RD

CITY JACKSONVILLE **STATE** FL

8. PATIENT STATUS
Single [X] Married [ ] Other [ ]

CITY JACKSONVILLE **STATE** FL

ZIP CODE 32231 **TELEPHONE (Include Area Code)** (999) 5550071

Employed [ ] Full-Time Student [ ] Part-Time Student [ ]

ZIP CODE 32231 **TELEPHONE (Include Area Code)** (999) 5550071

9. OTHER INSURED'S NAME (Last Name, First Name, Middle Initial)

10. IS PATIENT'S CONDITION RELATED TO:

11. INSURED'S POLICY GROUP OR FECA NUMBER

a. OTHER INSURED'S POLICY OR GROUP NUMBER

a. EMPLOYMENT? (Current or Previous)
YES [ ] NO [X]

a. INSURED'S DATE OF BIRTH MM DD YY **SEX** M [ ] F [ ]

b. OTHER INSURED'S DATE OF BIRTH MM DD YY **SEX** M [ ] F [ ]

b. AUTO ACCIDENT? PLACE (State)
YES [ ] NO [X]

b. EMPLOYER'S NAME OR SCHOOL NAME

c. EMPLOYER'S NAME OR SCHOOL NAME

c. OTHER ACCIDENT?
YES [ ] NO [X]

c. INSURANCE PLAN NAME OR PROGRAM NAME
NONE

d. INSURANCE PLAN NAME OR PROGRAM NAME

10d. RESERVED FOR LOCAL USE

d. IS THERE ANOTHER HEALTH BENEFIT PLAN?
YES [ ] NO [X] *If yes*, return to and complete item 9 a-d.

READ BACK OF FORM BEFORE COMPLETING & SIGNING THIS FORM.

12. PATIENT'S OR AUTHORIZED PERSON'S SIGNATURE I authorize the release of any medical or other information necessary to process this claim. I also request payment of government benefits either to myself or to the party who accepts assignment below.

SIGNED **SIGNATURE ON FILE** DATE **0709XXXX**

13. INSURED'S OR AUTHORIZED PERSON'S SIGNATURE I authorize payment of medical benefits to the undersigned physician or supplier for services described below.

SIGNED **SIGNATURE ON FILE**

14. DATE OF CURRENT: MM DD YY
02 15 XXXX
ILLNESS (First symptom) OR INJURY (Accident) OR PREGNANCY(LMP)

15. IF PATIENT HAS HAD SAME OR SIMILAR ILLNESS. GIVE FIRST DATE MM DD YY

16. DATES PATIENT UNABLE TO WORK IN CURRENT OCCUPATION MM DD YY
FROM TO

17. NAME OF REFERRING PROVIDER OR OTHER SOURCE
GEORGE BAILEY

17a. GB74625
17b. NPI

18. HOSPITALIZATION DATES RELATED TO CURRENT SERVICES MM DD YY
FROM TO

19. RESERVED FOR LOCAL USE

20. OUTSIDE LAB? YES [ ] NO [ ] **$ CHARGES** NONE

21. DIAGNOSIS OR NATURE OF ILLNESS OR INJURY (Relate Items 1, 2, 3 or 4 to Item 24E by Line)
1. M25 559
2. ___
3. ___
4. ___

22. MEDICAID RESUBMISSION CODE ORIGINAL REF. NO.

23. PRIOR AUTHORIZATION NUMBER

24. A. DATE(S) OF SERVICE From MM DD YY	To MM DD YY	B. PLACE OF SERVICE	C. EMG	D. PROCEDURES, SERVICES, OR SUPPLIES (Explain Unusual Circumstances) CPT/HCPCS	MODIFIER	E. DIAGNOSIS POINTER	F. $ CHARGES	G. DAYS OR UNITS	H. EPSDT Family Plan	I. ID. QUAL.	J. RENDERING PROVIDER ID. #
1	07 09 xxxx	07 09 xxxx	49		73223	LT 26	1	1500 00	1		NPI	8476293517
2											NPI	
3											NPI	
4											NPI	
5											NPI	
6											NPI	

25. FEDERAL TAX I.D. NUMBER 3897172465 SSN [ ] EIN [X]

26. PATIENT'S ACCOUNT NO.

27. ACCEPT ASSIGNMENT? (For govt. claims, see back) YES [X] NO [ ]

28. TOTAL CHARGE $ 1500 00

29. AMOUNT PAID $

30. BALANCE DUE $ 1500 00

31. SIGNATURE OF PHYSICIAN OR SUPPLIER INCLUDING DEGREES OR CREDENTIALS (I certify that the statements on the reverse apply to this bill and are made a part thereof.)

MIRANDA BAILEY MD 0709XXXX
SIGNED DATE

32. SERVICE FACILITY LOCATION INFORMATION
ULTRACARE IMAGING SERVICE
4610 W HILLSBORO BLVD
COCONUT CREEK FL 33073
a. 9537421683 b.

33. BILLING PROVIDER INFO & PH # (915) 4421833
MIRANDA BAILEY MD
4310 W HILLSBORO BLVD
COCONUT CREEK FL 33073
a. 8476293517 b.

NUCC Instruction Manual available at: www.nucc.org

APPROVED OMB-0938-0999 FORM CMS-1500 (08-05)

HEALTH INSURANCE CLAIM FORM

APPROVED BY NATIONAL UNIFORM CLAIM COMMITTEE 08/05

UNITED HEALTH CARE
450 COLUMBUS BLVD
HARTFORD CT 06103

☐☐ PICA | | | | | | | PICA ☐☐

1. MEDICARE ☐ (Medicare #)	MEDICAID ☐ (Medicaid #)	TRICARE CHAMPUS ☐ (Sponsor's SSN)	CHAMPVA ☐ (Member ID#)	GROUP HEALTH PLAN ☒ (SSN or ID)	FECA BLK LUNG ☐ (SSN)	OTHER ☐ (ID)	1a. INSURED'S I.D. NUMBER (For Program in Item 1)
							694712853

2. PATIENT'S NAME (Last Name, First Name, Middle Initial)
JACOBSEN ROBERT

3. PATIENT'S BIRTH DATE: MM 12 DD 10 YY 1950 SEX M ☒ F ☐

4. INSURED'S NAME (Last Name, First Name, Middle Initial)
JACOBSEN ROBERT

5. PATIENT'S ADDRESS (No., Street)
4546 DALLAS DR

6. PATIENT RELATIONSHIP TO INSURED: Self ☒ Spouse ☐ Child ☐ Other ☐

7. INSURED'S ADDRESS (No., Street)
4546 DALLAS DR

CITY **SAN FRANCISCO**   STATE **CA**

8. PATIENT STATUS: Single ☒ Married ☐ Other ☐

CITY **SAN FRANCISCO**   STATE **CA**

ZIP CODE **92564**   TELEPHONE (Include Area Code) **(901) 5452212**

Employed ☐ Full-Time Student ☐ Part-Time Student ☐

ZIP CODE **92564**   TELEPHONE (Include Area Code) **(901) 5452212**

9. OTHER INSURED'S NAME (Last Name, First Name, Middle Initial)

10. IS PATIENT'S CONDITION RELATED TO:

11. INSURED'S POLICY GROUP OR FECA NUMBER
9897

a. OTHER INSURED'S POLICY OR GROUP NUMBER

a. EMPLOYMENT? (Current or Previous) YES ☐ NO ☒

a. INSURED'S DATE OF BIRTH: MM 12 DD 10 YY 1950   SEX M ☒ F ☐

b. OTHER INSURED'S DATE OF BIRTH: MM DD YY   SEX M ☐ F ☐

b. AUTO ACCIDENT? YES ☐ NO ☒   PLACE (State)

b. EMPLOYER'S NAME OR SCHOOL NAME

c. EMPLOYER'S NAME OR SCHOOL NAME

c. OTHER ACCIDENT? YES ☐ NO ☐

c. INSURANCE PLAN NAME OR PROGRAM NAME

d. INSURANCE PLAN NAME OR PROGRAM NAME

10d. RESERVED FOR LOCAL USE

d. IS THERE ANOTHER HEALTH BENEFIT PLAN? YES ☐ NO ☒ If yes, return to and complete item 9 a-d.

READ BACK OF FORM BEFORE COMPLETING & SIGNING THIS FORM.

12. PATIENT'S OR AUTHORIZED PERSON'S SIGNATURE I authorize the release of any medical or other information necessary to process this claim. I also request payment of government benefits either to myself or to the party who accepts assignment below.

SIGNED **SIGNATURE ON FILE**   DATE **0412XXXX**

13. INSURED'S OR AUTHORIZED PERSON'S SIGNATURE I authorize payment of medical benefits to the undersigned physician or supplier for services described below.

SIGNED **SIGNATURE ON FILE**

14. DATE OF CURRENT: MM 03 DD 10 YY XXXX ILLNESS (First symptom) OR INJURY (Accident) OR PREGNANCY(LMP)

15. IF PATIENT HAS HAD SAME OR SIMILAR ILLNESS. GIVE FIRST DATE MM DD YY

16. DATES PATIENT UNABLE TO WORK IN CURRENT OCCUPATION   FROM MM DD YY   TO MM DD YY

17. NAME OF REFERRING PROVIDER OR OTHER SOURCE
GEORGE GARRISON

17a.
17b. NPI **5126487930**

18. HOSPITALIZATION DATES RELATED TO CURRENT SERVICES   FROM MM DD YY   TO MM DD YY

19. RESERVED FOR LOCAL USE

20. OUTSIDE LAB? YES ☐ NO ☐ $ CHARGES **NONE**

21. DIAGNOSIS OR NATURE OF ILLNESS OR INJURY (Relate Items 1, 2, 3 or 4 to Item 24E by Line)

1. **M54 30**   3.
2. **M25 559**   4.

22. MEDICAID RESUBMISSION CODE   ORIGINAL REF. NO.

23. PRIOR AUTHORIZATION NUMBER

24. A. DATE(S) OF SERVICE From MM DD YY	To MM DD YY	B. PLACE OF SERVICE	C. EMG	D. PROCEDURES, SERVICES, OR SUPPLIES CPT/HCPCS	MODIFIER	E. DIAGNOSIS POINTER	F. $ CHARGES	G. DAYS OR UNITS	H. EPSDT Family Plan	I. ID. QUAL.	J. RENDERING PROVIDER ID. #
1	04 12 XXXX	04 12 XXXX	49		97035		12	300 00	2		NPI	5126487930
2	04 12 XXXX	04 12 XXXX	49		97140		1	100 00	1		NPI	5126487930
3	04 12 XXXX	04 12 XXXX	49		97110		12	100 00	2		NPI	5126487930
4	04 12 XXXX	04 12 XXXX	49		97034		12	75 00	2		NPI	5126487930
5											NPI	
6											NPI	

25. FEDERAL TAX I.D. NUMBER **381796542** SSN ☐ EIN ☒

26. PATIENT'S ACCOUNT NO. **9950001654**

27. ACCEPT ASSIGNMENT? (For govt. claims, see back) YES ☐ NO ☒

28. TOTAL CHARGE $ **1050 00**

29. AMOUNT PAID $

30. BALANCE DUE $ **1050 00**

31. SIGNATURE OF PHYSICIAN OR SUPPLIER INCLUDING DEGREES OR CREDENTIALS (I certify that the statements on the reverse apply to this bill and are made a part thereof.)

ERIN MARTIN RPT   **0810XXXX**
SIGNED   DATE

32. SERVICE FACILITY LOCATION INFORMATION
NOVA CARE PHYSICAL THERAPY
3678 OAKLAND BLVD
SAN FRANCISCO CA 92564
a. **0914287356**   b.

33. BILLING PROVIDER INFO & PH # **(901) 5558412**
NOVA CARE PHYSICAL THERAPY CENTER
3678 OAKLAND BLVD
SAN FRANCISCO CA 92564
a. **0914287356**   b.

NUCC Instruction Manual available at: www.nucc.org

APPROVED OMB-0938-0999 FORM CMS-1500 (08-05)

1 FAITH UNITED HOSPITAL 1479 MAIN ST JACKSON MI 049021478	2		3a PAT. CNTL # 492379			4 TYPE OF BILL
			b. MED. REC. # 01429			111
			5 FED. TAX NO. 910478267	6 STATEMENT COVERS PERIOD FROM 012413 THROUGH 012513	7	

8 PATIENT NAME a	9 PATIENT ADDRESS a 4928 S HARPER ROAD				
b WATSON JESSICA	b JACKSON		c MI	d 04902	e

10 BIRTHDATE	11 SEX	12 DATE	ADMISSION 13 HR	14 TYPE	15 SRC	16 DHR	17 STAT	18	19	20	21	CONDITION CODES 22 23 24 25 26 27 28	29 ACDT STATE	30
07181971	F	012413	22	2	9	09	01							

31 OCCURRENCE CODE DATE	32 OCCURRENCE CODE DATE	33 OCCURRENCE CODE DATE	34 OCCURRENCE CODE DATE	35 OCCURRENCE SPAN CODE FROM THROUGH	36 OCCURRENCE SPAN CODE FROM THROUGH	37

38		39 VALUE CODES CODE AMOUNT	40 VALUE CODES CODE AMOUNT	41 VALUE CODES CODE AMOUNT
	a			
	b			
	c			
	d			

42 REV. CD.	43 DESCRIPTION	44 HCPCS / RATE / HIPPS CODE	45 SERV. DATE	46 SERV. UNITS	47 TOTAL CHARGES	48 NON-COVERED CHARGES	49
1 0120	ROOM-BOARD/SEMI	2115.00		1	2115 00		1
2 0258	IV SOLUTION			15	1455 32		2
3 0301	LAB CHEMISTRY			5	534 91		3
4 0307	LAB/UROLOGY			2	90 00		4
5 0350	CT SCAN			1	2973 00		5
6 0324	DX X-RAY CHEST			1	469 00		6
7 0483	ECHOCARDIOLOGY			1	2076 58		7
8 0730	EKG/ECG			5	1105 00		8
9							9
10							10
11							11
12							12
13							13
14							14
15							15
16							16
17							17
18							18
19							19
20							20
21							21
22							22
23	*PAGE* 1 *OF* 1		CREATION DATE 012613	TOTALS ▶	10818 81		23

50 PAYER NAME	51 HEALTH PLAN ID	52 REL INFO	53 ASG BEN.	54 PRIOR PAYMENTS	55 EST. AMOUNT DUE	56 NPI 7498978240	
A UNITED HEALTHCARE	4821792	N	Y	00 00		57 742139	A
B						OTHER	B
C						PRV ID	C

58 INSURED'S NAME	59 P.REL	60 INSURED'S UNIQUE ID	61 GROUP NAME	62 INSURANCE GROUP NO.	
A	18	AZ19ZX4T			A
B					B
C					C

63 TREATMENT AUTHORIZATION CODES	64 DOCUMENT CONTROL NUMBER	65 EMPLOYER NAME	
A			A
B			B
C			C

66 DX A40.9	I33.0		B	C	D	E	F	G	H	68
9		I	J	K	L	M	N	O	P	Q

69 ADMIT DX A40.9	70 PATIENT REASON DX a b c	71 PPS CODE	72 ECI a b c	73

74 PRINCIPAL PROCEDURE CODE DATE	a. OTHER PROCEDURE CODE DATE	b. OTHER PROCEDURE CODE DATE	75	76 ATTENDING NPI 111122222	QUAL IG UP123U
c. OTHER PROCEDURE CODE DATE	d. OTHER PROCEDURE CODE DATE	e. OTHER PROCEDURE CODE DATE		LAST LUCIDO	FIRST MARY JO
				77 OPERATING NPI	QUAL
				LAST	FIRST

80 REMARKS	81CC a		78 OTHER NPI	QUAL
	b		LAST	FIRST
	c		79 OTHER NPI	QUAL
	d		LAST	FIRST

UB-04 CMS-1450   APPROVED OMB NO. 0938-0997   NUBC National Uniform Billing Committee   THE CERTIFICATIONS ON THE REVERSE APPLY TO THIS BILL AND ARE MADE A PART HEREOF.

1500

HEALTH INSURANCE CLAIM FORM

APPROVED BY NATIONAL UNIFORM CLAIM COMMITTEE 08/05

MEDICARE PART B
PO BOX 5555
MARION IL 62959

☐☐ PICA   PICA ☐☐☐

1. MEDICARE	MEDICAID	TRICARE CHAMPUS	CHAMPVA	GROUP HEALTH PLAN	FECA BLK LUNG	OTHER	1a. INSURED'S I.D. NUMBER (For Program in Item 1)
☒ (Medicare #)	☐ (Medicaid #)	☐ (Sponsor's SSN)	☐ (Member ID#)	☐ (SSN or ID)	☐ (SSN)	☐ (ID)	425378961A

2. PATIENT'S NAME (Last Name, First Name, Middle Initial)	3. PATIENT'S BIRTH DATE	SEX	4. INSURED'S NAME (Last Name, First Name, Middle Initial)
MARTIN JOSEPH	MM 09 DD 15 YY 1940	M ☒ F ☐	MARTIN JOSEPH

5. PATIENT'S ADDRESS (No., Street)	6. PATIENT RELATIONSHIP TO INSURED	7. INSURED'S ADDRESS (No., Street)
7679 WILLSHIRE BLVD	Self ☒ Spouse ☐ Child ☐ Other ☐	7679 WILLSHIRE BLVD

CITY	STATE	8. PATIENT STATUS	CITY	STATE
CHICAGO	IL	Single ☐ Married ☐ Other ☒	CHICAGO	IL

ZIP CODE	TELEPHONE (Include Area Code)		ZIP CODE	TELEPHONE (Include Area Code)
62946	(319) 6151212	Employed ☐ Full-Time Student ☐ Part-Time Student ☐	62946	(319) 6151212

9. OTHER INSURED'S NAME (Last Name, First Name, Middle Initial)	10. IS PATIENT'S CONDITION RELATED TO:	11. INSURED'S POLICY GROUP OR FECA NUMBER

a. OTHER INSURED'S POLICY OR GROUP NUMBER	a. EMPLOYMENT? (Current or Previous) ☐ YES ☒ NO	a. INSURED'S DATE OF BIRTH MM 09 DD 15 YY 1940 SEX M ☒ F ☐

b. OTHER INSURED'S DATE OF BIRTH MM DD YY SEX M ☐ F ☐	b. AUTO ACCIDENT? ☐ YES ☒ NO PLACE (State)	b. EMPLOYER'S NAME OR SCHOOL NAME

c. EMPLOYER'S NAME OR SCHOOL NAME	c. OTHER ACCIDENT? ☐ YES ☒ NO	c. INSURANCE PLAN NAME OR PROGRAM NAME

d. INSURANCE PLAN NAME OR PROGRAM NAME	10d. RESERVED FOR LOCAL USE	d. IS THERE ANOTHER HEALTH BENEFIT PLAN? ☐ YES ☒ NO If yes, return to and complete item 9 a-d.

READ BACK OF FORM BEFORE COMPLETING & SIGNING THIS FORM.

12. PATIENT'S OR AUTHORIZED PERSON'S SIGNATURE I authorize the release of any medical or other information necessary to process this claim. I also request payment of government benefits either to myself or to the party who accepts assignment below.

SIGNED **SIGNATURE ON FILE**   DATE **1010XXXX**

13. INSURED'S OR AUTHORIZED PERSON'S SIGNATURE I authorize payment of medical benefits to the undersigned physician or supplier for services described below.

SIGNED **SIGNATURE ON FILE**

14. DATE OF CURRENT: ILLNESS (First symptom) OR INJURY (Accident) OR PREGNANCY(LMP) MM 10 DD 10 YY XXXX	15. IF PATIENT HAS HAD SAME OR SIMILAR ILLNESS. GIVE FIRST DATE MM DD YY	16. DATES PATIENT UNABLE TO WORK IN CURRENT OCCUPATION MM DD YY FROM TO

17. NAME OF REFERRING PROVIDER OR OTHER SOURCE	17a.	18. HOSPITALIZATION DATES RELATED TO CURRENT SERVICES MM DD YY FROM TO
	17b. NPI	

19. RESERVED FOR LOCAL USE	20. OUTSIDE LAB? ☐ YES ☐ NO $ CHARGES **NONE**

21. DIAGNOSIS OR NATURE OF ILLNESS OR INJURY (Relate Items 1, 2, 3 or 4 to Item 24E by Line)

1. I47 2
2. I48 91
3. ____ . ____
4. ____ . ____

22. MEDICAID RESUBMISSION CODE   ORIGINAL REF. NO.

23. PRIOR AUTHORIZATION NUMBER

24. A. DATE(S) OF SERVICE From MM DD YY To MM DD YY	B. PLACE OF SERVICE	C. EMG	D. PROCEDURES, SERVICES, OR SUPPLIES (Explain Unusual Circumstances) CPT/HCPCS MODIFIER	E. DIAGNOSIS POINTER	F. $ CHARGES	G. DAYS OR UNITS	H. EPSDT Family Plan	I. ID. QUAL	J. RENDERING PROVIDER ID. #
1	10 10 XXXX 10 10 XXXX	22		93620	26	12	1500 00	1		NPI	9071826354
2	10 10 XXXX 10 10 XXXX	22		93609	26	12	900 00	1		NPI	
3										NPI	
4										NPI	
5										NPI	
6										NPI	

25. FEDERAL TAX I.D. NUMBER SSN EIN	26. PATIENT'S ACCOUNT NO.	27. ACCEPT ASSIGNMENT? (For govt. claims, see back)	28. TOTAL CHARGE	29. AMOUNT PAID	30. BALANCE DUE
38724956 ☐ ☒		☐ YES ☒ NO	$ 2400 00	$	$ 2400 00

31. SIGNATURE OF PHYSICIAN OR SUPPLIER INCLUDING DEGREES OR CREDENTIALS (I certify that the statements on the reverse apply to this bill and are made a part thereof.) DAVID PINEGAR MD 1010XXXX SIGNED DATE	32. SERVICE FACILITY LOCATION INFORMATION NORTHWESTERN UNIVERSITY HOSPITAL 13789 MICHIGAN AVE CHICAGO IL 62957 a. 8975312640 b.	33. BILLING PROVIDER INFO & PH # (314) 5151459 DAVID PINEGAR MD PINEGAR HART ASSOCIATION 13752 MICHIGAN AVE CHICAGO IL 62957 a. 9071826354 b.

NUCC Instruction Manual available at: www.nucc.org

APPROVED OMB-0938-0999 FORM CMS-1500 (08-05)

Remittance Advice

Vendor: Marvin Klein MD
515 Somerset
Troy, MI 48098

Vendor ID: P14589
Tax ID #: 382014410
Check Date: 8/25/xxxx
Check Amt:

Provider Number: 14589   Provider Name: Marvin Klein, M.D.

Line Nbr	Reason Code	Status	QTY	Service Date	Rev/Proc Modifier Code	Billed Amt	Contractual Adjustment	Allowed Amt	Copay Amt	Coins Amt	Deductible Amt	Withhold Amt	Paid Amt
Member Name: Harvey Klein				Claim Number Case # 3		Member ID 322457149		HAP Number: 235678-01					
1	PAL04	P	1	07/13/xxxx	10060	$100.00		$95.00				$9.50	$85.50
Member Name: Harvey Klein				Claim Number G1 -3		Member ID 322457149		HAP Number: 235678-01					
1	PAL 04	P	1	07/29/xxxx	99212	$45.00		$40.50	$10.00			$4.05	$26.45
Vendor Totals	Nbr of Claims 2					$145.00		$135.50	$10.00			$13.55	$111.95

If you have any questions, please contact Claims investigation and Assessment at 248 443 4400
or 888 260 7003 outside Metro Detroit Area.

Status Legend: P- Payable, H- Held, D – Denied, I- Informational, IP in Process, C- Capitated, A-Adjusted, N- No check

REASON CODE LEGEND

CODE	DESCRIPTION
PAL 04	FEE SCHEDULE – REIMBURSED AT FEE

Aetna US Health Care
PO Box 2559
Fort Wayne IN 46801

EXPLANATION OF BENEFITS

PLEASE RETAIN FOR FUTURE REFERENCE

Date Printed – 9/10/xxxx
Tax ID #: 383214567
Check #: 678598234
Check Amt: $ 35.47

Nigel Brown MD
515 Somerset
Troy, MI 48098

Notes: The benefits listed below reflect your portion of this payment.

Patient Name: Melody Drew   Patient Acct #: 351641   ID# 06869-5
Member ID # 221960711
Relation: Child   Member: Harry

Service Dates	CPT Codes	PL	NUM SVC	Submitted Charges	Copay Amount	Not Payable	See Remarks	Deduct	Co-Ins	Patient Responsible	Payable Amount
08/01/xx	99212	11	1	$75.00	$25.00	$14.53	893			$39.53	$35.47
TOTALS				**$75.00**	**$25.00**	**$14.53**				**$39.53**	**$35.47**

Remark Code 893: Not authorized by Primary Care Physician – reduced reimbursement

For Questions regarding this claim Call 888-6979356 For Assistance. Please use ID number for reference to this claim	Total Patient Responsibility $39.53

TCF Bank   Check #: 678598234
56624 Highland Rd
Waterford MI 48327   9/10/xxxx

PAY THIRTY-FIVE & 47/100**

******* $35.47

TO THE ODER OF:
NIGEL BROWN MD
515 SOMERSET
TROY MI 48098

NICHOLAS JONES

Sun Valley PPO
PO Box 16750
Lansing MI 48275

EXPLANATION OF BENEFITS

PLEASE RETAIN FOR FUTURE REFERENCE

Date Printed – 8/25/xxxx
Tax ID #: 382014410
Check #: 3567895234
Check Amt: $

Benjamin Matthews
186 Maple Ave
Livonia MI 48476

Notes: The benefits listed below reflect your portion of this payment.

Patient Name: Melody Duncan
Patient Acct #: 25631   Patient ID# 268631
Member ID # 977653741
Relation: Spouse   Member: Mark

Service Dates	CPT Codes	PL	NUM SVC	Submitted Charges	Copay Amount	Not Payable	See Remarks	Deduct	Co-Ins	Patient Resp	Payable Amount
08/01/xx	99203	11	1	$115.00	$25.00	$19.44	345			$25.00	$70.56
08/01/xx	93000	11	1	$ 55.00		$ 29.69	345				$25.31
TOTALS				**$170.00**	**$25.00**	**$49.13**				**$25.00**	**$95.87**

Remark Code 345: Contractual write off as a participating physician.

For Questions regarding this claim Call 888-6979356 For Assistance. Please use ID number for reference to this claim	Total Patient Responsibility	$25.00

TCF Bank   Check #: 3567895234
56624 Highland Rd
Waterford MI 48327   8/25/xxxx

PAY FORTY FIVE AND NO/100**

******** $95.87

TO THE ODER OF:
DEREK SHEPHERD MD
186 MAPLE AVE
LIVONIA MI 48476

NICHOLAS JONES _____

Sun Valley PPO
PO Box 16750
Lansing MI 48275

EXPLANATION OF BENEFITS

PLEASE RETAIN FOR FUTURE REFERENCE

Date Printed – 8/25/xxxx
Tax ID #: 382014410
Check #: 3567895234
Check Amt: $ 30.00

Marvin Klein MD
515 Somerset
Troy, MI 48098

Notes: The benefits listed below reflect your portion of this payment.

Patient Name: Jose Martino
Patient Acct #: 25871   Patient ID# 2145556
Member ID # 998741368
Relation: Self   Member: Jose

Service Dates	CPT Codes	PL	NUM SVC	Submitted Charges	Copay Amount	Not Payable	See Remarks	Deduct	Co-Ins	Patient Resp	Payable Amount
07/13/xx	99202	11	1	$115.00		$115.00	231	$115.00		$115.00	
07/13/xx	93000	11	1	$ 55.00		$ 25.00	231	$ 25.00		$ 25.00	$30.00
TOTALS				**$170.00**		**$140.00**		**$140.00**		**$140.00**	**$30.00**

Remark Code 231: Provider not in network. Patient's Responsibility

For Questions regarding this claim Call 888-6979356 For Assistance. Please use ID number for reference to this claim	Total Patient Responsibility	$140.00

TCF Bank   Check #: 3567895234
56624 Highland Rd
Waterford MI 48327   8/25/xxxx

PAY Forty five and no/100**

******** $30.00

TO THE ODER OF:
MARVIN KLEIN MD
515 SOMERSET
TROY MI 48098

Nicholas Jones

397

PATIENT INFORMATION

YOUR NAME: _____
(FIRST)   (MIDDLE)   (LAST)

BIRTH DATE: _____ SEX: MALE___ FEMALE___ S.S.#:____-___-_____

MARITAL STATUS: S___ M___ D___ W___ HOME PHONE #: (___)____-_____

HOME ADDRESS:_____

CITY:_____ STATE:_____ ZIP CODE:_____

EMPLOYER:_____ WK PHONE: (___)____-_____

NAME OF SPOUSE:_____ BIRTH DATE:___/___/_____

SPOUSE'S SOCIAL SECURITY #:____-___-_____ WORK PHONE: (___)____-_____

****

IN CASE OF EMERGENCY CONTACT (NAME)_____
(FIRST)   (LAST)

RELATIONSHIP TO PATIENT:_____ HOME PHONE #: (___)____-_____

WORK PHONE: (___)____-_____

PLEASE SEE OTHER SIDE

FINANCIAL AGREEMENT

1. Payment in full is due at the time. We accept cash, checks, VISA, MasterCard or Discover cards. Your insurance coverage is not a guarantee of payment. Your **insurance carrier may decide that the services that were rendered were not medically necessary or not a covered benefit** and they **may not pay the** claim. Any balance not paid by your insurance carrier will be your responsibility.

2. All Co-Pays must be paid in full at the time of service. The co-pay amount is set by a contract between you and your insurance carrier. Failure to pay your co-pay at the time of service will force us to contact your insurance carrier that you are not compliant with your contract with them.

3. If your insurance company requires that lab work or specimens need to be sent to a specific laboratory, it is YOUR responsibility to know which laboratory your insurance company participates with. It is also your responsibility to let our office know which lab.

4. In the case of estranged or divorced parents, the custodial parent is responsible for payment for all services rendered, **regardless of any insurance arrangements or divorce decree**. This is per the law from the State of Michigan regarding minor children. We will gladly furnish a receipt when payment is made by you so that you can turn this into friend of the court.

5. If you are experiencing financial difficulties, please talk to our billing department at _____ or our office manager, in order to arrange a suitable payment schedule.

6. The physicians are not experts on the many insurance contracts and cannot be aware of all financial arrangements. Please discuss all insurance problems and financial issues with our billing department at _____ or speak with our office manager.

7. All accounts overdue by more than 90 days may be turned over to a collection agency. If your insurance company has not paid your claim within 120 days the balance will be turned over to you for payment. Our past experience now requires us to adopt this policy in order to stay in business.

8. **There is an additional $25.00 returned check fee added plus the amount of your check** to your account in addition to the amount of your check that did not clear.

9. **When you do not call to cancel your appointment 24 hours in advance there will be a $25.00 NO SHOW fee added to your account.**

I UNDERSTAND AND ACCEPT THE ABOVE STATEMENTS.

_____   _____
PATIENT OR DPOA OR Guardian   Date

					3a PAT. CNTL # 525252			4 TYPE OF BILL
1 FAITH UNITED HOSPITAL		2			b. MED. REC. # 555999			0131
700 LaCross Ave					5 FED. TAX NO.	6 STATEMENT COVERS PERIOD	7	
City XX 12345						FROM	THROUGH	
9892223333					12-3456789	0119013	012013	

8 PATIENT NAME	a		9 PATIENT ADDRESS	a 2014 ANNIE ST					
b STRONG WENDY			b DETROIT			c MI	d 48234	e	

10 BIRTHDATE	11 SEX	12 DATE	ADMISSION 13 HR	14 TYPE	15 SRC	16 DHR	17 STAT	18	19	20	21	CONDITION CODES 22	23	24	25	26	27	28	29 ACDT STATE	30
07241951	F	011913	22	2	1	04	01													

31 OCCURRENCE CODE	DATE	32 OCCURRENCE CODE	DATE	33 OCCURRENCE CODE	DATE	34 OCCURRENCE CODE	DATE	35 CODE	OCCURRENCE SPAN FROM	THROUGH	36 CODE	OCCURRENCE SPAN FROM	THROUGH	37	
a															a
b															b

38			39 CODE	VALUE CODES AMOUNT	40 CODE	VALUE CODES AMOUNT	41 CODE	VALUE CODES AMOUNT
		a						
		b						
		c						
		d						

42 REV. CD.	43 DESCRIPTION	44 HCPCS / RATE / HIPPS CODE	45 SERV. DATE	46 SERV. UNITS	47 TOTAL CHARGES	48 NON-COVERED CHARGES	49
1 0300	LAB	80101	011913	1	65:00		1
2 0300	LAB	82055	011913	1	60:00		2
3 0300	LAB	86001	011913	1	1269:00		3
4 0637	DRUG/SELF ADMIN	9928525	011913	1	5:12	5:12	4
5							5
6							6
7							7
8							8
9							9
10							10
11							11
12							12
13							13
14							14
15							15
16							16
17							17
18							18
19							19
20							20
21							21
22						1399:12	5:12	22
23	PAGE 1 OF 1	CREATION DATE 012513	TOTALS ➡		1399:12	5:12	23

50 PAYER NAME	51 HEALTH PLAN ID	52 REL INFO	53 ASG. BEN.	54 PRIOR PAYMENTS	55 EST. AMOUNT DUE	56 NPI 1234512345	
A MECIDARE	XXX	Y	Y	00		57 OTHER 999888	A
B						PRV ID	B
C							C

58 INSURED'S NAME	59 P.REL	60 INSURED'S UNIQUE ID	61 GROUP NAME	62 INSURANCE GROUP NO.	
A STRONG WENDY	18	333222555			A
B					B
C					C

63 TREATMENT AUTHORIZATION CODES	64 DOCUMENT CONTROL NUMBER	65 EMPLOYER NAME	
A			A
B			B
C			C

66 DX F32.9	F45.0	F10.10	I10	C	D	E	F	G	H	68
9	I	J	K	L	M	N	O	P	Q	

69 ADMIT DX F45.0	70 PATIENT REASON DX	a	b	c	71 PPS CODE	72 ECI			73

74 PRINCIPAL PROCEDURE CODE DATE	a. OTHER PROCEDURE CODE DATE	b. OTHER PROCEDURE CODE DATE	75	76 ATTENDING NPI 111122222	QUAL IG UP1234
				LAST LUCIDO	FIRST MARY JO
c. OTHER PROCEDURE CODE DATE	d. OTHER PROCEDURE CODE DATE	e. OTHER PROCEDURE CODE DATE		77 OPERATING NPI	QUAL
				LAST	FIRST
80 REMARKS	81CC a		78 OTHER NPI	QUAL
	b		LAST	FIRST
	c		79 OTHER NPI	QUAL
	d		LAST	FIRST

UB-04 CMS-1450   APPROVED OMB NO. 0938-0997   NUBC National Uniform Billing Committee   THE CERTIFICATIONS ON THE REVERSE APPLY TO THIS BILL AND ARE MADE A PART HEREOF.

400

WISCONSIN PHYSICIAN SERVICES
PO BOX 5555
MARION IL 62959
866-234-7331

MEDICARE
REMITTANCE
NOTICE

MARSHA BROOKS MD
503 MEDICAL TOWERS
TROY MI 48098

PROVIDER #: 0352681
PAGE #: 1 OF 1
DATE: 0813xxxx
CHECK/EFT #: 560784

PERF PROV	SERV DATE	POS NOS	PROC	MODS	BILLED	ALLOWED	DEDUCT	COINS	GRP/RC – AMT		PROV PD
NAME	GRAHAM MITCHELL		HIC 392594611A		ACNT	CASE C-14	ICN	1234679		ASGY	MAO MAO1
0352681	0714 0714xxxx	11 001	99205		200.00	188.07	0.00	37.61	CO-42	11.93	150.46
	0714 0714xxxx	11 001	81001		15.00	5.25	0.00	1.05	CO-42	4.75	4.20
PT RESP	38.66		CLAIM TOTAL		215.00	193.32		38.66		16.68	154.66
ADJS: PREVS PD	0.00	PD TO BENE	0.00		INT	0.00	PRIMARY	0.00		OTHER	0.00
										154.66	NET
NAME	JOHNSTONE MARY ALICE		HIC 292995651C1		ACNT	CASE 13	ICN	1234680		ASGY	MA0 MA01
0352681	0724 0724xxxx	11 001	99205		200.00	188.07	0.00	37.61	CO-42	11.93	150.46
M34	0724 0724xxxx	11 001	84443		15.00	15.00	0.00		CO-17		
	0724 0724xxxx	11 001	84480		20.00	9.75	0.00	1.95	CO-42	10.25	7.80
PT RESP	22.18		CLAIM TOTAL		235.00	212.82		41.51		22.18	158.26
ADJS: PREVS PD	0.00	PD TO BENE	0.00		INT	0.00	PRIMARY	0.00		OTHER	0.00
										158.26	NET
NAME	POWELL BRANDON		HIC 372529175A		ACNT	CASE 15	ICN	1234681		ASG Y	MAO MA01
0352681	0714 0714xxxx	22 001	93510		500.00	280.35	0.00	56.07	CO-42	219.65	224.28
	0714 0714xxxx	22 001	93545		30.00	16.97	0.00	3.39	CO-42	13.03	13.58
	0714 0714xxxx	22 001	93543		35.00	22.80	0.00	4.56	CO-42	12.20	18.24
	0714 0714xxxx	22 001	93555		50.00	48.04	0.00	9.61	CO-42	1.96	38.43
	0714 0714xxxx	22 001	93556		55.00	49.21	0.00	5.84	CO-42	5.79	43.37
PT RESP	79.47		CLAIM TOTAL		670.00	417.37		79.47		252.63	337.90
ADJS: PREVS PD	0.00	PD TO BENE	0.00		INT	0.00	PRIMARY	0.00		OTHER	0.00
CLAIM TRANSFERRED TO BCBS										337.90	NET

TOTALS	TOTAL CLAIMS	TOTAL BILLED	TOTAL ALLOWED	TOTAL DEDUCT	TOTAL COINS	TOTAL RC AMT	TOTAL PROV PD
	3	1120.00	808.51		157.69	291.49	650.82

ADJS	TOTAL PREV PD	TOTAL PD TO BENE	TOTAL INT	TOTAL PRIMARY	TOTAL OFFSET	TOTAL OTHER ADJS	AMOUNT OF CHECK
	0.00 650.82	0.00	0.00	0.00	0.00	0.00	

GLOSSARY: GROUP, REASON, MOA AND REMARK CODES

CO   CONTRACTUAL OBLIGATION. AMOUNT FOR WHICH THE PROVIDE IS FINANCIALLY LIABLE. THE PATIENT MAY NOT BE BILLED FOR THIS AMOUNT.

42   CHARGES EXCEED OUR FEE SCHEDULE OR MAXIMUM ALLOWABLE AMOUNT

MA01   IF YOU DO NOT AGREE WITH WHAT WE APPROVED FOR THESE SERVICES, YOU MAY APPEAL OUR DECISION. TO MAKE SURE THAT WE ARE FAIR TO YOU, WE REQUIRE ANOTHER INDIVIDUAL THAT DID NOT PROCESS YOU INTIAL CLAIM TO CONDUCT THE REVIEW. HOWEVER, IN ORDER TO BE ELIGIBLE FOR A REVIEW, YOU MUST WRITE TO US WITHIN 120 DAYS OF THE DATE OF THIS NOTICE, UNLESS YOU HAVE A GOOD REASON FOR BEING LATE.

401

Global Insurance Co.
PO Box 3000
Grand Rapids MI 49175

EXPLANATION OF BENEFITS

PLEASE RETAIN FOR FUTURE REFERENCE

Date Printed – 8/25/xxxx
Tax ID #: 344102810
Check #: 3565987234
Check Amt: $

Marvin Klein MD
515 Somerset
Troy, MI 48098

Notes: The benefits listed below reflect your portion of this payment.

Patient Name: Joseph Martino
Patient Acct #: Case # 2 Patient ID# 2145556
Member ID # 342556630
Relation: Self   Member: Joseph

Service Dates	CPT Codes	PL	NUM SVC	Submitted Charges	Copay Amount	Not Payable	See Remarks	Deduct	Co-Insurance	Patient Responsible	Payable Amount
07/13/xx	99202	11	1	$75.00				$75.00		$75.00	
07/13/xx	93000	11	1	$45.00							$45.00
TOTALS				**$120.00**				**$75.00**		**$75.00**	**$45.00**

For Questions regarding this claim Call 888-6539797 For Assistance. Please use ID number for reference to this claim	Total Patient Responsibility	$75.00

TCF Bank   Check #: 3567895234
56624 Highland Rd
Waterford MI 48327   8/25/xxxx

PAY Forty five AND NO/100**

******** $45.00

TO THE ODER OF:
MARVIN KLEIN MD
515 SOMERSET
TROY MI 48098

NICHOLAS JONES

[RP009321] Insurance
GARAGE FAMILY PHYSICIANS
USER - MLS

Aged Outstanding Claims

DATE   1/28/2009
TIME   14:45
PAGE   1

CLAIM #	PATIENT #	PATIENT NAME			DATE FILED	DATE REFILED	DATE OF SERVICE	[CURRENT	31-60	61-90	90+]	B [AGE] I
564889	58680	WARD	RICHARD	M	01/03/08		12/07/07				68.00	390
232354	546882	HODGENS	JAMIE	K	01/03/08	01/15/09	06/02/08				270.00	237
357512	755588	SMITH	KATIE	J	10/16/08		09/24/08				82.00	103
314854	68144	JONES	CARRIE	A	11/03/08		11/03/08			74.00		85
355568	152235	SMEDLEY	KAREN	L	11/13/08		10/30/08			74.00		75
535541	55422	BARRETT	WILLIAM	D	11/26/08		11/06/08			145.00		62
535545	579869	JACKSON	STERLING	A	12/08/08	01/15/09	12/05/08		74.00			50
598878	684489	GABRIEL	LOLA	F	12/15/08		11/24/08		155.00			43
354875	900846	CHRISTENSEN	EMMA	C	12/29/08		12/23/08	74.00				29
546688	578880	JENSEN	EVA	E	01/08/09		01/06/09	178.00				20
648500	586687	GUNTHER	ELIZABETH	L	01/15/09		10/29/07	205.00				13

INS CO# 2 MEDICARE	PHONE # 313 225 8222	TOTAL	CURRENT	31-60	61-90	OVER 90
	11 CLAIMS TOTALING	1,399.00	457.00	229.00	293.00	420.00

CLAIM #	PATIENT #	PATIENT NAME			DATE FILED	DATE REFILED	DATE OF SERVICE	[CURRENT	31-60	61-90	90+]	B [AGE] I
946540	315540	BROWN	DOROTHY	M	12/17/06	05/14/08	03/30/06				50.00	772
235008	350005	STAFFORD	DENNIS	K	08/08/07		08/21/07				68.00	538
564658	135849	ALLRED	SANDRA	J	05/16/08		05/01/08				150.00	256
435689	54611	RICHARDSON	RANDALL	A	11/10/08		11/03/08			74.00		78
955400	564604	MATTHEWS	DAVID	L	01/20/09		01/20/09	74.00				8
984050	468764	MANN	JIM	D	01/22/09		01/20/09	74.00				6
780031	564846	WRIGHT	REBEKAH	A	01/22/09		01/22/09	110.00				6
135498	79645	STEVENSON	RYAN	F	01/26/09		01/23/09	8.00				2

INS CO# 3 BCBSM	PHONE # 800 482 5141	TOTAL	CURRENT	31-60	61-90	OVER 90
	8 CLAIMS TOTALING	608.00	266.00	0.00	74.00	268.00

Date	Patient Name	Claim Number	3rd Party Payer	Amount Billed	Date Paid	Paid by Payer	Remainder	Action
3/15/09	Arnold, James	819211	Advance Insurance 123 Action Ave. Regalstown, MD 23216	$640.00	4/21/09	$600.00	$40.00	$40.00 coinsurance billed to patient
3/16/09	Breznick, Alisa	819230	Singular Insurance Company 10 Park Place Westchester, WA 67511	$178.00				
3/16/09	Milton, Alex	819231	Protection United 244 East End Ave. Dayton, OH 34421	$92.00	4/27/09	$0.00	$92.00	Rejection on being reviewed

STATEMENT

PAYMENTS MADE AFTER 04/08/2007
WILL APPEAR ON NEXT STATEMENT
QUESTIONS REGARDING THIS INVOICE
CAN BE DIRECTED TO THE OFFICE
BETWEEN 1:00PM AND 4:00PM DAILY

ADDRESS SERVICE REQUESTED

			SHOW AMOUNT PAID HERE	$ _____
	05/04/07		01	168.12
OFFICE PHONE NUMBER	CLOSING DATE	YOUR ACCOUNT NUMBER	PAGE NO.	PATIENT BALANCE

:

|||||||||||||||||||||||||||||||||||||||||||||||||| ||||||||||||||||||||||||||||||||||||||||||||||||||

NOTE: Charges and payments not appearing on this
statement will appear on next month's statement.

PLEASE RETURN THIS PORTION WITH PAYMENT

CHARGES APPEARING ON THIS STATEMENT ARE NOT INCLUDED ON ANY HOSPITAL BILL OR STATEMENT

DATE	PROVIDER NAME	EXPLANATION OF ACTIVITY	PATIENT NAME	CHARGES AND DEBITS	PAYMENTS AND CREDITS
072905		INITIAL INPTN CONSULT COMP HISTORY AN		365.00	
073005		FOLLOW CONSULT		250.00	
060205		MEDICARE # 11545 Filed			
092605		PAYMENT MEDICARE c# 115451			-291.17
092605		WRITE-OFF MEDICARE c# 115451			-251.04
092605		Co-ins 72.79			
080105		FOLLOW UP CONSULTATION INPT		720.00	
060205		MEDICARE # 11546 Filed			
092605		PAYMENT MEDICARE c# 115461			-319.68
092605		WRITE-OFF MEDICARE c# 115461			-320.40
092605		Co-ins 79.92			
080905		HOSPITAL DISCHARGE MANAGEMENT 30 MINU		100.00	
060205		MEDICARE # 11547 Filed			
092605		PAYMENT MEDICARE c# 115471			-61.64
092605		WRITE-OFF MEDICARE c# 115471			-22.95
092605		Co-ins 15.41			

STATEMENT CLOSING DATE: **05/04/07** PLEASE INDICATE YOUR ACCOUNT NUMBER WHEN CALLING OUR OFFICE:

CURRENT	30-60 DAYS	60-90 DAYS	> 90 DAYS	TOTAL	INS PENDING	PATIENT BALANCE PAY THIS AMOUNT
			168.12	168.12	0.00	168.12

SEND INQUIRIES TO:

Form CMS-1500
At A Glance

1. MEDICARE	MEDICAID	CHAMPUS	CHAMPVA	GROUP HEALTH PLAN (SSN or ID)	FECA BLK LUNG (SSN)	OTHER	
(Medicare #)	(Medicaid #)	(Sponsor's SSN)	(VA File #)			(ID)	
2. PATIENT'S NAME (Last Name, First Name, Middle Initial)				3. PATIENT'S BIRTH DATE MM | DD | YY		SEX M ☐ F ☐	
5. PATIENT'S ADDRESS (No., Street)				6. PATIENT RELATIONSHIP TO INSURED			

■ What is the Form CMS-1500?

The Form CMS-1500 is the standard paper claim form used by health care professionals and suppliers to bill Medicare Carriers or Part A/B and Durable Medical Equipment Medicare Administrative Contractors (A/B MACs and DME MACs).

A claim is a request for payment of Medicare benefits for services furnished by a health care professional or supplier. Claims must be submitted within one year from the date of service and Medicare beneficiaries cannot be charged for completing or filing a claim. Offenders may be subject to penalty for violations.

■ Exceptions to Mandatory Electronic Claim Submission

The Administrative Simplification Compliance Act (ASCA) prohibits payment of services or supplies not submitted to Medicare electronically, with limited exceptions. Medicare will receive and process paper claims from health care professionals and suppliers who meet the exceptions to the requirements set forth in the ASCA.

Some circumstances *always* meet the exception criteria

Health care professionals and suppliers that experience one of these unusual circumstances are automatically waived from the electronic claim submission requirement for either the indicated claim type or the period when the unusual circumstance exists.

A listing of these definitive exceptions and the latest information on CMS regulations regarding the limited acceptance of paper claims in lieu of electronic billing may be found at http://www.cms.gov/ElectronicBillingEDITrans/05_ASCASelfAssessment.asp on the CMS website. These circumstances include:

- A physician, practitioner, or supplier that bills a Medicare Carrier, A/B MAC, or DME MAC and has fewer than 10 Full-Time Equivalent (FTE) employees.

- A health care professional or supplier experiencing a disruption in electricity and communication connections that is beyond its control expected to last more than two business days.

Health care professionals and suppliers are to self-assess to determine if they meet one or more of these situations and should not submit a waiver request to their contractor. If one of these circumstances applies, they may submit claims to Medicare on paper or via other non-electronic means.

Chapter 26 of the "Medicare Claims Processing Manual" (Pub. 100-04) provides detailed information on completing the Form CMS-1500. This manual may be found at http://www.cms.gov/manuals/downloads/clm104c26.pdf on the CMS website.

Other waiver request circumstances may meet the exception criteria
Medicare pre-approval must be obtained to submit paper claims in the following situations:

- Any situation where a health care professional or supplier can demonstrate that the applicable adopted Health Insurance Portability and Accountability Act (HIPAA) claim standard does not permit submission of a particular type of claim electronically;
- Disability of all members of a health care professional or supplier's staff prevents use of a computer for electronic submission of claims; and
- Other rare situations that cannot be anticipated by the Centers for Medicare & Medicaid Services (CMS) where a health care professional or supplier can establish that due to conditions outside of their control, it would be against equity and good conscience for CMS to enforce this requirement.

Requests for this type of waiver must be sent by letter to the Medicare Contractor. Visit http://www.cms.gov/ElectronicBillingEDITrans/07_ASCAWaiver.asp for more information.

> Note that Medicare Secondary Payer (MSP) claims submission is not an exception to mandatory electronic claims submission unless there is more than one primary payer to Medicare.

■ Form CMS-1500 (08/05)

The Form CMS-1500 is maintained by the National Uniform Claim Committee (NUCC).

The NUCC previously updated the Form CMS-1500 to accommodate the National Provider Identifier (NPI), a unique provider number mandated by HIPAA.

The form is designated as Form CMS-1500 (8/05) and was developed through a collaborative effort led by NUCC, in consultation with CMS. **The Form CMS-1500 (08/05) is the only version accepted by Medicare.**

■ Crosswalk of Paper Form CMS-1500 Fields to Electronic Form Equivalent Fields

The Accredited Standards Committee (ASC) X12N 837 Professional is the standard format for transmitting health care claims electronically. The NUCC has developed a crosswalk between the ASC X12N 837 Professional and the Form CMS-1500 located at http://www.nucc.org on the web. Medicare Carriers, A/B MACs, and DME MACS may also include a crosswalk on their websites.

■ Purchasing the Form CMS-1500

Health care professionals and suppliers are responsible for purchasing their own claim forms. The Form CMS-1500 is available in single, multipart snap-out sets or in continuous pin-feed formats and may be obtained from the United States Government Printing Office (GPO). Contact the GPO at 1-202-512-1800 or visit http://bookstore.gpo.gov on the Internet. It is also available from printing companies and office supply stores, as long as it follows the CMS approved specifications. These specifications may be found in the "Medicare Claims Processing Manual" (Pub. 100-04, Chapter 26, Section 30) at http://www.cms.gov/manuals/downloads/clm104c26.pdf on the CMS website.

You may download a sample of the form by visiting http://www.cms.gov/CMSForms/CMSForms/list.asp on the CMS website. Under the search options, select "Show only items containing the following word" and enter "CMS 1500" in the corresponding field. Then, select the "Show Items" button to locate the form.

■ Completing the Form CMS-1500

Since most paper claims submitted to Medicare are electronically read using Optical Character Recognition (OCR) equipment, the only acceptable claim forms are those printed in OCR Red, J6983, (or exact match) ink.

Claims submitted on forms that cannot be read by the OCR equipment will be returned. Claims must be submitted as originals. Photocopied claims are not accepted.

Form CMS-1500 completion instructions, as well as the print specifications, may be found in the "Medicare Claims Processing Manual" at http://www.cms.gov/manuals/downloads/clm104c26.pdf on the CMS website.

Visit the NUCC "1500 Health Insurance Claim Form Reference Instruction Manual" at http://www.nucc.org for additional information. From the top of the website, select "1500 Claim Form," then "1500 Instructions."

> Note that some payers may give different instructions on how to complete certain Item Numbers on the claim form.

Health care professionals and suppliers should always refer to the most current Federal, State, or other payer instructions for specific requirements applicable to using the Form CMS-1500. Health care professionals and suppliers should always confirm that payers accept claim forms with pre-printed information.

■ Timely Filing

The timely filing period for both paper and electronic Medicare claims for services furnished on or after January 1, 2010, is one calendar year after the date of service.

Claims will be denied if they arrive after the deadline date. When a claim is denied for having been filed after the timely filing period, such a denial does not constitute an "initial determination." As such, the determination that a claim was not filed timely is not subject to appeal.

■ Claim Errors

"Unprocessable claims" is a term used by Medicare for claims that contain certain incomplete or invalid information and are returned to the provider. For example, a claim may be returned as unprocessable because the contractor requires additional information or a correction to the submitted claim data. Because there is no initial determination on the claim, health care professionals and suppliers who submit unprocessable claims have no appeal rights.

The phrase "return as unprocessable" does not mean that in every case a claim is physically returned. Contractors may return the actual unprocessable claim (or a copy of it) to the health care professional or supplier with a letter of explanation or generate a Remittance Advice (RA), which we will discuss later in this fact sheet. Some contractors may suspend a claim that contains incomplete or invalid information, and then provide notice of the errors to the provider and afford a period of time for corrections to be submitted. When adequate corrections are submitted, the contractor will then resume processing of the claim.

Providers need to be aware that an unprocessable claim that has been returned for correction and resubmission does not toll the timely filing period. A correct claim must be resubmitted within the timely filing period. Where a contractor has suspended a claim and allowed a period for submission of corrections, the timely filing requirements will have been met if the corrections are received within the allotted time.

Form CMS-1500 incomplete and invalid claims processing guidelines may be found in the "Medicare Claims Processing Manual" at http://www.cms.gov/manuals/downloads/clm104c01.pdf starting at Section 80.3.1.

■ Tips for submitting error-free paper claims

TROUBLESHOOTING BASICS:

- Use only an original red-ink-on-white-paper Form CMS-1500 claim form.
- Use dark ink.
- Do not print, hand-write, or stamp any extraneous data on the form.
- Do not staple, clip, or tape anything to the Form CMS-1500 claim form.
- Remove pin-fed edges at side perforations.
- Use only lift-off correction tape to make corrections.
- Place all necessary documentation in the envelope with the Form CMS-1500 claim form.

FORMAT HINTS:

- Do not use italics or script.
- Do not use dollar signs, decimals, or punctuation.
- Use only upper-case (CAPITAL) letters.
- Use 10- or 12-pitch (pica) characters and standard dot matrix fonts.
- Do not include titles (e.g., Dr., Mr., Mrs., Rev., M.D.) as part of the beneficiary's name.
- Enter all information on the same horizontal plane within the designated field.
- Follow the correct Health Insurance Claim Number (HICN) format. No hyphens or dashes should be used. The alpha prefix or suffix is part of the HICN and should not be omitted. Be especially careful with spouses who have a similar HICN with a different alpha prefix or suffix.
- Ensure data is in the appropriate field and does not overlap into other fields.
- Use an individual's name in the provider signature field, not a facility or practice name.

ACCURATE INFORMATION IS KEY:

- Put the beneficiary's name and Medicare number on each piece of documentation submitted. Always use the beneficiary's name exactly as it appears on the beneficiary's Medicare card.
- Include all applicable NPIs on the claim, including the NPI for the referring provider.
- Indicate the correct address, including a valid ZIP code, where the service was rendered to the beneficiary. Any missing, incomplete, or invalid information in the Service Facility Location Information field will cause the claim to be unprocessable. Any claims received with the word "SAME" in fields indicating that the information is the same as in another field are unacceptable. A post office box address is unacceptable in the field for the location where the service was rendered.
- Include special certification numbers for services such as mammography (FDA number) and clinical laboratory (CLIA number).
- Ensure that the number of units/days and the date of service range are not contradictory.
- Ensure that the number of units/days and the quantity indicated in the procedure code's description are not contradictory.

CODING TIPS:

- Use current valid diagnosis codes and code them to the highest level of specificity (maximum number of digits) available. Also make sure that the diagnosis codes used are appropriate for the gender of the beneficiary.
- Use current valid procedure codes as described in the Current Procedural Terminology (CPT) or Healthcare Common Procedure Coding System (HCPCS) manuals.
- Use only Level II HCPCS codes, not local codes.
- Use current valid modifiers when necessary.

Page 4

■ More Troubleshooting Tips...

Item 11: If Medicare is the primary payer, enter the word "None" in Item 11. If Medicare is not the primary payer, include the primary payer's information and a copy of the primary payer's Explanation of Benefits or Remittance Advice.

Item 17: Enter the name of the referring or ordering physician if the service or item was ordered or referred by a physician.

■ Remittance Advice

After a claim has been received and processed, the Medicare Contractor sends the health care professional or supplier a notice of payments and adjustments explaining the reimbursement decisions including the reasons for adjustments of processed claims. This notice is called a Remittance Advice (RA).

The RA may serve as a companion to a claim payment or as an explanation when there is no payment. The explanation of the errors will be provided in the form of a description or a code.

Note that unprocessable claims returned with a Remittance Advice can be identified by the presence of code MA130 and an explanation of the specific rejection reason.

For more information on the Remittance Advice, visit http://www.cms.gov/MLNProducts/downloads/RA_Guide_Full_03-22-06.pdf on the CMS website.

■ Web Resources

"Medicare Claims Processing Manual" (Pub. 100-04, Chapter 26)
http://www.cms.gov/manuals/downloads/clm104c26.pdf

Electronic Billing & EDI Transactions – Professional Paper Claim Form (CMS-1500) Web Page
http://www.cms.gov/ElectronicBillingEDITrans/16_1500.asp

"National Uniform Claim Committee 1500 Health Insurance Claim Form Reference Instruction Manual"
http://www.nucc.org

Administrative Simplification Compliance Act
http://www.cms.gov/HIPAAGenInfo/Downloads/ASCALaw.pdf

"Medicare Physician Guide: A Resource for Residents, Practicing Physicians, and Other Health Care Professionals"
http://www.cms.gov/MLNProducts/downloads/physicianguide.pdf

"Understanding the Remittance Advice: A Guide for Medicare Providers, Physicians, Suppliers, and Billers"
http://www.cms.gov/MLNProducts/downloads/RA_Guide_Full_03-22-06.pdf

Form CMS-1500 Web-based Tutorial
http://www.cms.gov/MLNEdWebGuide

CMS Electronic Mailing Lists
http://www.cms.gov/AboutWebsite/EmailUpdates/list.asp

Medicare Learning Network® (MLN) Web Page
http://www.cms.gov/MLNGenInfo

MLN Matters® Articles
http://www.cms.gov/MLNMattersArticles

Carrier & A/B MAC Contact Information
http://www.cms.gov/MLNProducts/downloads/CallCenterTollNumDirectory.zip

Looking for the latest online educational resources? Visit the Medicare Learning Network® (MLN) at http://www.cms.gov/MLNGenInfo on the CMS website.

1500

HEALTH INSURANCE CLAIM FORM

APPROVED BY NATIONAL UNIFORM CLAIM COMMITTEE 08/05

☐☐ PICA

PICA ☐☐☐

1. MEDICARE MEDICAID TRICARE CHAMPUS CHAMPVA GROUP HEALTH PLAN FECA BLK LUNG OTHER	1a. INSURED'S I.D. NUMBER (For Program in Item 1)
☐ (Medicare #) ☐ (Medicaid #) ☐ (Sponsor's SSN) ☐ (Member ID#) ☐ (SSN or ID) ☐ (SSN) ☐ (ID)	

2. PATIENT'S NAME (Last Name, First Name, Middle Initial)	3. PATIENT'S BIRTH DATE MM DD YY SEX M ☐ F ☐	4. INSURED'S NAME (Last Name, First Name, Middle Initial)

5. PATIENT'S ADDRESS (No., Street)	6. PATIENT RELATIONSHIP TO INSURED Self ☐ Spouse ☐ Child ☐ Other ☐	7. INSURED'S ADDRESS (No., Street)
CITY STATE	8. PATIENT STATUS Single ☐ Married ☐ Other ☐	CITY STATE
ZIP CODE TELEPHONE (Include Area Code) ( )	Employed ☐ Full-Time Student ☐ Part-Time Student ☐	ZIP CODE TELEPHONE (Include Area Code) ( )

9. OTHER INSURED'S NAME (Last Name, First Name, Middle Initial)	10. IS PATIENT'S CONDITION RELATED TO:	11. INSURED'S POLICY GROUP OR FECA NUMBER
a. OTHER INSURED'S POLICY OR GROUP NUMBER	a. EMPLOYMENT? (Current or Previous) ☐ YES ☐ NO	a. INSURED'S DATE OF BIRTH MM DD YY SEX M ☐ F ☐
b. OTHER INSURED'S DATE OF BIRTH MM DD YY SEX M ☐ F ☐	b. AUTO ACCIDENT? PLACE (State) ☐ YES ☐ NO	b. EMPLOYER'S NAME OR SCHOOL NAME
c. EMPLOYER'S NAME OR SCHOOL NAME	c. OTHER ACCIDENT? ☐ YES ☐ NO	c. INSURANCE PLAN NAME OR PROGRAM NAME
d. INSURANCE PLAN NAME OR PROGRAM NAME	10d. RESERVED FOR LOCAL USE	d. IS THERE ANOTHER HEALTH BENEFIT PLAN? ☐ YES ☐ NO If yes, return to and complete item 9 a-d.

READ BACK OF FORM BEFORE COMPLETING & SIGNING THIS FORM.

12. PATIENT'S OR AUTHORIZED PERSON'S SIGNATURE I authorize the release of any medical or other information necessary to process this claim. I also request payment of government benefits either to myself or to the party who accepts assignment below.

SIGNED _____ DATE _____

13. INSURED'S OR AUTHORIZED PERSON'S SIGNATURE I authorize payment of medical benefits to the undersigned physician or supplier for services described below.

SIGNED _____

14. DATE OF CURRENT: MM DD YY ILLNESS (First symptom) OR INJURY (Accident) OR PREGNANCY(LMP)	15. IF PATIENT HAS HAD SAME OR SIMILAR ILLNESS. GIVE FIRST DATE MM DD YY	16. DATES PATIENT UNABLE TO WORK IN CURRENT OCCUPATION FROM MM DD YY TO MM DD YY
17. NAME OF REFERRING PROVIDER OR OTHER SOURCE	17a. ___ 17b. NPI ___	18. HOSPITALIZATION DATES RELATED TO CURRENT SERVICES FROM MM DD YY TO MM DD YY
19. RESERVED FOR LOCAL USE		20. OUTSIDE LAB? ☐ YES ☐ NO $ CHARGES

21. DIAGNOSIS OR NATURE OF ILLNESS OR INJURY (Relate Items 1, 2, 3 or 4 to Item 24E by Line)

1. |___.___| 3. |___.___|
2. |___.___| 4. |___.___|

22. MEDICAID RESUBMISSION CODE ___ ORIGINAL REF. NO. ___

23. PRIOR AUTHORIZATION NUMBER

24. A. DATE(S) OF SERVICE From To MM DD YY MM DD YY	B. PLACE OF SERVICE	C. EMG	D. PROCEDURES, SERVICES, OR SUPPLIES (Explain Unusual Circumstances) CPT/HCPCS MODIFIER	E. DIAGNOSIS POINTER	F. $ CHARGES	G. DAYS OR UNITS	H. EPSDT Family Plan	I. ID. QUAL.	J. RENDERING PROVIDER ID. #
1									NPI
2									NPI
3									NPI
4									NPI
5									NPI
6									NPI

25. FEDERAL TAX I.D. NUMBER SSN EIN ☐☐	26. PATIENT'S ACCOUNT NO.	27. ACCEPT ASSIGNMENT? (For govt. claims, see back) ☐ YES ☐ NO	28. TOTAL CHARGE $	29. AMOUNT PAID $	30. BALANCE DUE $

31. SIGNATURE OF PHYSICIAN OR SUPPLIER INCLUDING DEGREES OR CREDENTIALS (I certify that the statements on the reverse apply to this bill and are made a part thereof.) SIGNED _____ DATE _____	32. SERVICE FACILITY LOCATION INFORMATION a. NPI b.	33. BILLING PROVIDER INFO & PH # ( ) a. NPI b.

NUCC Instruction Manual available at: www.nucc.org   **PLEASE PRINT OR TYPE**   APPROVED OMB-0938-0999 FORM CMS-1500 (08-05)

CMS 1500 claim form requirements

To complete this form, follow the instructions below. **Each field on the form has a corresponding number. Claims submitted with missing or invalid required fields may be rejected and/or returned for correction and resubmission.**

Requirements	Field	Description
	1:	Type of Health Insurance Show the type of health insurance coverage applicable to this claim by checking the appropriate box.
Required	1A:	**Insured's Identification Number** Enter the three-digit alpha prefix and identification number of the insured *exactly as shown on the member card*.
Required	2:	**Patient's Name** Enter the last name, first name, and middle initial (if known) of the patient exactly as shown on the member card. *Do not use nicknames.*
Required	3:	**Patient's Birth Date and Sex** Enter the eight-digit month, day, century, and year of the patient's birth (MMDDCCYY). Check the appropriate box to identify patient's gender.
Required	4:	**Insured's Name** Enter the last name, first name, and middle initial of the insured as shown on the member card. If the patient is the insured, enter the word "same".
Required	5:	**Patient's Address** Enter the patient's complete address.
Required	6:	**Patient's Relationship to Insured** Check self, spouse, child or other.
	7:	Insured's Address Complete if the patient *is not* the insured.
	8:	Patient Status Check the appropriate box.
Recommended	9:	**Other Insured's Name** Enter the name of the insured with other insurance coverage.
Recommended	9A:	**Other Insured's Policy or Group Number** Enter the policy and/or group number of the other insurance coverage.
Recommended	9B:	**Other Insured's Date of Birth** Enter the information available to you in eight-digit format (MMDDCCYY).
	9C:	Employer's Name or School Name Enter the complete name.
	9D:	Insurance Plan Name or Program Name Enter the name of the insurance plan.
Required	10:	**Is Patient's Condition Related to** Check the correct boxes in a., b. and c.

Requirements	Field	Description
	10D:	Reserved for Local Use Leave blank.
Required	11:	**Insured's Policy or FECA Number** Enter the group number of the insured as shown on the member card. **Exception:** If a member card from another Blue Cross and/or BlueShield Plan does not show a group number - leave the field blank or populate the field with a numeric (e.g., 99999999)
Recommended	11A:	**Insured's Date of Birth** Use eight-digit date form if submitting.
	11B:	Employer's Name or School Name
	11C:	Insurance Plan Name or Program Name
	11D:	Additional Benefit Plans
	12:	Patient's or Authorized Person's Signature Have patient sign if your office requires it.
	13:	Insured's or Authorized Person's Signature May be left blank.
Required for accidents or injuries **Recommended for all other**	14:	**Date of Current illness, Injury, Pregnancy** Enter the date of the current illness, injury or pregnancy.
	15:	If Patient has had Same or Similar illness Enter the date the patient first consulted you for this condition.
	16:	Dates Patient Unable to Work in Current Occupation Leave blank.
	17:	Name of Referring Provider or Other Source List the name of the referring, ordering or supervising physician or other health care professional.
	17A:	Shaded Area - Other ID # Enter the assigned ID number for the physician or other health care professional listed in field 17. The qualifier indicating what the number represents is reported in the qualifier field to the immediate right of 17a. Qualifiers include: ZZ – Provider Taxonomy
See BlueCard requirements in description	17B:	NPI # Enter the assigned NPI of the physician or other health care professional listed in field 17. **The referring provider NPI number required for independent clinical laboratories, durable medical equipment suppliers and specialty pharmacy claims for BlueCard members.**

Requirements	Field	Description
Recommended	18:	**Hospitalization Dates Related to Current Services**
	19:	Reserved for Local Use Leave blank.
	20:	Outside Lab If your patient had lab work done, check the correct box *even if you are not billing for the lab work*. Do not list charges in this field.
Required	21:	**Diagnosis or Nature of illness or Injury** Identify the patient's condition(s) by entering up to four ICD-9-CM codes in order of relevance. **Codes must be carried out to the highest possible (4th or 5th) digit. Non-specific diagnoses, such as 780, may result in denials.**
	22:	Medicaid Resubmission Leave blank.
	23:	Prior Authorization Number Leave blank.
Recommended	24A – 24G:	**Shaded Area – National Drug Code (NDC)** In the shaded area above "Date(s) of Service", enter the two digit Product ID Qualifier "N4" identifying the type of number being provided. Enter the 11-digit NDC number immediately after the Product ID Qualifier. **Valid Unit of Measurement Qualifiers are:** F2 – International unit GR – Gram ML – Milliliter UN – Unit The HCPCS code should be entered in Field 24D "Procedures, Services, or Supplies", the charges in Field 24F and the units in Field 24G.
Required	24A:	**Date(s) of Service** Enter the date(s) of service. If only one service is provided, the date can be entered as a "from date" or a "to date".

414

Requirements	Field	Description
Required	24B:	**Place of Services** Indicate where services were provided by entering the appropriate two-digit place of service code. Valid codes are as follows: 11 Office 12 Home 17 Walk-in Retail Health Clinic 21 Inpatient Hospital 22 Outpatient Hospital 23 Emergency Room 24 Ambulatory Surgery Center 25 Birthing Center 26 Military Treatment Center 31 Skilled Nursing Facility 32 Nursing Facility 33 Custodial Care Facility 34 Hospice 41 Ambulance (land) 42 Ambulance (air or water) 51 Inpatient Psychiatric Facility 52 Psychiatric Facility Partial Hospitalization 53 Community Mental Health Facility 54 Intermediate Care Facility/Mentally Retarded 55 Residential Substance Abuse Treatment Facility 56 Psychiatric Residential Treatment Center 61 Comprehensive Inpatient Rehabilitation Facility 62 Comprehensive Outpatient Rehabilitation Facility 65 End-Stage Renal Disease Treatment Facility
	24C:	Emergency Indicator (EMG Leave blank.
Required	24D:	**Procedures, Services, or Supplies: CPT/HCPCS, Modifier** Enter a valid procedure code best describing each service or supply. Explain unusual services or situations with procedure code modifiers. If a CPT and a HCPCS code describe the same service, use the CPT code. **Claims with an invalid or missing procedure code may be denied or returned for correction and resubmission.**
Required	24E:	**Diagnosis Pointer** Enter one diagnosis code reference number per claim line (i.e., up to four ICD-9-CM codes) as shown in item 21, to relate the date of service and the procedures performed to the appropriate diagnosis.
Required	24F:	**Charges** Enter your charge for each listed service.
Required	24G:	**Days or Units** Enter the number of services billed on the line. For anesthesia services, report time and modifier units on separate lines.

Requirements	Field	Description
	24H:	EPSDT Family Plan Leave blank.
Taxonomy required if applicable for Regence MedAdvantage beginning January 1, 2012	24I:	**Shaded Area - ID Qualifier** Enter the qualifier identifying if the number is a non-NPI. The Other ID# of the rendering provider is reported in 24J in the shaded area. Qualifiers include: ZZ – Provider Taxonomy
Required if applicable (Taxonomy code is required if applicable for Regence MedAdvantage beginning January 1, 2012)	24J:	**Rendering Provider ID # (split field)** The individual performing/rendering the service. **The rendering provider ID # is required when different than the billing provider found in Field 33**. Please submit only one provider per claim. **Unlabeled Shaded Field** – Enter the code or number that corresponds with the ID Qualifier used in 24I. **NPI Field** – Enter your Type 1 individual NPI number.
Required	25:	**Federal Tax ID Number** Enter the provider's tax identification number as given by the Internal Revenue Service.
Recommended	26:	**Patient's Account Number** If you use patient account numbers, enter the number for this patient.
Required for Medicare only	27:	**Accept Assignment** Please check applicable box.
Required	28:	**Total Charge** Enter the total of all charges submitted on this claim.
Recommended	29:	**Amount Paid** Enter the exact amount the patient and/or other insurance carrier has paid to you for these services. Entering the words patient paid' without indicating the exact amount may cause claims delays and inaccurate processing.
	30:	**Balance Due** Enter the difference between Field 28 and Field 29.
Required	31:	**Signature of Physician or Supplier** Sign and date the form. Stamped and preprinted signatures that include the degree are acceptable for all products except Regence MedAdvantage. Claims for this product must be signed or have a preprinted signature including degree.
Required if applicable	32:	**Service Facility Location Information** Enter name and address of the location where the services were rendered.
Required if applicable	32A:	**NPI #** Enter the service facility NPI number (Type 2) of the service facility location, if known.

Requirements	Field	Description
Taxonomy required if applicable for Regence MedAdvantage beginning January 1, 2012	**32B:**	**Other ID** Enter the two-digit ID qualifier identifying the non-NPI number followed by the ID number. Do not enter a space, hyphen or other separator between the qualifier and number. ZZ – Provider Taxonomy
Required	**33:**	**Billing Provider Information and Phone #** Enter the billing provider's name, address, zip code, and telephone number.
Required (Required for paper submitted claims beginning January 1, 2012)	**33A:**	**NPI #** Enter the NPI number (Type 1 or 2) of the billing provider.
Taxonomy is required for Regence MedAdvantage beginning January 1, 2012 **Recommended for all other lines of business**	**33B:**	**Other ID** Enter the two-digit ID qualifier identifying the non-NPI number followed by the ID number. Do not enter a space, hyphen or other separator between the qualifier and number. Qualifiers include: ZZ – Provider Taxonomy

Sample *CMS-1500* (08-05) claim form

1500

HEALTH INSURANCE CLAIM FORM
APPROVED BY NATIONAL UNIFORM CLAIM COMMITTEE 08/05

☐☐ PICA   PICA ☐☐

CARRIER

1. MEDICARE ☐ (Medicare #) MEDICAID ☐ (Medicaid #) TRICARE CHAMPUS ☐ (Sponsor's SSN) CHAMPVA ☐ (Member ID#) GROUP HEALTH PLAN ☐ (SSN or ID) FECA BLK LUNG ☐ (SSN) OTHER ☐ (ID)	1a. INSURED'S I.D. NUMBER (For Program in Item 1)
2. PATIENT'S NAME (Last Name, First Name, Middle Initial)	3. PATIENT'S BIRTH DATE MM	DD	YY SEX M ☐ F ☐	4. INSURED'S NAME (Last Name, First Name, Middle Initial)
5. PATIENT'S ADDRESS (No., Street)	6. PATIENT RELATIONSHIP TO INSURED Self ☐ Spouse ☐ Child ☐ Other ☐	7. INSURED'S ADDRESS (No., Street)
CITY STATE	8. PATIENT STATUS Single ☐ Married ☐ Other ☐	CITY STATE
ZIP CODE TELEPHONE (Include Area Code) ( )	Employed ☐ Full-Time Student ☐ Part-Time Student ☐	ZIP CODE TELEPHONE (Include Area Code) ( )

PATIENT AND INSURED INFORMATION

9. OTHER INSURED'S NAME (Last Name, First Name, Middle Initial)	10. IS PATIENT'S CONDITION RELATED TO:	11. INSURED'S POLICY GROUP OR FECA NUMBER
a. OTHER INSURED'S POLICY OR GROUP NUMBER	a. EMPLOYMENT? (Current or Previous) ☐ YES ☐ NO	a. INSURED'S DATE OF BIRTH MM	DD	YY SEX M ☐ F ☐
b. OTHER INSURED'S DATE OF BIRTH MM	DD	YY SEX M ☐ F ☐	b. AUTO ACCIDENT? PLACE (State) ☐ YES ☐ NO	b. EMPLOYER'S NAME OR SCHOOL NAME
c. EMPLOYER'S NAME OR SCHOOL NAME	c. OTHER ACCIDENT? ☐ YES ☐ NO	c. INSURANCE PLAN NAME OR PROGRAM NAME
d. INSURANCE PLAN NAME OR PROGRAM NAME	10d. RESERVED FOR LOCAL USE	d. IS THERE ANOTHER HEALTH BENEFIT PLAN? ☐ YES ☐ NO If yes, return to and complete item 9 a-d.

READ BACK OF FORM BEFORE COMPLETING & SIGNING THIS FORM.
12. PATIENT'S OR AUTHORIZED PERSON'S SIGNATURE I authorize the release of any medical or other information necessary to process this claim. I also request payment of government benefits either to myself or to the party who accepts assignment below.	13. INSURED'S OR AUTHORIZED PERSON'S SIGNATURE I authorize payment of medical benefits to the undersigned physician or supplier for services described below.
SIGNED _____ DATE _____	SIGNED _____

14. DATE OF CURRENT: ILLNESS (First symptom) OR INJURY (Accident) OR PREGNANCY(LMP) MM	DD	YY	15. IF PATIENT HAS HAD SAME OR SIMILAR ILLNESS. GIVE FIRST DATE MM	DD	YY	16. DATES PATIENT UNABLE TO WORK IN CURRENT OCCUPATION FROM MM	DD	YY TO MM	DD	YY
17. NAME OF REFERRING PROVIDER OR OTHER SOURCE	17a. 17b. NPI	18. HOSPITALIZATION DATES RELATED TO CURRENT SERVICES FROM MM	DD	YY TO MM	DD	YY
19. RESERVED FOR LOCAL USE		20. OUTSIDE LAB? ☐ YES ☐ NO $ CHARGES
21. DIAGNOSIS OR NATURE OF ILLNESS OR INJURY (Relate Items 1, 2, 3 or 4 to Item 24E by Line) 1. └___ . ___ 3. └___ . ___ 2. └___ . ___ 4. └___ . ___		22. MEDICAID RESUBMISSION CODE _____ ORIGINAL REF. NO. 23. PRIOR AUTHORIZATION NUMBER

PHYSICIAN OR SUPPLIER INFORMATION

24. A. DATE(S) OF SERVICE From To MM DD YY MM DD YY	B. PLACE OF SERVICE	C. EMG	D. PROCEDURES, SERVICES, OR SUPPLIES (Explain Unusual Circumstances) CPT/HCPCS	MODIFIER	E. DIAGNOSIS POINTER	F. $ CHARGES	G. DAYS OR UNITS	H. EPSDT Family Plan	I. ID. QUAL.	J. RENDERING PROVIDER ID. #
									NPI	
									NPI	
									NPI	
									NPI	
									NPI	
									NPI	

25. FEDERAL TAX I.D. NUMBER SSN ☐ EIN ☐	26. PATIENT'S ACCOUNT NO.	27. ACCEPT ASSIGNMENT? (For govt. claims, see back) ☐ YES ☐ NO	28. TOTAL CHARGE $	29. AMOUNT PAID $	30. BALANCE DUE $
31. SIGNATURE OF PHYSICIAN OR SUPPLIER INCLUDING DEGREES OR CREDENTIALS (I certify that the statements on the reverse apply to this bill and are made a part thereof.) SIGNED _____ DATE _____	32. SERVICE FACILITY LOCATION INFORMATION a. NPI b.	33. BILLING PROVIDER INFO & PH # ( ) a. NPI b.

NUCC Instruction Manual available at: www.nucc.org

Regence BlueCross BlueShield of Oregon is an Independent Licensee of the Blue Cross and Blue Shield Association

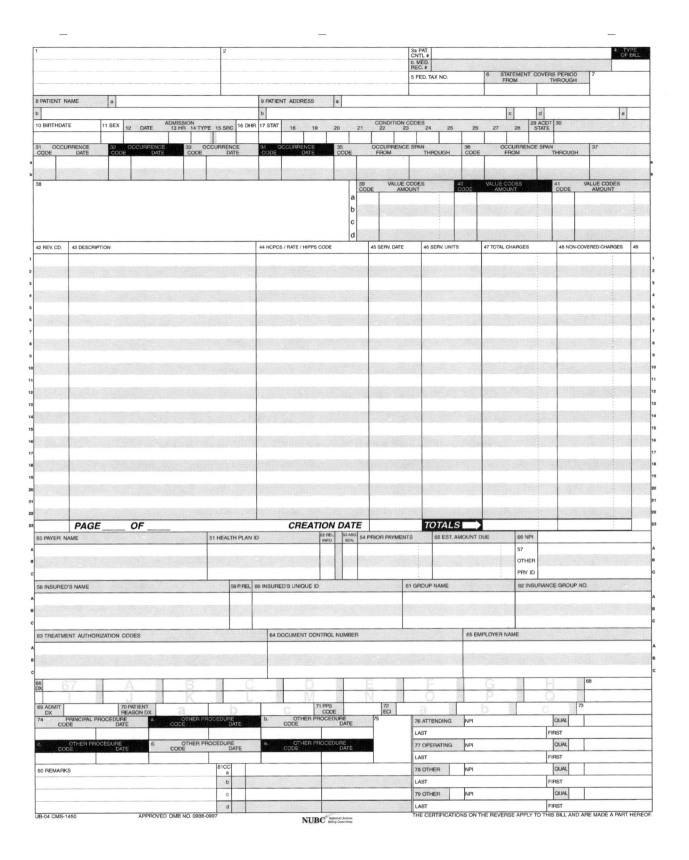

Coding and Billing Audit Form

A. CLAIM INFORMATION

Patient Name: _____   Provider Name: _____

Medical Record # _____   Invoice # _____

Place of Service_____   Type of Service_____

Date of Service _____

WAS THIS ICD-10 CODE CORRECT? YES   NO

ICD-10 Code Billed _____   Corrected ICD-10 Code _____

WAS THE AMOUNT CHARGED CORRECT? YES   NO

Charge Amount_____   Corrected Charge Amount _____

B. REASON(S) FOR REFUND (indicate all that apply)

☐ **Incorrect of Missing Modifier (If the modifier is payment related)**
☐ **Incorrect OASIS Code**
☐ **Incorrect ICD-10 Code (If correct ICD-10 code results in a non-reimbursable service)**
☐ **Incorrect Place of Service (If correct POS results in a lower or non-reimbursable service)**
☐ **Duplicate Reimbursement (same charge submitted more than once)**
☐ **Insufficient documentation for level billed (MUST indicate reason)**

_____

C. ADDITIONAL INFORMATION/COMMENTS/STEPS TO IMPROVE COMPLIANCE _____

D. SIGNATURES/AUTHORIZATIONS

Auditor   **Telephone**   **Date**

Compliance Officer   **Telephone**   **Date**

BILLING RECORD AUDIT FORM

example

Patient Name			I.D. #				
Physican			Specialty:				
Auditor			Audit date:				
Level billed:		Diagnosis:		Payer			
Indicator					**Yes**	**No**	**N/A**
Patient signed consent for assignment of benefits/payment							
Insurance verified before providing services							
Primary diagnosis coded correctly							
Documentation meets level billed							
Correct Evaluation and Management code billed							
Correct CPT code identified by provider on encounter form							
Correct ICD-9 code identified by provider on encounter form							
All information on encounter form and progress notes match							
CPT and ICD-9 codes on claim form reflect documentation							
Patient information entered correctly into computer							
Authorization number assigned to visit (if applicable)							
Was claim paid?							
Was follow-up made if claim not paid?							
Was follow up made on unpaid claim timely?							
Was Co-pay collected at time of service?							
If billing for counseling/Coordination of care (more than 50% of the time) was the accurate amount of time documented?							
If ABN in use, was it completed properly							
Financial Hardship form in chart if "write-off"							
Suggested E&M code:							
Auditor's note / Comments / Suggestions:							

Documentation of Patient Services Audit Form

Patient Name: _____   Physician: _____

Medical Record # _____   Invoice # _____

Place of Service: _____   Date of Service _____

(ICD-10 Code) _____   Type of Service _____

Auditor's Name and Telephone Number _____

Compliance Officer's Name and Telephone Number _____

Is the documentation in the patient's chart sufficient? _____Yes _____ No

Does the documentation support the billing level? _____Yes _____ No

Is the patient chart in Compliance with our policies? _____Yes _____ No

If the answer to any of the above questions was no, complete the following.

Non-Compliance resulted from: _____

_____

_____

People Contacted: _____

_____

_____

What was discussed? _____

_____

_____

Steps taken to correct this now and in the future: _____

_____

_____

_____

_____

_____

_____

Medicare/Medicaid Complaint and Resolution Form

Name of person bringing the issue to our attention _____

Address _____

City/State/Zip _____

Phone _____ Fax _____ e-mail _____

Physician(s) involved _____

Medical Record # and Invoice # _____

Date and Place of Service: _____

Level of Service Coded: (CPT Code) _____

Type of Service _____

Name of employee completing this form _____

Address _____

City/State/Zip _____

Date issue first brought to our attention _____

Employee Contacted _____

By phone, in person, other _____

Was the person referred to someone else? Y N. If yes, Name of employee _____

What did the person say: _____
_____
_____
_____

What was the person told: _____
_____
_____
_____

What was done to resolve this issue: _____
_____